ne
& Hana

13

STORY AND ART BY

Yuki Shiwasu

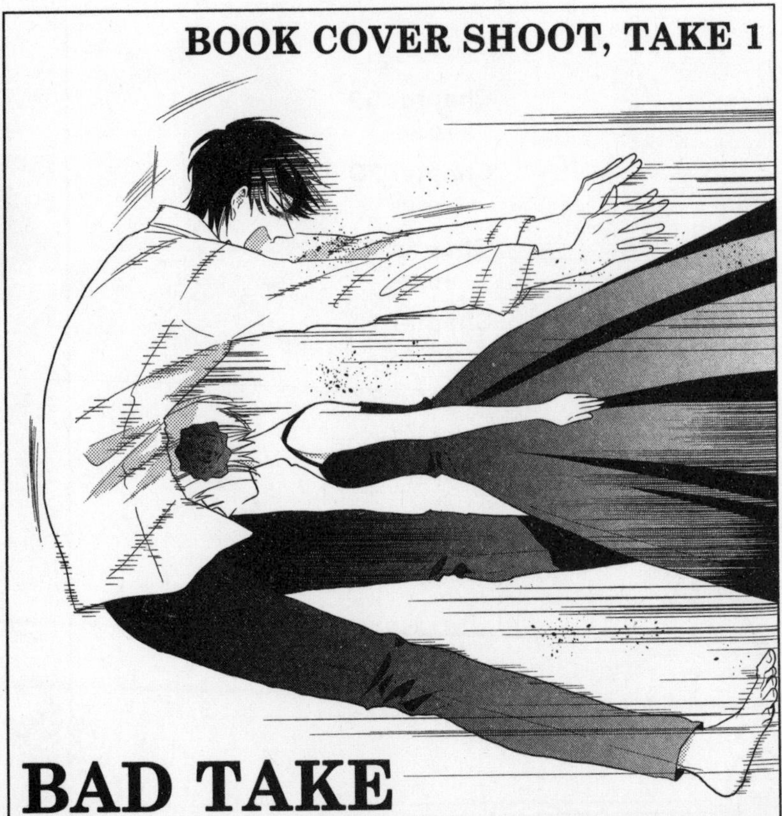
BOOK COVER SHOOT, TAKE 1
BAD TAKE

Takane & Hana

13

Takane Conference ①

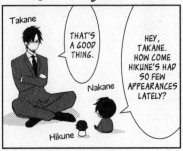

Takane
Nakane
Hikune
HEY, TAKANE. HOW COME HIKUNE'S HAD SO FEW APPEARANCES LATELY?
THAT'S A GOOD THING.
HOW IS THAT GOOD? HIKUNE'S THE MASCOT IN THE TAKANE WORLD!
YOU NEED TO ACTIVELY TRY TO SHRINK MORE.
SHUSH.
Taka
I'M THE MASCOT. WE DON'T NEED ANOTHER ONE!
IN WHAT POSSIBLE WAY ARE YOU A MASCOT?
MY EARLOBES ARE SURPRISINGLY SOFT AND CUTE!
AS IF ANYONE KNOWS THAT!
Naka

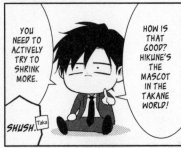

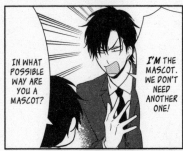

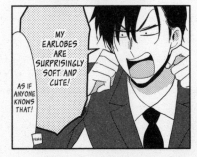

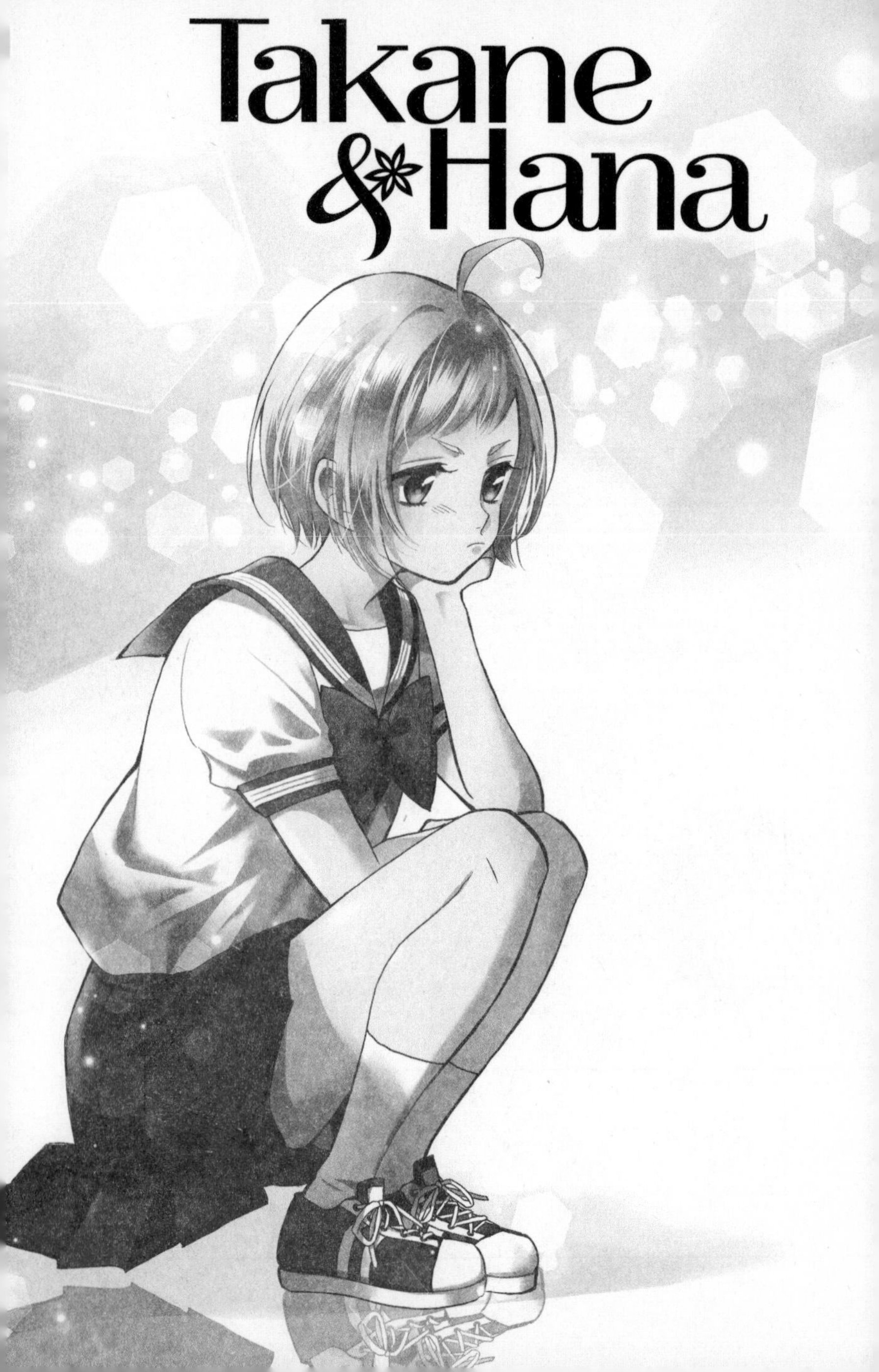
Takane & Hana

Chapter 69

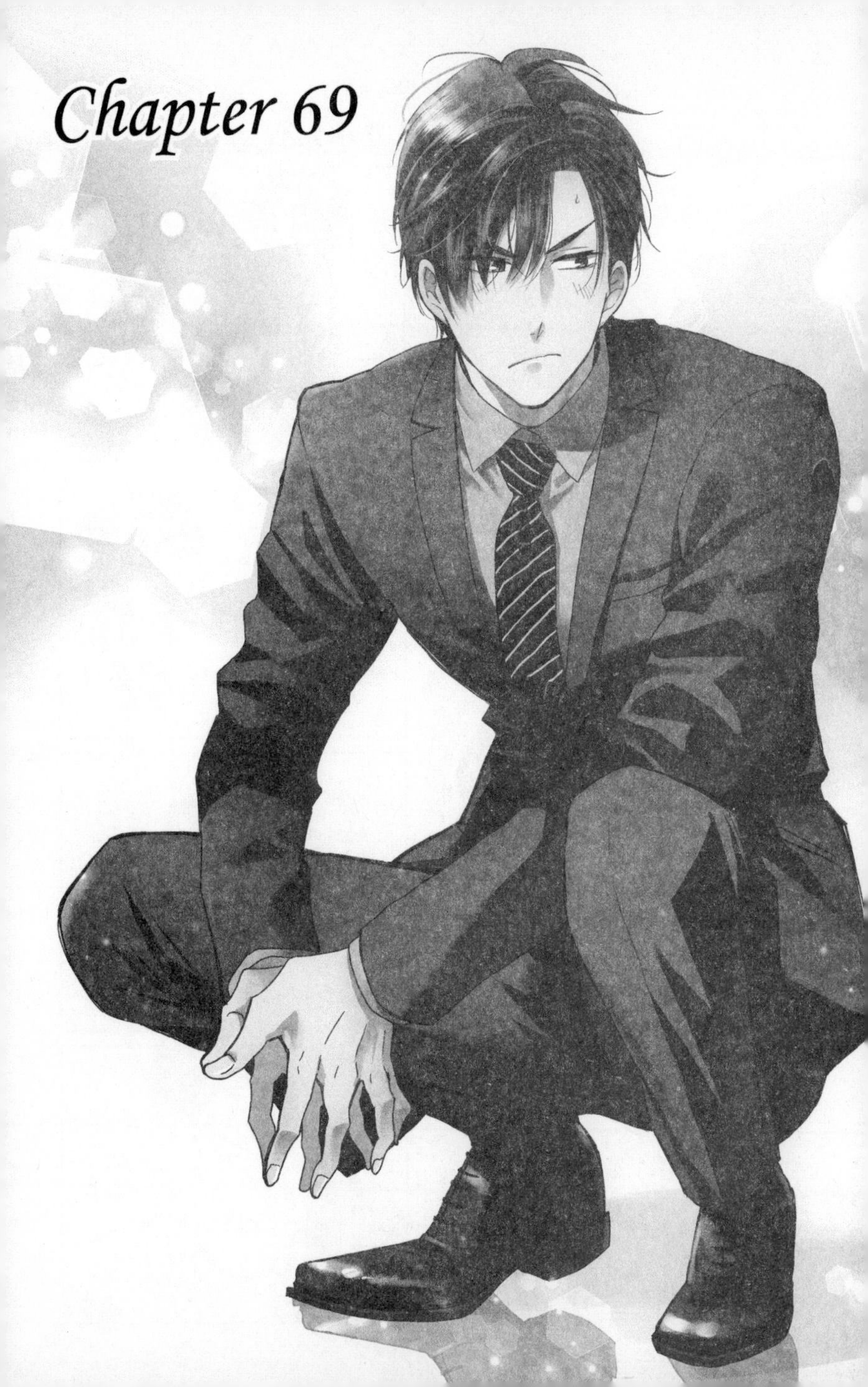

Takane Conference ②

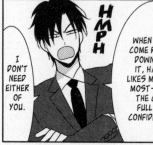

WHEN YOU COME RIGHT DOWN TO IT, HANA LIKES ME THE MOST—ME, THE GUY FULL OF CONFIDENCE.
HMPH
I DON'T NEED EITHER OF YOU.
WELL, LET ME ASK YOU THIS.
HAS SHE EVER PATTED YOUR HEAD? CARRIED YOU IN HER ARMS?
...
WE'RE THE ONES WHO BRING OUT HER MATERNAL INSTINCTS. THAT'S OUR ROLE AS SMALL TAKANES.
Get a clue.
YEAH, BUT I'M THE ONE SHE LECTURES THE MOST!
SHE TREATS ME THE MOST LIKE A CHILD.
Naka
DON'T BRAG ABOUT THAT.

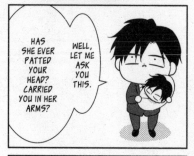

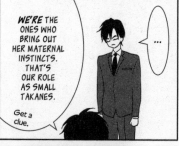

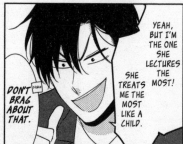

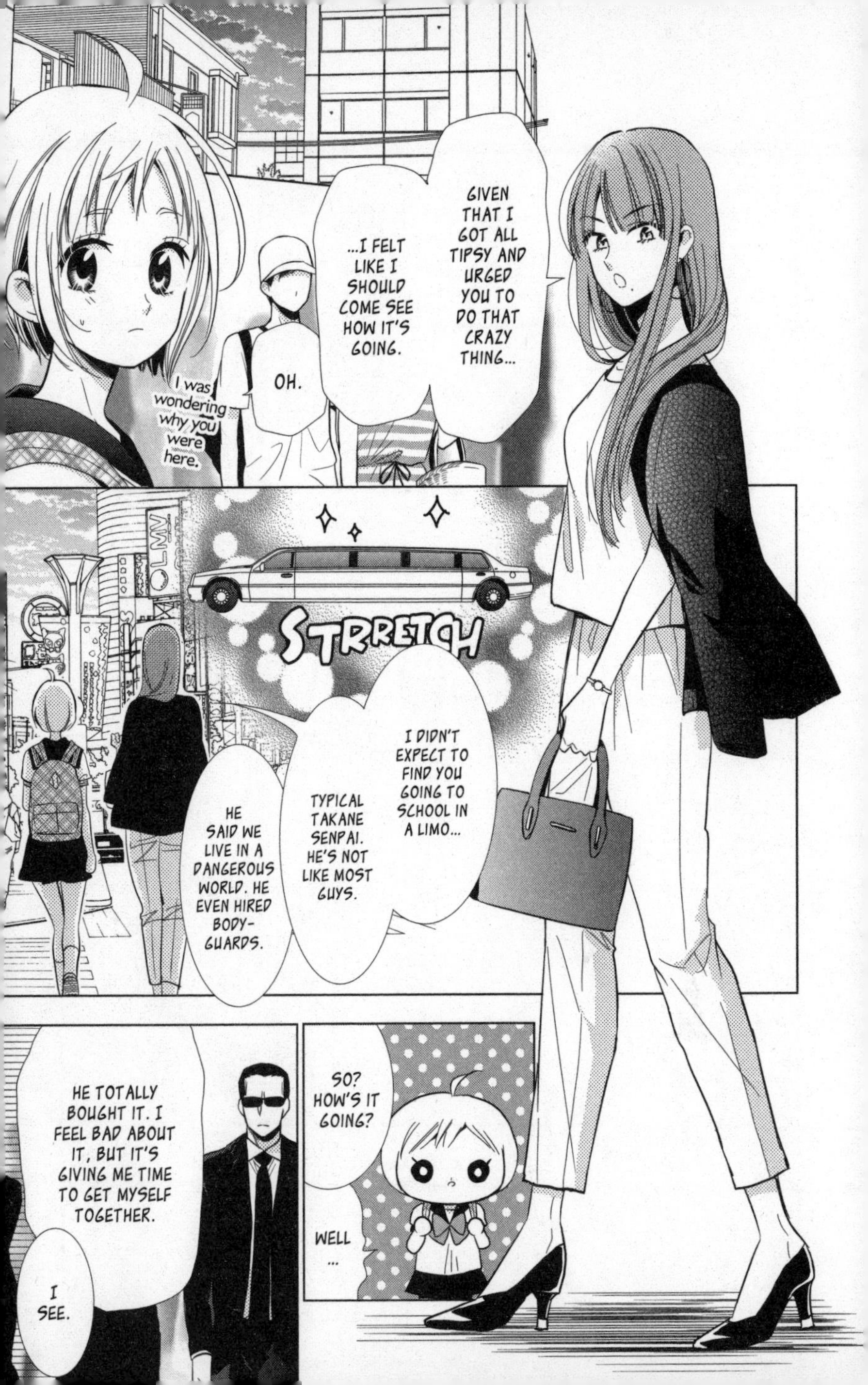
GIVEN THAT I GOT ALL TIPSY AND URGED YOU TO DO THAT CRAZY THING...
...I FELT LIKE I SHOULD COME SEE HOW IT'S GOING.
OH.
I was wondering why you were here.
STRRETCH
I DIDN'T EXPECT TO FIND YOU GOING TO SCHOOL IN A LIMO...
TYPICAL TAKANE SENPAI. HE'S NOT LIKE MOST GUYS.
HE SAID WE LIVE IN A DANGEROUS WORLD. HE EVEN HIRED BODY-GUARDS.
SO? HOW'S IT GOING?
WELL ...
HE TOTALLY BOUGHT IT. I FEEL BAD ABOUT IT, BUT IT'S GIVING ME TIME TO GET MYSELF TOGETHER.
I SEE.

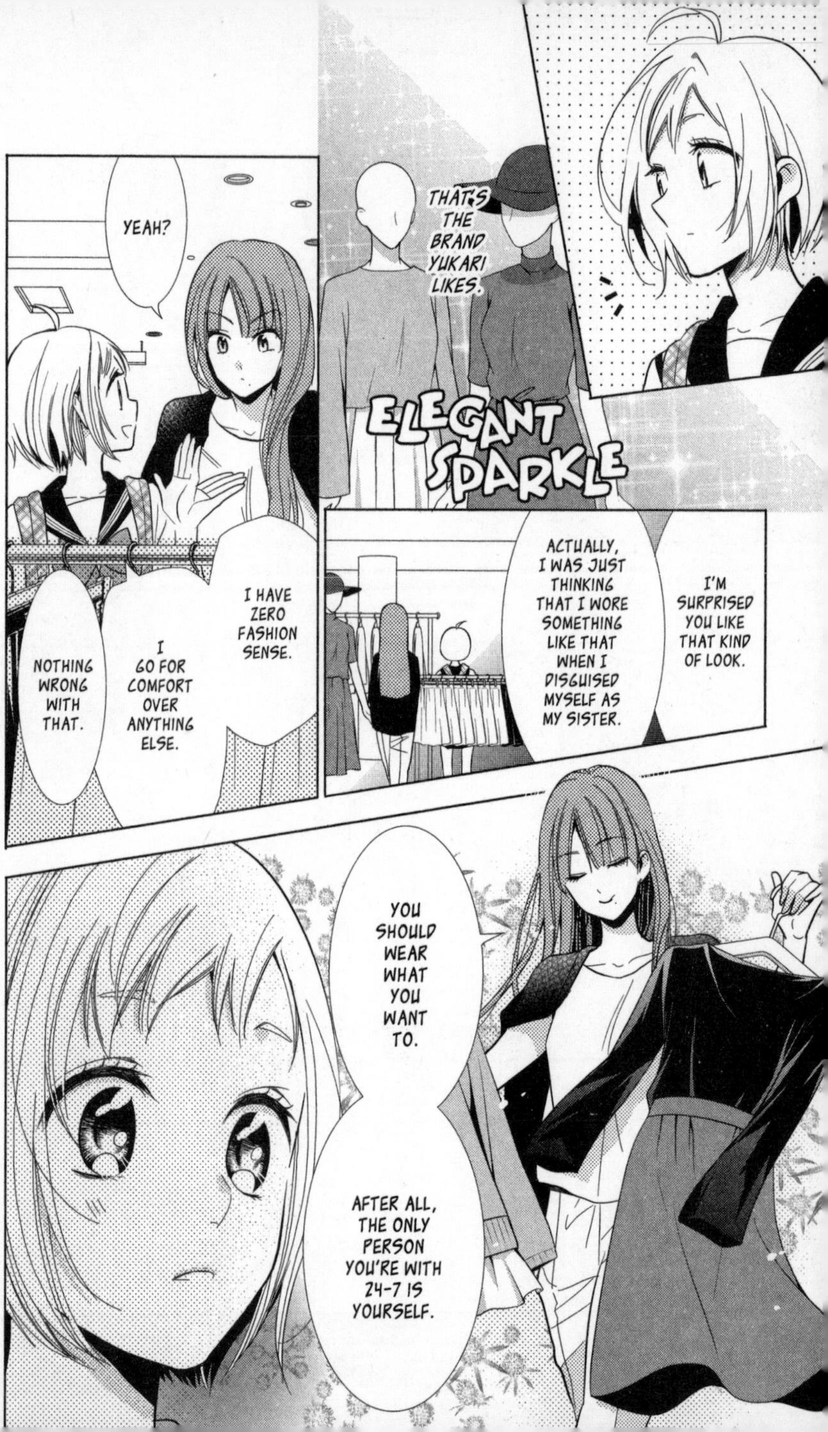
THAT'S THE BRAND YUKARI LIKES.
ELEGANT SPARKLE
I'M SURPRISED YOU LIKE THAT KIND OF LOOK.
ACTUALLY, I WAS JUST THINKING THAT I WORE SOMETHING LIKE THAT WHEN I DISGUISED MYSELF AS MY SISTER.
YEAH?
I HAVE ZERO FASHION SENSE.
I GO FOR COMFORT OVER ANYTHING ELSE.
NOTHING WRONG WITH THAT.
YOU SHOULD WEAR WHAT YOU WANT TO.
AFTER ALL, THE ONLY PERSON YOU'RE WITH 24-7 IS YOURSELF.

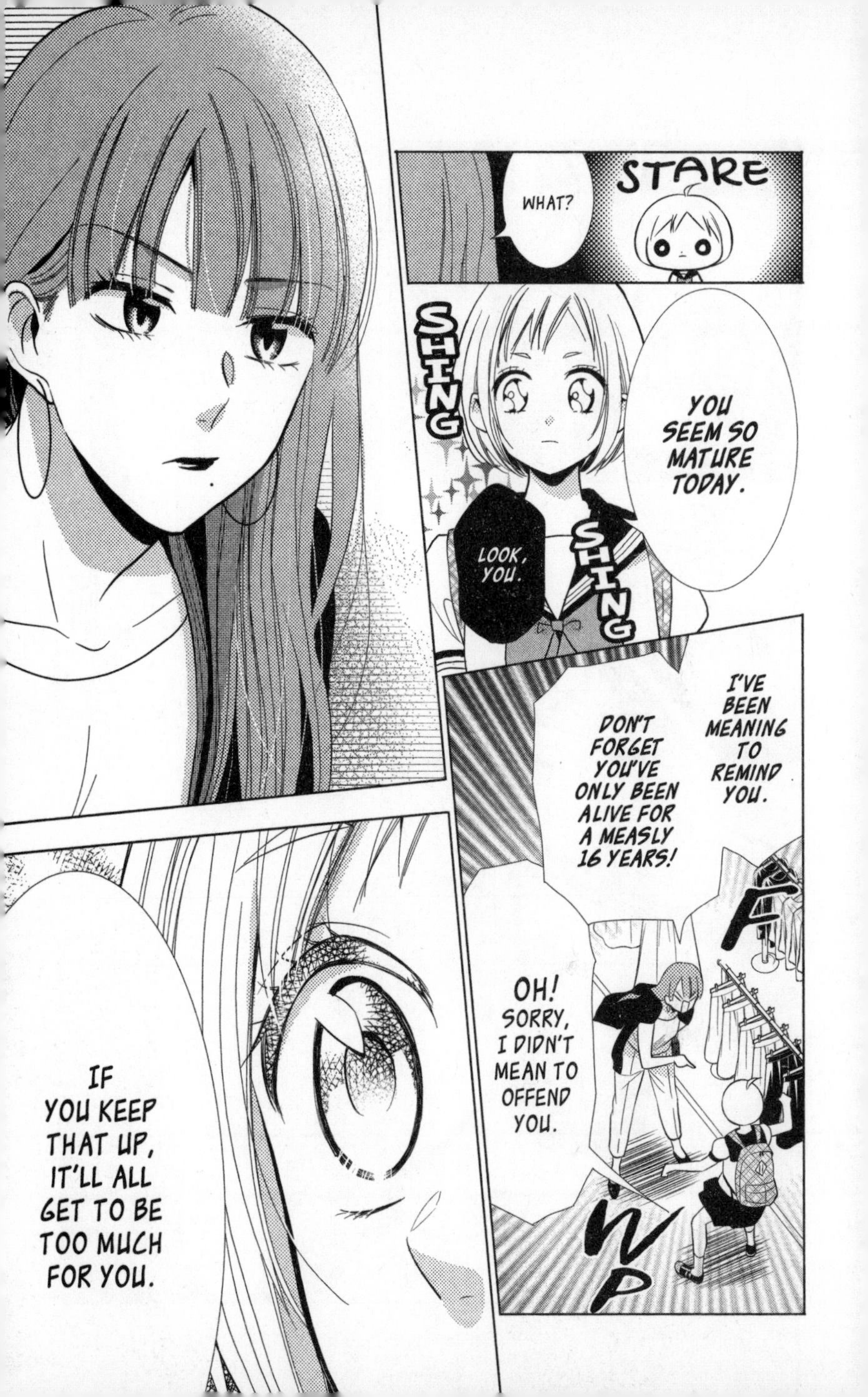
STARE
WHAT?
YOU SEEM SO MATURE TODAY.
SHING
SHING
LOOK, YOU.
I'VE BEEN MEANING TO REMIND YOU.
DON'T FORGET YOU'VE ONLY BEEN ALIVE FOR A MEASLY 16 YEARS!
OH! SORRY, I DIDN'T MEAN TO OFFEND YOU.
IF YOU KEEP THAT UP, IT'LL ALL GET TO BE TOO MUCH FOR YOU.

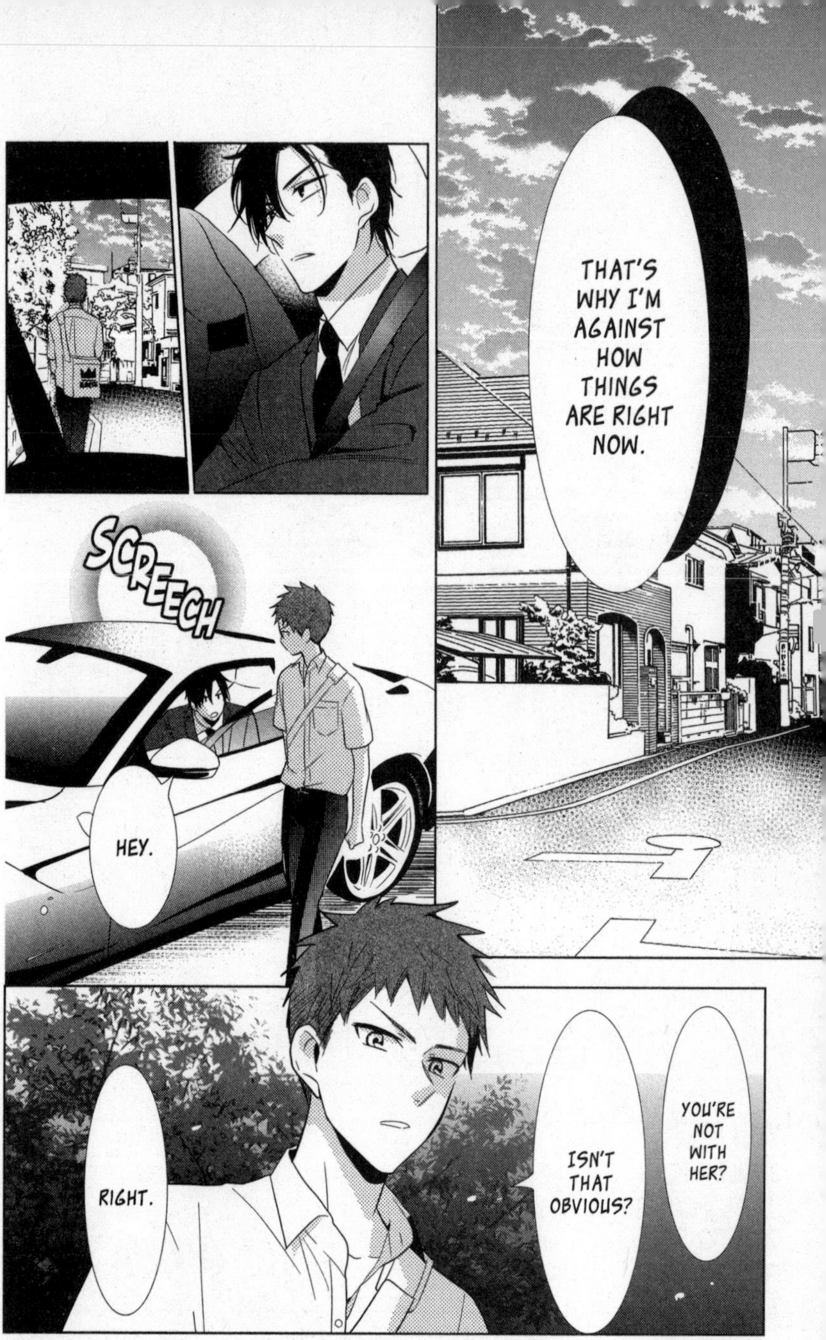
THAT'S WHY I'M AGAINST HOW THINGS ARE RIGHT NOW.
SCREECH
HEY.
YOU'RE NOT WITH HER?
ISN'T THAT OBVIOUS?
RIGHT.

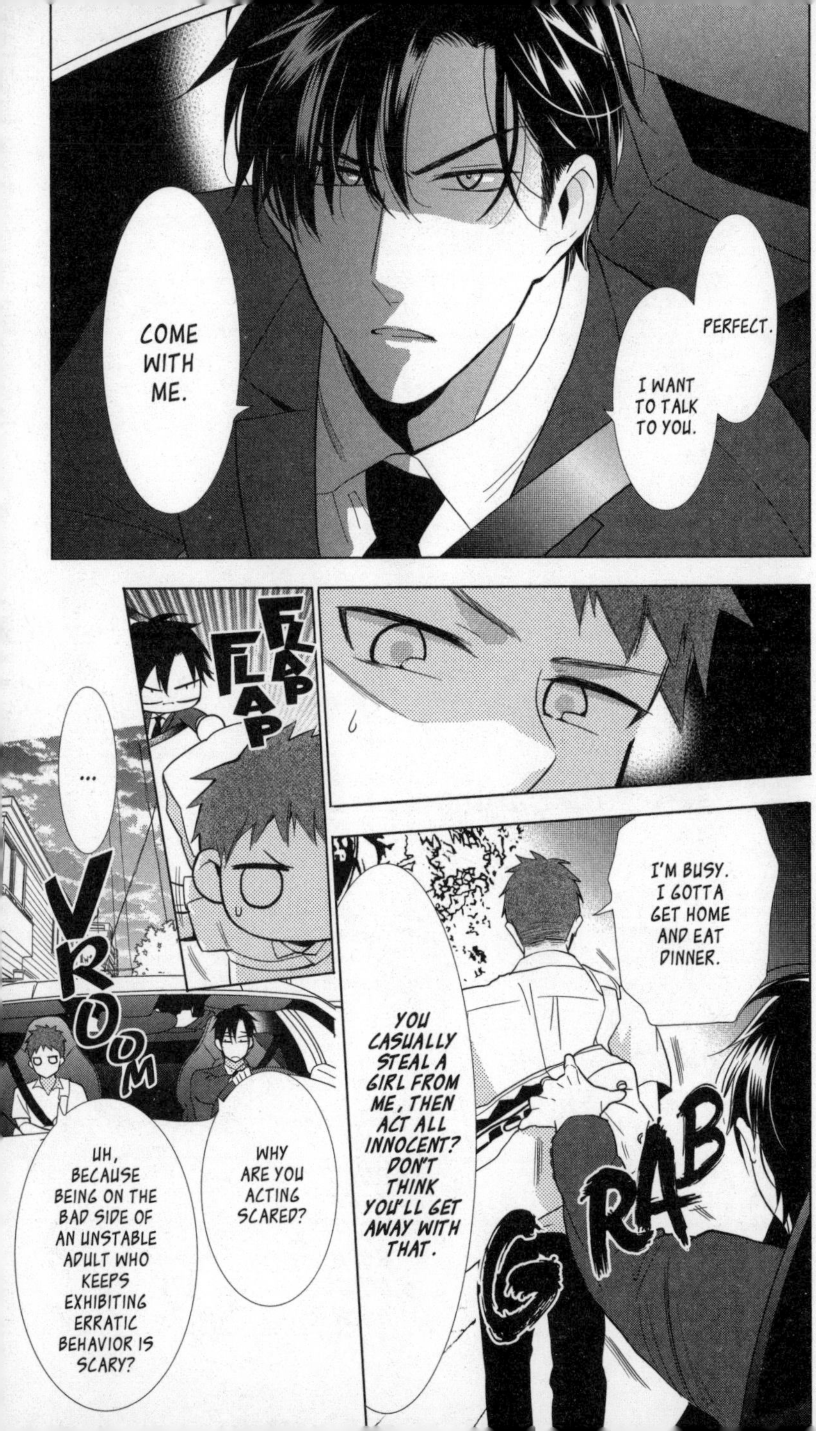
PERFECT.
I WANT TO TALK TO YOU.
COME WITH ME.
FLAP FLAP
...
I'M BUSY. I GOTTA GET HOME AND EAT DINNER.
YOU CASUALLY STEAL A GIRL FROM ME, THEN ACT ALL INNOCENT? DON'T THINK YOU'LL GET AWAY WITH THAT.
GRAB
VROOM
WHY ARE YOU ACTING SCARED?
UH, BECAUSE BEING ON THE BAD SIDE OF AN UNSTABLE ADULT WHO KEEPS EXHIBITING ERRATIC BEHAVIOR IS SCARY?

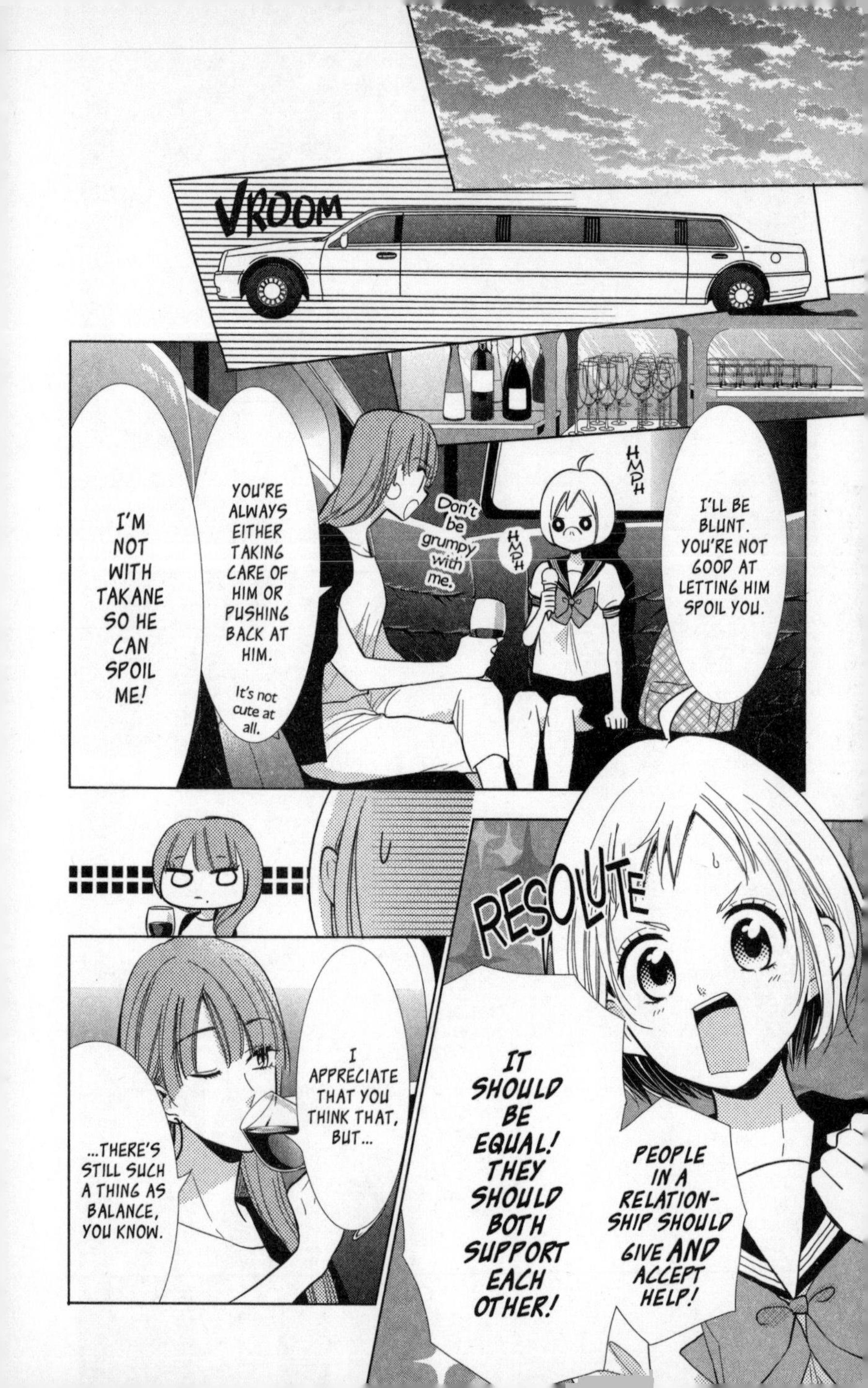
VROOM
I'LL BE BLUNT. YOU'RE NOT GOOD AT LETTING HIM SPOIL YOU.
HMPH
HMPH
Don't be grumpy with me.
YOU'RE ALWAYS EITHER TAKING CARE OF HIM OR PUSHING BACK AT HIM.
It's not cute at all.
I'M NOT WITH TAKANE SO HE CAN SPOIL ME!
RESOLUTE
PEOPLE IN A RELATION-SHIP SHOULD GIVE AND ACCEPT HELP!
IT SHOULD BE EQUAL! THEY SHOULD BOTH SUPPORT EACH OTHER!
I APPRECIATE THAT YOU THINK THAT, BUT...
...THERE'S STILL SUCH A THING AS BALANCE, YOU KNOW.

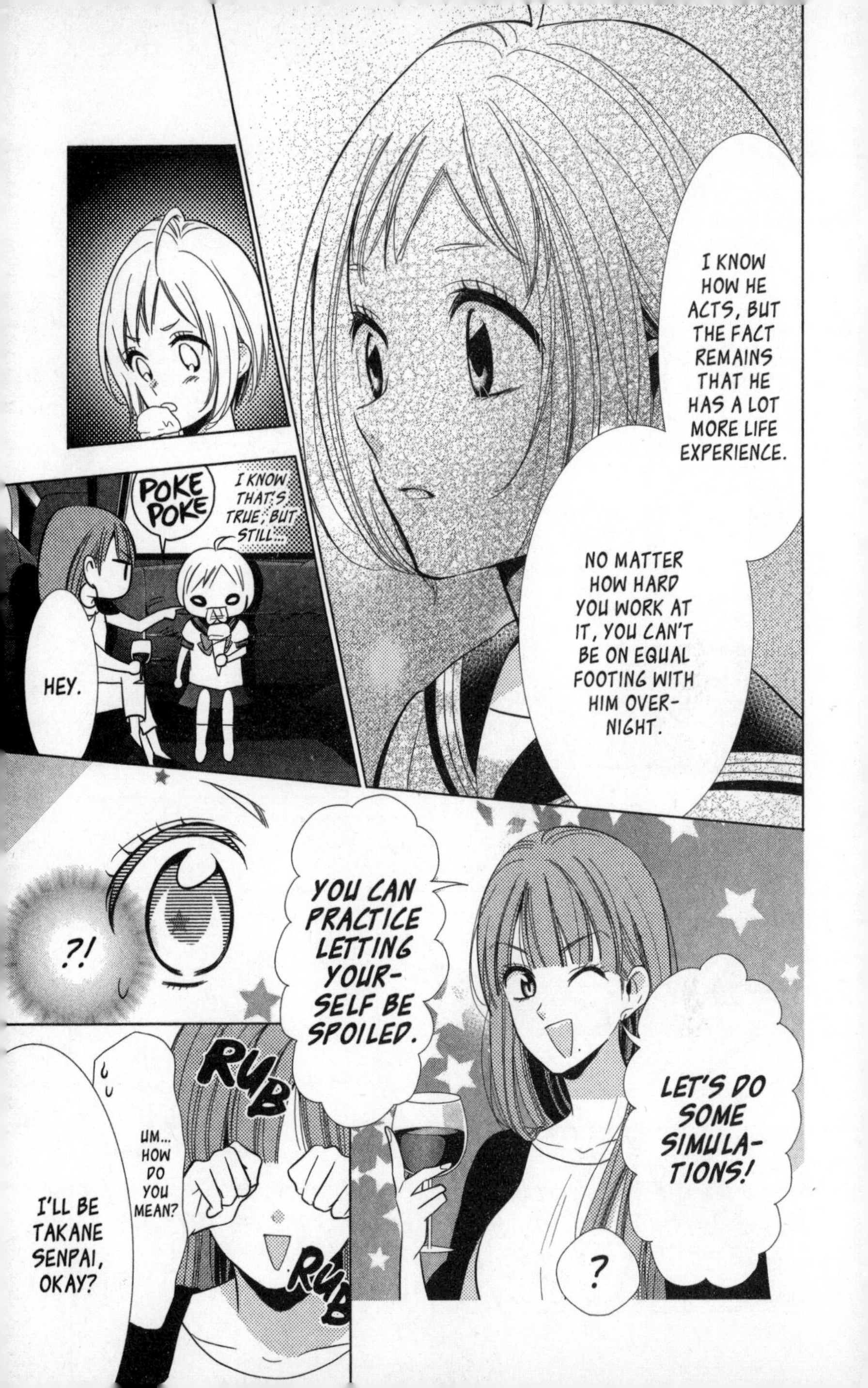
I KNOW HOW HE ACTS, BUT THE FACT REMAINS THAT HE HAS A LOT MORE LIFE EXPERIENCE.
NO MATTER HOW HARD YOU WORK AT IT, YOU CAN'T BE ON EQUAL FOOTING WITH HIM OVER-NIGHT.
I KNOW THAT'S TRUE, BUT STILL...
POKE POKE
HEY.
YOU CAN PRACTICE LETTING YOUR-SELF BE SPOILED.
?!
LET'S DO SOME SIMULA-TIONS!
?
RUB RUB
UM... HOW DO YOU MEAN?
I'LL BE TAKANE SENPAI, OKAY?

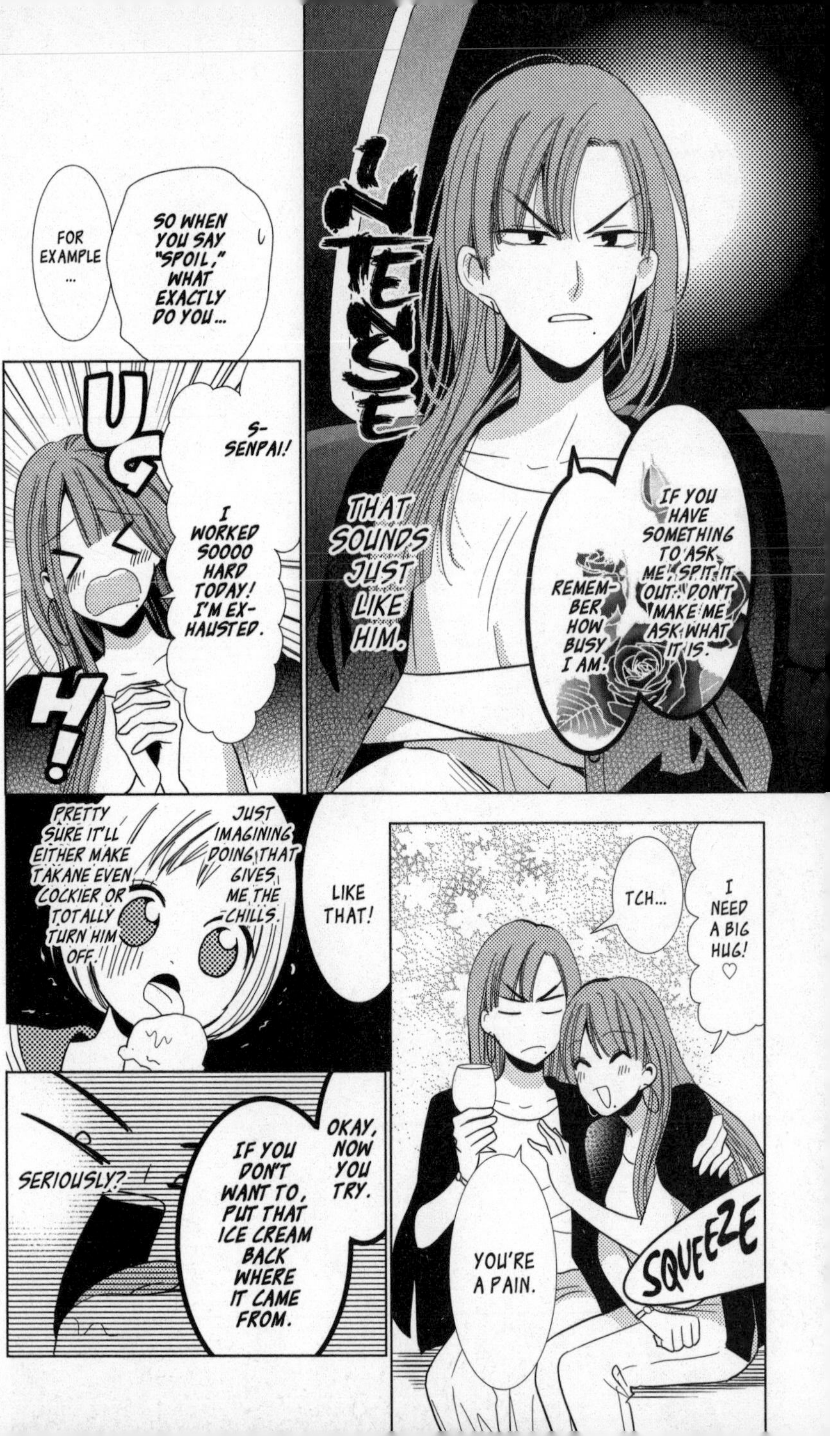
SO WHEN YOU SAY "SPOIL," WHAT EXACTLY DO YOU...
FOR EXAMPLE...
UGH!
S-SENPAI!
I WORKED SOOOO HARD TODAY! I'M EXHAUSTED.
TENSE
IF YOU HAVE SOMETHING TO ASK ME, SPIT IT OUT. DON'T MAKE ME ASK WHAT IT IS.
REMEMBER HOW BUSY I AM.
THAT SOUNDS JUST LIKE HIM.
I NEED A BIG HUG! ♡
TCH...
SQUEEZE
YOU'RE A PAIN.
LIKE THAT!
JUST IMAGINING DOING THAT GIVES ME THE CHILLS.
PRETTY SURE IT'LL EITHER MAKE TAKANE EVEN COCKIER OR TOTALLY TURN HIM OFF.
OKAY, NOW YOU TRY.
IF YOU DON'T WANT TO, PUT THAT ICE CREAM BACK WHERE IT CAME FROM.
SERIOUSLY?

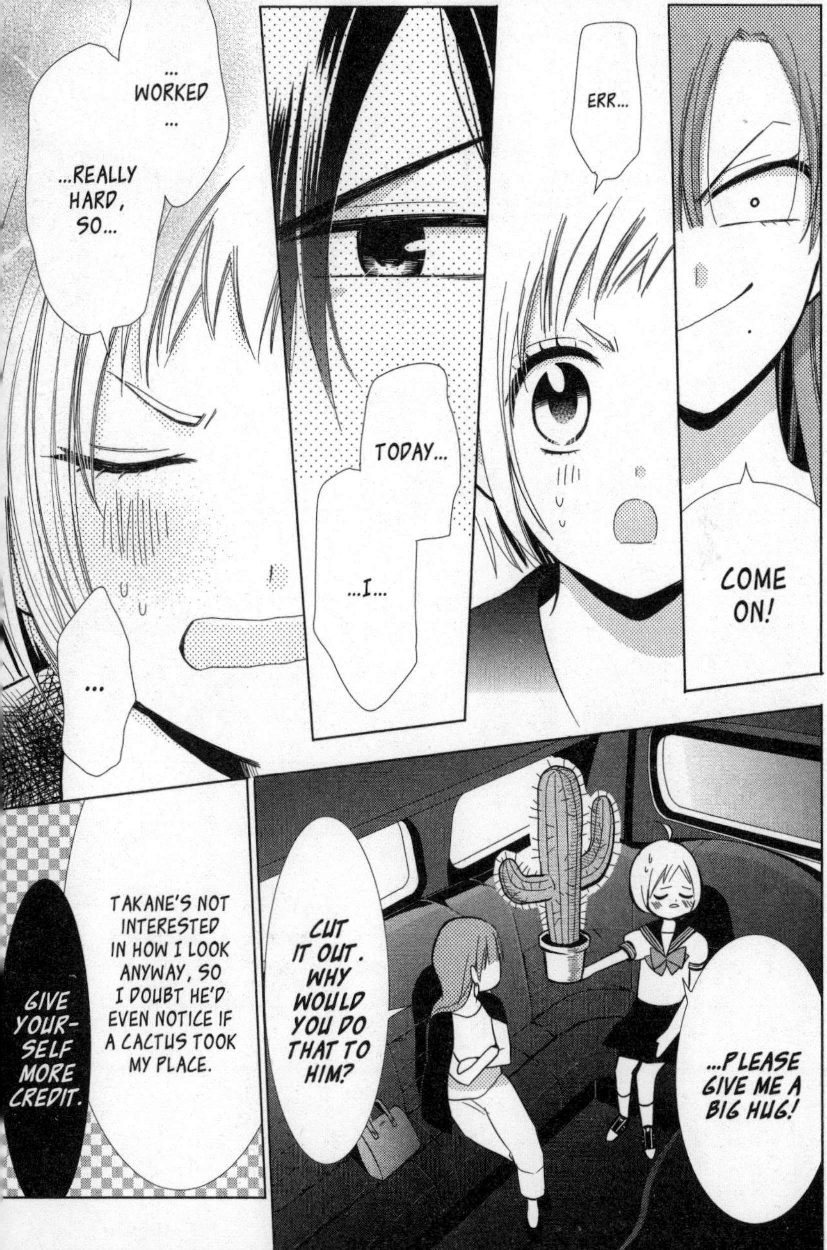
COME ON!
ERR...
TODAY...
...I...
... WORKED ...
...REALLY HARD, SO...
...
...PLEASE GIVE ME A BIG HUG!
CUT IT OUT. WHY WOULD YOU DO THAT TO HIM?
TAKANE'S NOT INTERESTED IN HOW I LOOK ANYWAY, SO I DOUBT HE'D EVEN NOTICE IF A CACTUS TOOK MY PLACE.
GIVE YOURSELF MORE CREDIT.

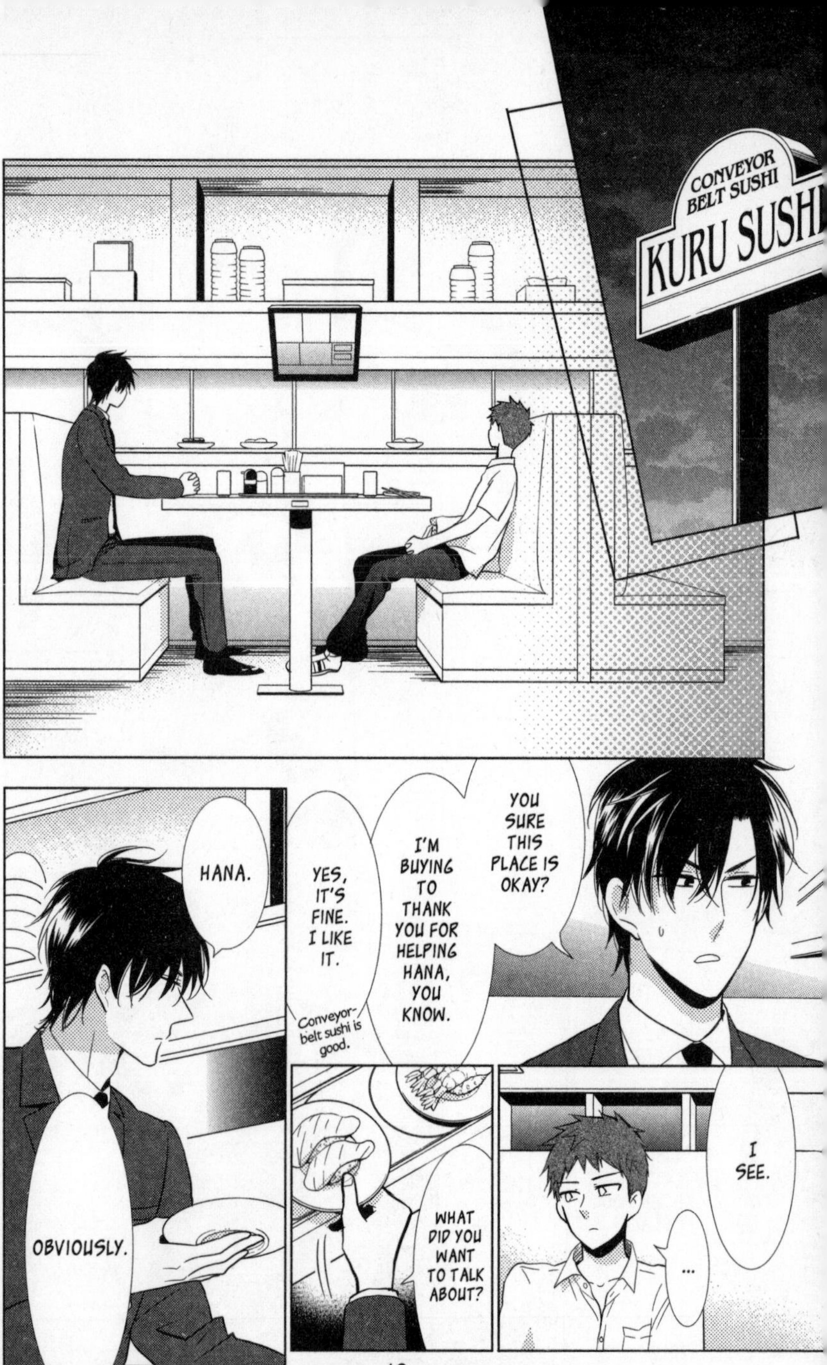
CONVEYOR BELT SUSHI
KURU SUSH
YOU SURE THIS PLACE IS OKAY?
I'M BUYING TO THANK YOU FOR HELPING HANA, YOU KNOW.
YES, IT'S FINE. I LIKE IT.
Conveyor-belt sushi is good.
I SEE.
...
WHAT DID YOU WANT TO TALK ABOUT?
HANA.
OBVIOUSLY.

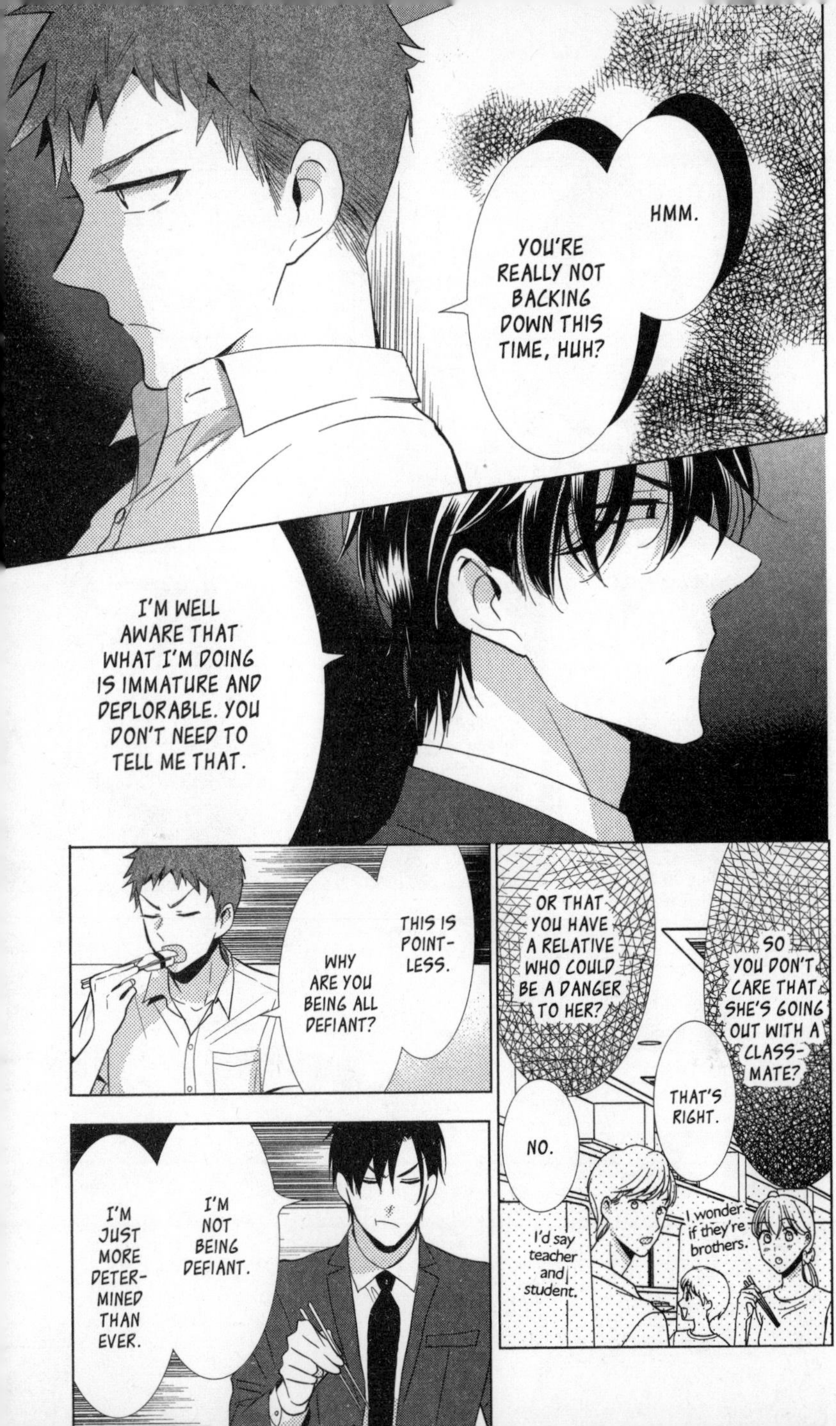
HMM.
YOU'RE REALLY NOT BACKING DOWN THIS TIME, HUH?
I'M WELL AWARE THAT WHAT I'M DOING IS IMMATURE AND DEPLORABLE. YOU DON'T NEED TO TELL ME THAT.
SO YOU DON'T CARE THAT SHE'S GOING OUT WITH A CLASS-MATE?
THAT'S RIGHT.
OR THAT YOU HAVE A RELATIVE WHO COULD BE A DANGER TO HER?
NO.
I wonder if they're brothers.
I'd say teacher and student.
THIS IS POINT-LESS.
WHY ARE YOU BEING ALL DEFIANT?
I'M NOT BEING DEFIANT.
I'M JUST MORE DETER-MINED THAN EVER.

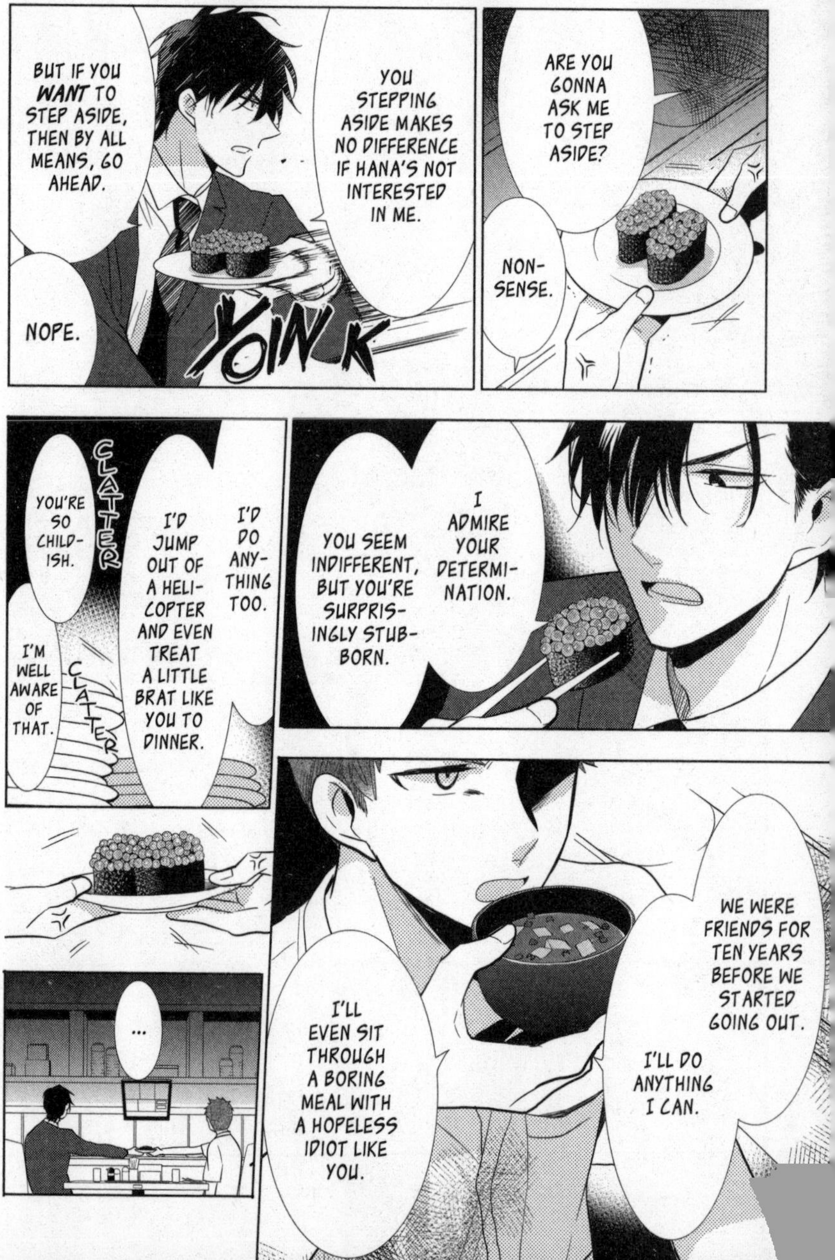
ARE YOU GONNA ASK ME TO STEP ASIDE?
NON-SENSE.
YOU STEPPING ASIDE MAKES NO DIFFERENCE IF HANA'S NOT INTERESTED IN ME.
BUT IF YOU *WANT* TO STEP ASIDE, THEN BY ALL MEANS, GO AHEAD.
YOINK
NOPE.
I ADMIRE YOUR DETERMI-NATION.
YOU SEEM INDIFFERENT, BUT YOU'RE SURPRIS-INGLY STUB-BORN.
I'D DO ANY-THING TOO.
I'D JUMP OUT OF A HELI-COPTER AND EVEN TREAT A LITTLE BRAT LIKE YOU TO DINNER.
CLATTER
YOU'RE SO CHILD-ISH.
I'M WELL AWARE OF THAT.
CLATTER
WE WERE FRIENDS FOR TEN YEARS BEFORE WE STARTED GOING OUT.
I'LL DO ANYTHING I CAN.
I'LL EVEN SIT THROUGH A BORING MEAL WITH A HOPELESS IDIOT LIKE YOU.
...

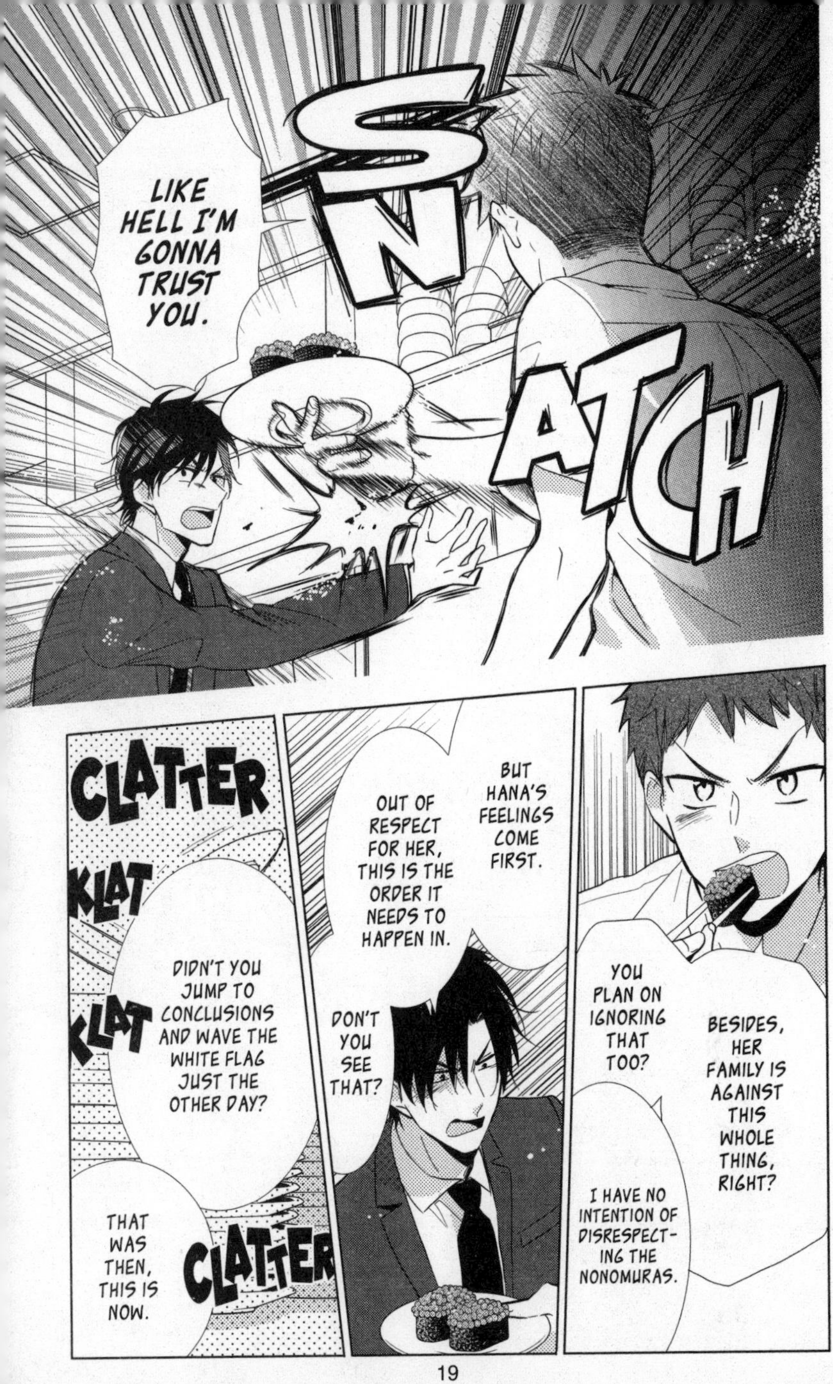
LIKE HELL I'M GONNA TRUST YOU.
SNATCH
BESIDES, HER FAMILY IS AGAINST THIS WHOLE THING, RIGHT?
YOU PLAN ON IGNORING THAT TOO?
I HAVE NO INTENTION OF DISRESPECTING THE NONOMURAS.
BUT HANA'S FEELINGS COME FIRST.
OUT OF RESPECT FOR HER, THIS IS THE ORDER IT NEEDS TO HAPPEN IN.
DON'T YOU SEE THAT?
CLATTER
KLAT
KLAT
DIDN'T YOU JUMP TO CONCLUSIONS AND WAVE THE WHITE FLAG JUST THE OTHER DAY?
CLATTER
THAT WAS THEN, THIS IS NOW.

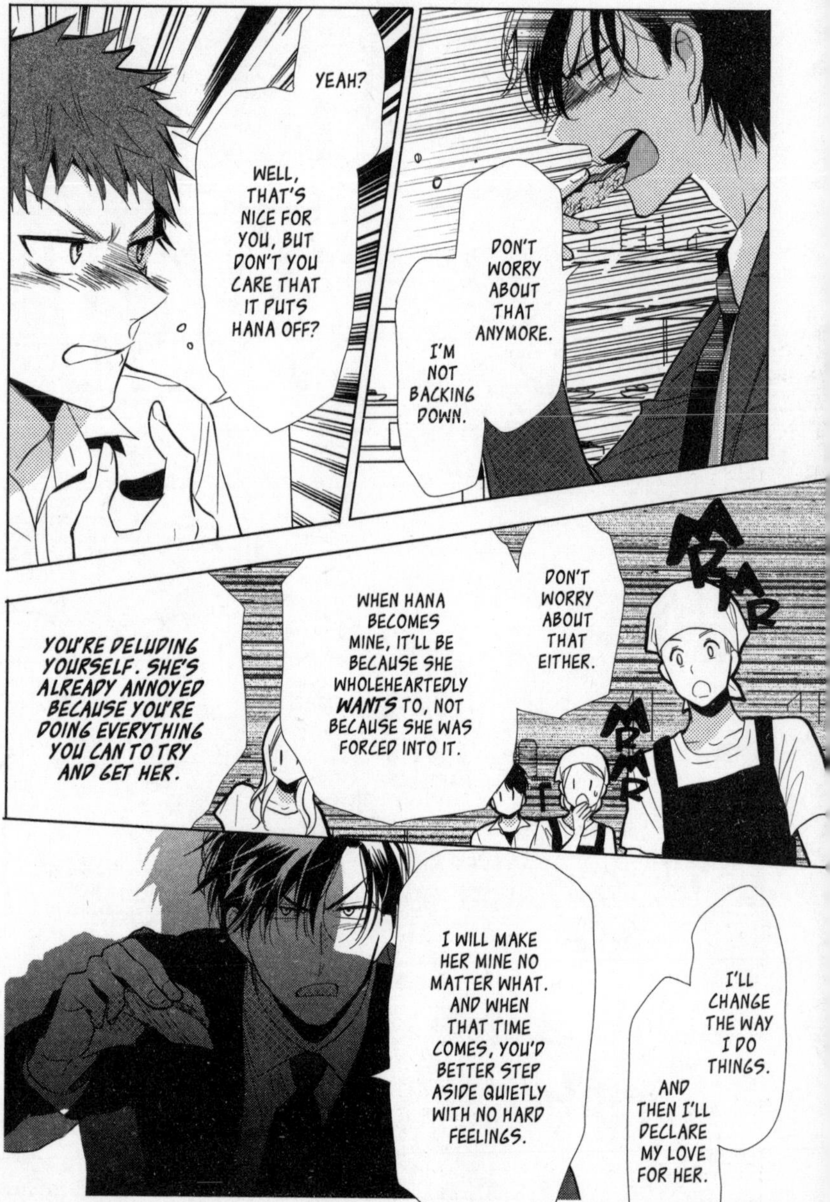
DON'T WORRY ABOUT THAT ANYMORE.
I'M NOT BACKING DOWN.
YEAH?
WELL, THAT'S NICE FOR YOU, BUT DON'T YOU CARE THAT IT PUTS HANA OFF?
MRMR
DON'T WORRY ABOUT THAT EITHER.
WHEN HANA BECOMES MINE, IT'LL BE BECAUSE SHE WHOLEHEARTEDLY **WANTS** TO, NOT BECAUSE SHE WAS FORCED INTO IT.
MRMR
YOU'RE DELUDING YOURSELF. SHE'S ALREADY ANNOYED BECAUSE YOU'RE DOING EVERYTHING YOU CAN TO TRY AND GET HER.
I'LL CHANGE THE WAY I DO THINGS.
AND THEN I'LL DECLARE MY LOVE FOR HER.
I WILL MAKE HER MINE NO MATTER WHAT. AND WHEN THAT TIME COMES, YOU'D BETTER STEP ASIDE QUIETLY WITH NO HARD FEELINGS.

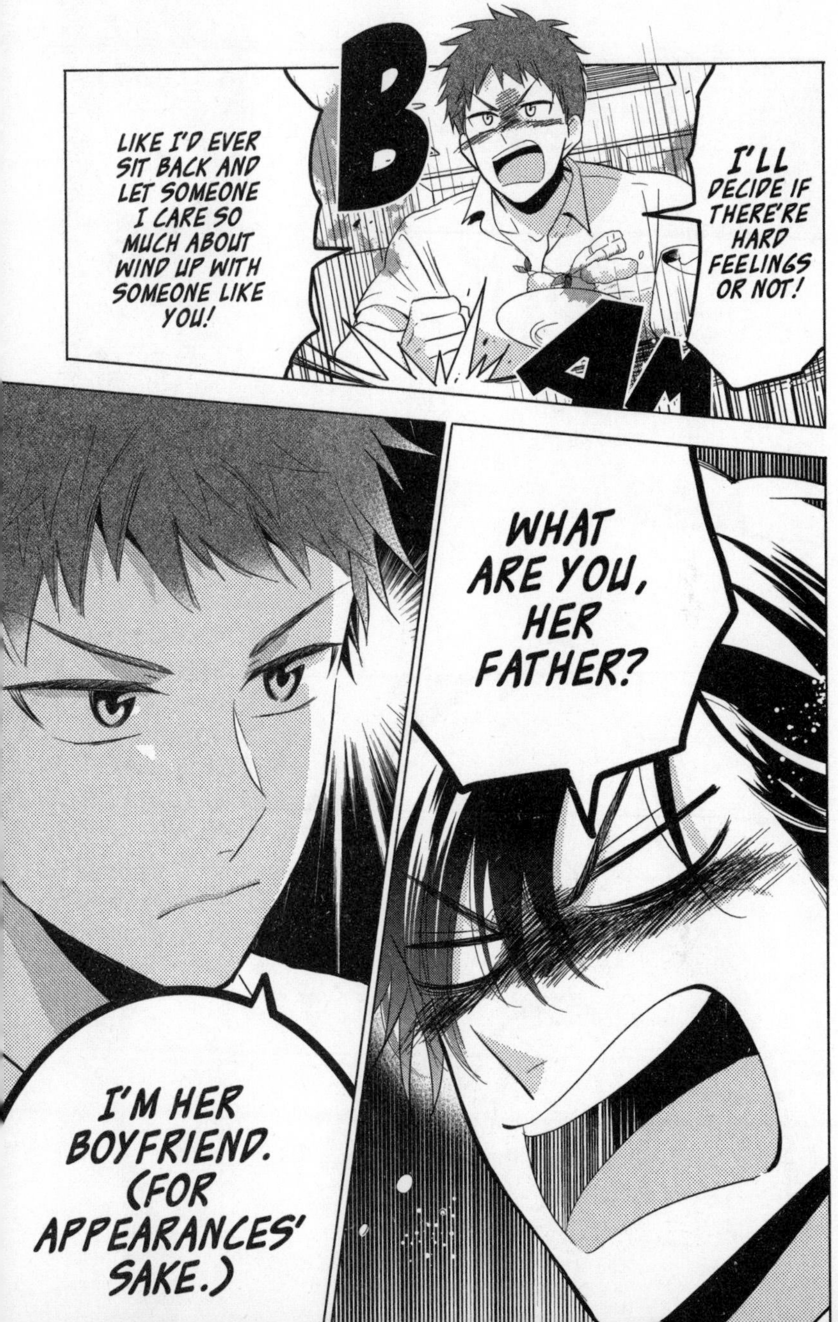
I'LL DECIDE IF THERE'RE HARD FEELINGS OR NOT!
BAM
LIKE I'D EVER SIT BACK AND LET SOMEONE I CARE SO MUCH ABOUT WIND UP WITH SOMEONE LIKE YOU!
WHAT ARE YOU, HER FATHER?
I'M HER BOYFRIEND. (FOR APPEARANCES' SAKE.)

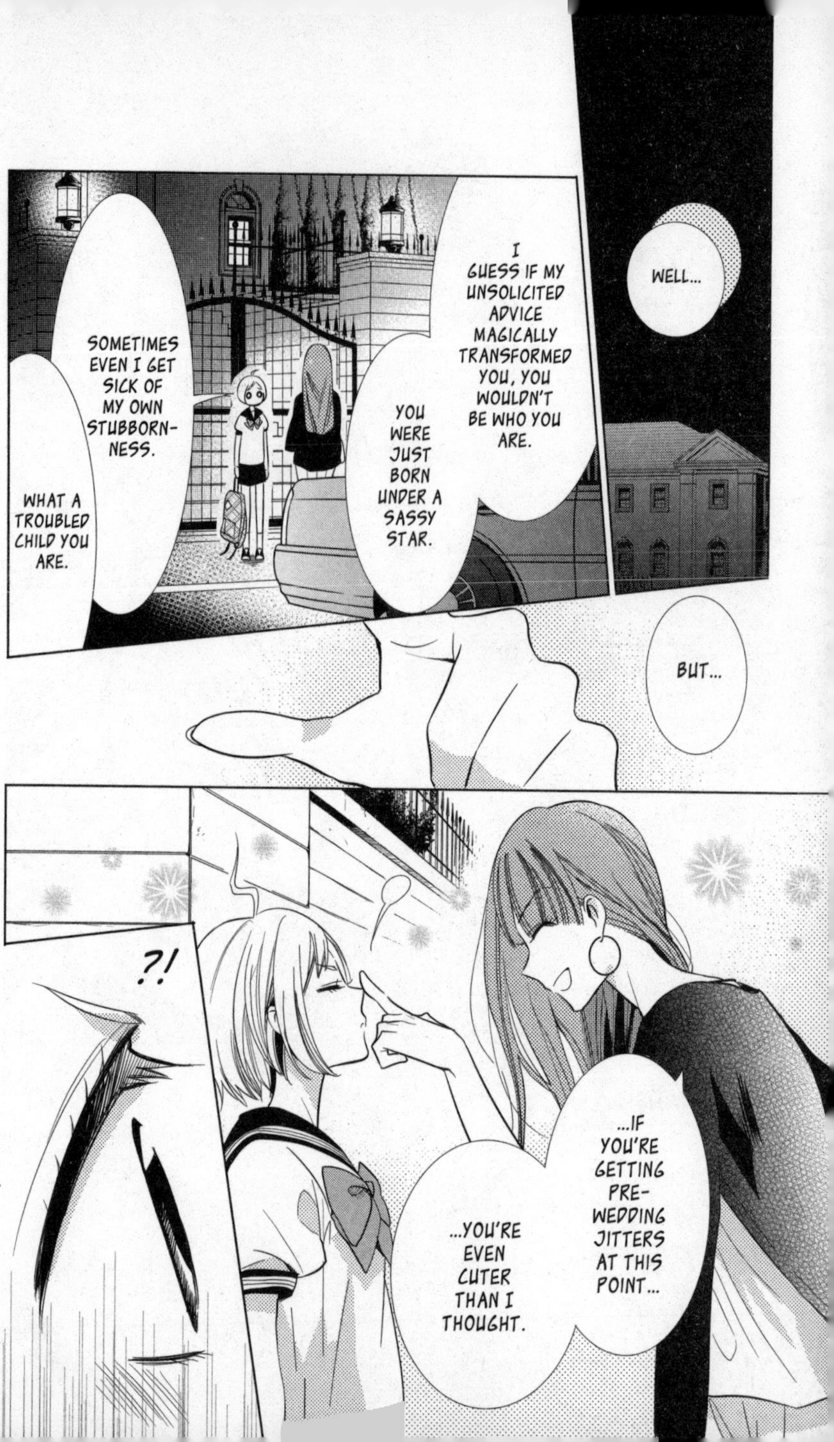
WELL...
I GUESS IF MY UNSOLICITED ADVICE MAGICALLY TRANSFORMED YOU, YOU WOULDN'T BE WHO YOU ARE.
YOU WERE JUST BORN UNDER A SASSY STAR.
SOMETIMES EVEN I GET SICK OF MY OWN STUBBORN-NESS.
WHAT A TROUBLED CHILD YOU ARE.
BUT...
...IF YOU'RE GETTING PRE-WEDDING JITTERS AT THIS POINT...
...YOU'RE EVEN CUTER THAN I THOUGHT.
?!

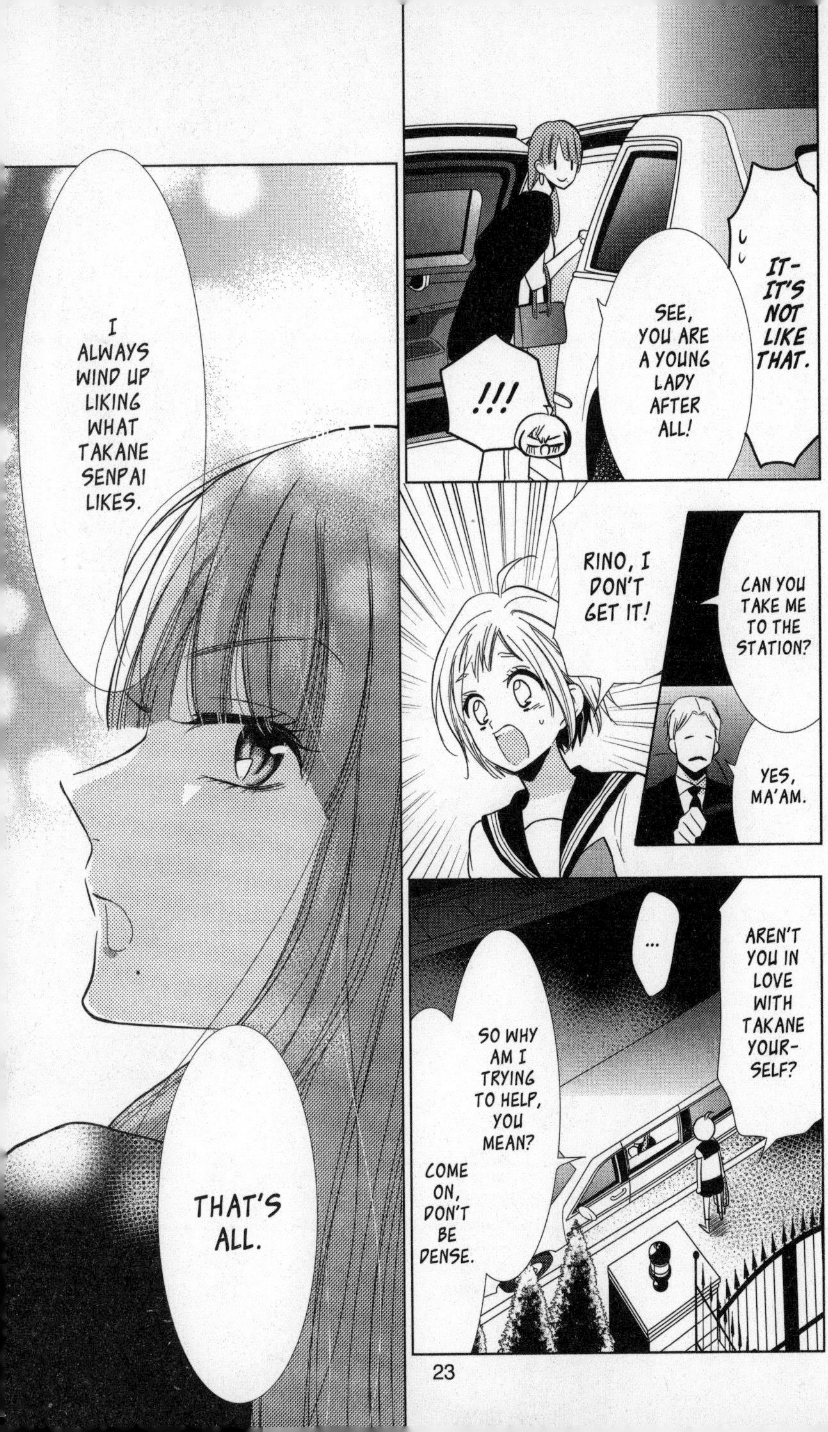
IT-IT'S NOT LIKE THAT.
SEE, YOU ARE A YOUNG LADY AFTER ALL!
!!!
CAN YOU TAKE ME TO THE STATION?
YES, MA'AM.
RINO, I DON'T GET IT!
AREN'T YOU IN LOVE WITH TAKANE YOUR-SELF?
...
SO WHY AM I TRYING TO HELP, YOU MEAN?
COME ON, DON'T BE DENSE.
I ALWAYS WIND UP LIKING WHAT TAKANE SENPAI LIKES.
THAT'S ALL.

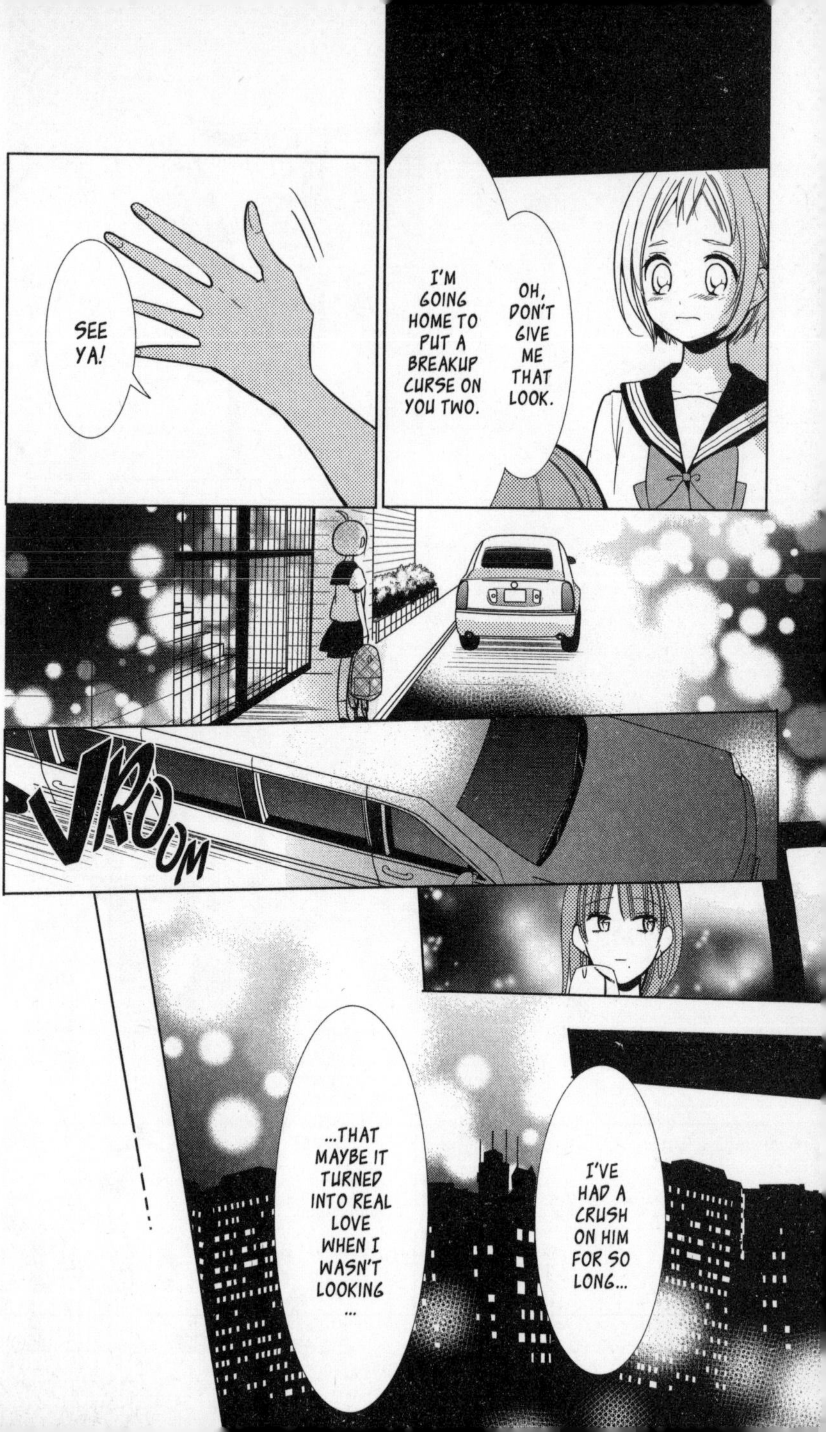
OH, DON'T GIVE ME THAT LOOK.
I'M GOING HOME TO PUT A BREAKUP CURSE ON YOU TWO.
SEE YA!
VROOM
I'VE HAD A CRUSH ON HIM FOR SO LONG...
...THAT MAYBE IT TURNED INTO REAL LOVE WHEN I WASN'T LOOKING...

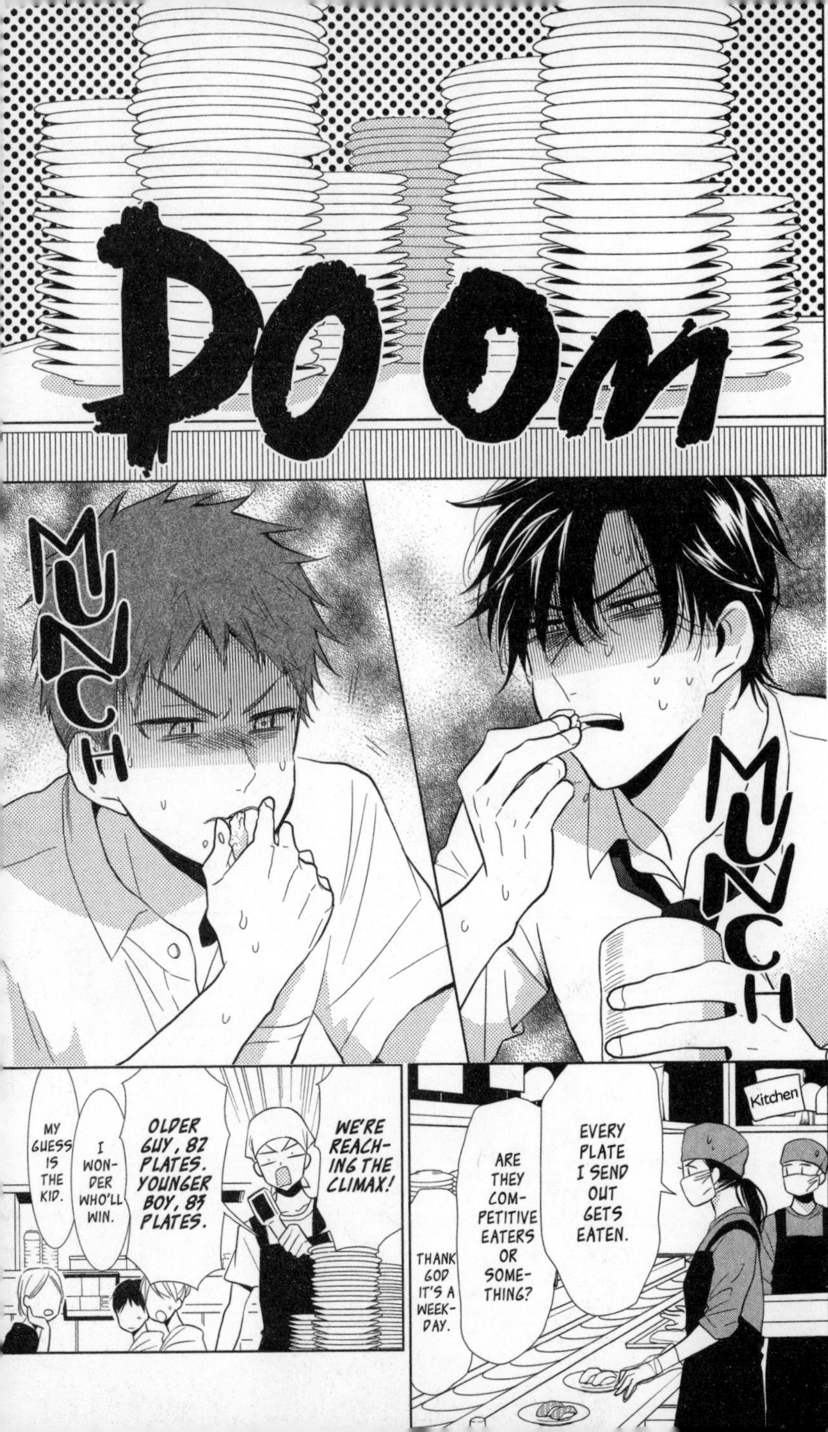
DOOM
MUNCH
MUNCH
Kitchen
EVERY PLATE I SEND OUT GETS EATEN.
ARE THEY COMPETITIVE EATERS OR SOMETHING?
THANK GOD IT'S A WEEKDAY.
WE'RE REACHING THE CLIMAX!
OLDER GUY, 82 PLATES. YOUNGER BOY, 83 PLATES.
I WONDER WHO'LL WIN.
MY GUESS IS THE KID.

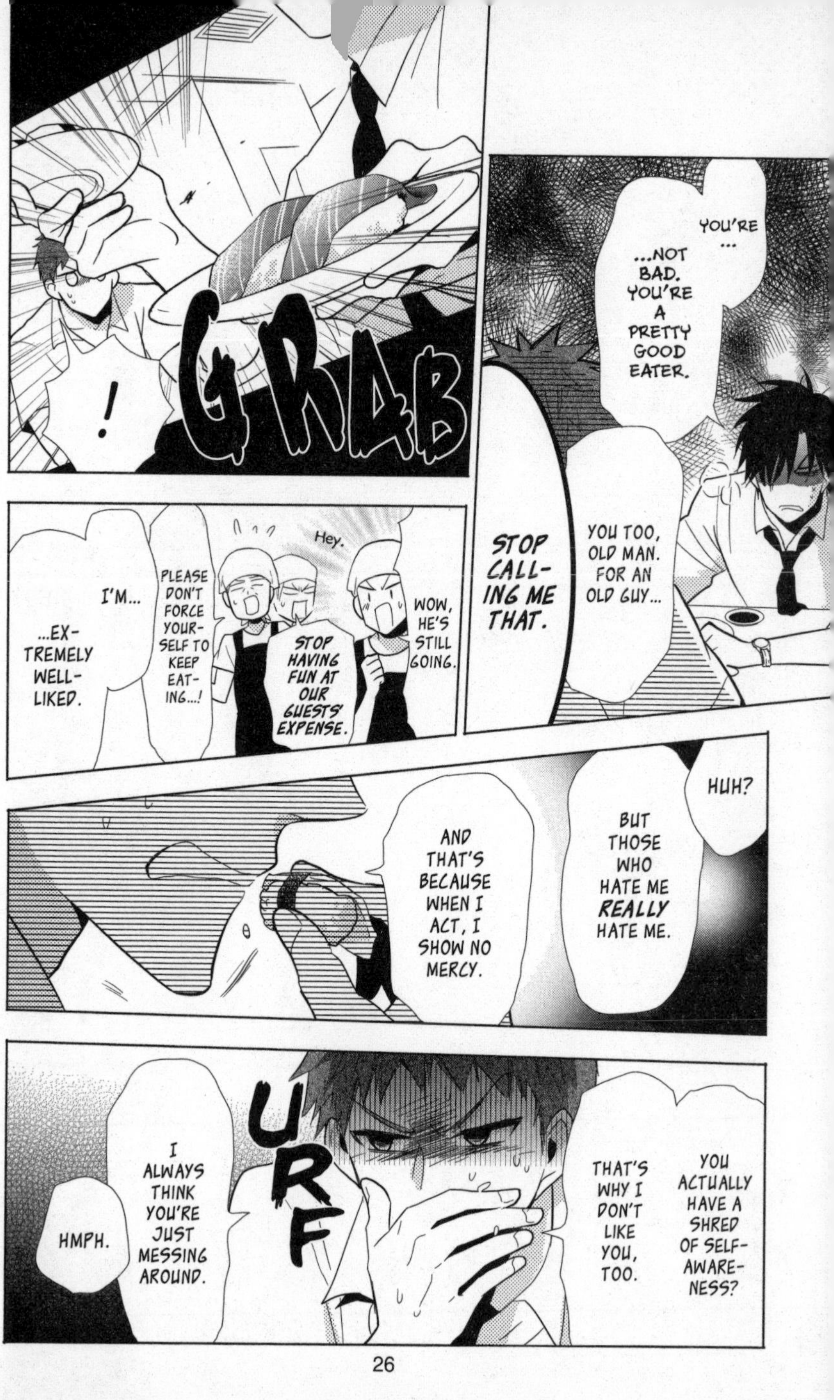
GRAB
!
YOU'RE ...
...NOT BAD. YOU'RE A PRETTY GOOD EATER.
YOU TOO, OLD MAN. FOR AN OLD GUY...
STOP CALLING ME THAT.
WOW, HE'S STILL GOING.
Hey.
STOP HAVING FUN AT OUR GUESTS' EXPENSE.
PLEASE DON'T FORCE YOURSELF TO KEEP EATING...!
I'M...
...EXTREMELY WELL-LIKED.
HUH?
BUT THOSE WHO HATE ME REALLY HATE ME.
AND THAT'S BECAUSE WHEN I ACT, I SHOW NO MERCY.
YOU ACTUALLY HAVE A SHRED OF SELF-AWARENESS?
THAT'S WHY I DON'T LIKE YOU, TOO.
URF
I ALWAYS THINK YOU'RE JUST MESSING AROUND.
HMPH.

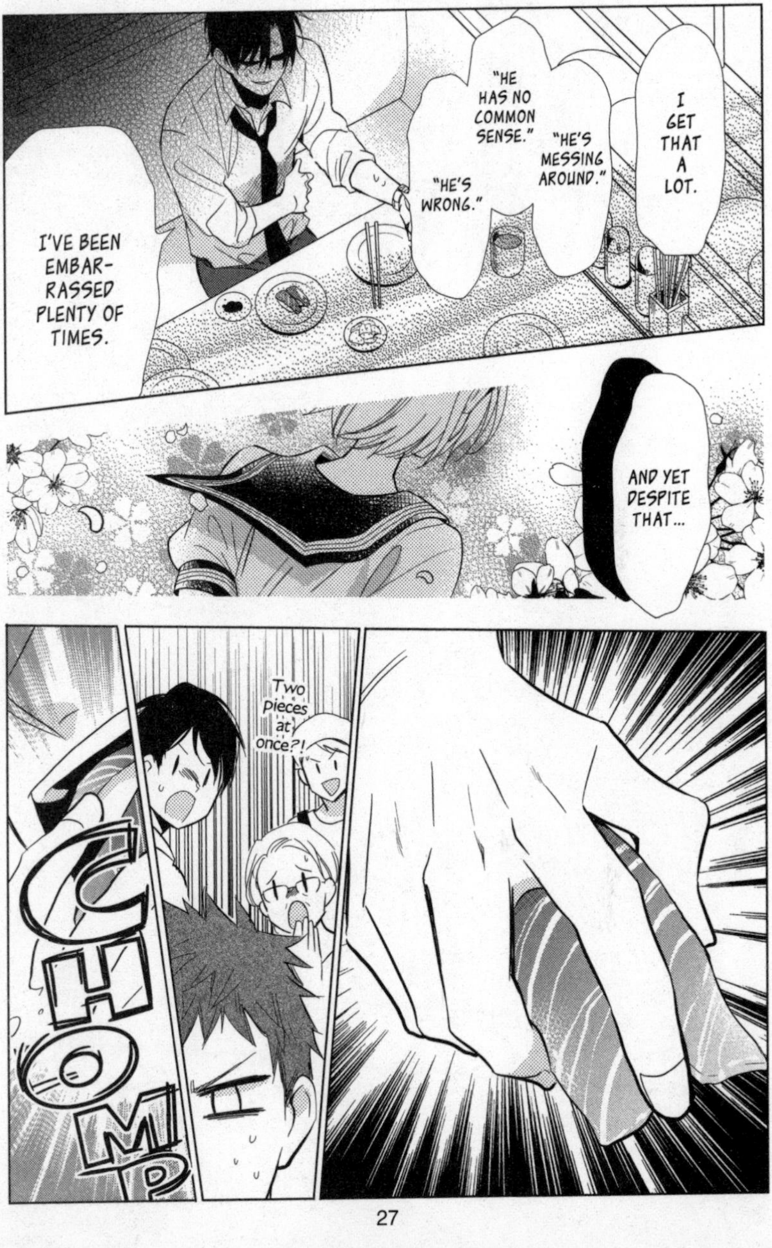
I GET THAT A LOT.
"HE HAS NO COMMON SENSE."
"HE'S MESSING AROUND."
"HE'S WRONG."
I'VE BEEN EMBAR-RASSED PLENTY OF TIMES.
AND YET DESPITE THAT...
Two pieces at once?!
CHOMP

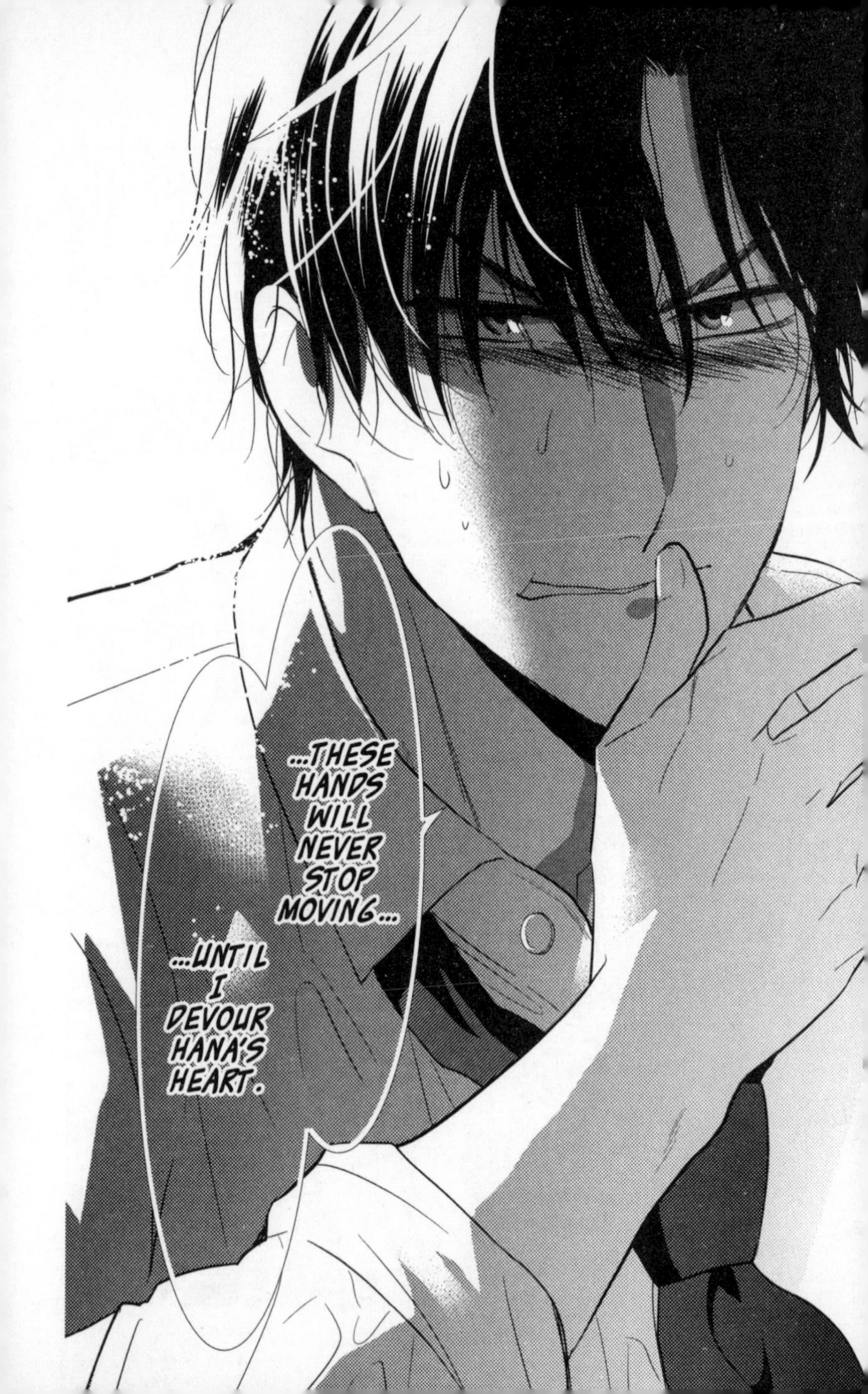
...THESE HANDS WILL NEVER STOP MOVING...
...UNTIL I DEVOUR HANA'S HEART.

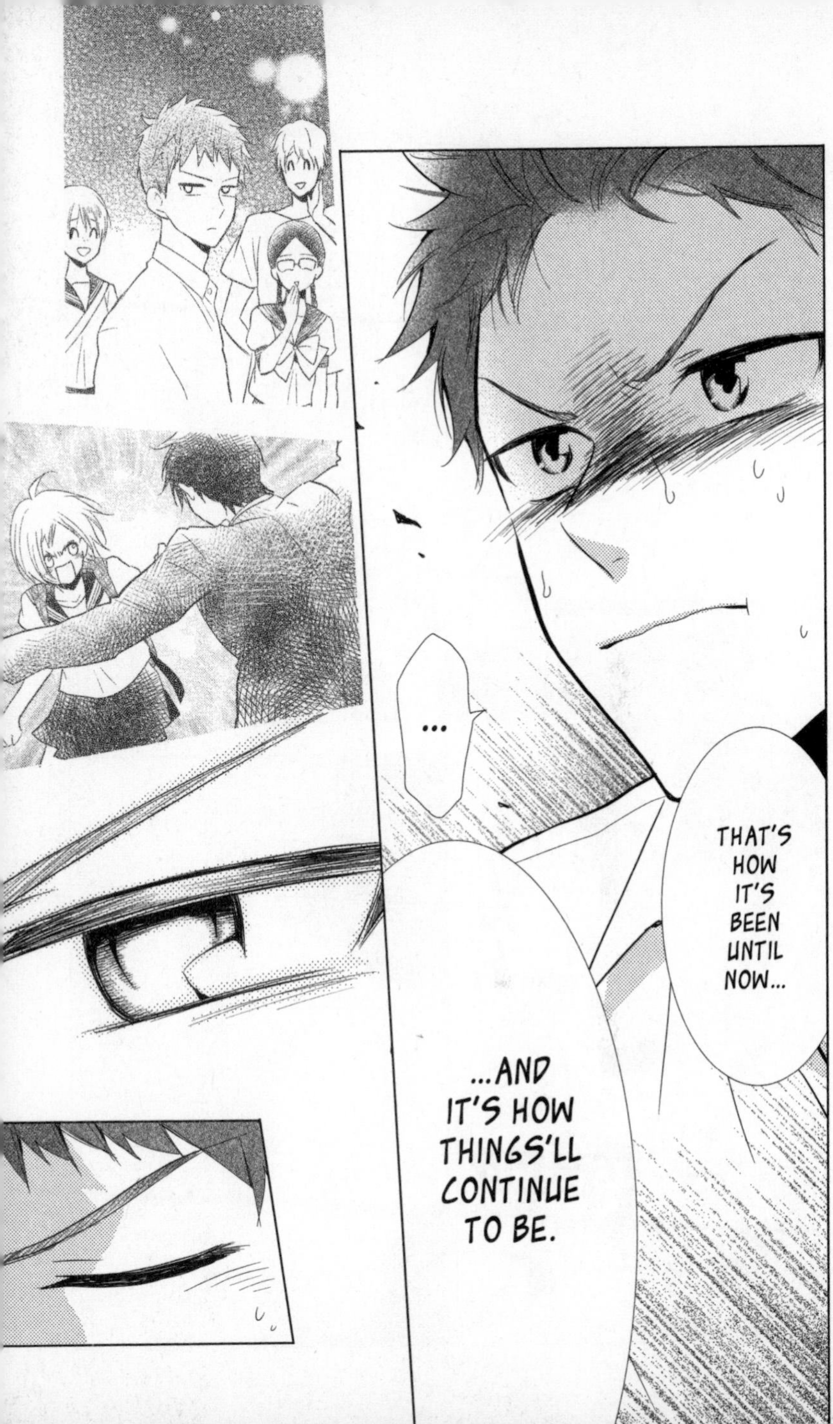
...
THAT'S HOW IT'S BEEN UNTIL NOW...
...AND IT'S HOW THINGS'LL CONTINUE TO BE.

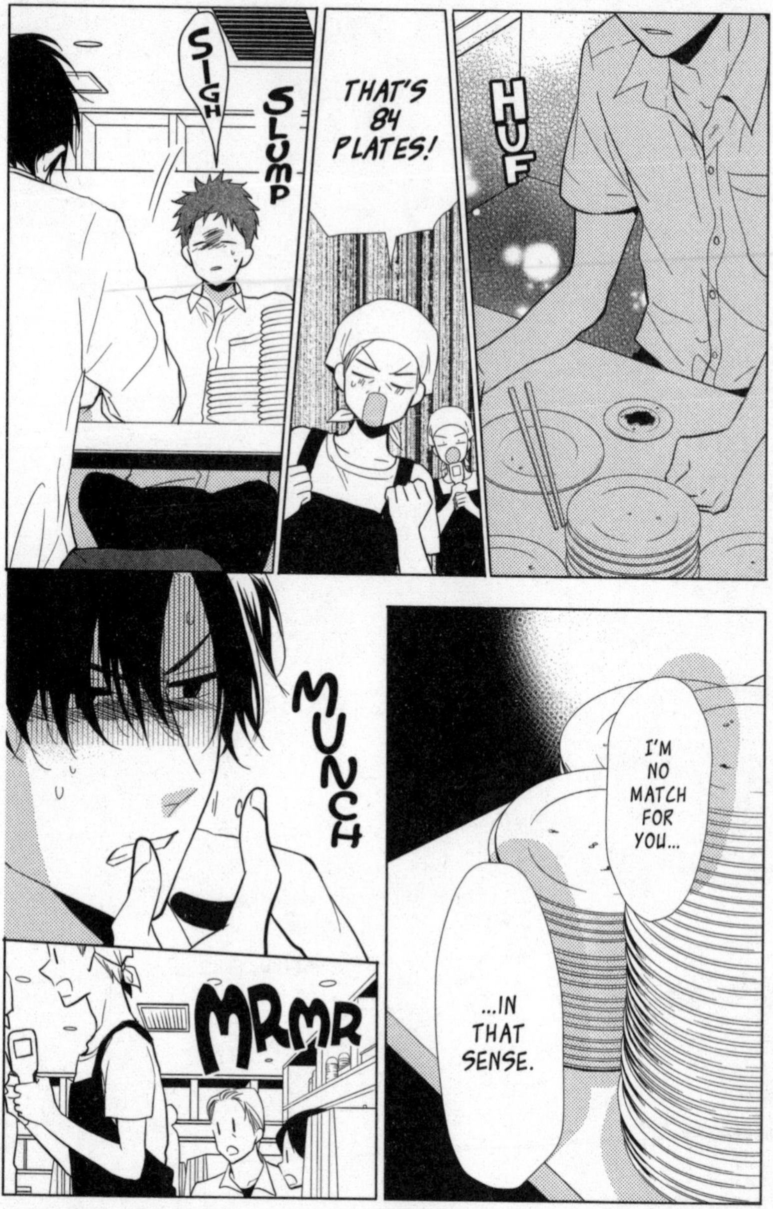
HUF
THAT'S 84 PLATES!
SIGH
SLUMP
I'M NO MATCH FOR YOU...
...IN THAT SENSE.
MUNCH
MRMR

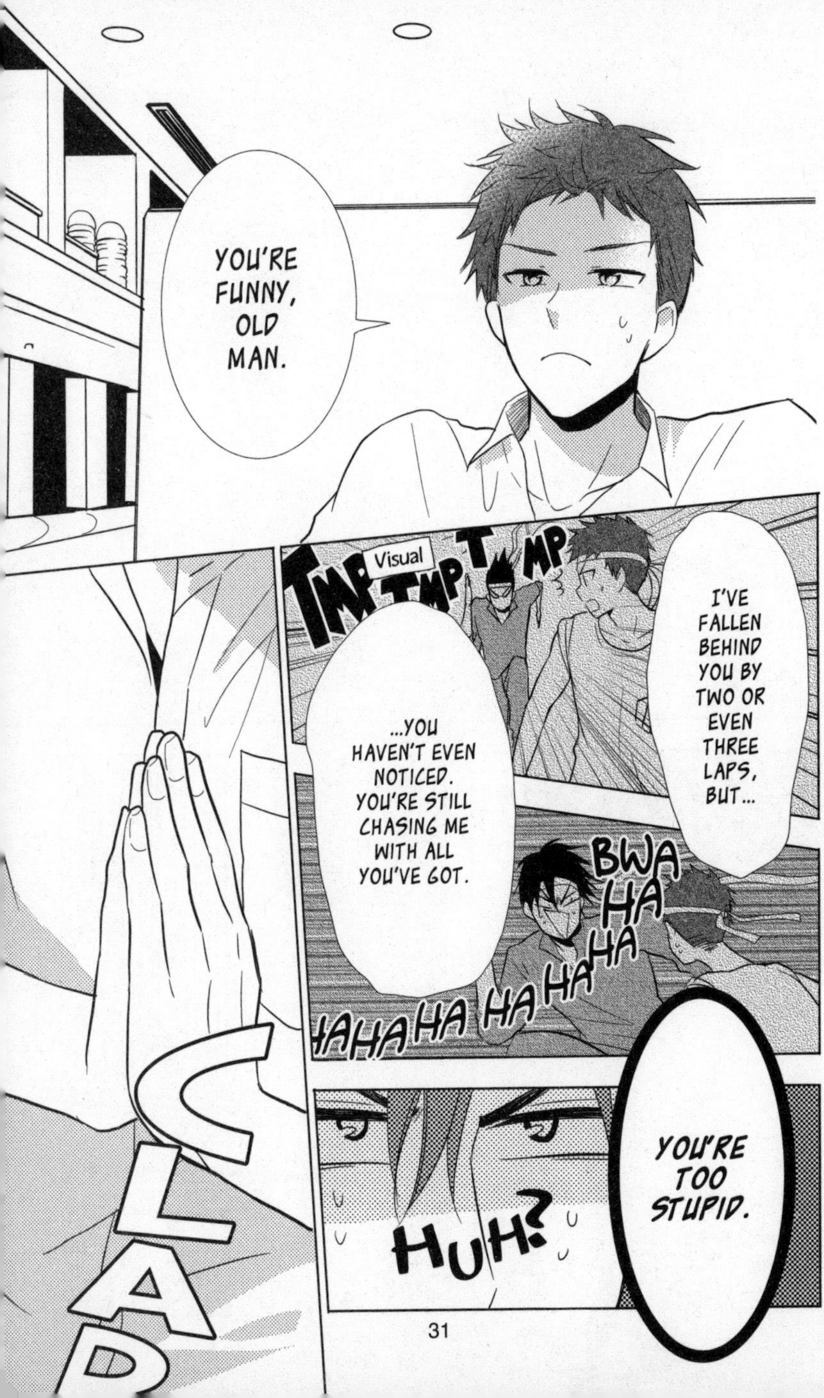
YOU'RE FUNNY, OLD MAN.
TMP TMP TMP TMP
Visual
I'VE FALLEN BEHIND YOU BY TWO OR EVEN THREE LAPS, BUT...
...YOU HAVEN'T EVEN NOTICED. YOU'RE STILL CHASING ME WITH ALL YOU'VE GOT.
BWA HA HA HA HA HA HA HA HA
YOU'RE TOO STUPID.
HUH?
CLAP

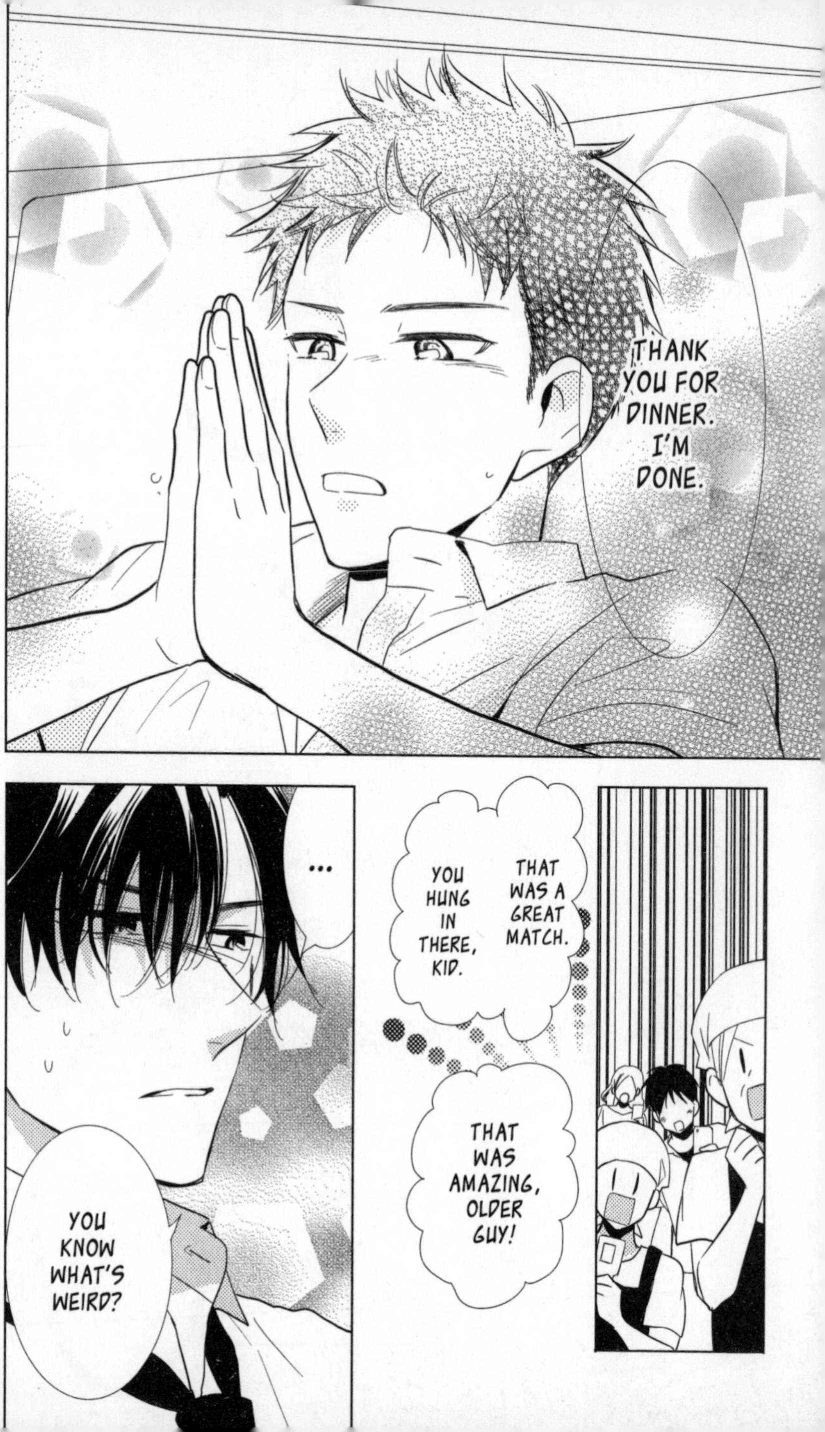
THANK YOU FOR DINNER. I'M DONE.
THAT WAS A GREAT MATCH.
YOU HUNG IN THERE, KID.
THAT WAS AMAZING, OLDER GUY!
...
YOU KNOW WHAT'S WEIRD?

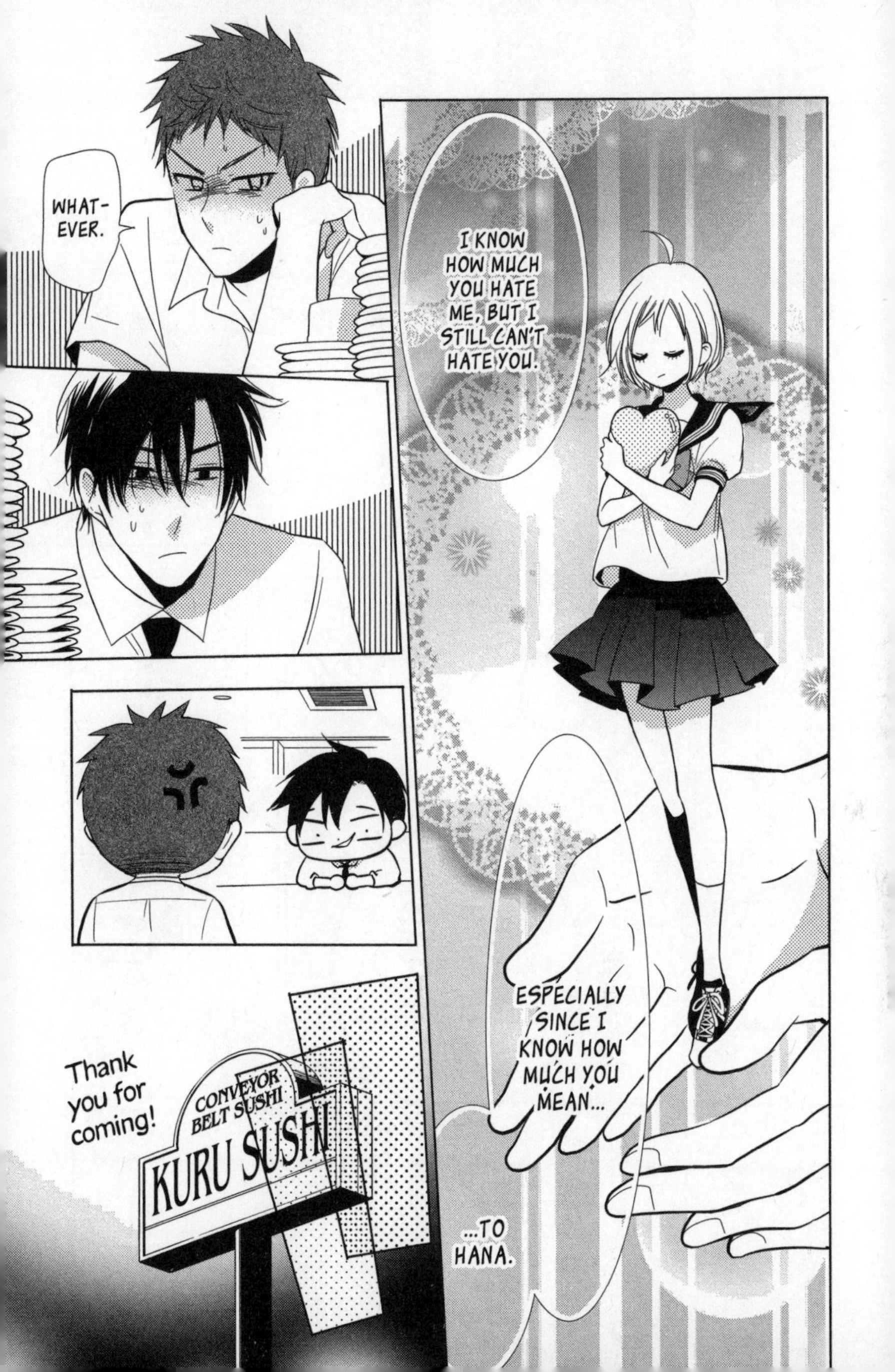
I KNOW HOW MUCH YOU HATE ME, BUT I STILL CAN'T HATE YOU.
ESPECIALLY SINCE I KNOW HOW MUCH YOU MEAN...
...TO HANA.
WHAT-EVER.
Thank you for coming!
CONVEYOR BELT SUSHI
KURU SUSHI

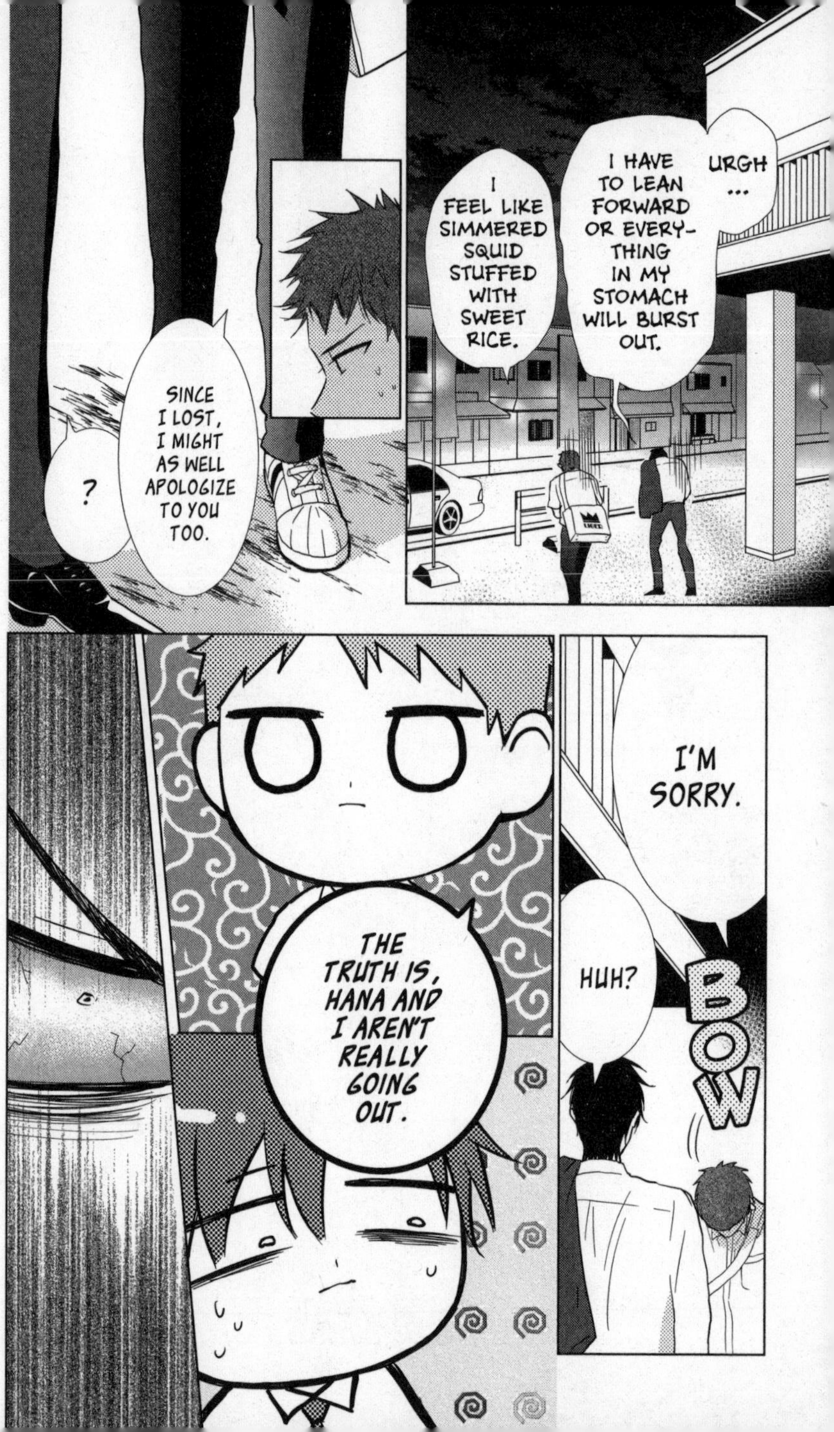
URGH...
I HAVE TO LEAN FORWARD OR EVERY-THING IN MY STOMACH WILL BURST OUT.
I FEEL LIKE SIMMERED SQUID STUFFED WITH SWEET RICE.
SINCE I LOST, I MIGHT AS WELL APOLOGIZE TO YOU TOO.
?
I'M SORRY.
BOW
HUH?
THE TRUTH IS, HANA AND I AREN'T REALLY GOING OUT.

A Heated Sushi Battle

People who have significant weaknesses also have strengths, and people who have significant strengths also have weaknesses. I've always wanted to draw characters like that.

But wait...

Does Okamon have any weaknesses?

As I asked myself that, I looked back and saw that his grades were always less than stellar. But to a certain extent, that's unavoidable—he's so busy with club activities and working at the restaurant.

As I was working on this sushi-battle story line, it made me realize again that one of Okamon's main attributes is that when he gets mad, he tends to go on and on with sound arguments.

That's not necessarily a weakness, but it shows a human side to the normally cool and sweet Okamon, so that was fun to draw.

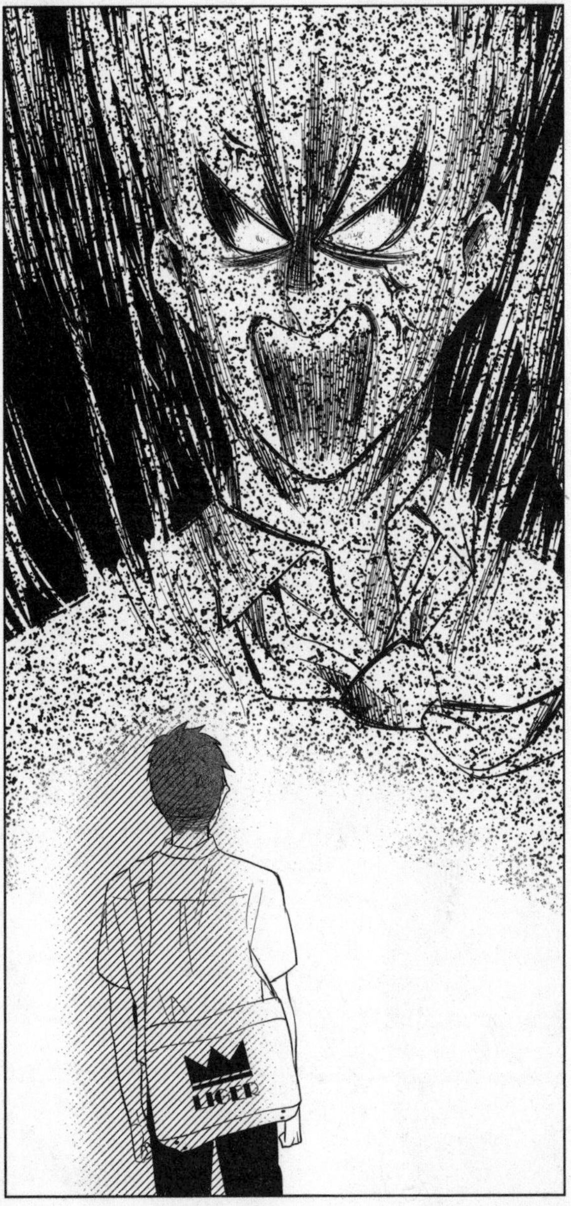

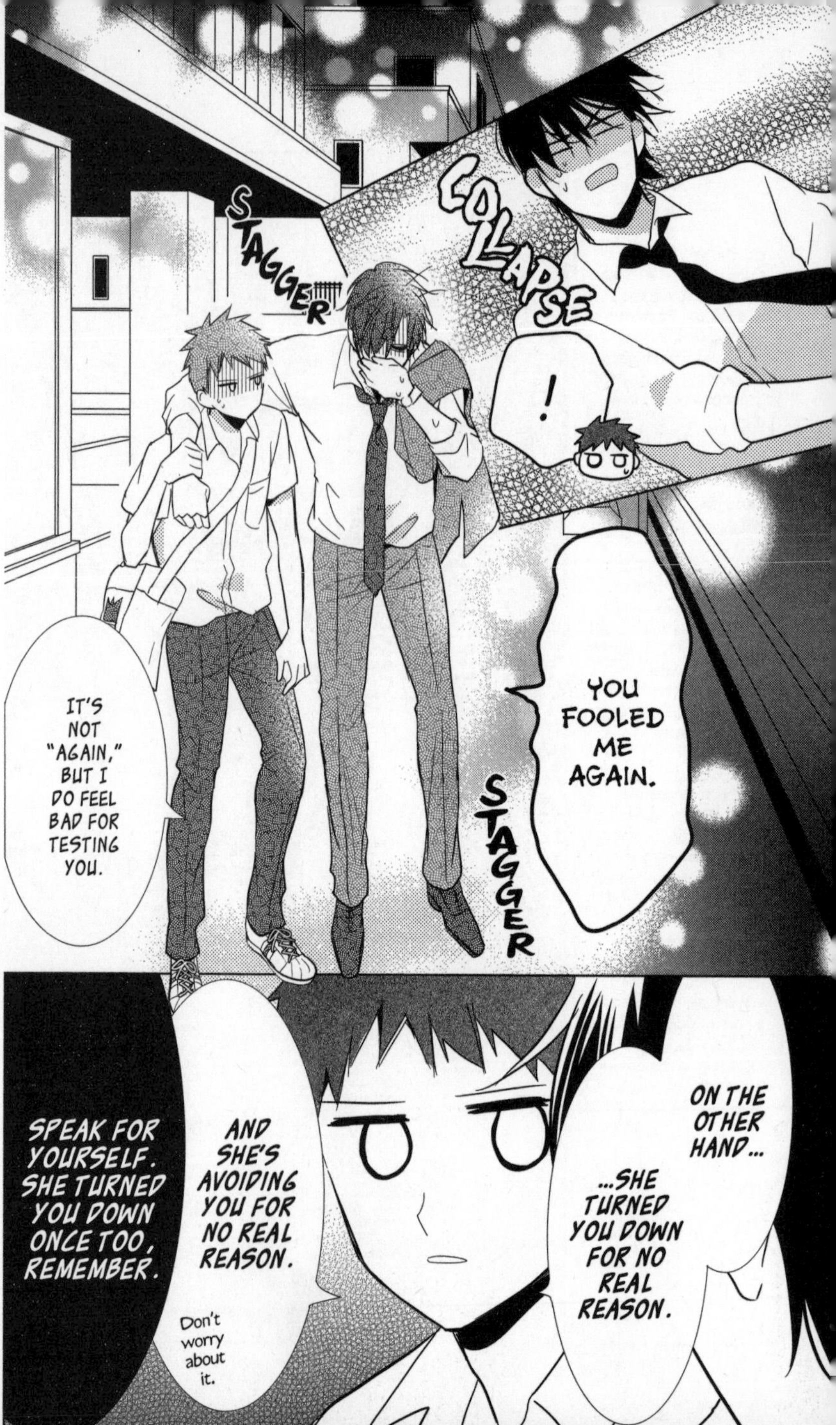
COLLAPSE
!
STAGGER
YOU FOOLED ME AGAIN.
STAGGER
IT'S NOT "AGAIN," BUT I DO FEEL BAD FOR TESTING YOU.
ON THE OTHER HAND...
...SHE TURNED YOU DOWN FOR NO REAL REASON.
AND SHE'S AVOIDING YOU FOR NO REAL REASON.
Don't worry about it.
SPEAK FOR YOURSELF. SHE TURNED YOU DOWN ONCE TOO, REMEMBER.

Chapter 70

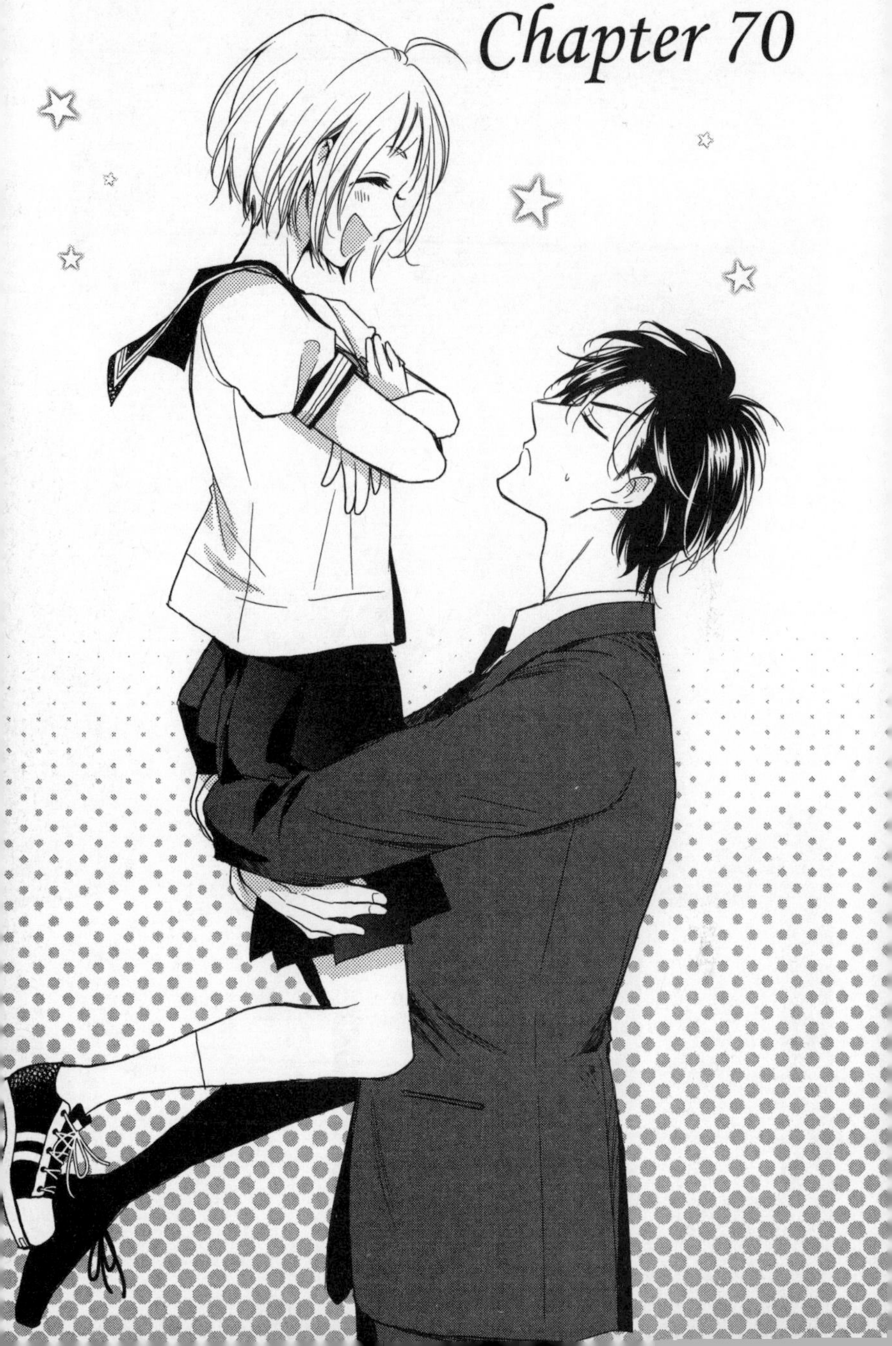

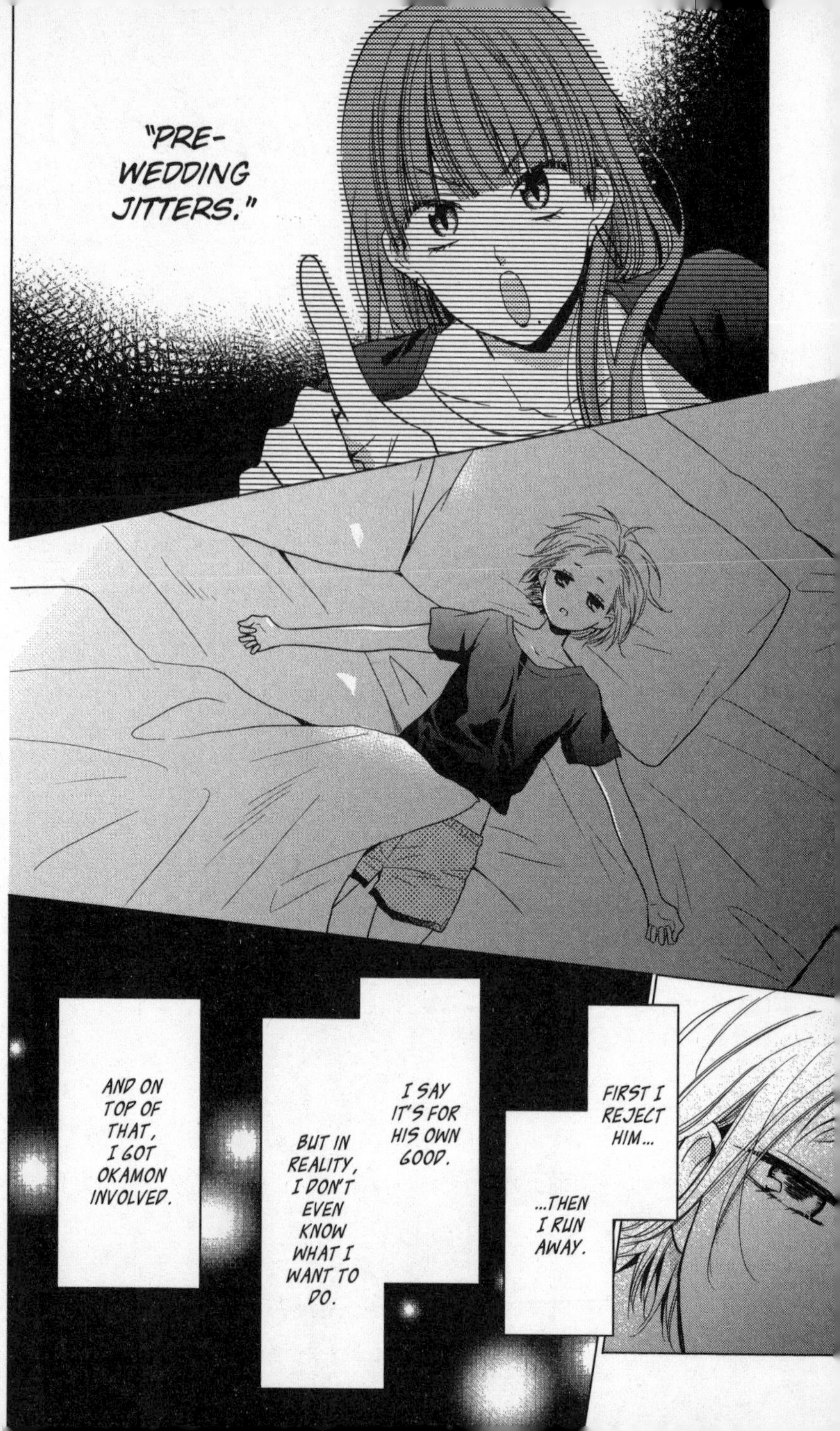
"PRE-WEDDING JITTERS."
FIRST I REJECT HIM...
...THEN I RUN AWAY.
I SAY IT'S FOR HIS OWN GOOD.
BUT IN REALITY, I DON'T EVEN KNOW WHAT I WANT TO DO.
AND ON TOP OF THAT, I GOT OKAMON INVOLVED.

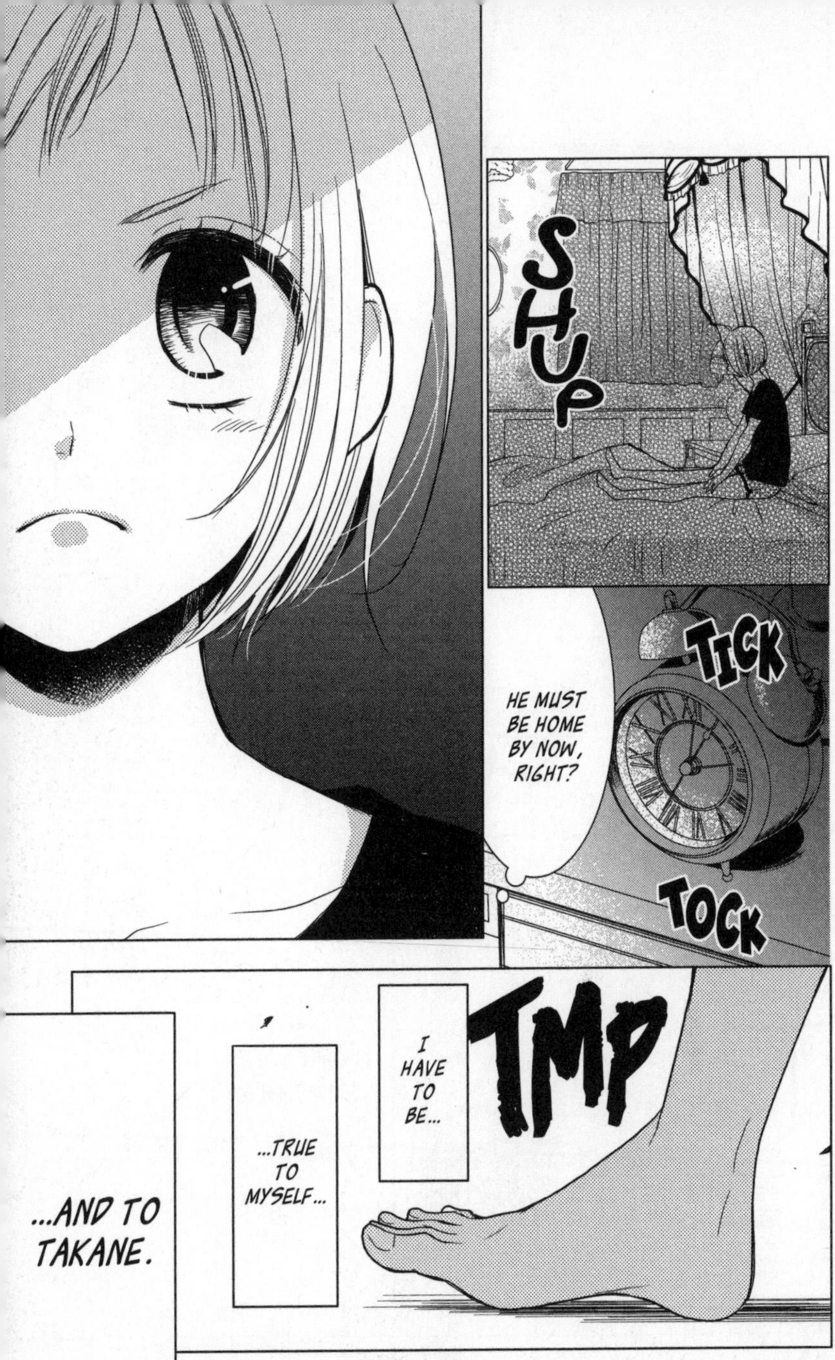
SHUP
TICK
HE MUST BE HOME BY NOW, RIGHT?
TOCK
TMP
I HAVE TO BE...
...TRUE TO MYSELF...
...AND TO TAKANE.

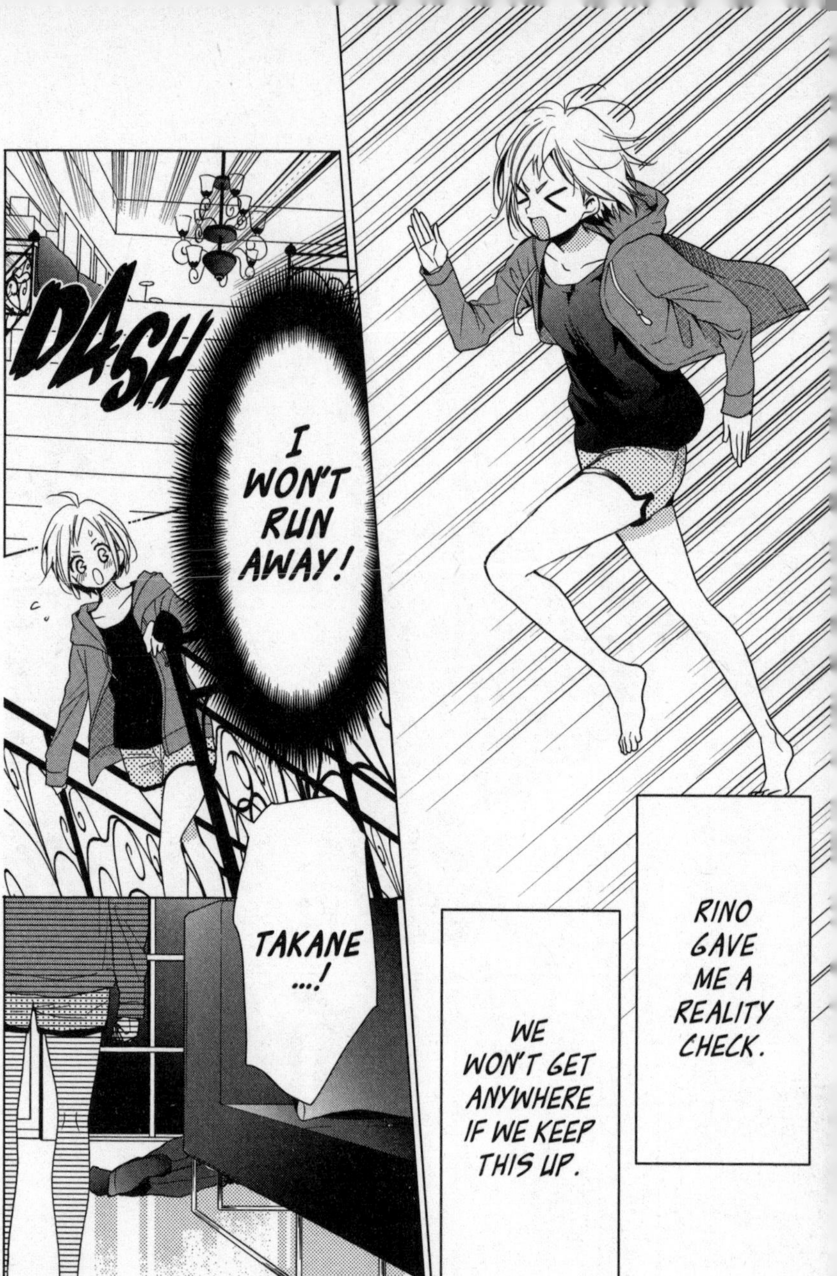
RINO GAVE ME A REALITY CHECK.
WE WON'T GET ANYWHERE IF WE KEEP THIS UP.
I WON'T RUN AWAY!
DASH
TAKANE ...!

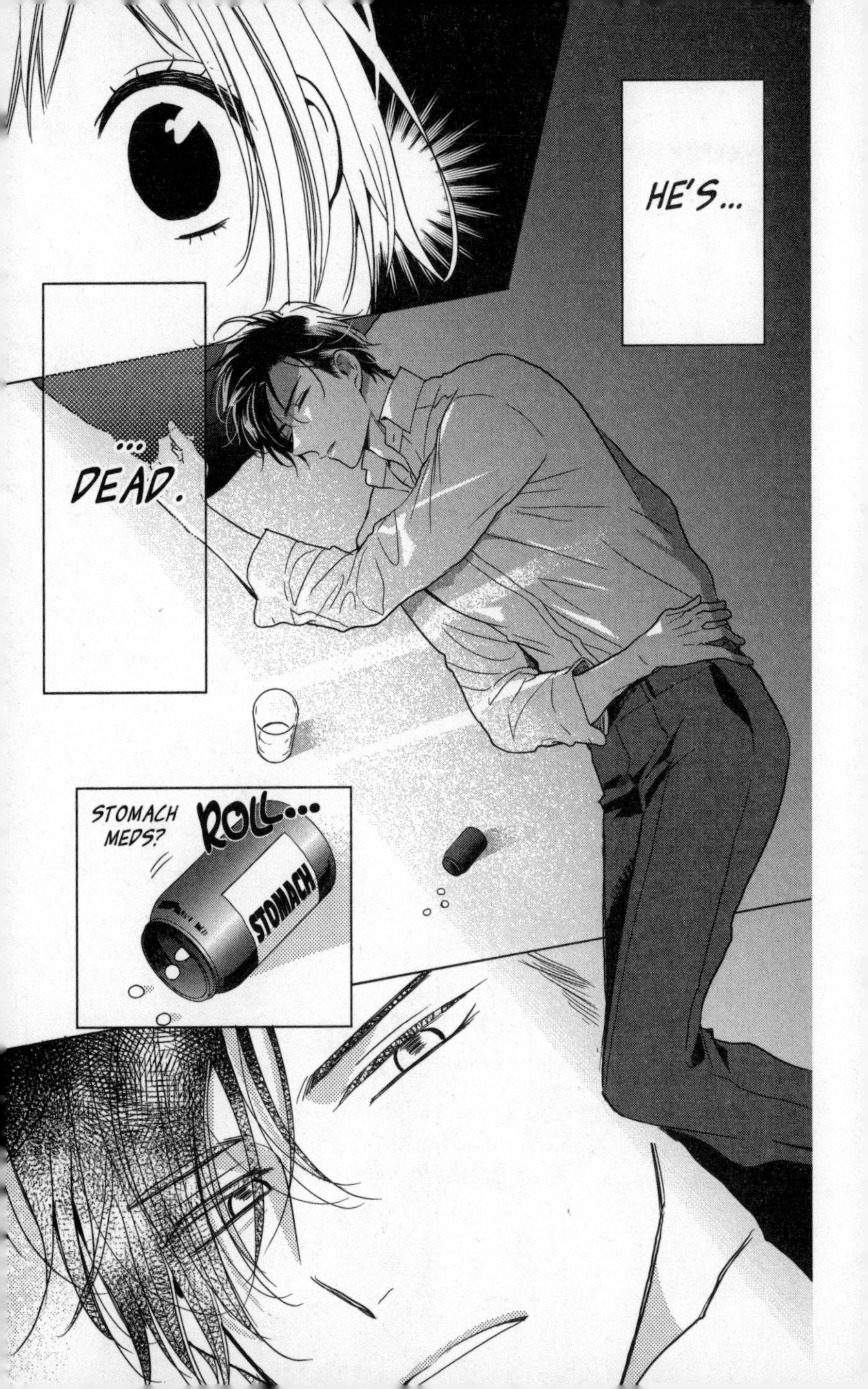
HE'S...
... DEAD.
ROLL...
STOMACH MEDS?
STOMACH

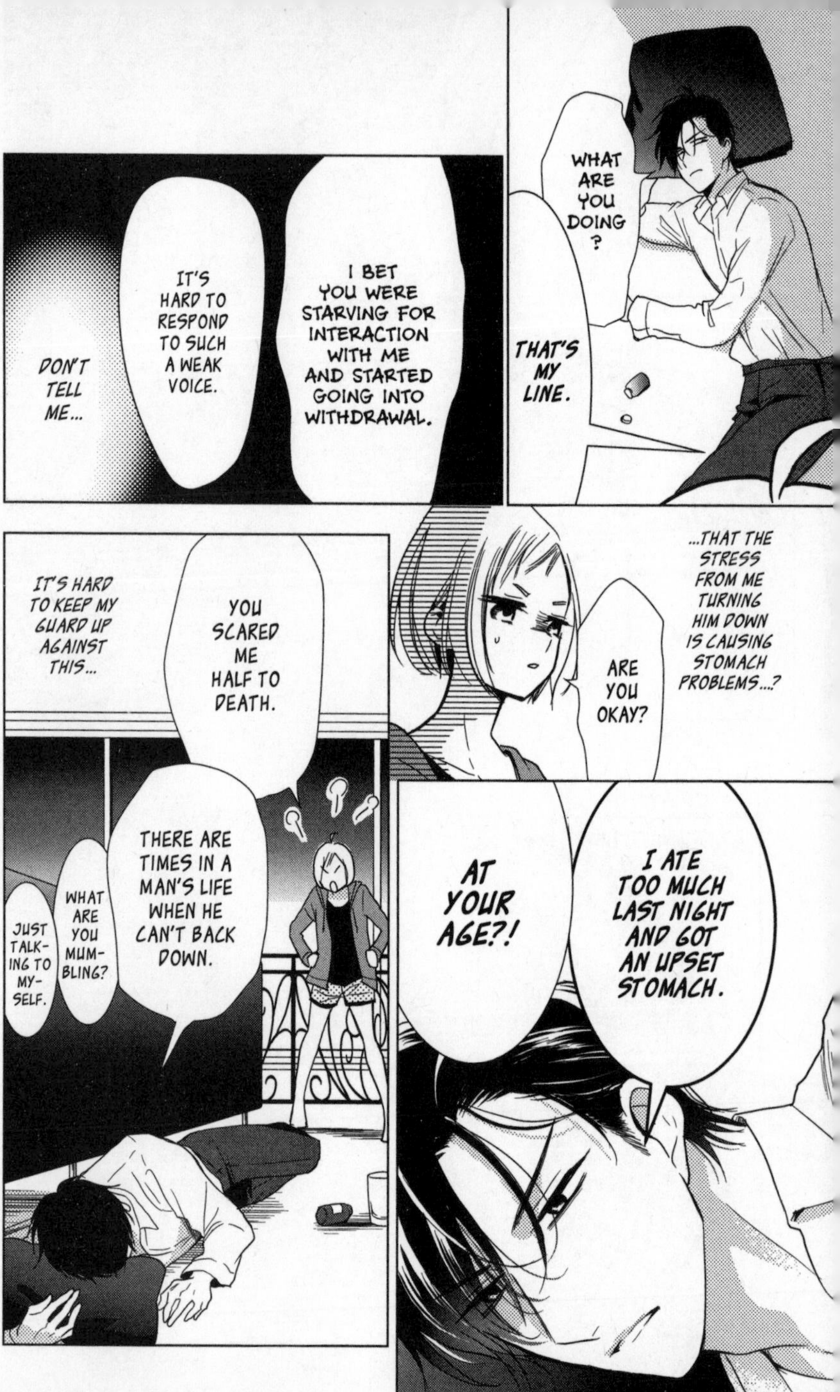

WHAT ARE YOU DOING?
THAT'S MY LINE.
I BET YOU WERE STARVING FOR INTERACTION WITH ME AND STARTED GOING INTO WITHDRAWAL.
IT'S HARD TO RESPOND TO SUCH A WEAK VOICE.
DON'T TELL ME...
...THAT THE STRESS FROM ME TURNING HIM DOWN IS CAUSING STOMACH PROBLEMS...?
ARE YOU OKAY?
I ATE TOO MUCH LAST NIGHT AND GOT AN UPSET STOMACH.
AT YOUR AGE?!
YOU SCARED ME HALF TO DEATH.
IT'S HARD TO KEEP MY GUARD UP AGAINST THIS...
THERE ARE TIMES IN A MAN'S LIFE WHEN HE CAN'T BACK DOWN.
WHAT ARE YOU MUMBLING?
JUST TALKING TO MYSELF.

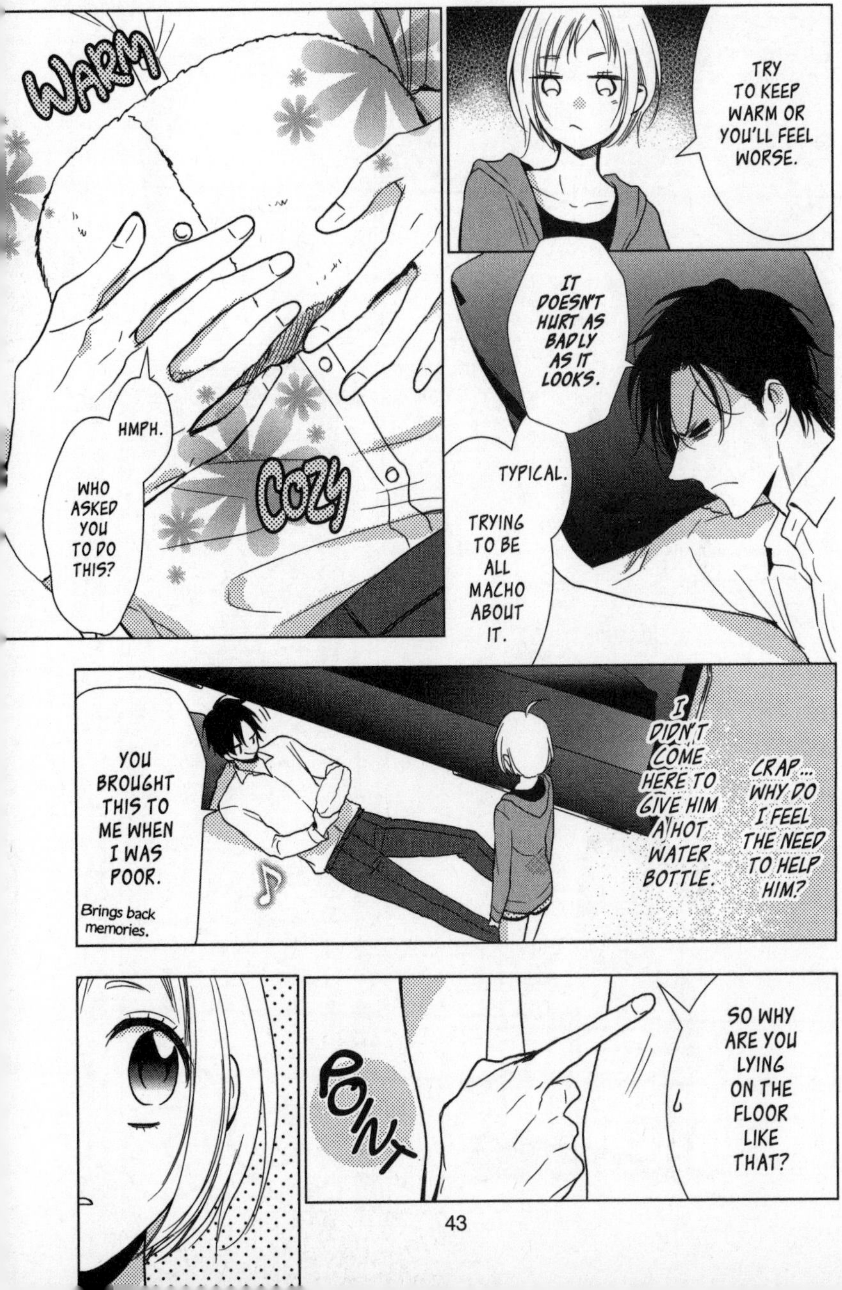
TRY TO KEEP WARM OR YOU'LL FEEL WORSE.
IT DOESN'T HURT AS BADLY AS IT LOOKS.
TYPICAL.
TRYING TO BE ALL MACHO ABOUT IT.
WARM
HMPH.
WHO ASKED YOU TO DO THIS?
COZY
CRAP... WHY DO I FEEL THE NEED TO HELP HIM?
I DIDN'T COME HERE TO GIVE HIM A HOT WATER BOTTLE.
YOU BROUGHT THIS TO ME WHEN I WAS POOR.
Brings back memories.
SO WHY ARE YOU LYING ON THE FLOOR LIKE THAT?
POINT

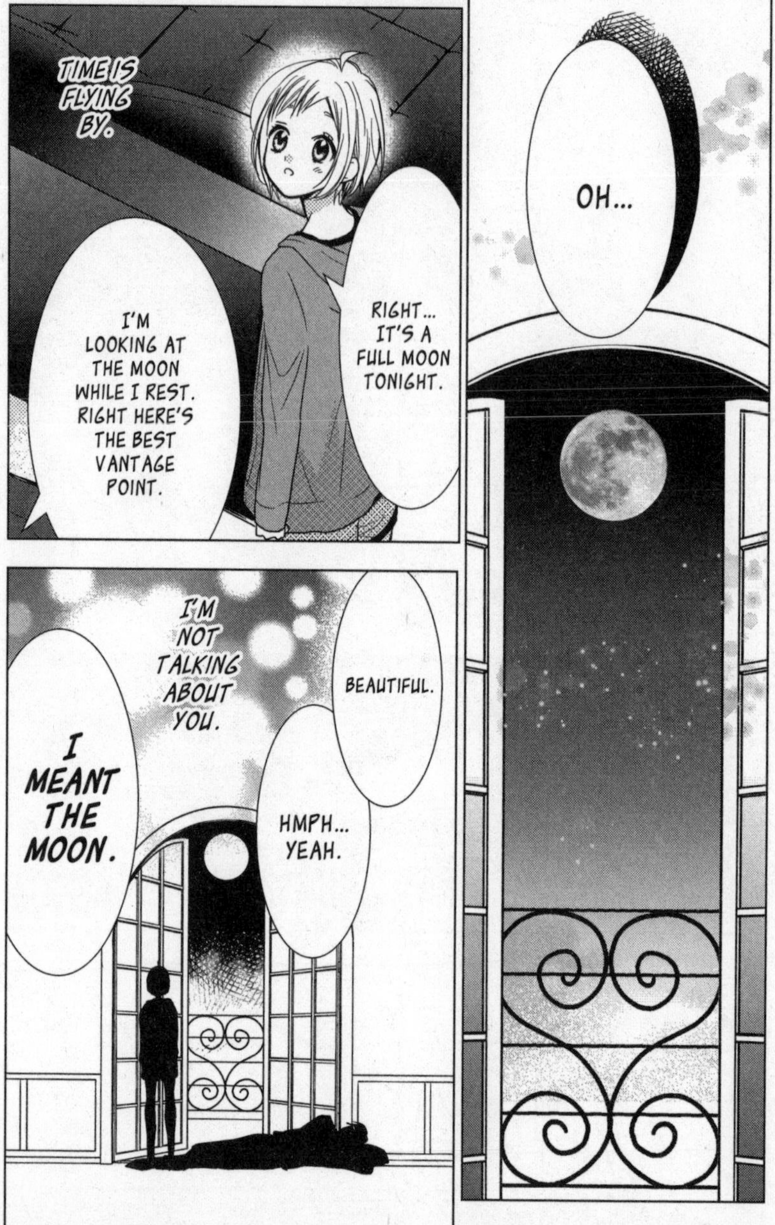
OH...
RIGHT... IT'S A FULL MOON TONIGHT.
TIME IS FLYING BY.
I'M LOOKING AT THE MOON WHILE I REST. RIGHT HERE'S THE BEST VANTAGE POINT.
BEAUTIFUL.
HMPH... YEAH.
I'M NOT TALKING ABOUT YOU.
I MEANT THE MOON.

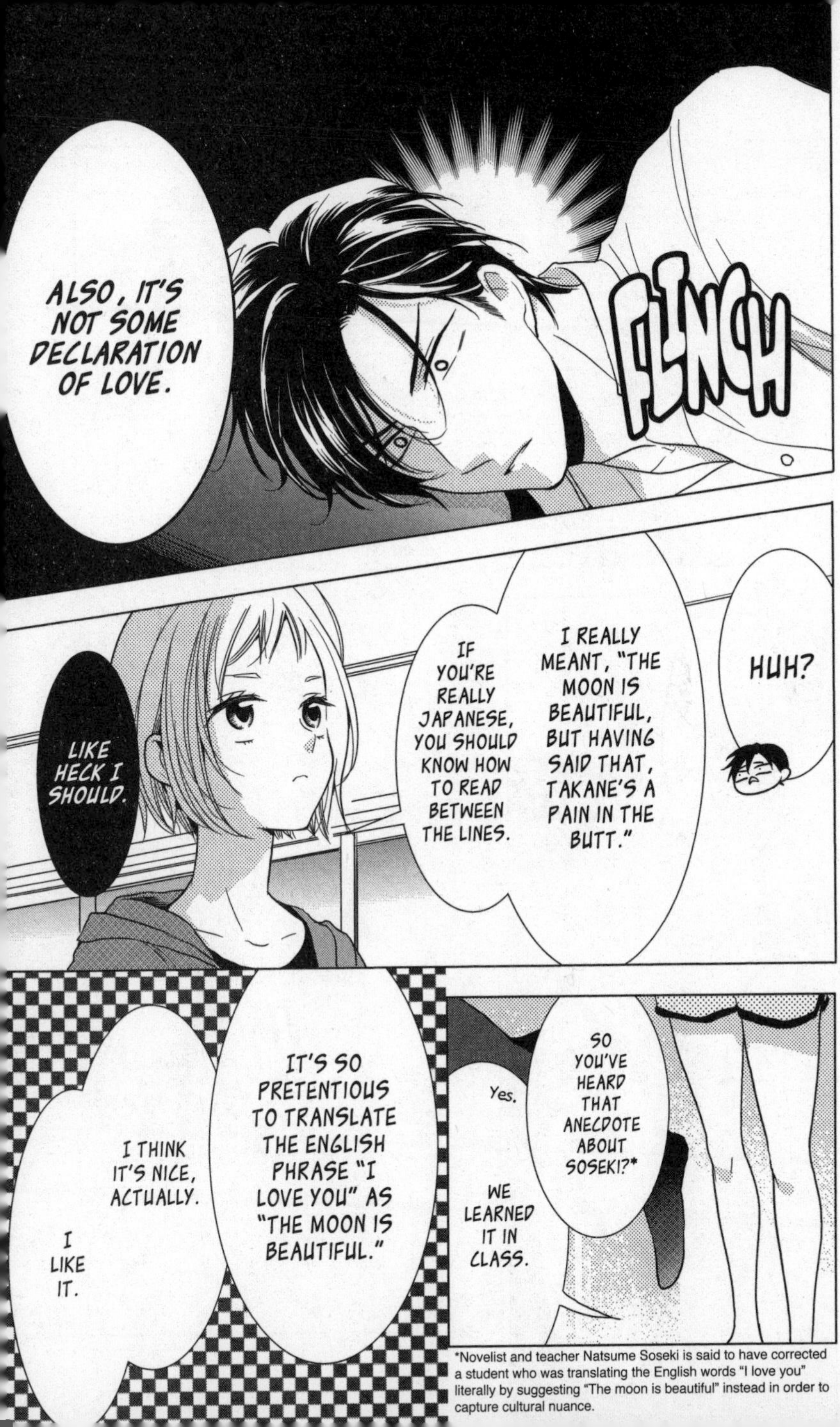

ALSO, IT'S NOT SOME DECLARATION OF LOVE.
FLINCH
HUH?
I REALLY MEANT, "THE MOON IS BEAUTIFUL, BUT HAVING SAID THAT, TAKANE'S A PAIN IN THE BUTT."
IF YOU'RE REALLY JAPANESE, YOU SHOULD KNOW HOW TO READ BETWEEN THE LINES.
LIKE HECK I SHOULD.
SO YOU'VE HEARD THAT ANECDOTE ABOUT SOSEKI?*
Yes.
WE LEARNED IT IN CLASS.
IT'S SO PRETENTIOUS TO TRANSLATE THE ENGLISH PHRASE "I LOVE YOU" AS "THE MOON IS BEAUTIFUL."
I THINK IT'S NICE, ACTUALLY.
I LIKE IT.

*Novelist and teacher Natsume Soseki is said to have corrected a student who was translating the English words "I love you" literally by suggesting "The moon is beautiful" instead in order to capture cultural nuance.

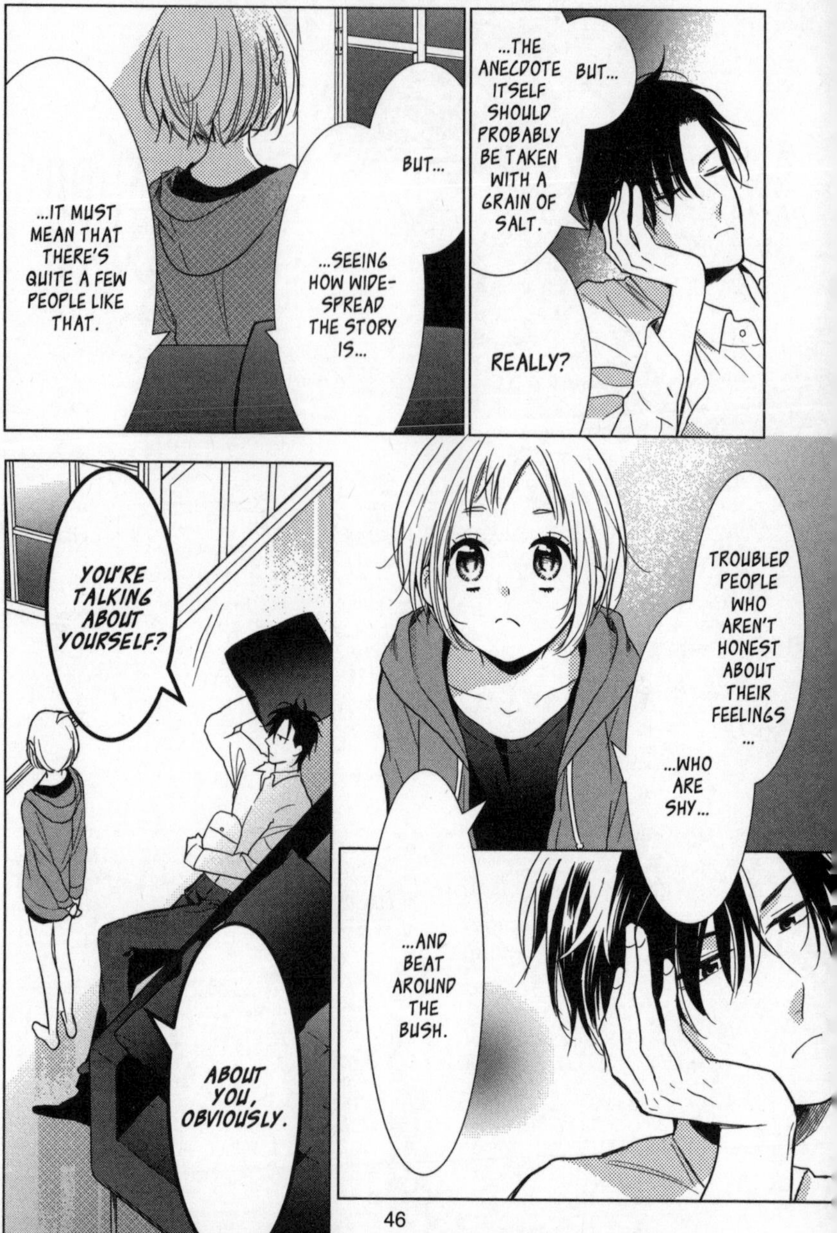
BUT...
...THE ANECDOTE ITSELF SHOULD PROBABLY BE TAKEN WITH A GRAIN OF SALT.
REALLY?
BUT...
...SEEING HOW WIDE-SPREAD THE STORY IS...
...IT MUST MEAN THAT THERE'S QUITE A FEW PEOPLE LIKE THAT.
TROUBLED PEOPLE WHO AREN'T HONEST ABOUT THEIR FEELINGS ...
...WHO ARE SHY...
...AND BEAT AROUND THE BUSH.
YOU'RE TALKING ABOUT YOURSELF?
ABOUT YOU, OBVIOUSLY.

A first-ever limited edition drama CD!

There are two versions of volume 13 in Japan—the regular edition and the limited edition that comes with a drama CD. The drama CD is a voice dramatization of chapters 67 through 70. Since it's all four chapters, some of the details had to be left out, but there's still quite a bit of material.

There was also a free drama CD that came with the *Hana and Yume* issue that went on sale at the same time as volume 13. That drama CD is a voice dramatization of chapter 72, the hiking story. There's also an extra anecdote about Okamon and Luciano on that CD.

In the bonus stories at the end of volume 13, you will see those extra anecdotes as a four-panel comic, so please have a look.

Rather than giving them completely new lines, I wanted them to have lines that were representative of each character, so what you see is a déjà vu type of interaction between the two.

At the time of this writing, the recording is pretty much done. I can't wait to hear the finished product!

WELL, I GUESS WE'RE BOTH LIKE THAT.

...

DIDN'T YOU COME HERE TO TALK ABOUT SOMETHING?

OH...

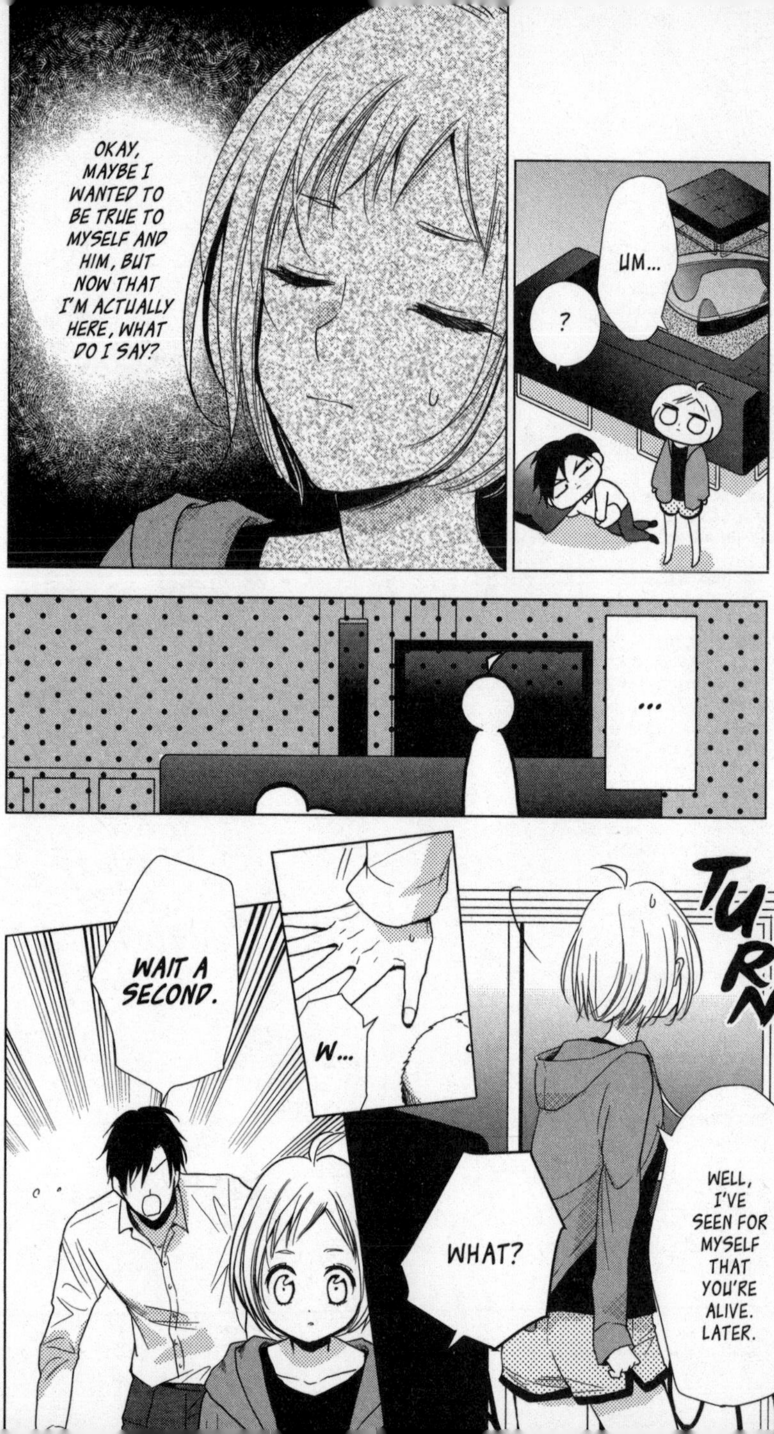
UM...
?
OKAY, MAYBE I WANTED TO BE TRUE TO MYSELF AND HIM, BUT NOW THAT I'M ACTUALLY HERE, WHAT DO I SAY?
...
TURN
WELL, I'VE SEEN FOR MYSELF THAT YOU'RE ALIVE. LATER.
WHAT?
W...
WAIT A SECOND.

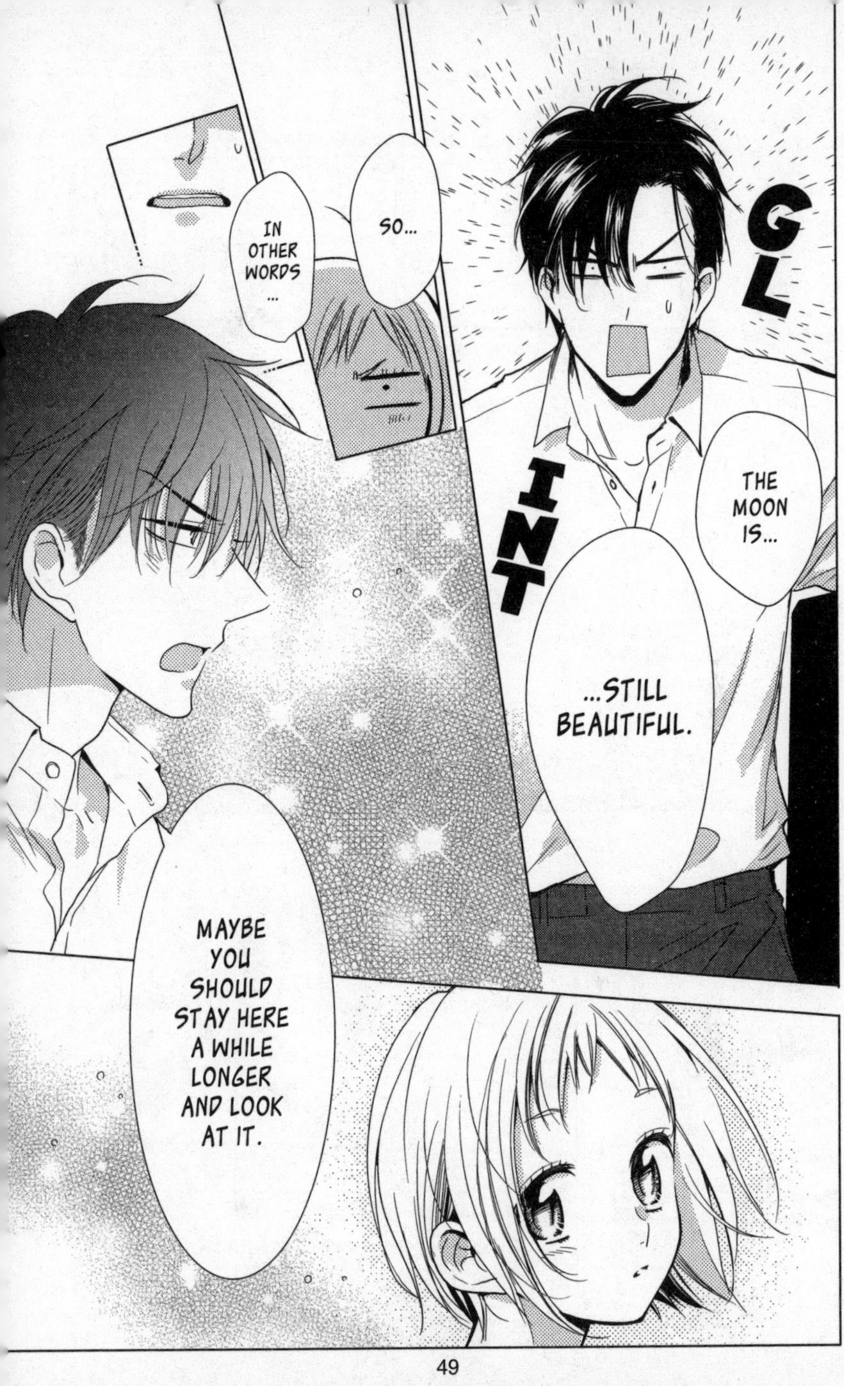
GLINT
THE MOON IS...
...STILL BEAUTIFUL.
SO...
IN OTHER WORDS ...
MAYBE YOU SHOULD STAY HERE A WHILE LONGER AND LOOK AT IT.

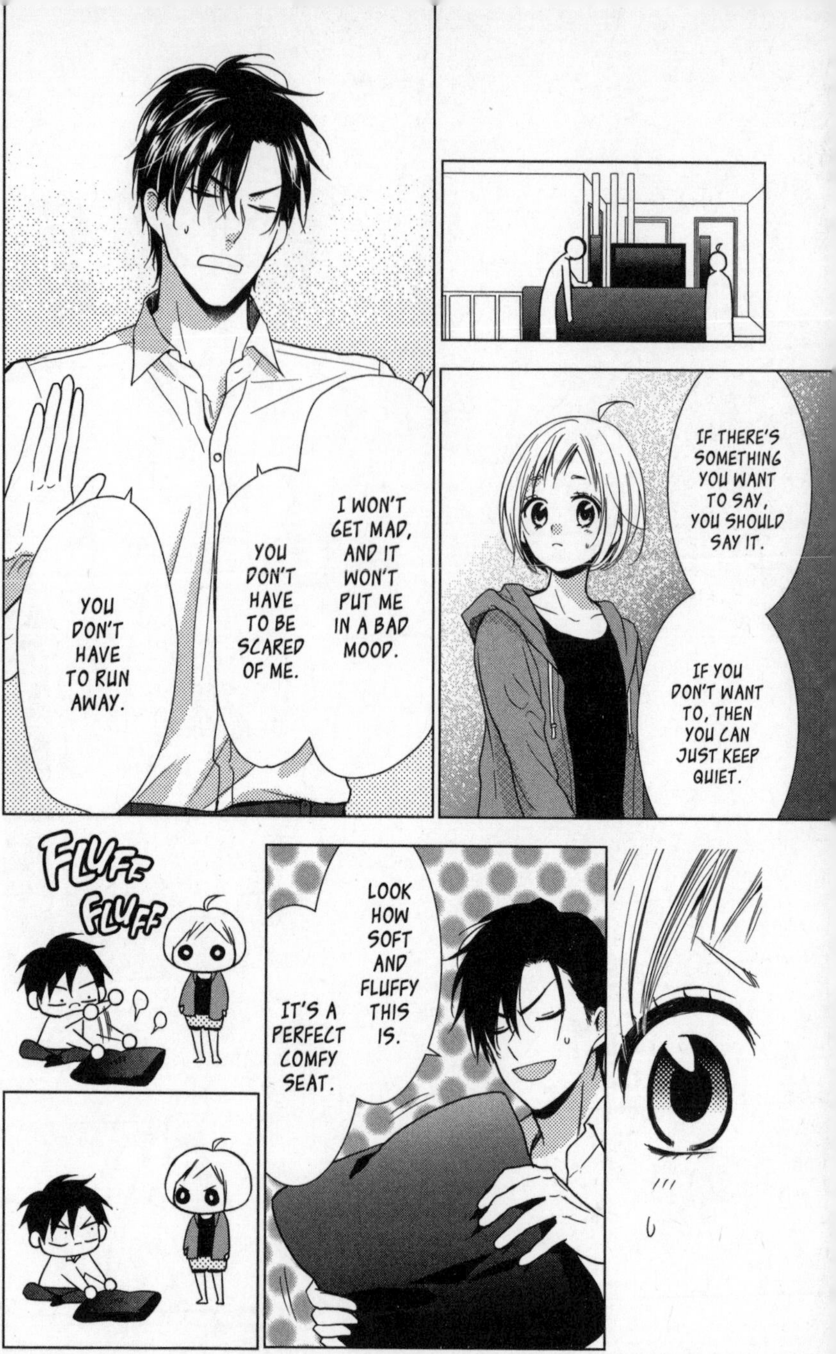
IF THERE'S SOMETHING YOU WANT TO SAY, YOU SHOULD SAY IT.
IF YOU DON'T WANT TO, THEN YOU CAN JUST KEEP QUIET.
I WON'T GET MAD, AND IT WON'T PUT ME IN A BAD MOOD.
YOU DON'T HAVE TO BE SCARED OF ME.
YOU DON'T HAVE TO RUN AWAY.
LOOK HOW SOFT AND FLUFFY THIS IS.
IT'S A PERFECT COMFY SEAT.
FLUFF FLUFF

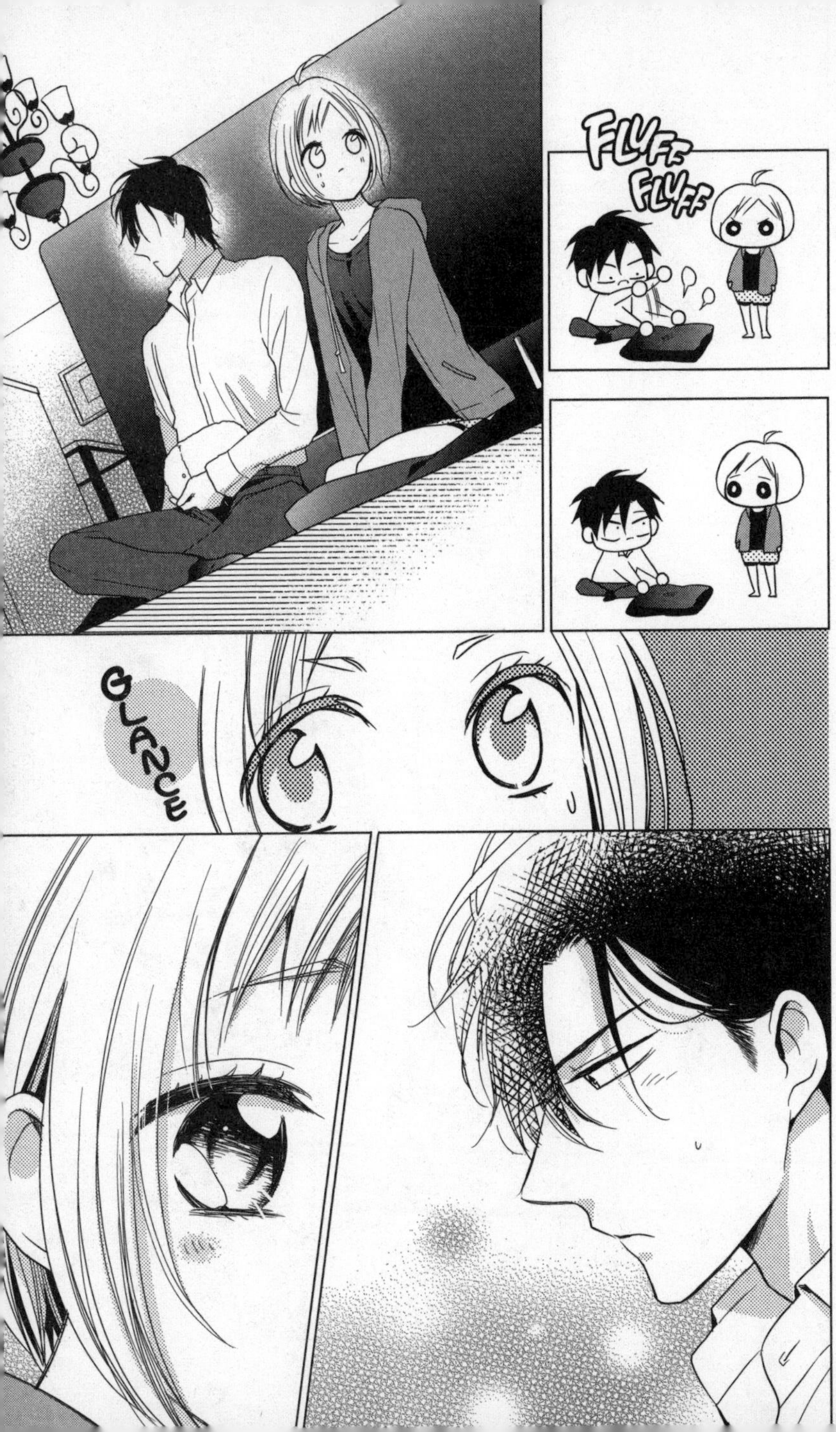
FLUFF FLUFF
GLANCE

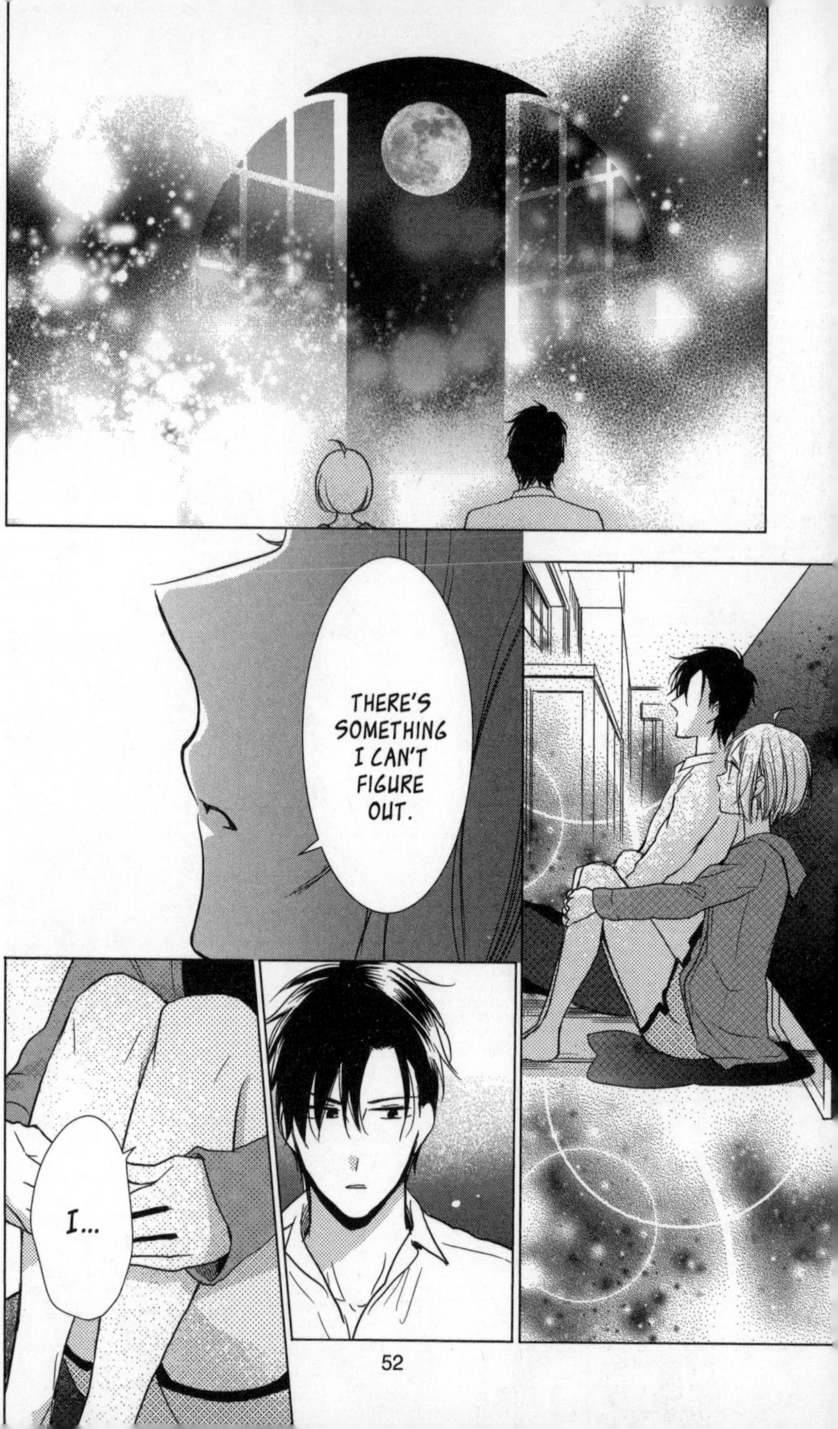
THERE'S SOMETHING I CAN'T FIGURE OUT.
I...

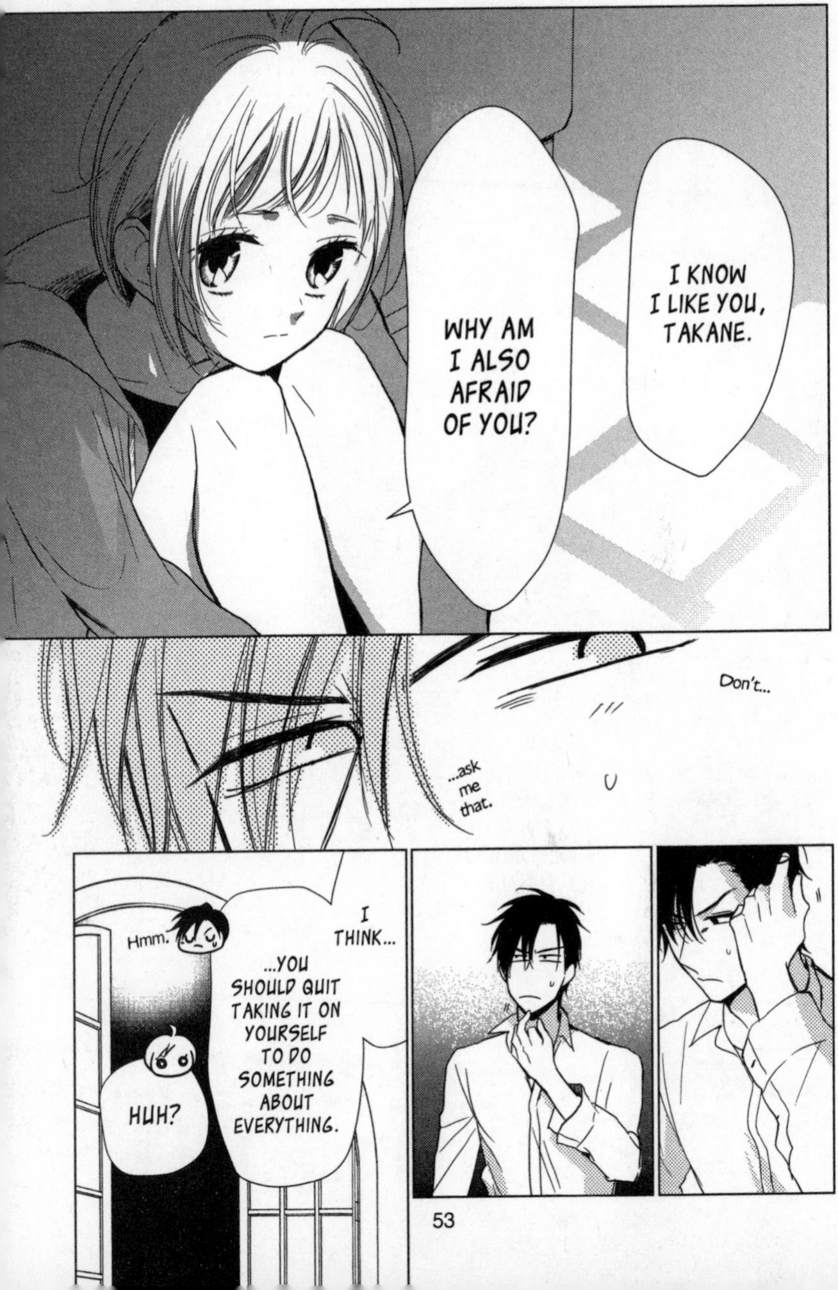
I KNOW I LIKE YOU, TAKANE.
WHY AM I ALSO AFRAID OF YOU?
Don't...
...ask me that.
I THINK...
...YOU SHOULD QUIT TAKING IT ON YOURSELF TO DO SOMETHING ABOUT EVERYTHING.
Hmm.
HUH?

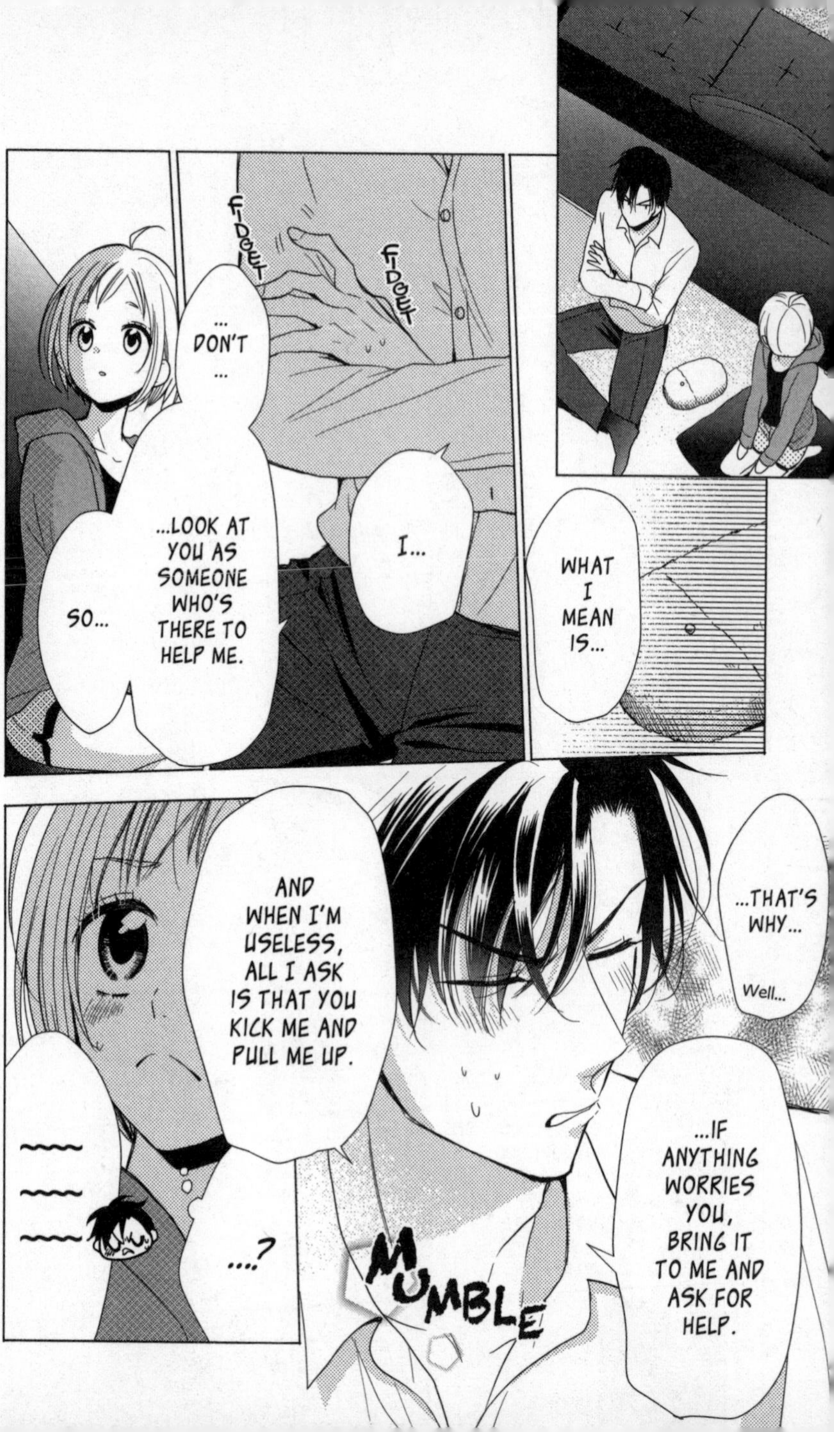
WHAT I MEAN IS...
FIDGET
FIDGET
I...
... DON'T ...
...LOOK AT YOU AS SOMEONE WHO'S THERE TO HELP ME.
SO...
...THAT'S WHY...
Well...
...IF ANYTHING WORRIES YOU, BRING IT TO ME AND ASK FOR HELP.
MUMBLE
AND WHEN I'M USELESS, ALL I ASK IS THAT YOU KICK ME AND PULL ME UP.
~~~~ ~~~~ ~~~~
...?
~~~~

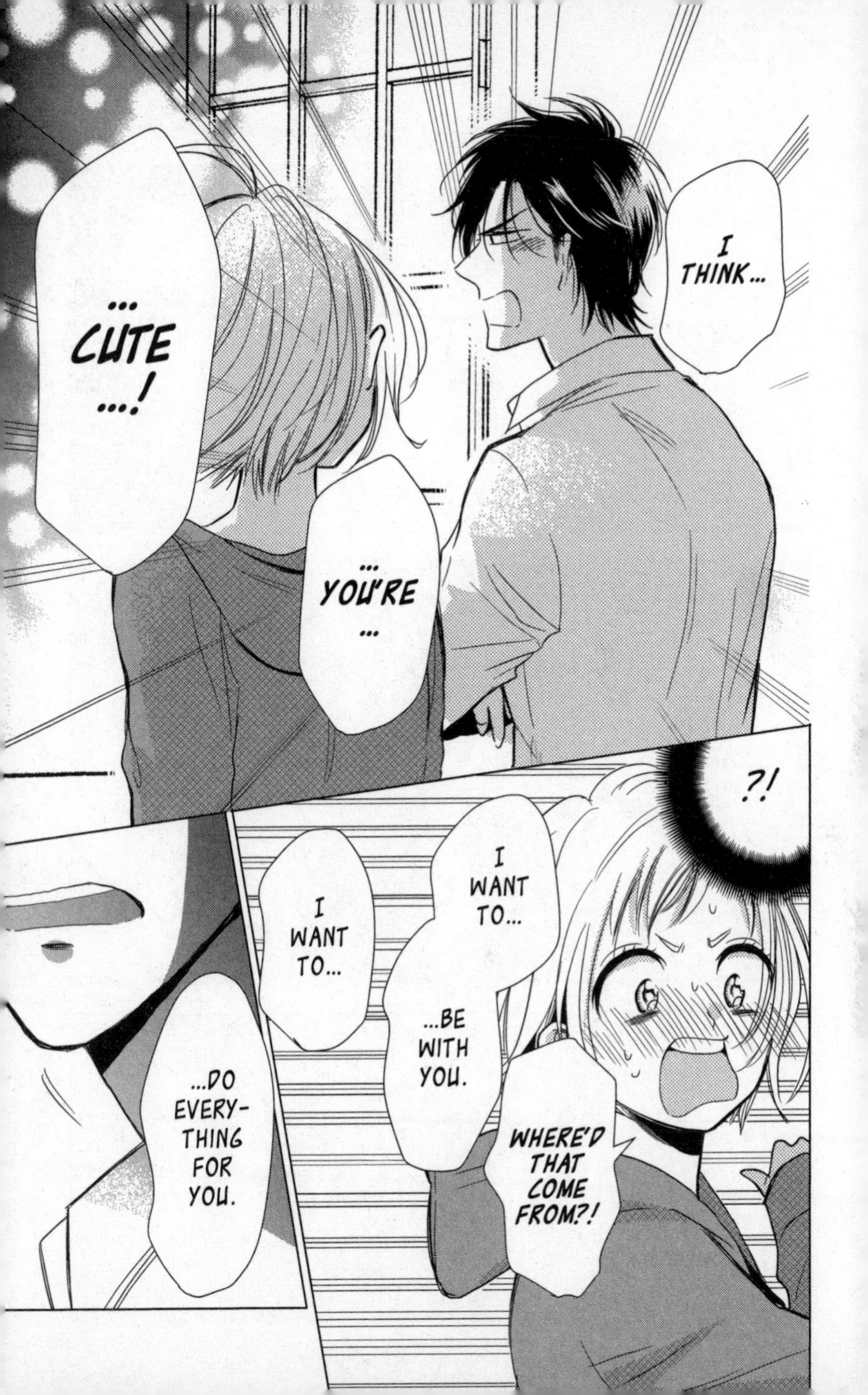
I THINK...
...YOU'RE...
...CUTE...!
?!
I WANT TO...
...BE WITH YOU.
I WANT TO...
...DO EVERYTHING FOR YOU.
WHERE'D THAT COME FROM?!

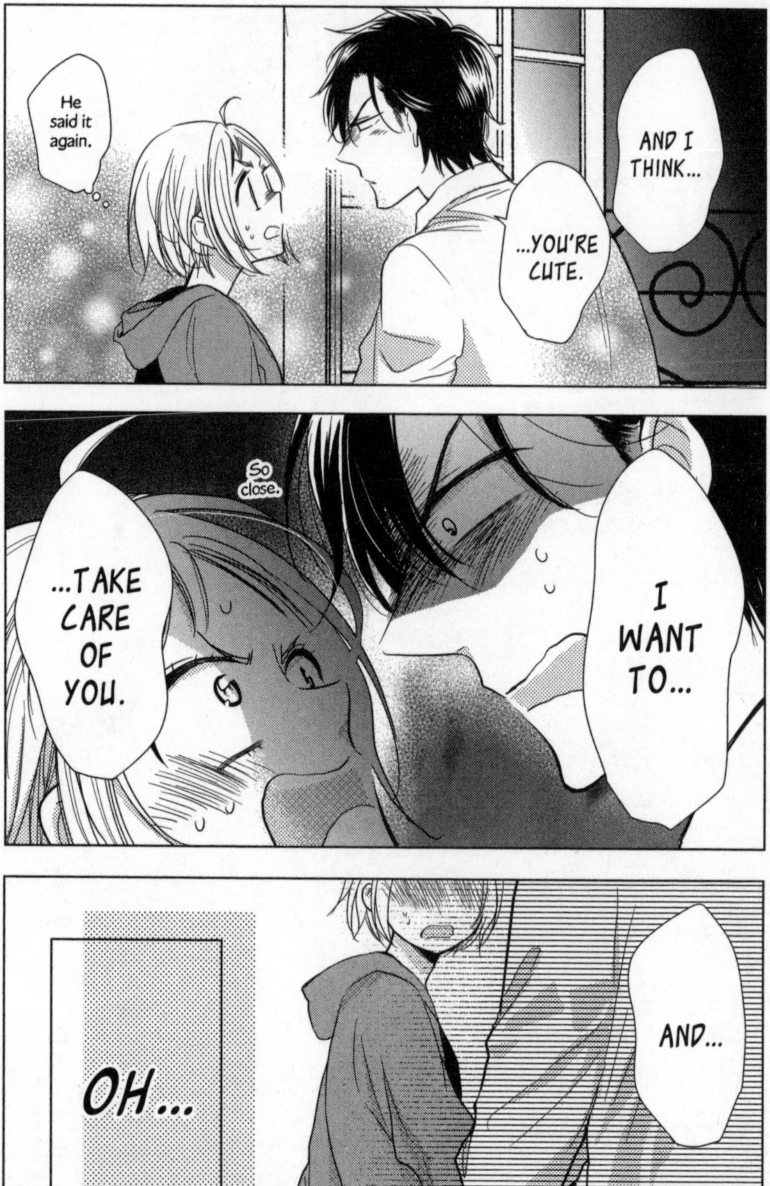
AND I THINK...
...YOU'RE CUTE.
He said it again.
I WANT TO...
So close.
...TAKE CARE OF YOU.
AND...
OH...

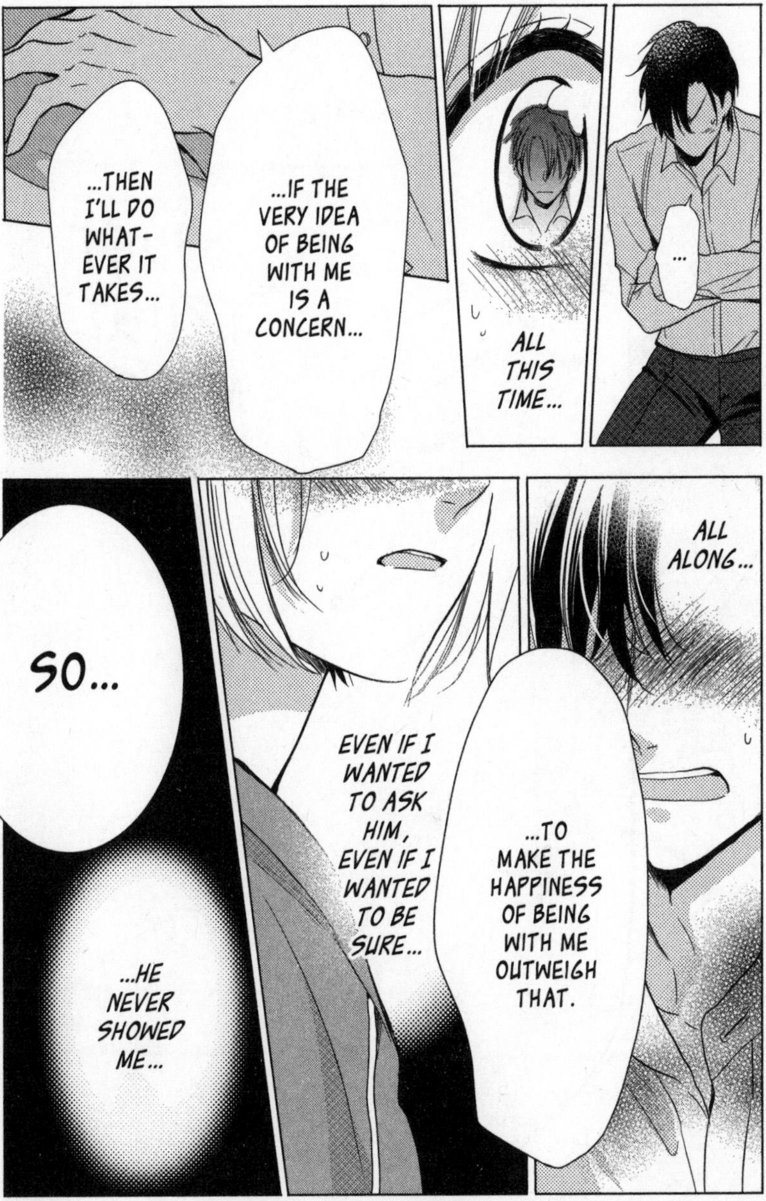
...
ALL THIS TIME...
...IF THE VERY IDEA OF BEING WITH ME IS A CONCERN...
...THEN I'LL DO WHAT-EVER IT TAKES...
ALL ALONG...
...TO MAKE THE HAPPINESS OF BEING WITH ME OUTWEIGH THAT.
EVEN IF I WANTED TO ASK HIM, EVEN IF I WANTED TO BE SURE...
SO...
...HE NEVER SHOWED ME...

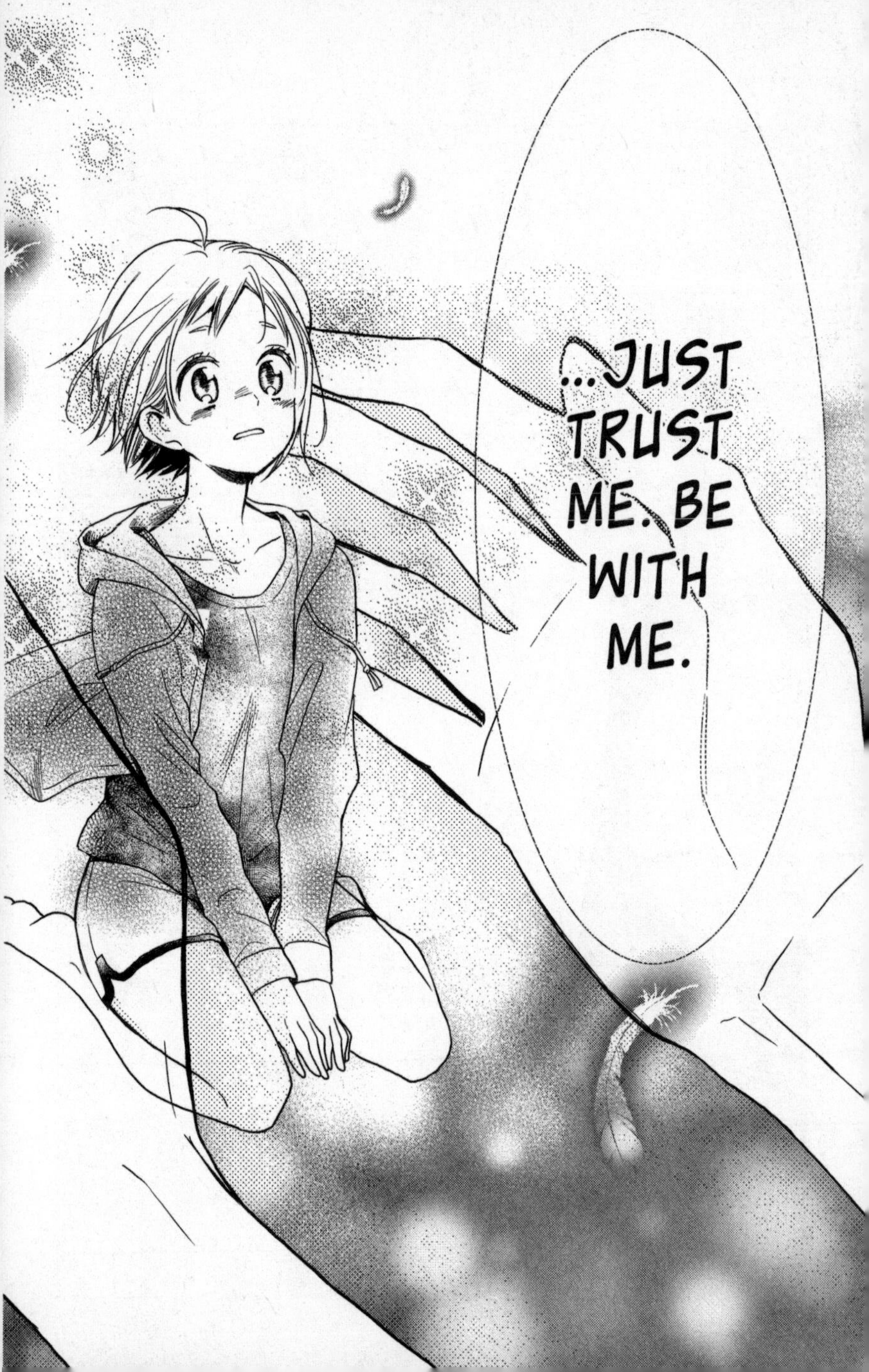
...JUST TRUST ME. BE WITH ME.

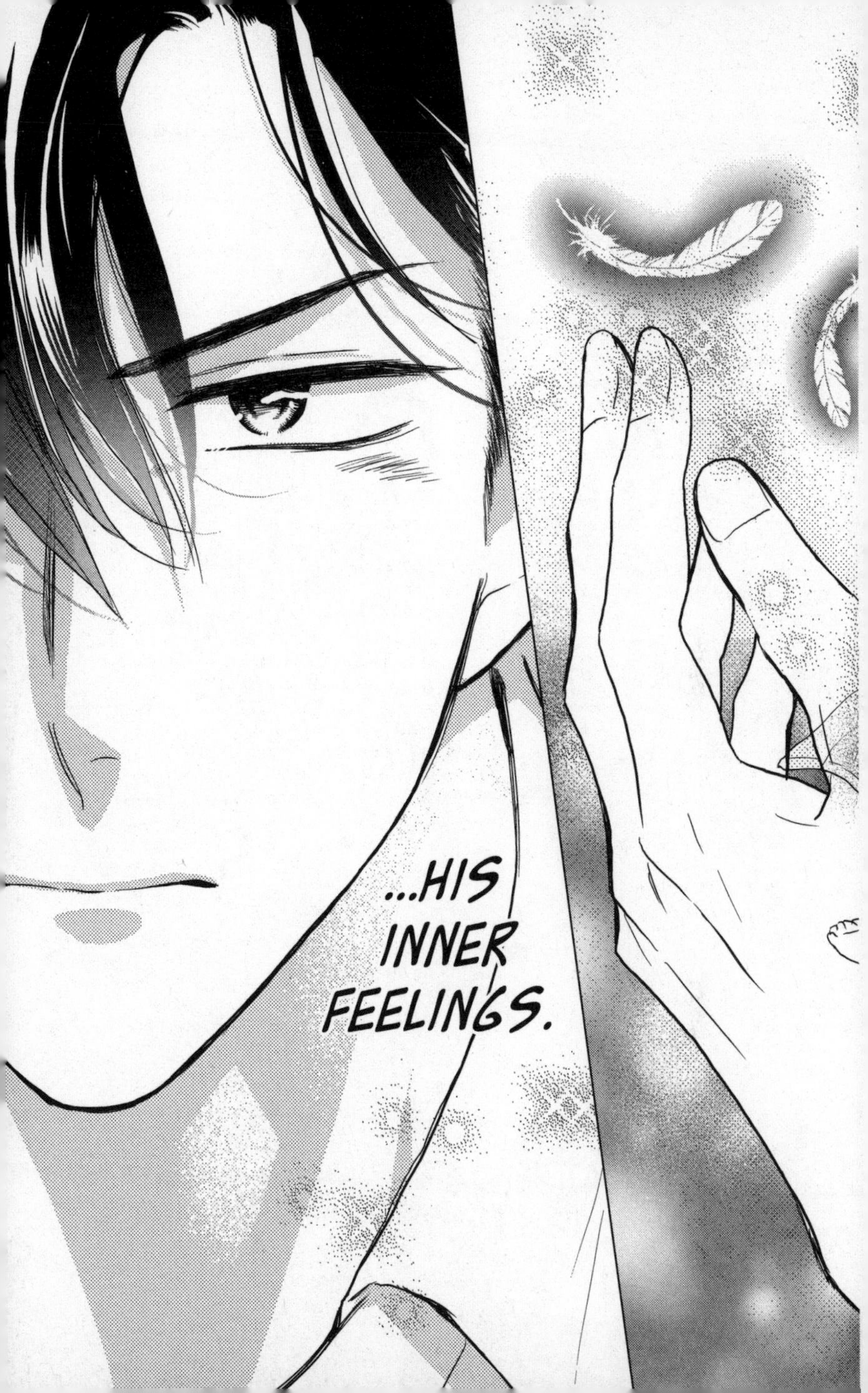
...HIS INNER FEELINGS.

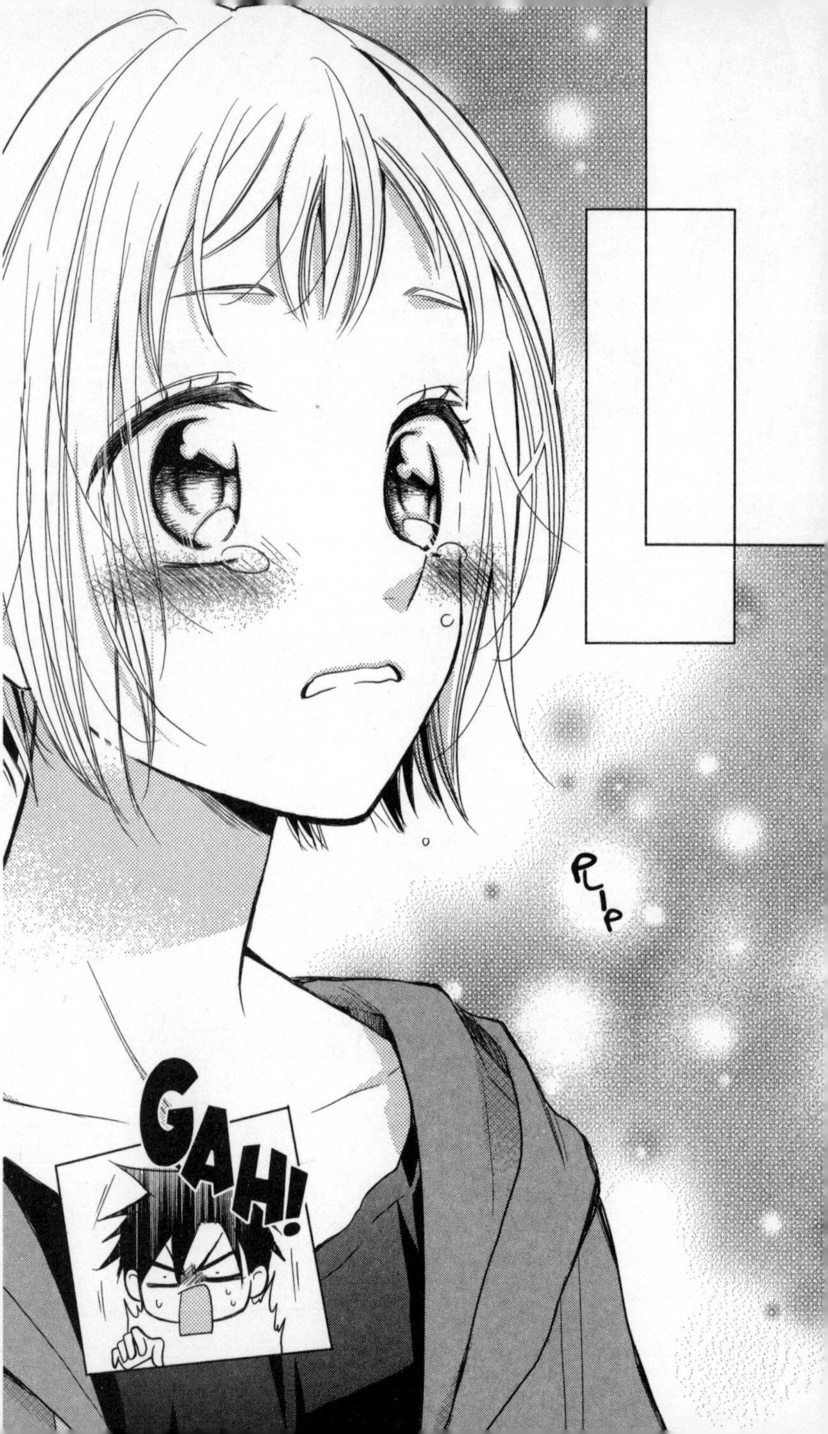
PLIP
GAH!

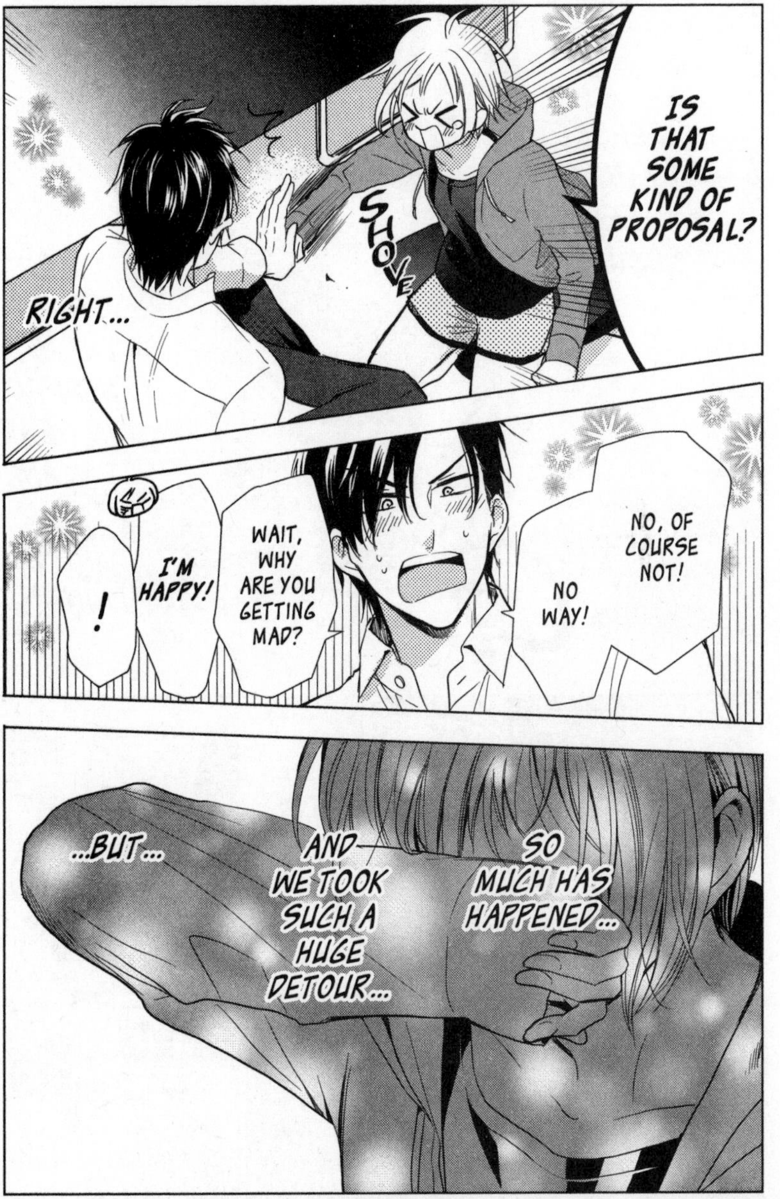
IS THAT SOME KIND OF PROPOSAL?
SHOVE
RIGHT...
NO, OF COURSE NOT!
NO WAY!
WAIT, WHY ARE YOU GETTING MAD?
I'M HAPPY!
!
SO MUCH HAS HAPPENED...
AND WE TOOK SUCH A HUGE DETOUR...
...BUT...

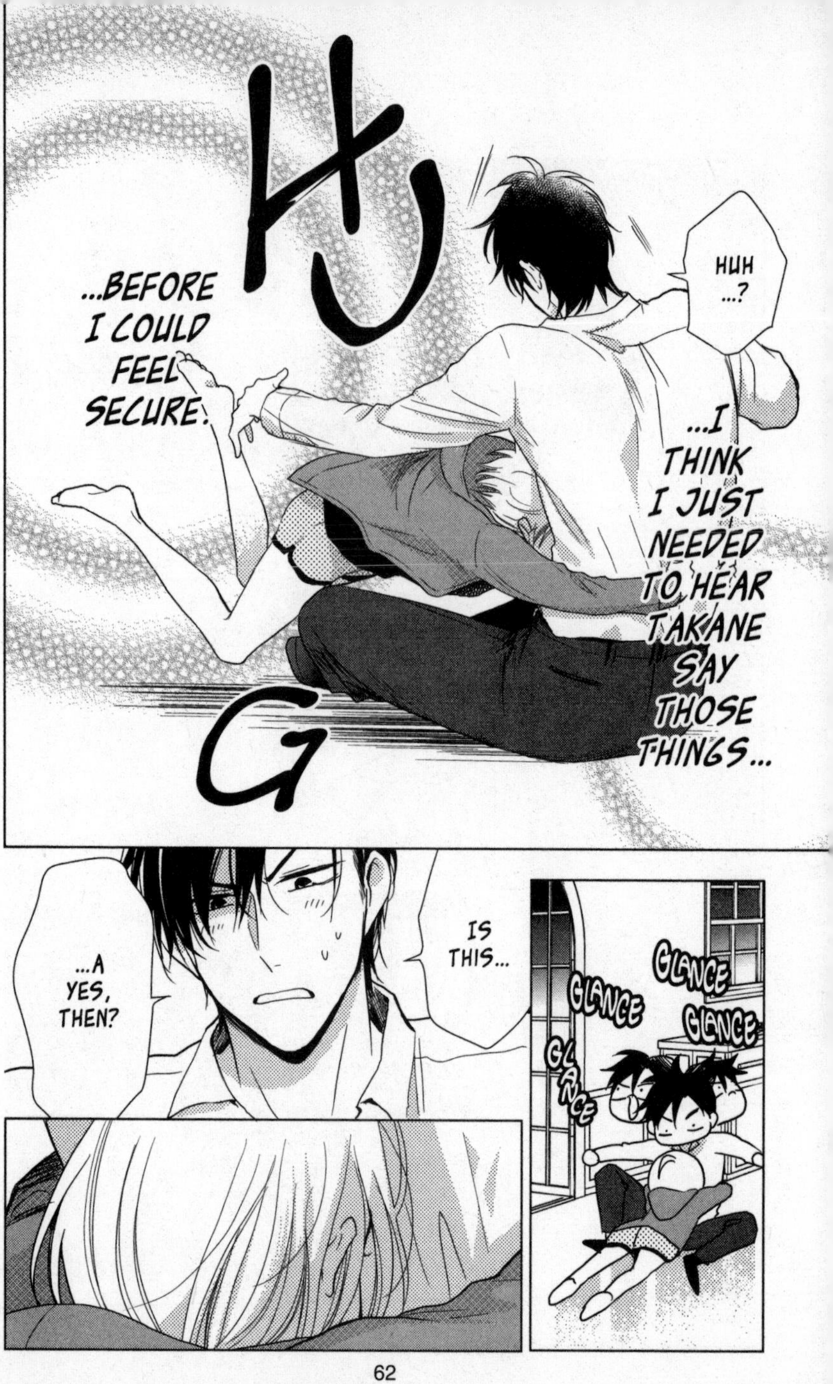
HUH ...?
...I THINK I JUST NEEDED TO HEAR TAKANE SAY THOSE THINGS...
...BEFORE I COULD FEEL SECURE.
HUG
GLANCE
GLANCE
GLANCE
GLANCE
IS THIS...
...A YES, THEN?

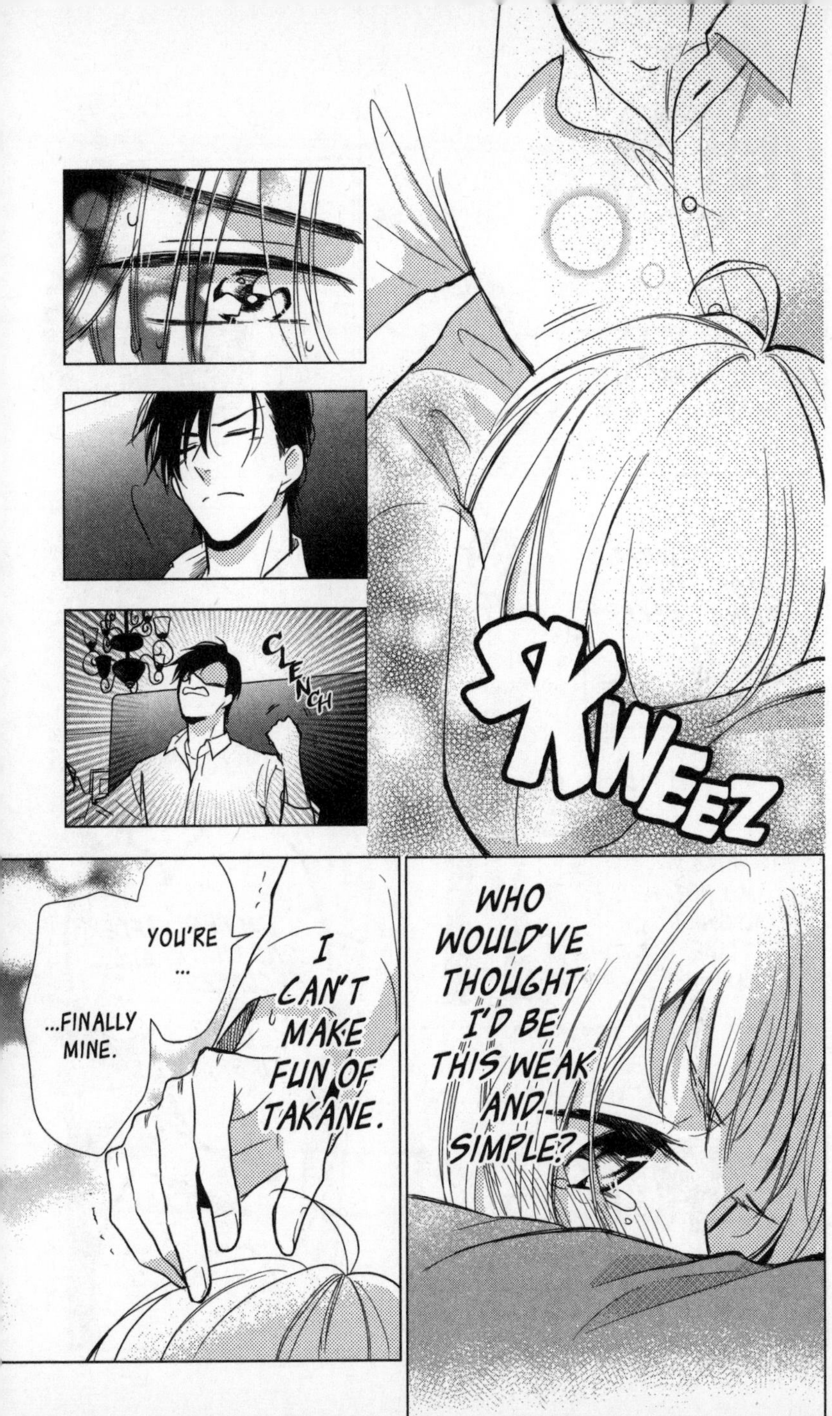
SKWEEZ
CLENCH
WHO WOULD'VE THOUGHT I'D BE THIS WEAK AND SIMPLE?
I CAN'T MAKE FUN OF TAKANE.
YOU'RE ...
...FINALLY MINE.

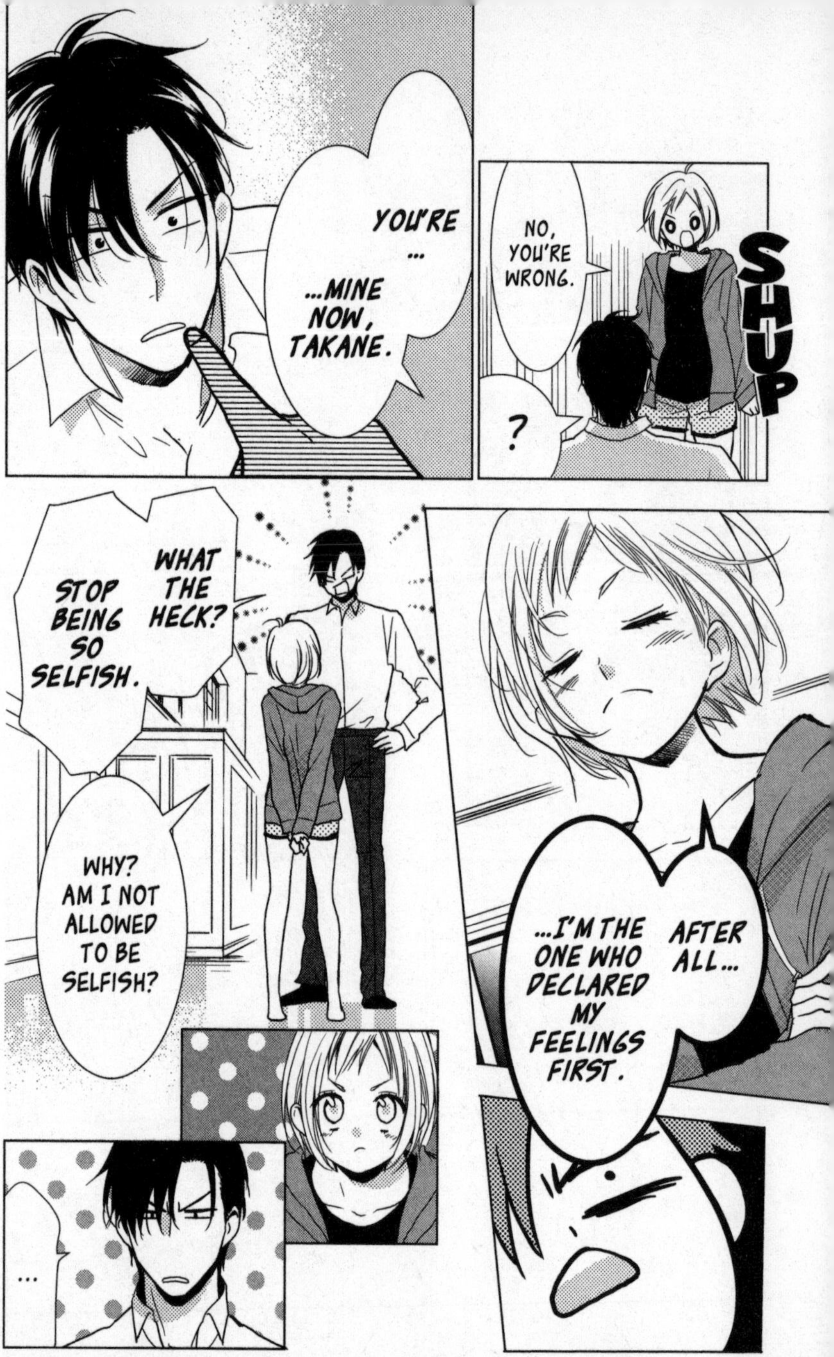
YOU'RE ...
...MINE NOW, TAKANE.
NO, YOU'RE WRONG.
?
SHUP
AFTER ALL...
...I'M THE ONE WHO DECLARED MY FEELINGS FIRST.
WHAT THE HECK?
STOP BEING SO SELFISH.
WHY? AM I NOT ALLOWED TO BE SELFISH?
...

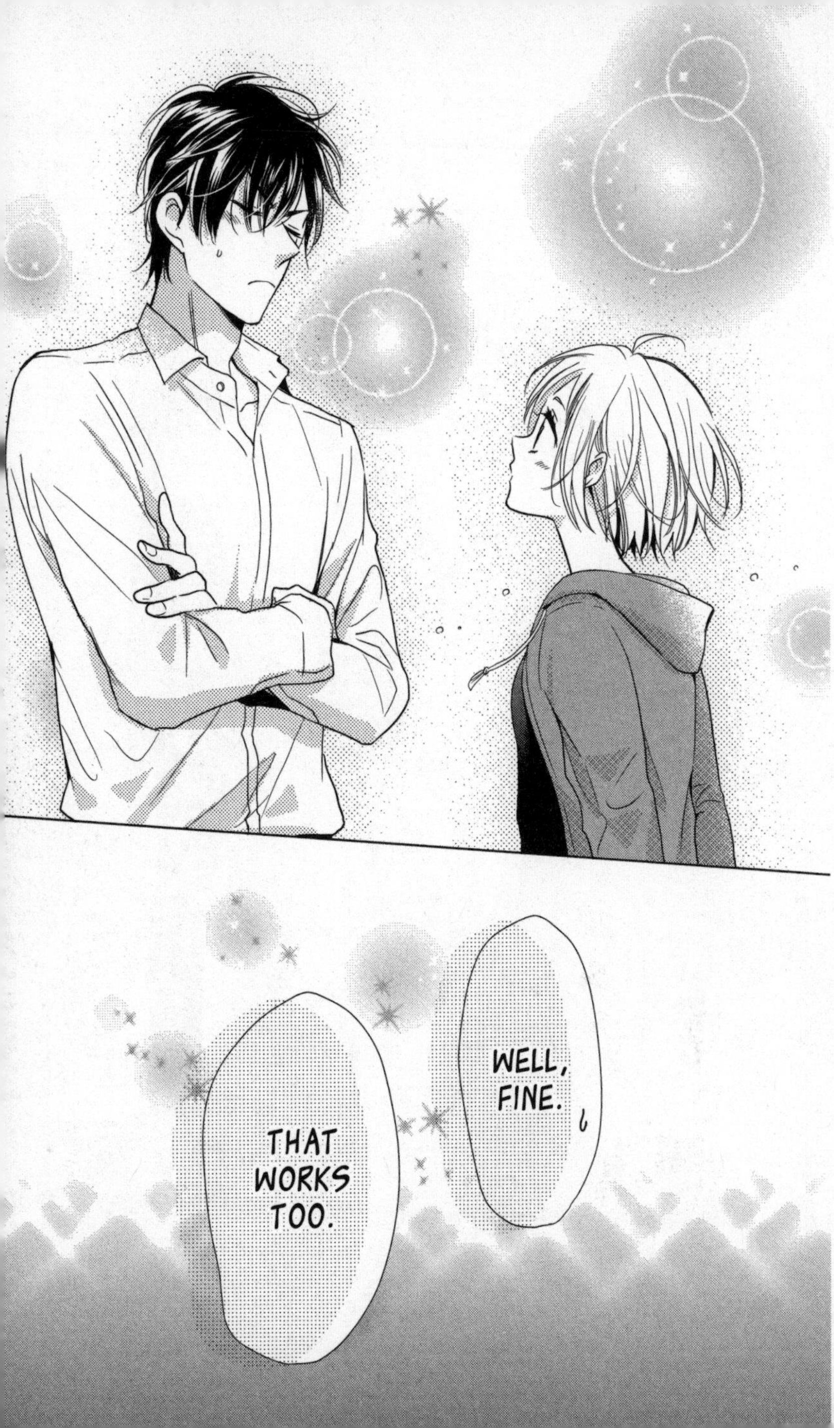
WELL, FINE.
THAT WORKS TOO.

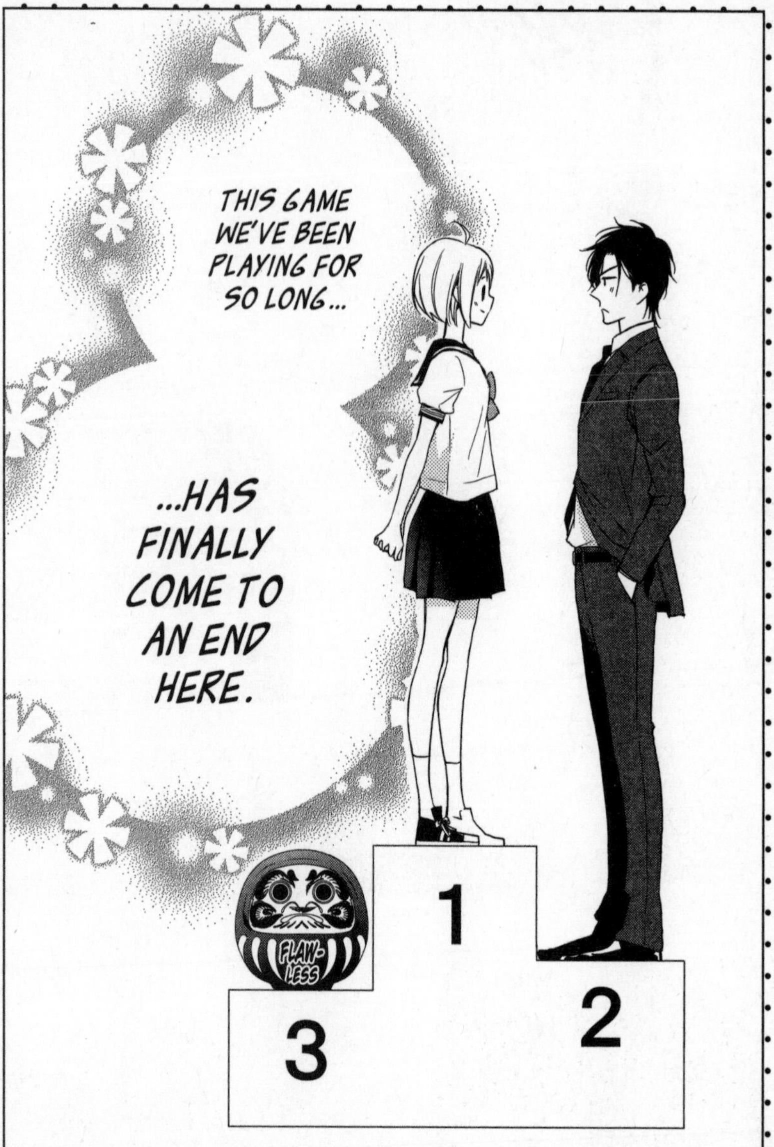
THIS GAME WE'VE BEEN PLAYING FOR SO LONG...
...HAS FINALLY COME TO AN END HERE.
FLAW-LESS
1
2
3

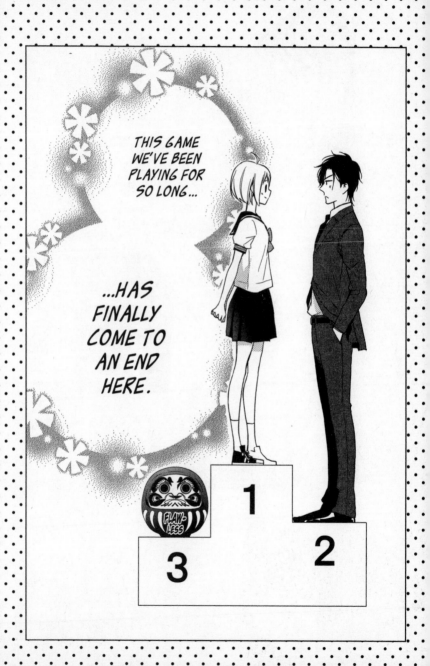

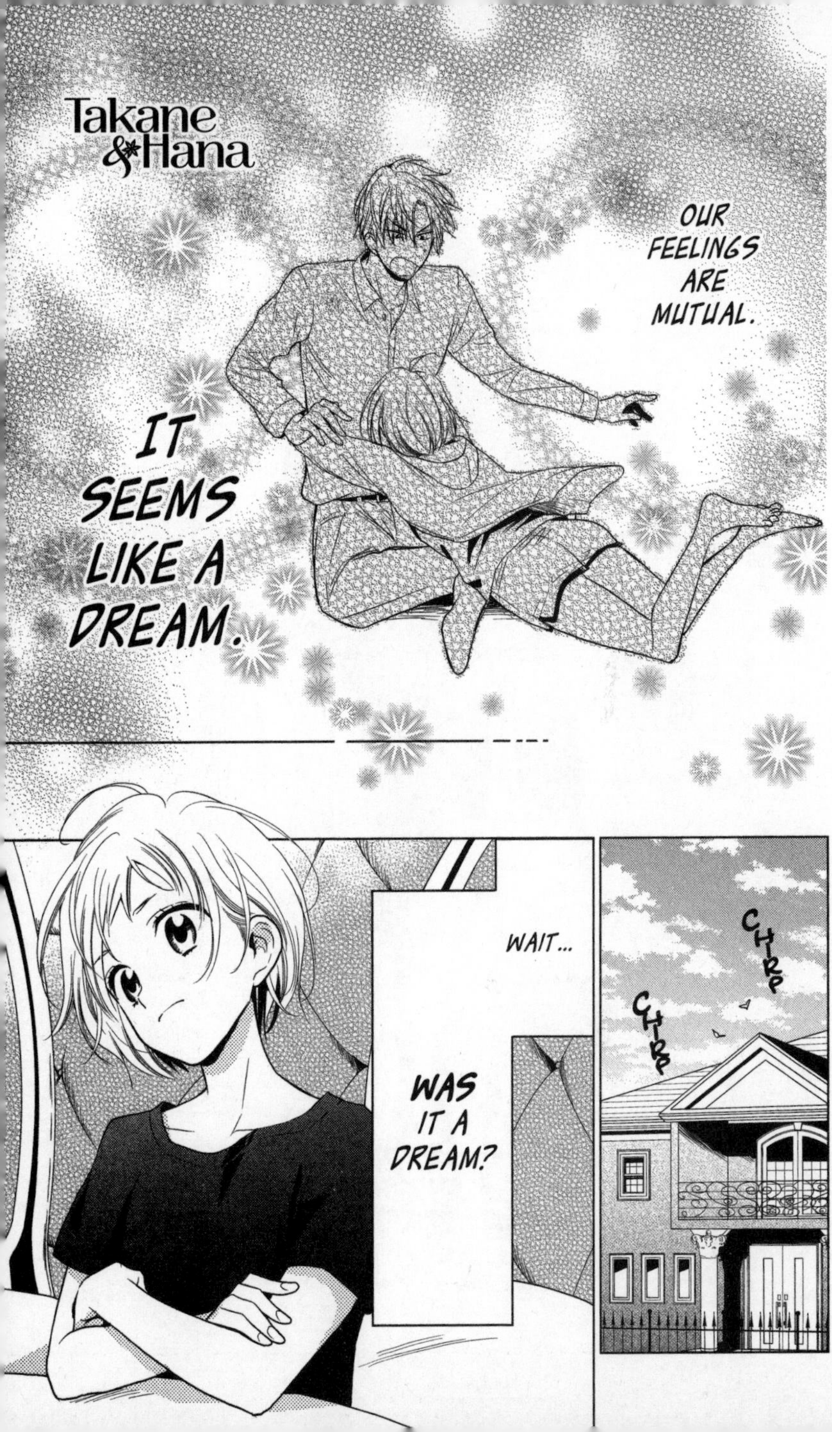
Takane & Hana
OUR FEELINGS ARE MUTUAL.
IT SEEMS LIKE A DREAM.
CHIRP
CHIRP
WAIT...
WAS IT A DREAM?

Chapter 71

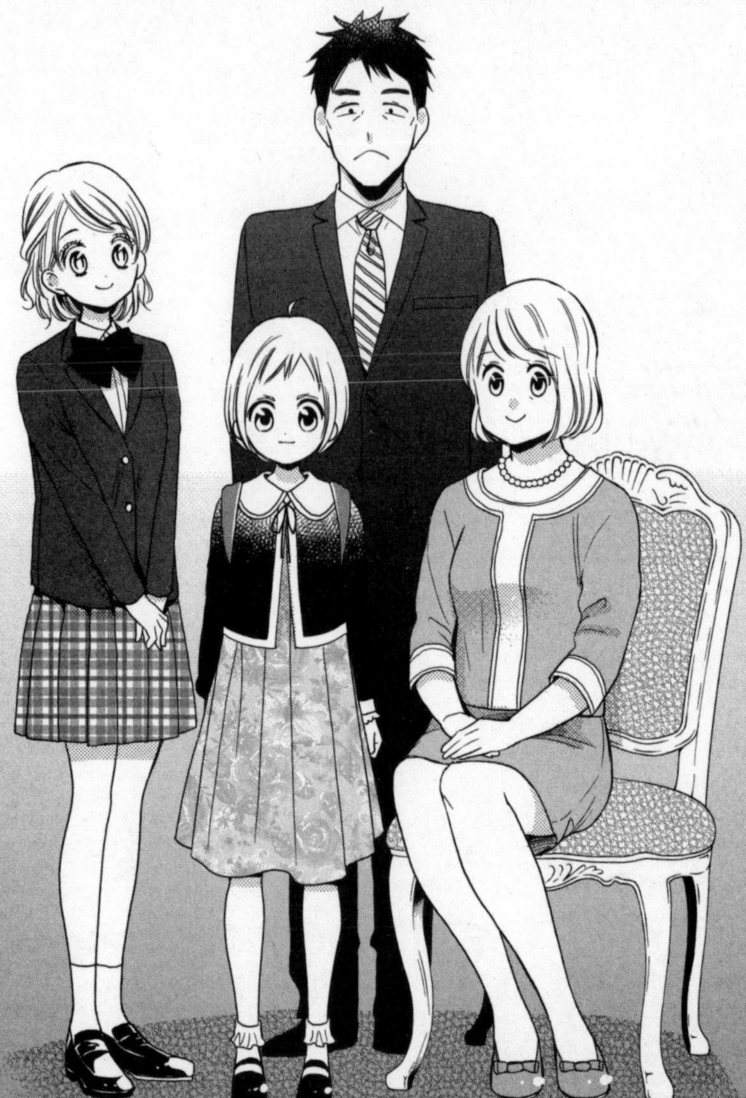

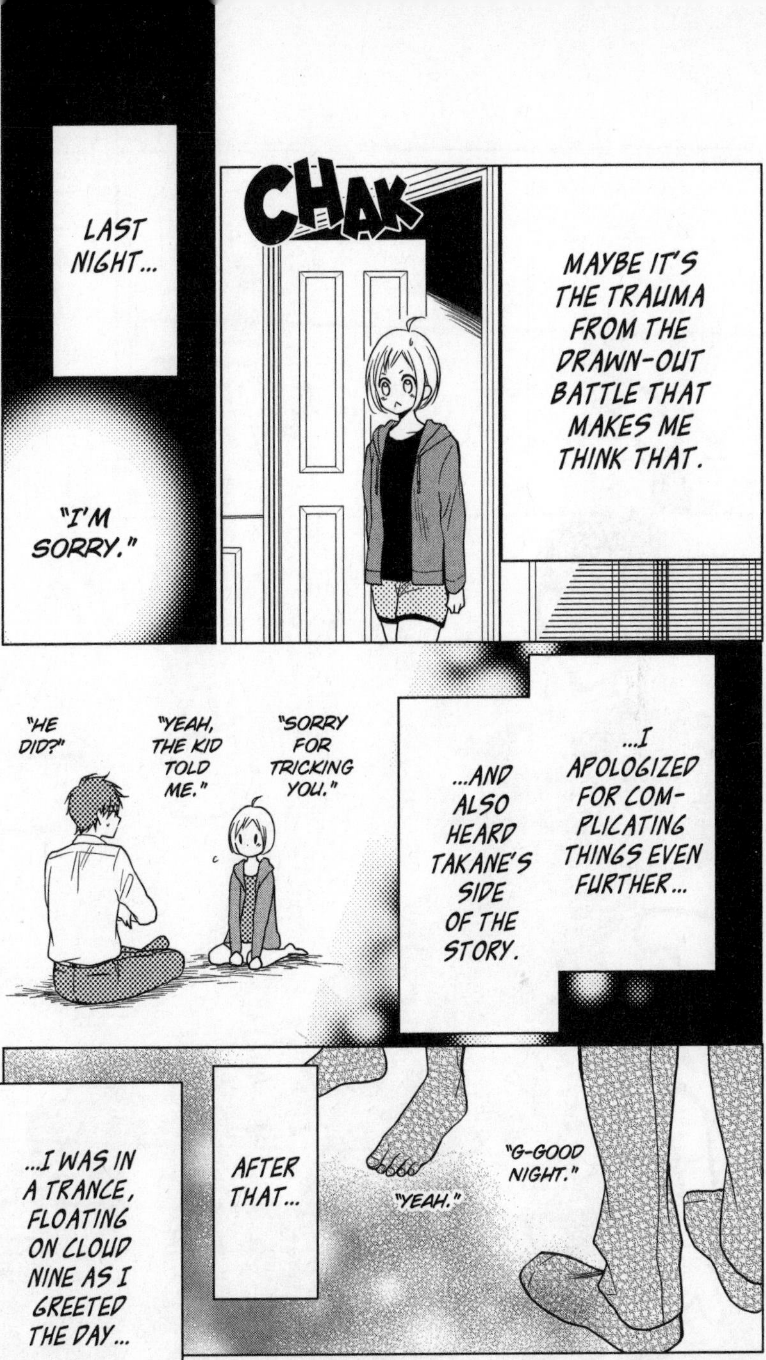
MAYBE IT'S THE TRAUMA FROM THE DRAWN-OUT BATTLE THAT MAKES ME THINK THAT.
CHAK
LAST NIGHT...
"I'M SORRY."
...I APOLOGIZED FOR COM-PLICATING THINGS EVEN FURTHER...
...AND ALSO HEARD TAKANE'S SIDE OF THE STORY.
"SORRY FOR TRICKING YOU."
"YEAH, THE KID TOLD ME."
"HE DID?"
"G-GOOD NIGHT."
"YEAH."
AFTER THAT...
...I WAS IN A TRANCE, FLOATING ON CLOUD NINE AS I GREETED THE DAY...

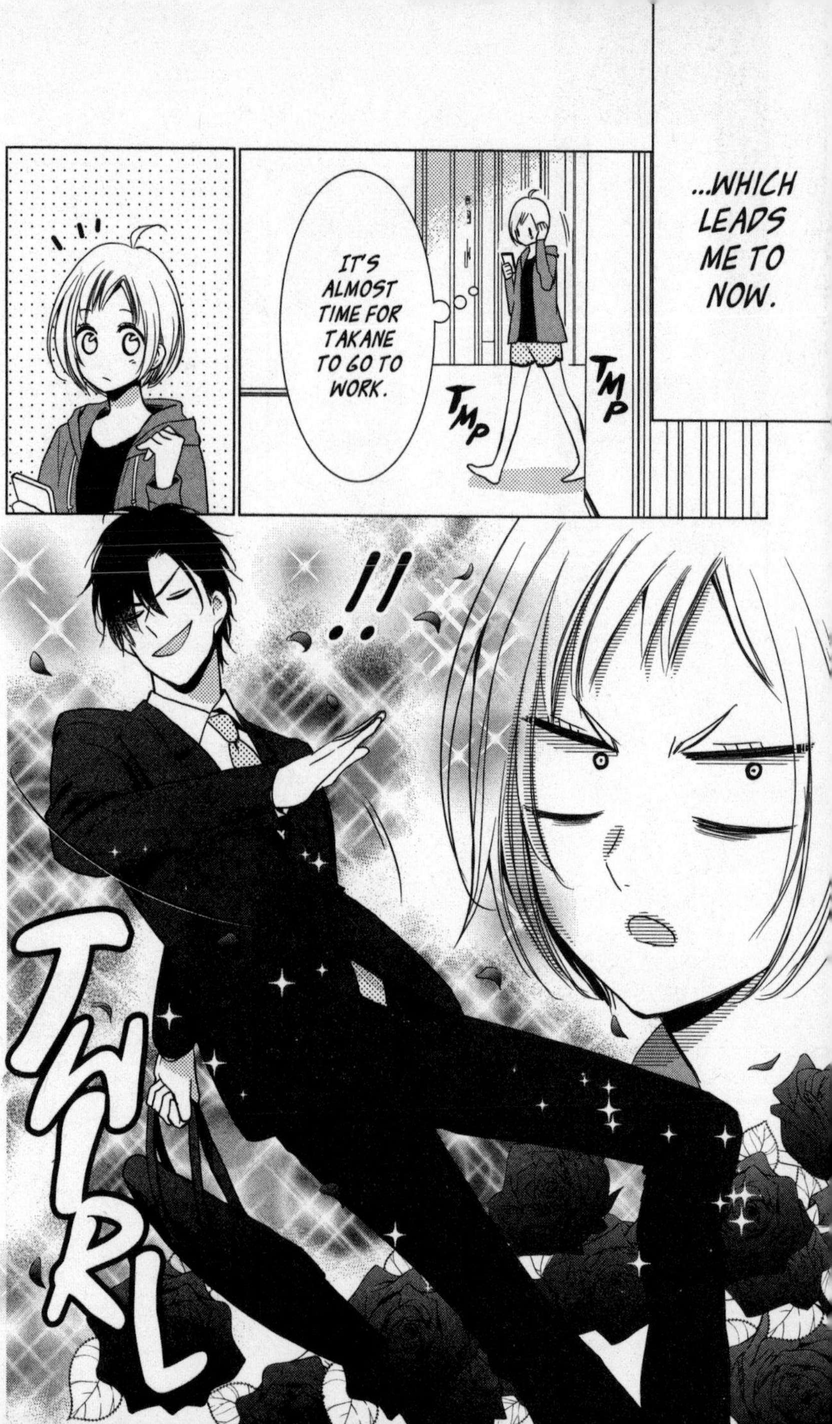
...WHICH LEADS ME TO NOW.
IT'S ALMOST TIME FOR TAKANE TO GO TO WORK.
TMP
TMP
..!!
TWIRL

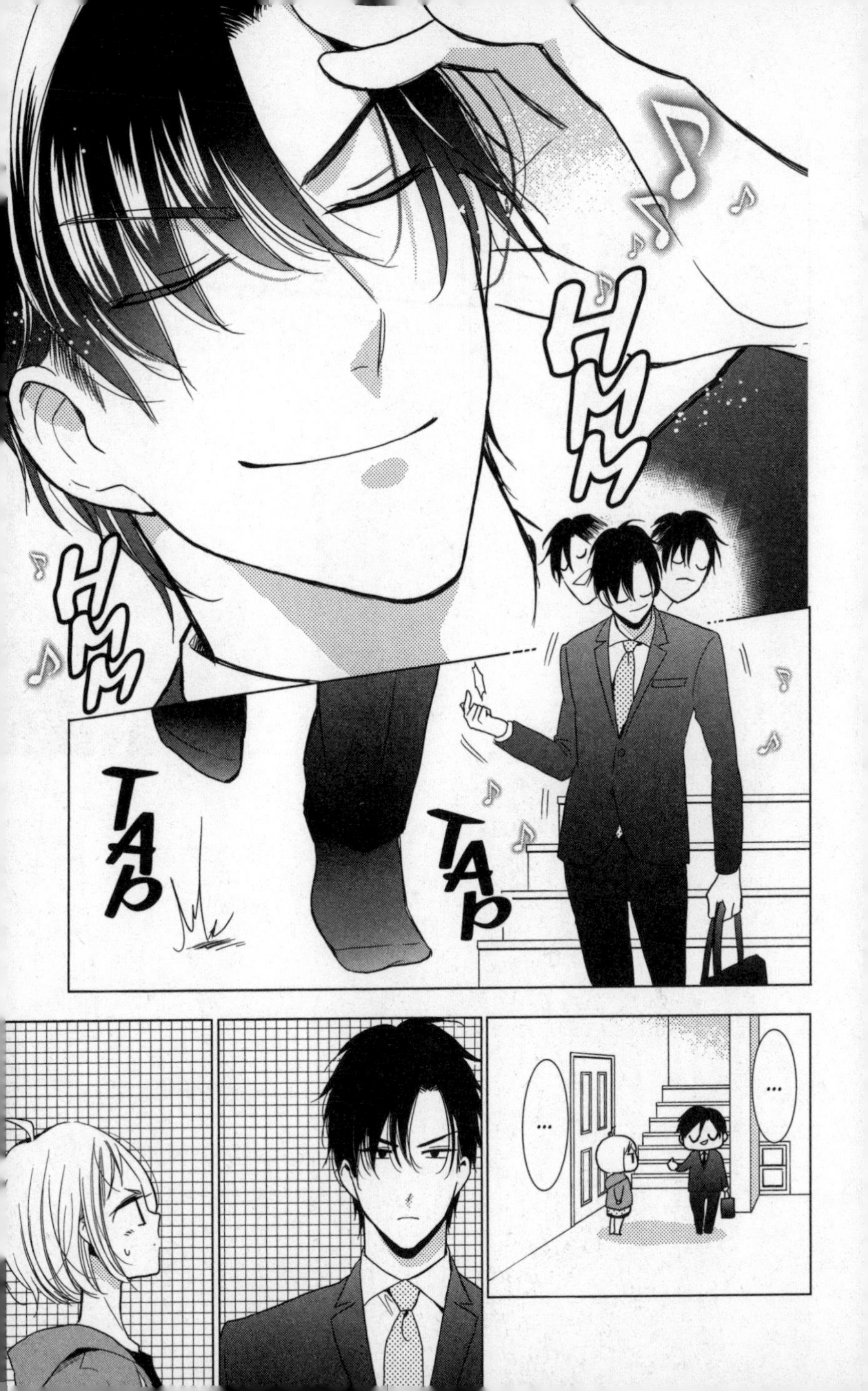
HMM
HMM
TAP
TAP
...
...

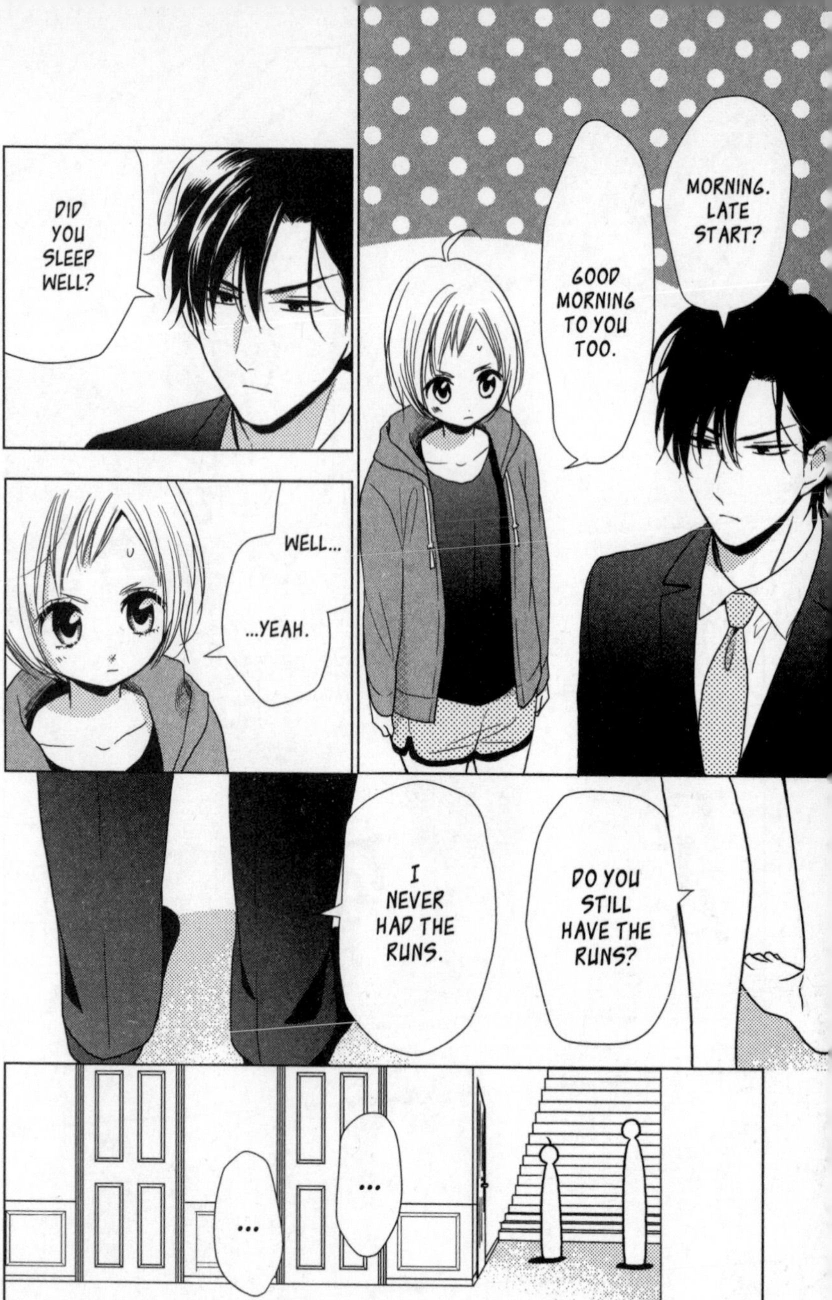
MORNING. LATE START?
GOOD MORNING TO YOU TOO.
DID YOU SLEEP WELL?
WELL...
...YEAH.
DO YOU STILL HAVE THE RUNS?
I NEVER HAD THE RUNS.
...
...

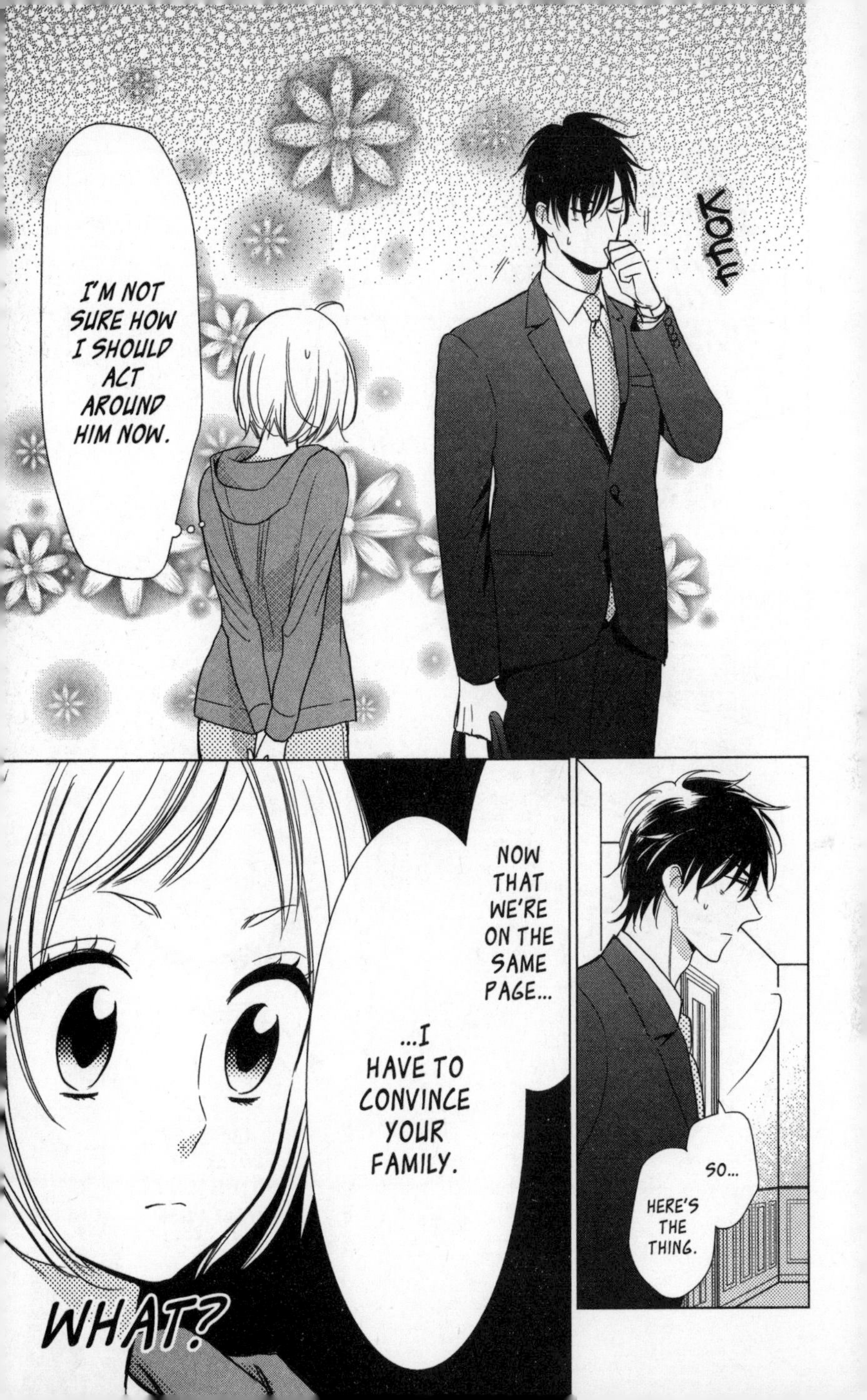
KOFF
I'M NOT SURE HOW I SHOULD ACT AROUND HIM NOW.
SO... HERE'S THE THING.
NOW THAT WE'RE ON THE SAME PAGE...
...I HAVE TO CONVINCE YOUR FAMILY.
WHAT?

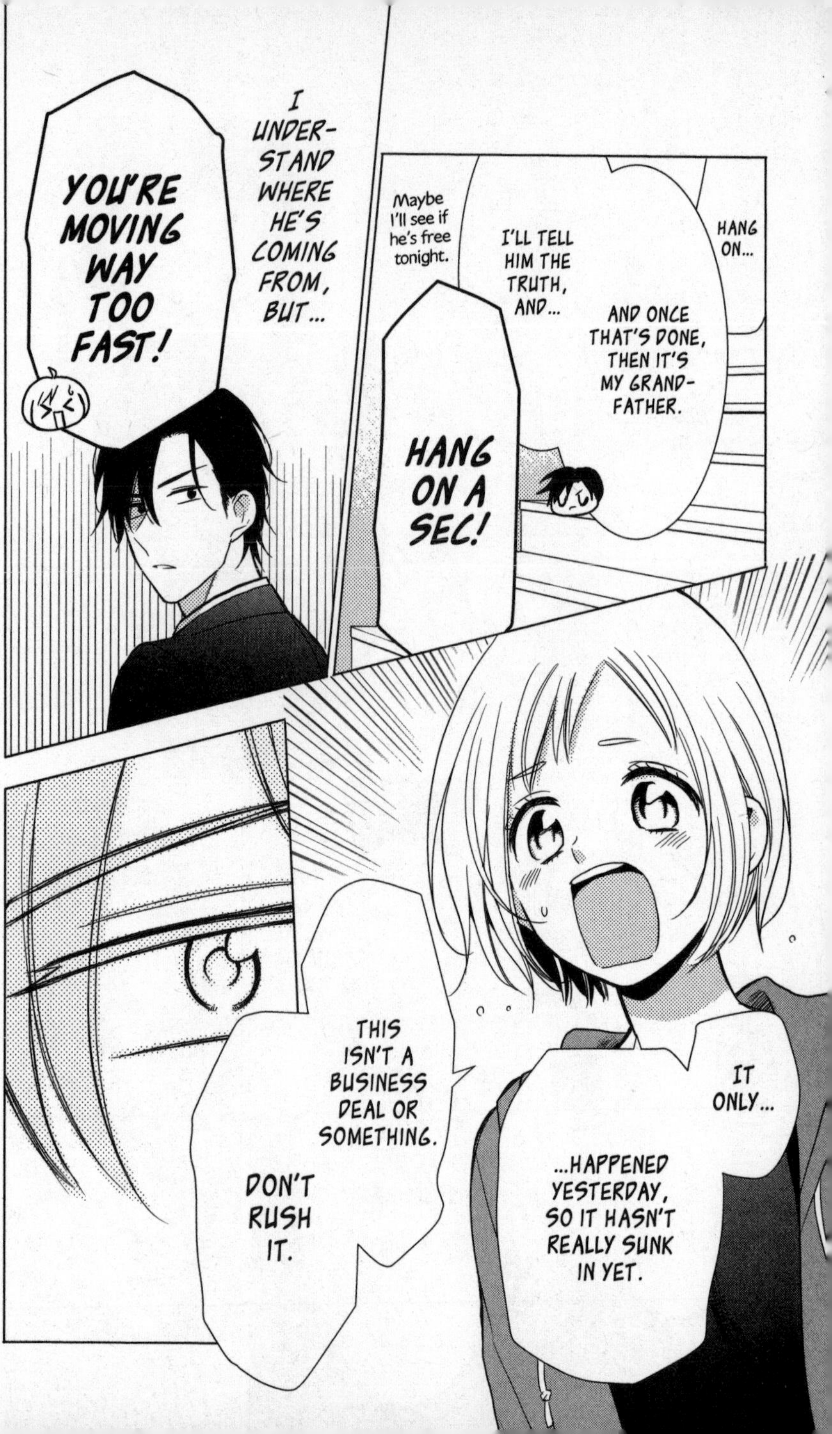
HANG ON...
I'LL TELL HIM THE TRUTH, AND...
AND ONCE THAT'S DONE, THEN IT'S MY GRANDFATHER.
Maybe I'll see if he's free tonight.
HANG ON A SEC!
I UNDERSTAND WHERE HE'S COMING FROM, BUT...
YOU'RE MOVING WAY TOO FAST!
IT ONLY...
...HAPPENED YESTERDAY, SO IT HASN'T REALLY SUNK IN YET.
THIS ISN'T A BUSINESS DEAL OR SOMETHING.
DON'T RUSH IT.

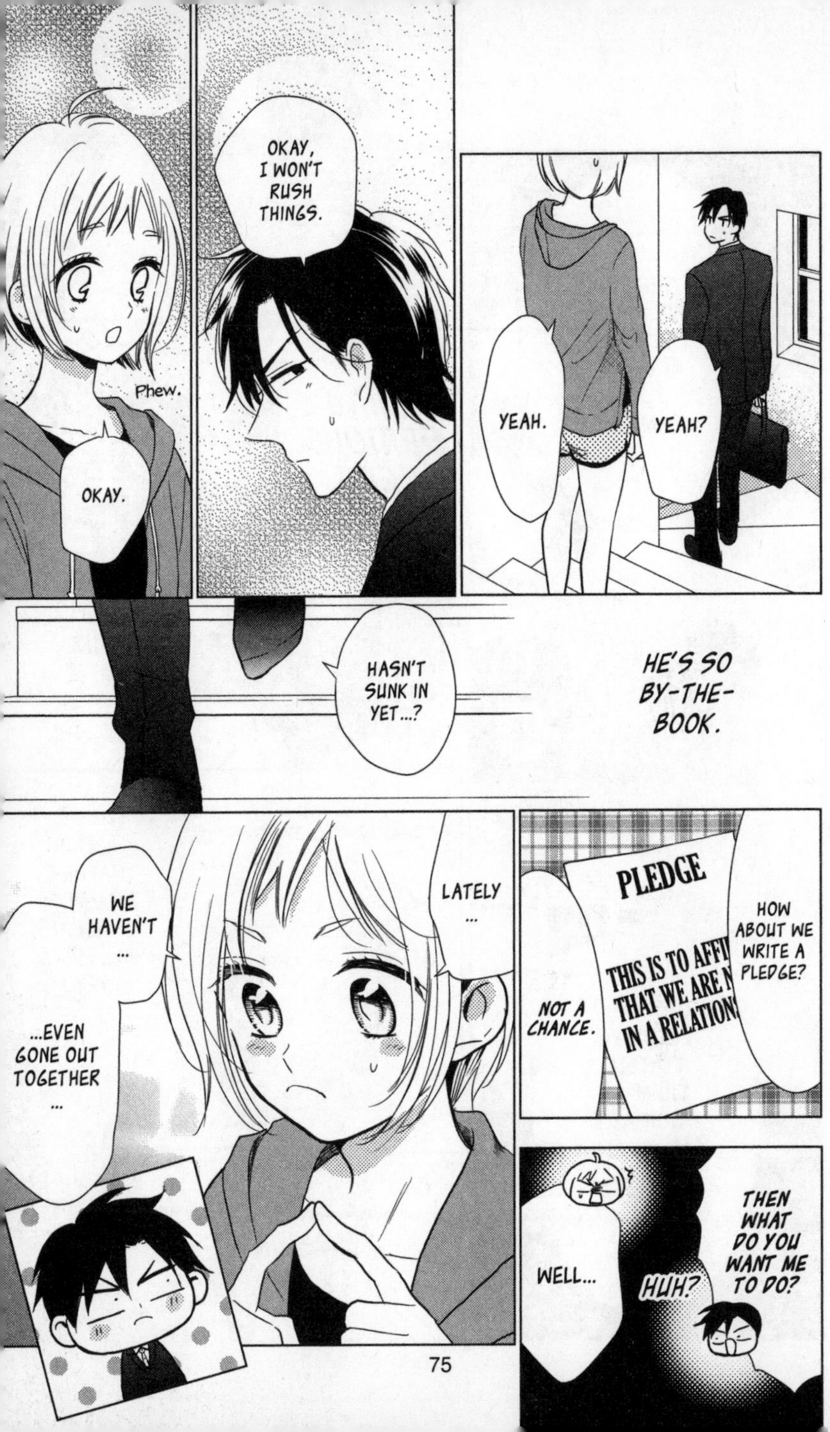
YEAH?
YEAH.
OKAY, I WON'T RUSH THINGS.
Phew.
OKAY.
HE'S SO BY-THE-BOOK.
HASN'T SUNK IN YET...?
HOW ABOUT WE WRITE A PLEDGE?
PLEDGE
THIS IS TO AFFI
THAT WE ARE N
IN A RELATIONS
NOT A CHANCE.
THEN WHAT DO YOU WANT ME TO DO?
HUH?
WELL...
LATELY ...
WE HAVEN'T ...
...EVEN GONE OUT TOGETHER ...

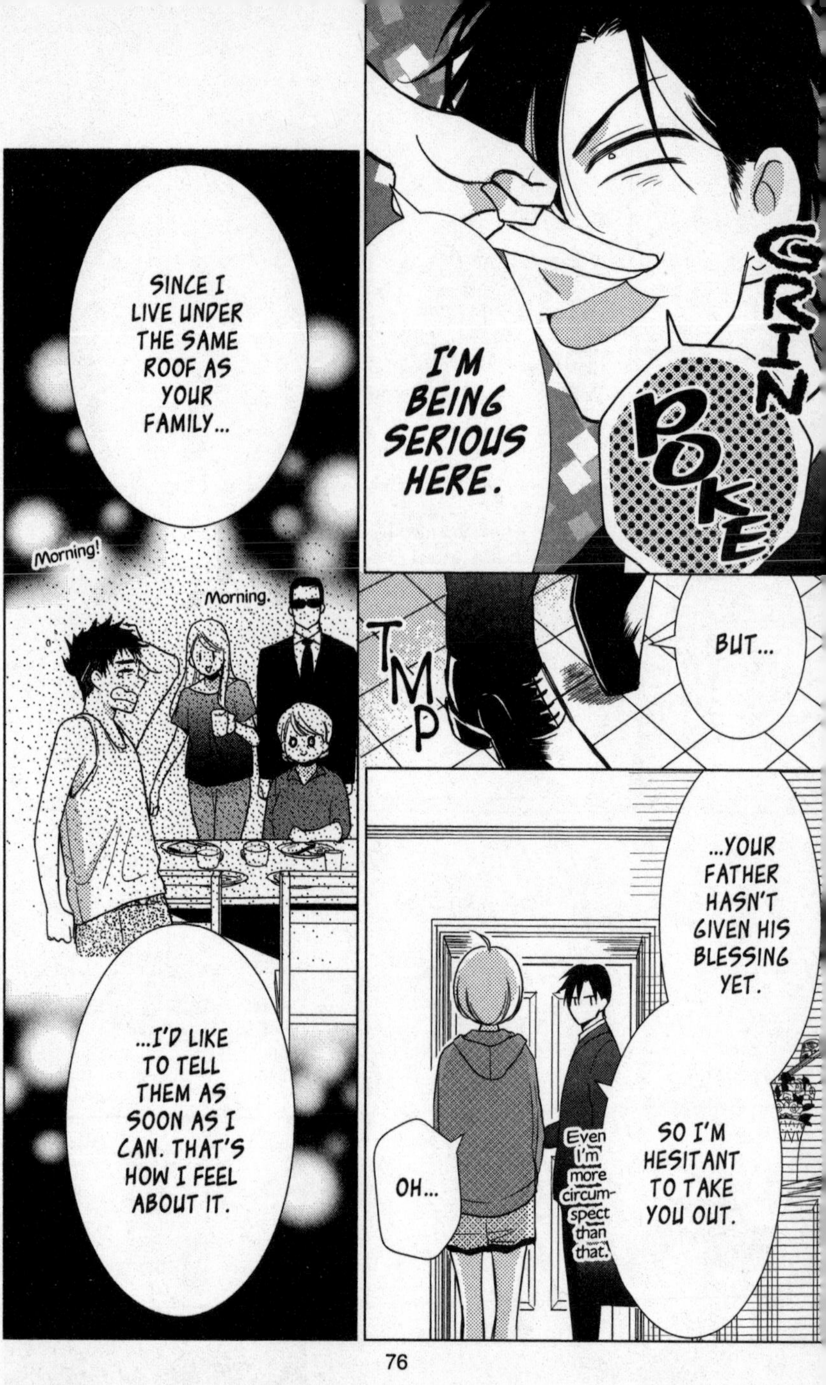
GRIN
POKE
I'M BEING SERIOUS HERE.
BUT...
TMP
...YOUR FATHER HASN'T GIVEN HIS BLESSING YET.
SO I'M HESITANT TO TAKE YOU OUT.
Even I'm more circumspect than that.
OH...
SINCE I LIVE UNDER THE SAME ROOF AS YOUR FAMILY...
Morning!
Morning.
...I'D LIKE TO TELL THEM AS SOON AS I CAN. THAT'S HOW I FEEL ABOUT IT.

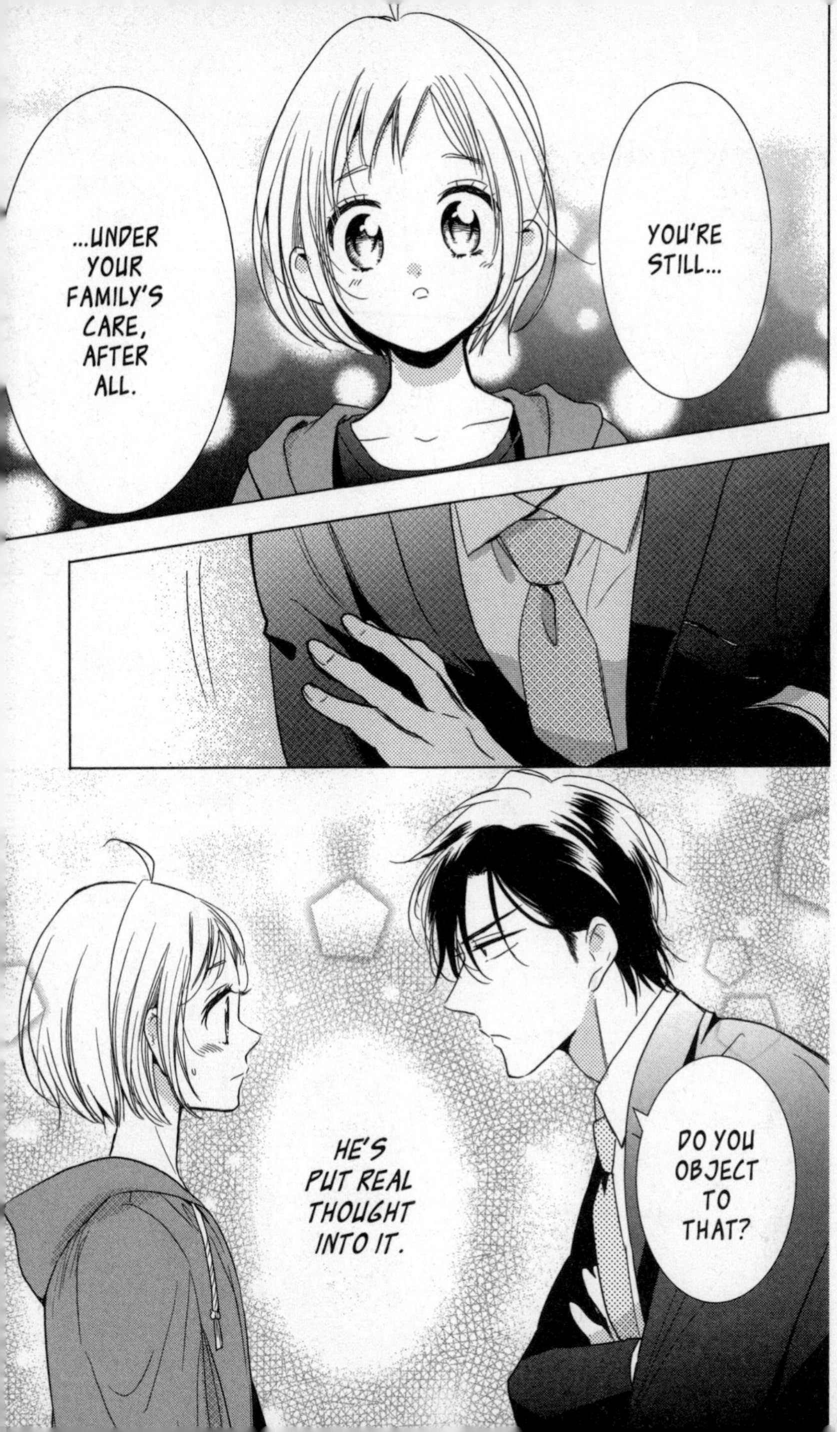
YOU'RE STILL...
...UNDER YOUR FAMILY'S CARE, AFTER ALL.
DO YOU OBJECT TO THAT?
HE'S PUT REAL THOUGHT INTO IT.

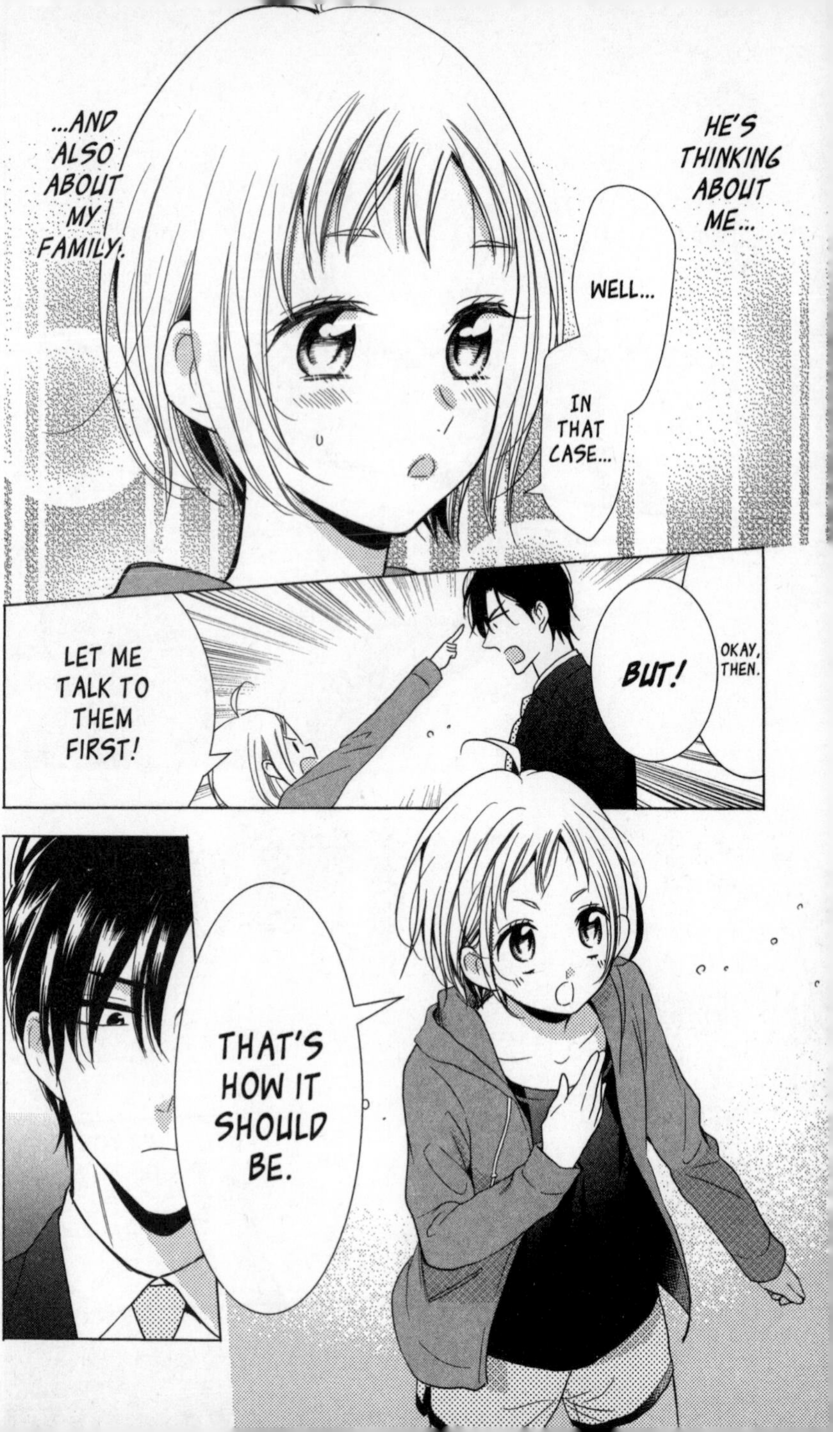
HE'S THINKING ABOUT ME...
...AND ALSO ABOUT MY FAMILY.
WELL... IN THAT CASE...
OKAY, THEN.
BUT!
LET ME TALK TO THEM FIRST!
THAT'S HOW IT SHOULD BE.

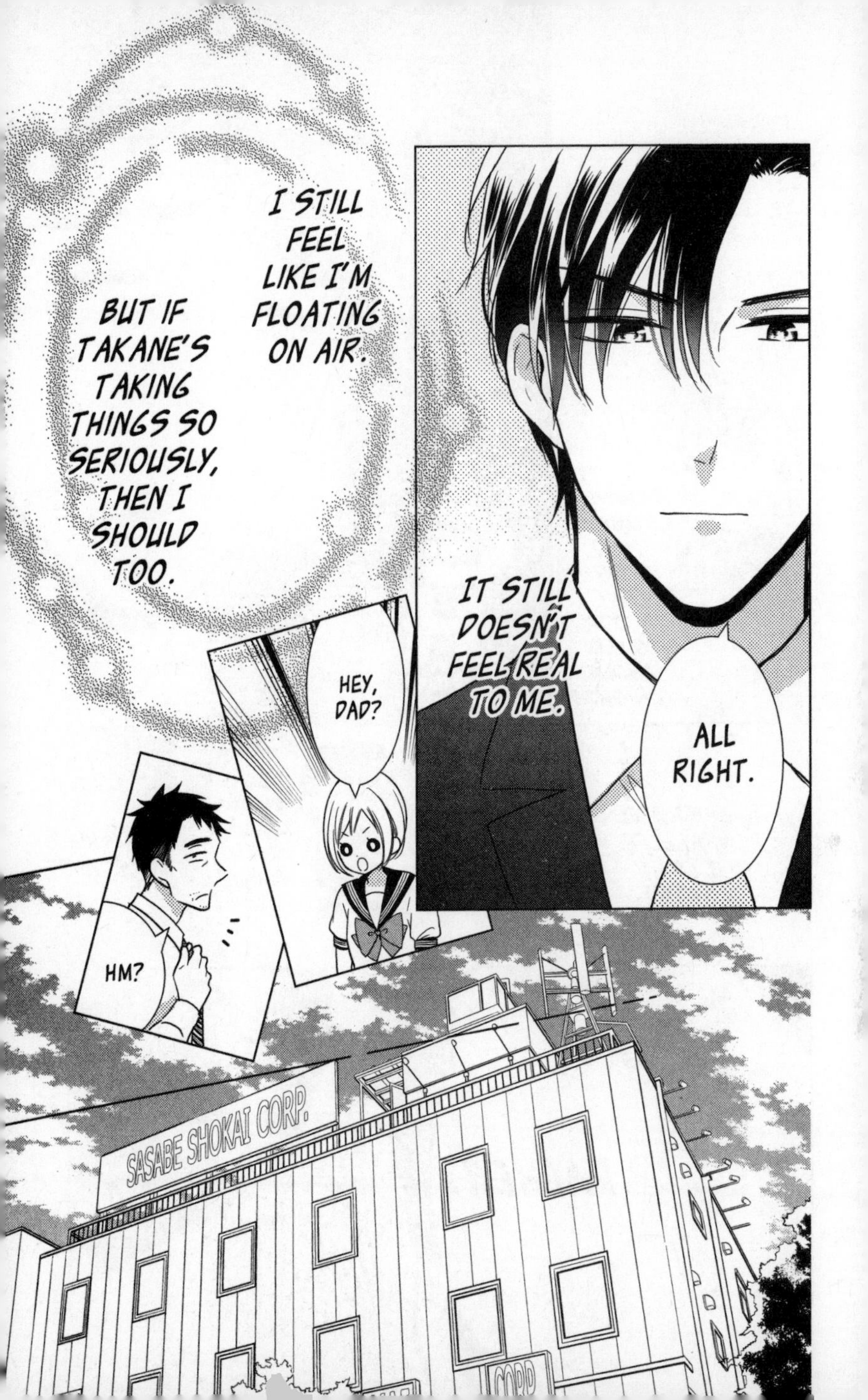
ALL RIGHT.
IT STILL DOESN'T FEEL REAL TO ME.
I STILL FEEL LIKE I'M FLOATING ON AIR.
BUT IF TAKANE'S TAKING THINGS SO SERIOUSLY, THEN I SHOULD TOO.
HEY, DAD?
...
HM?
SASABE SHOKAI CORP.

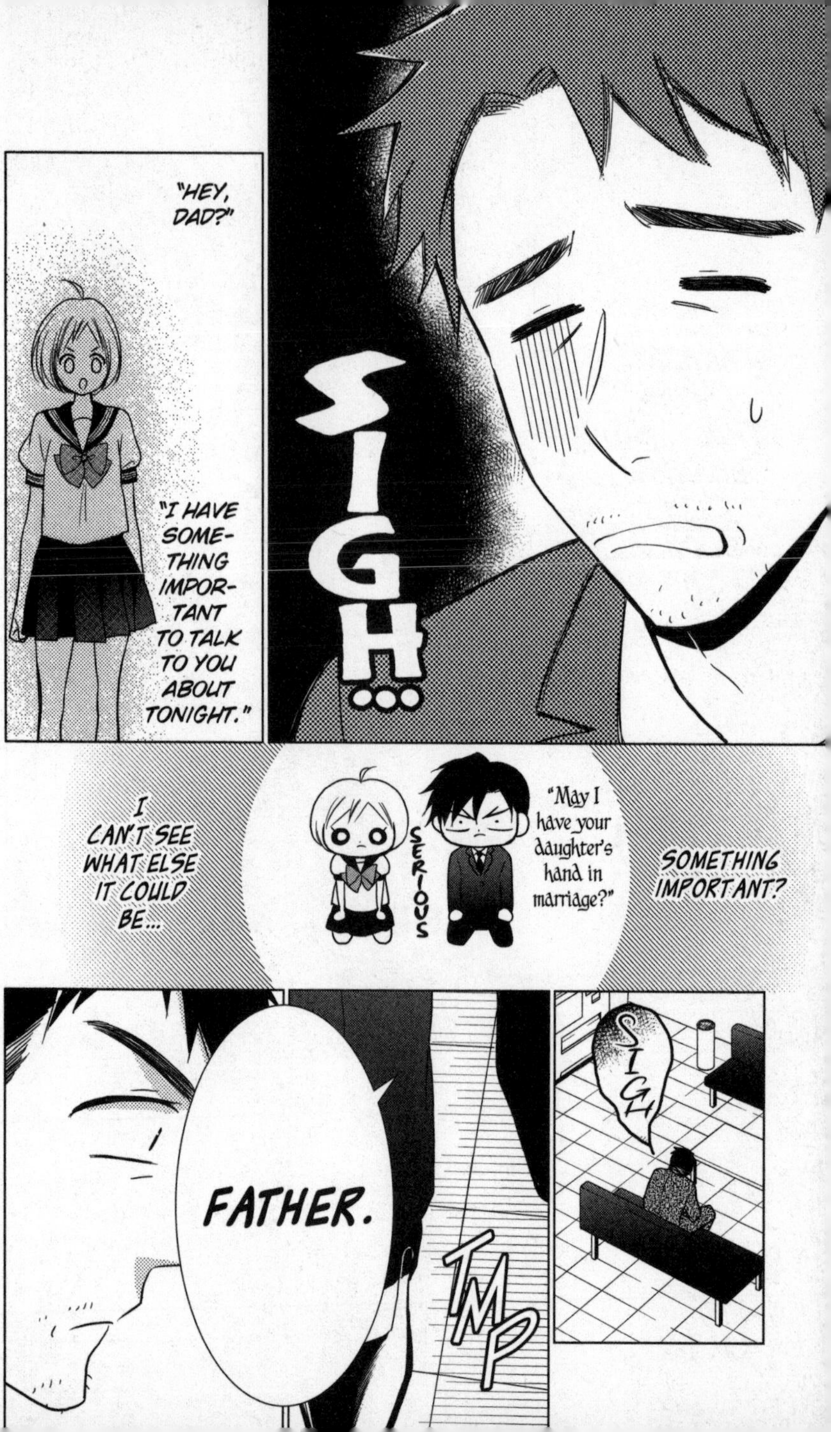
SIGH...
"HEY, DAD?"
"I HAVE SOMETHING IMPORTANT TO TALK TO YOU ABOUT TONIGHT."
SOMETHING IMPORTANT?
"May I have your daughter's hand in marriage?"
SERIOUS
I CAN'T SEE WHAT ELSE IT COULD BE...
SIGH
TMP
FATHER.

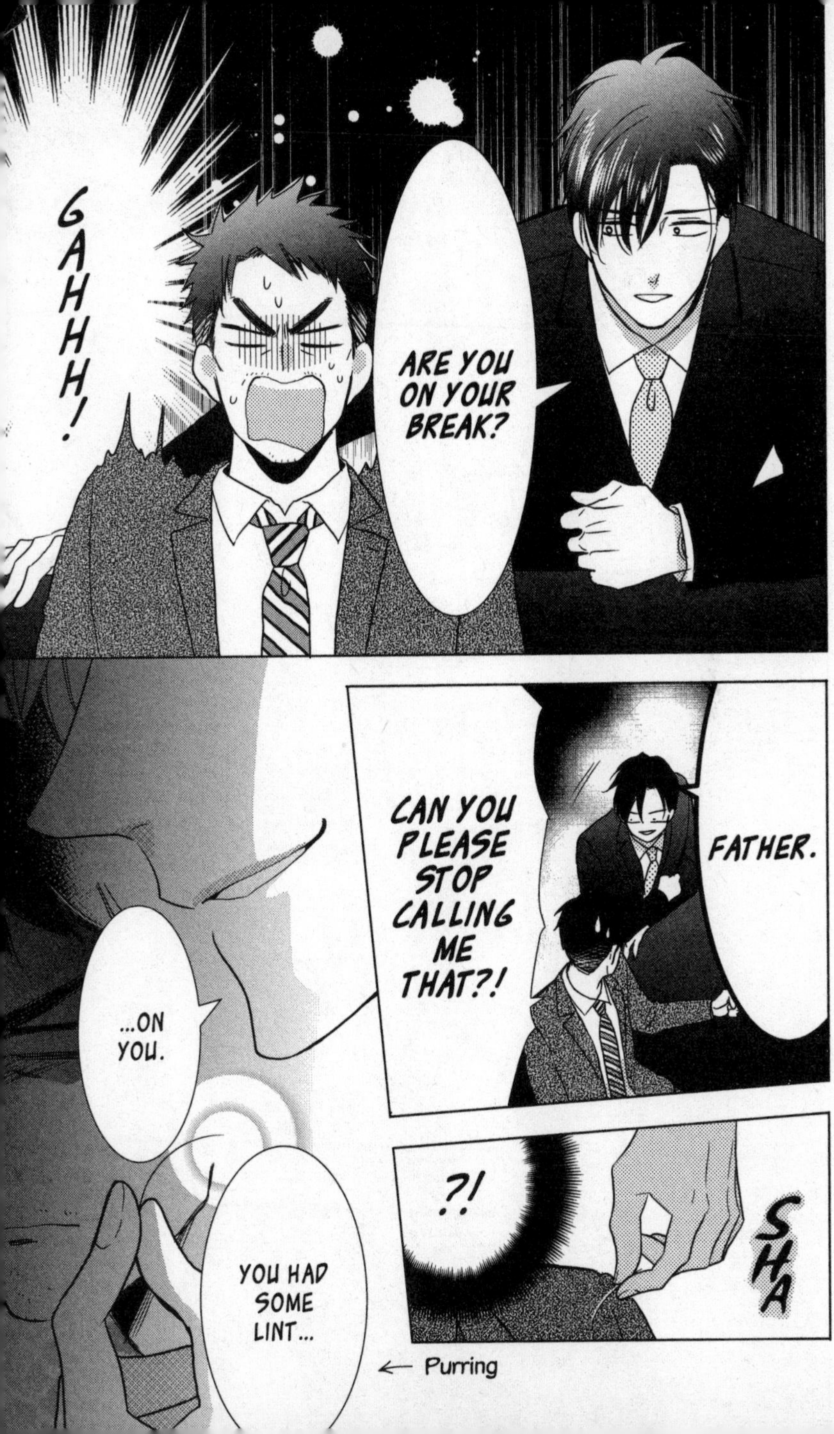
ARE YOU ON YOUR BREAK?
GAHHHH!
FATHER.
CAN YOU PLEASE STOP CALLING ME THAT?!
SHA
?!
YOU HAD SOME LINT...
...ON YOU.
← Purring

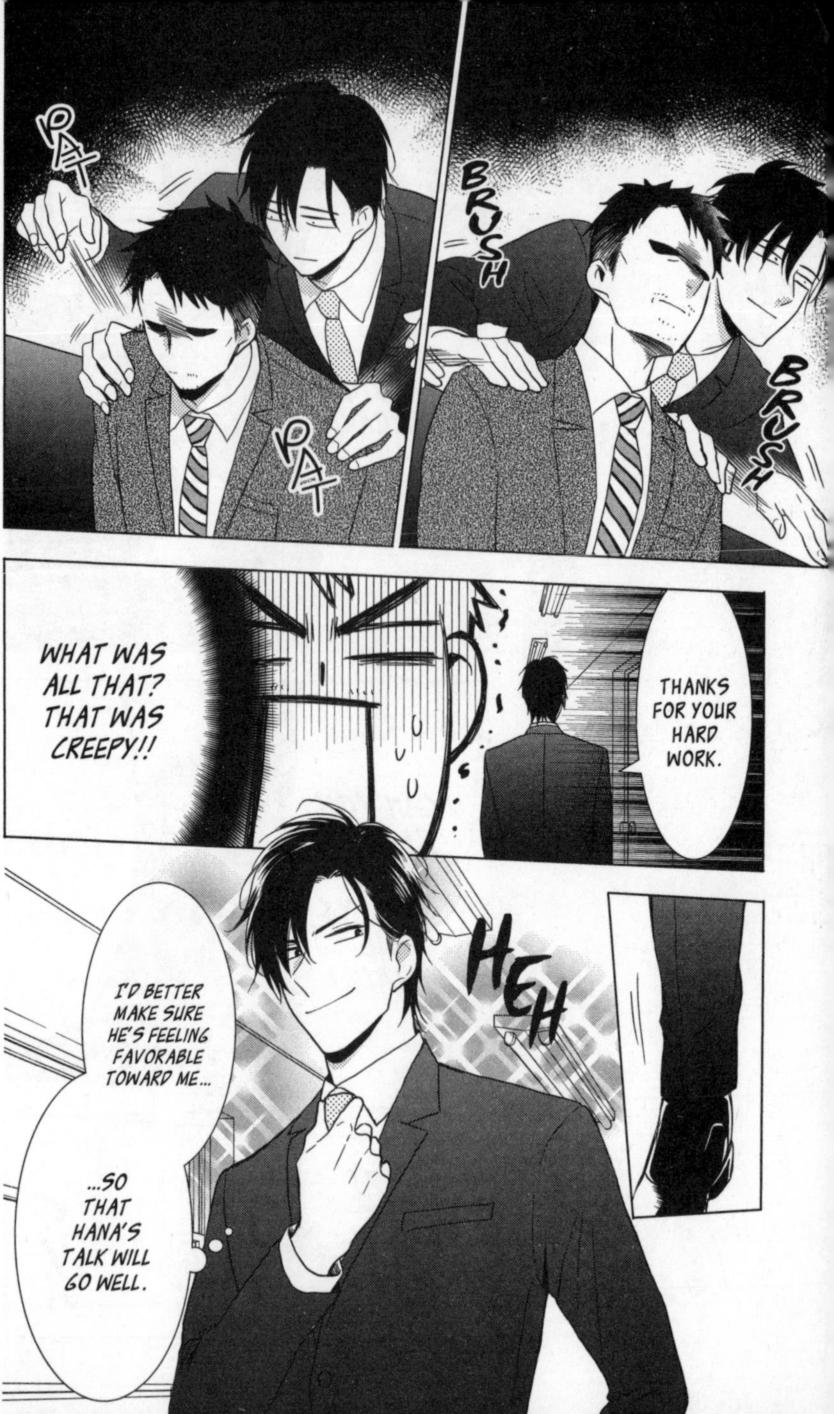
BRUSH
BRUSH
PAT
PAT
THANKS FOR YOUR HARD WORK.
WHAT WAS ALL THAT? THAT WAS CREEPY!!
HEH
I'D BETTER MAKE SURE HE'S FEELING FAVORABLE TOWARD ME...
...SO THAT HANA'S TALK WILL GO WELL.

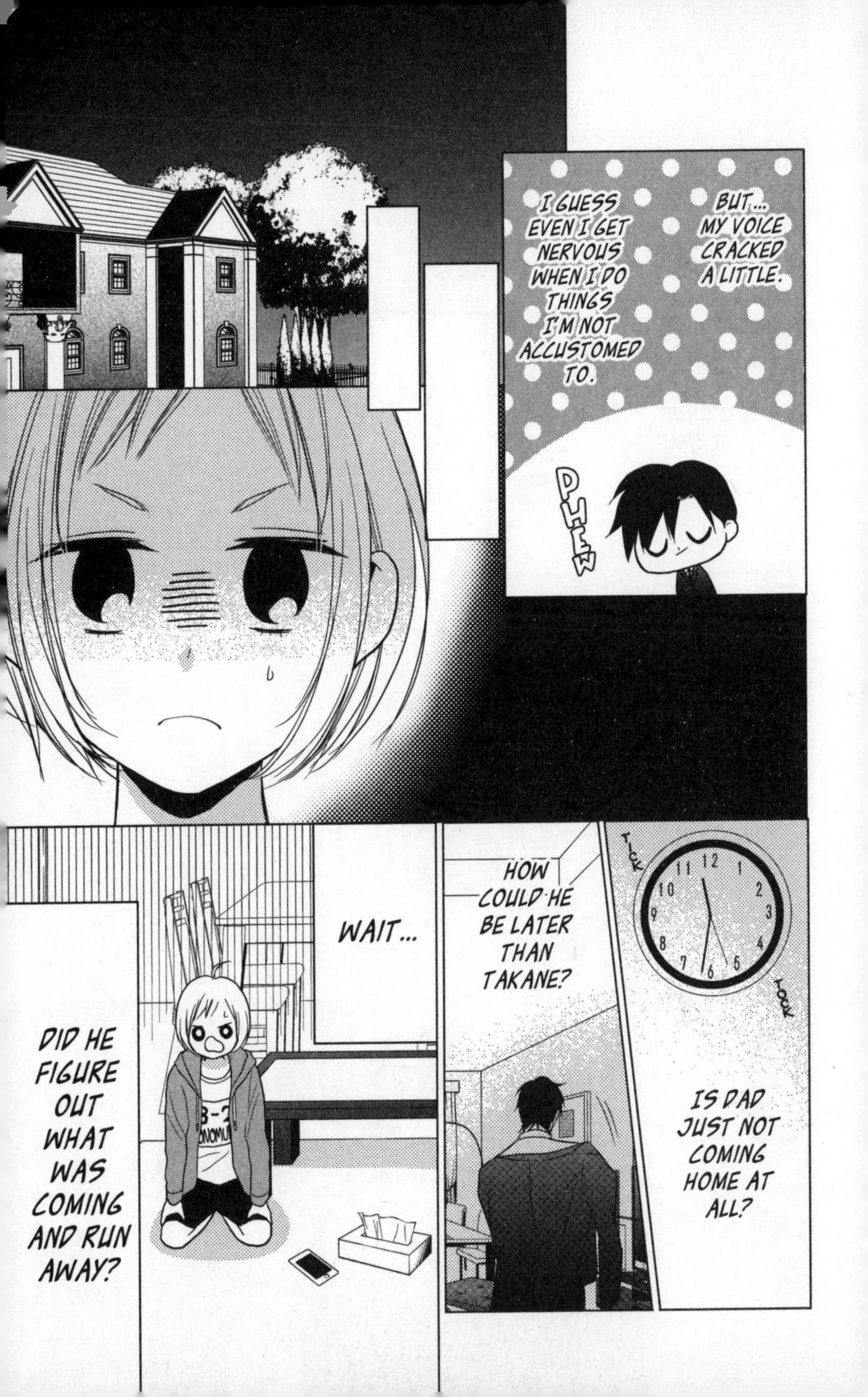
BUT... MY VOICE CRACKED A LITTLE.
I GUESS EVEN I GET NERVOUS WHEN I DO THINGS I'M NOT ACCUSTOMED TO.
PHEW
TICK
TOCK
HOW COULD HE BE LATER THAN TAKANE?
IS DAD JUST NOT COMING HOME AT ALL?
WAIT...
DID HE FIGURE OUT WHAT WAS COMING AND RUN AWAY?

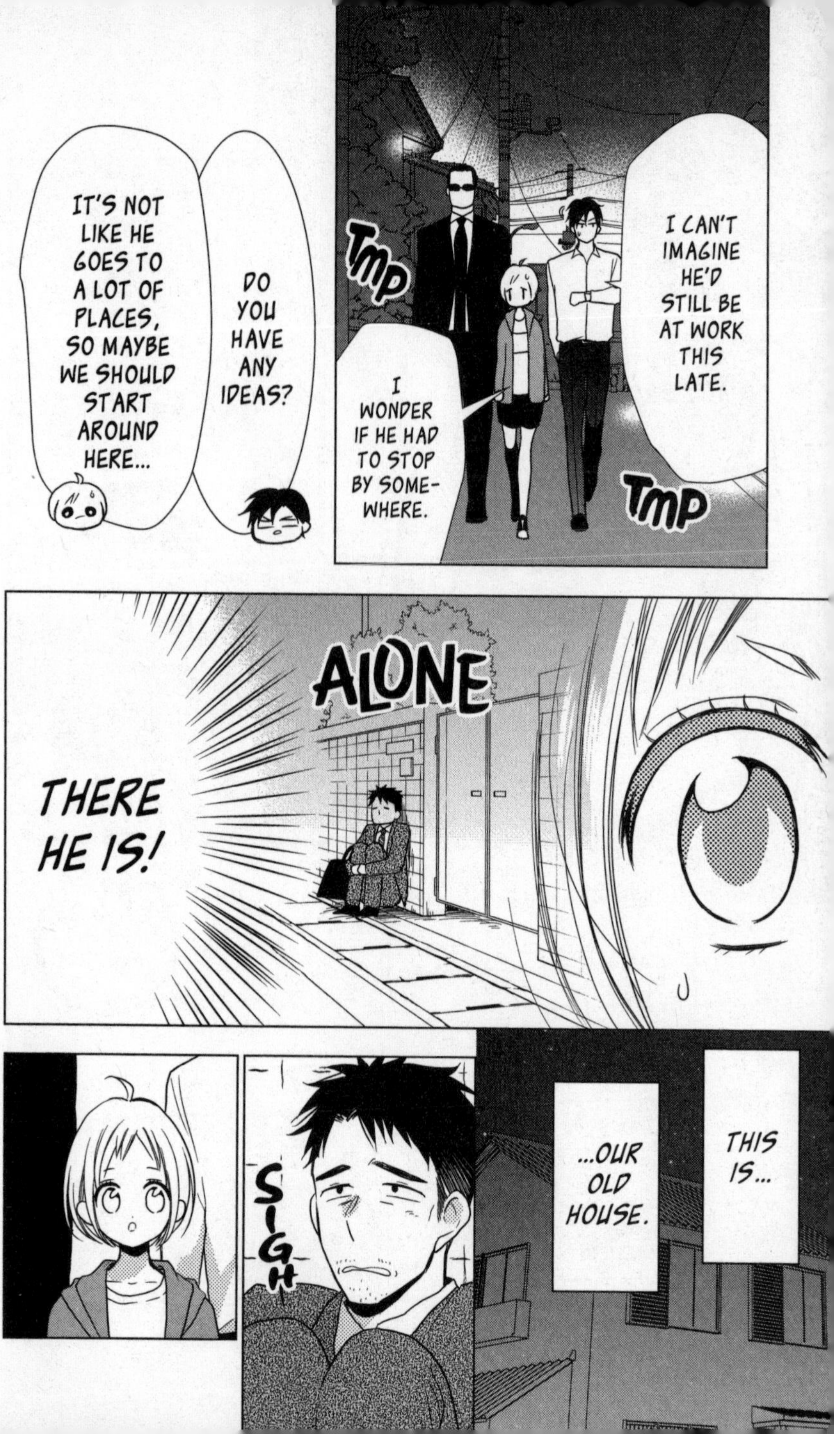

I CAN'T IMAGINE HE'D STILL BE AT WORK THIS LATE.
TMP
TMP
I WONDER IF HE HAD TO STOP BY SOME-WHERE.
DO YOU HAVE ANY IDEAS?
IT'S NOT LIKE HE GOES TO A LOT OF PLACES, SO MAYBE WE SHOULD START AROUND HERE...
ALONE
THERE HE IS!
THIS IS...
...OUR OLD HOUSE.
SIGH

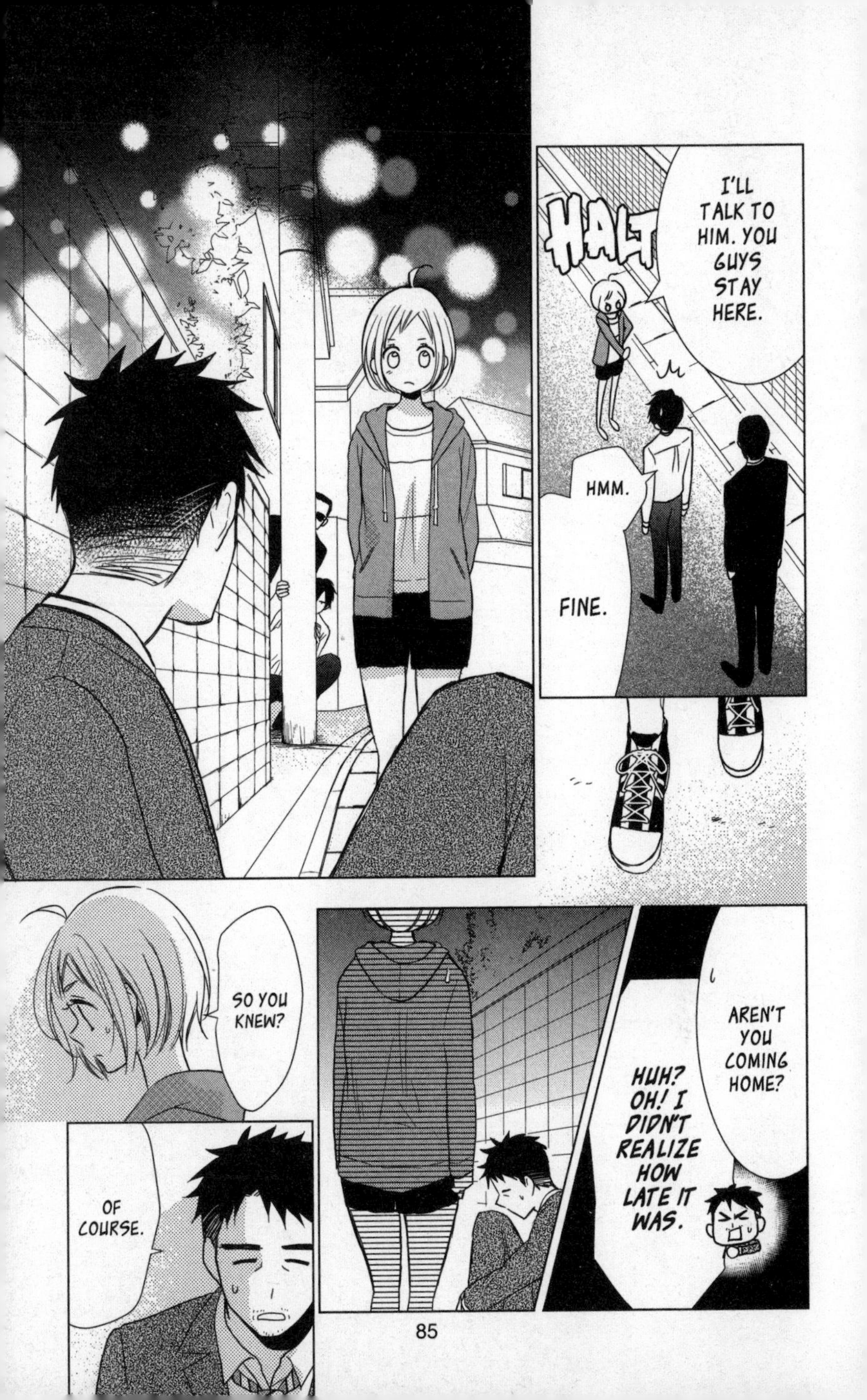
HALT
I'LL TALK TO HIM. YOU GUYS STAY HERE.
HMM.
FINE.
AREN'T YOU COMING HOME?
HUH? OH! I DIDN'T REALIZE HOW LATE IT WAS.
SO YOU KNEW?
OF COURSE.

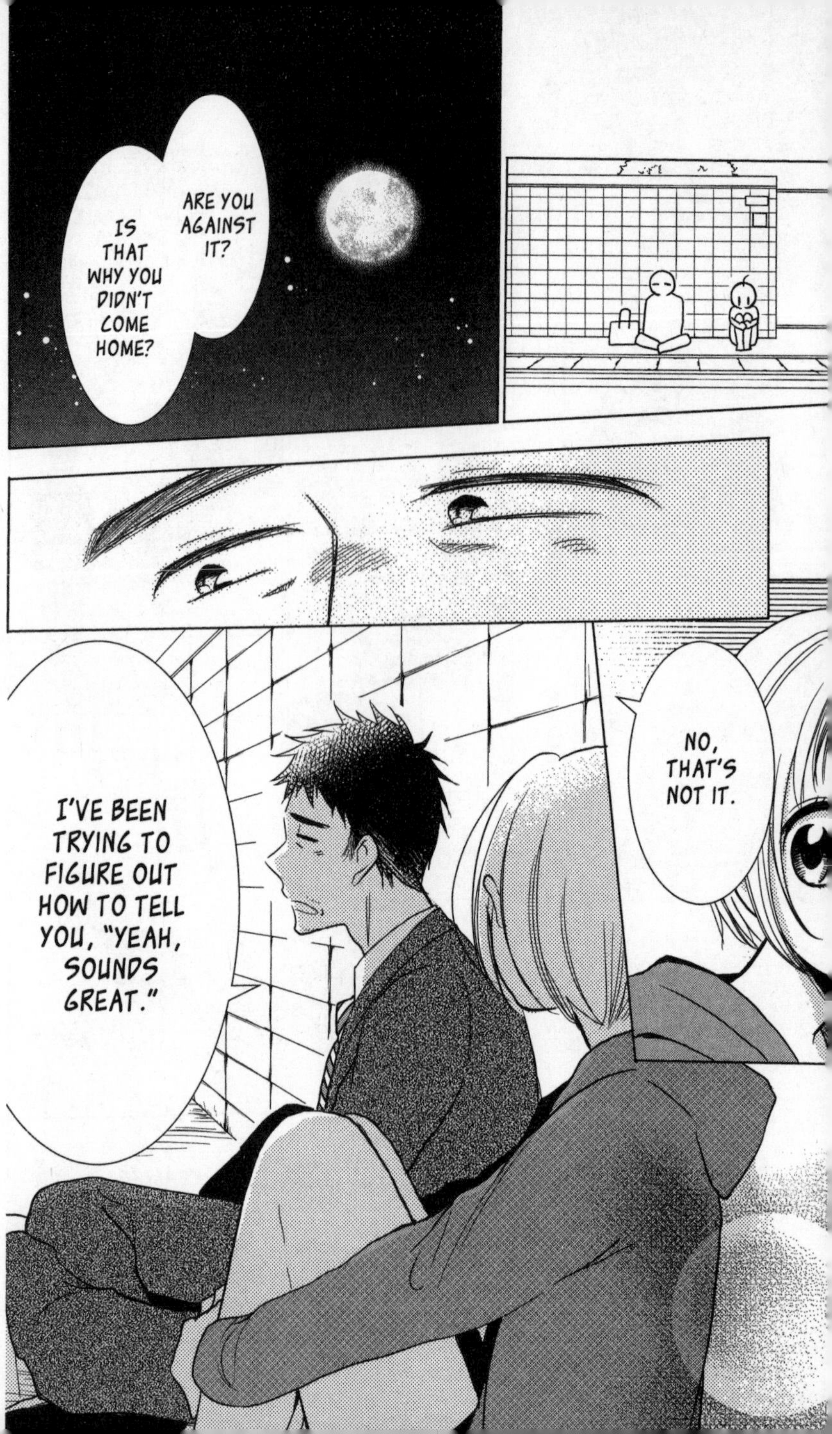
ARE YOU AGAINST IT?
IS THAT WHY YOU DIDN'T COME HOME?
NO, THAT'S NOT IT.
I'VE BEEN TRYING TO FIGURE OUT HOW TO TELL YOU, "YEAH, SOUNDS GREAT."

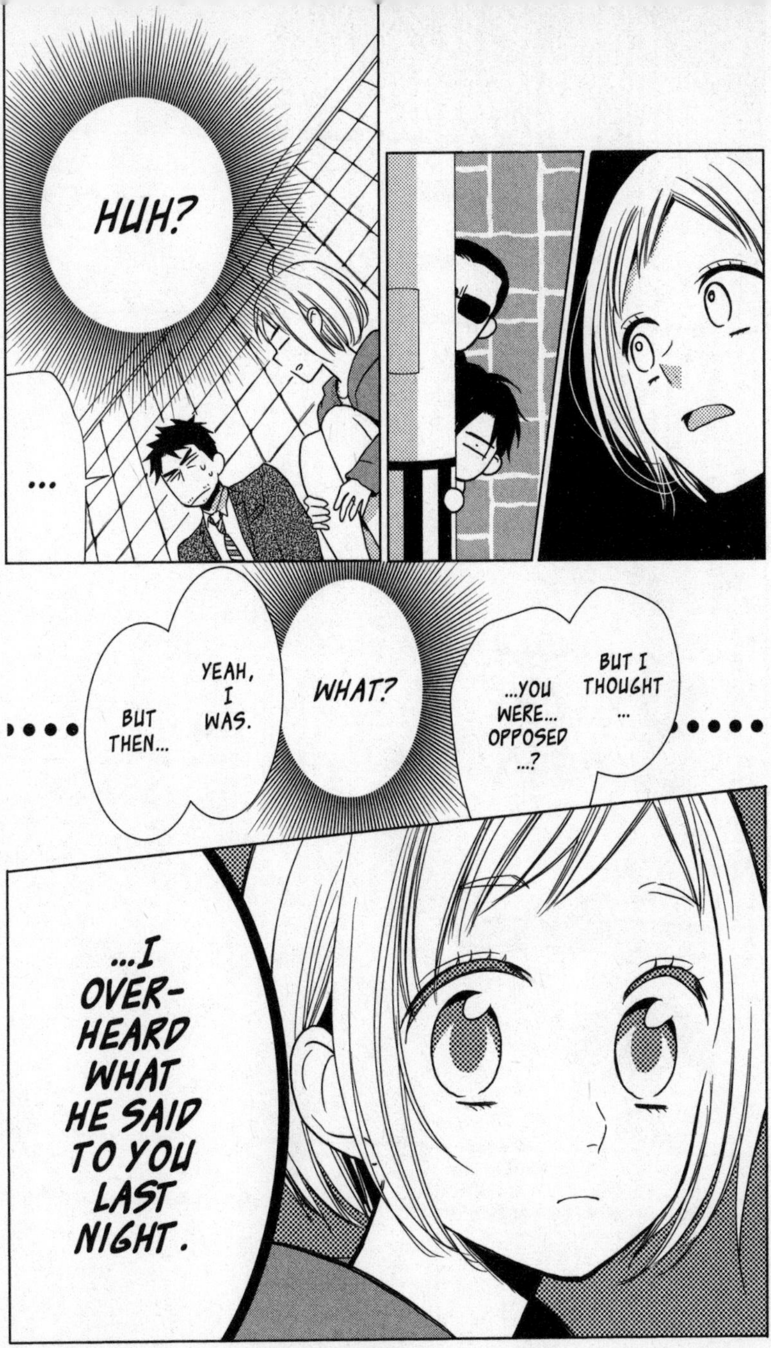
HUH?
...
BUT I THOUGHT... ...YOU WERE... OPPOSED...?
WHAT?
YEAH, I WAS. BUT THEN...
...I OVER-HEARD WHAT HE SAID TO YOU LAST NIGHT.

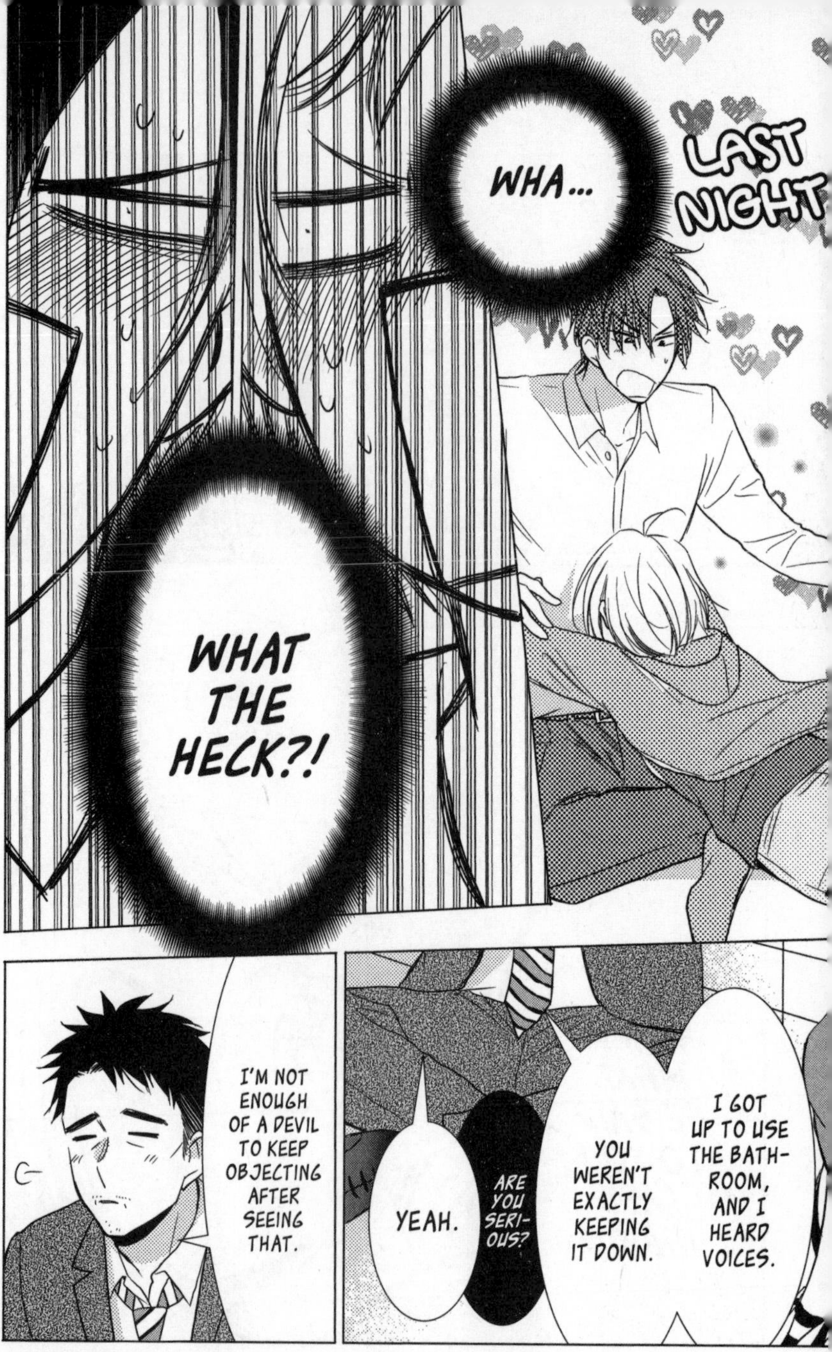
LAST NIGHT
WHA...
WHAT THE HECK?!
I GOT UP TO USE THE BATHROOM, AND I HEARD VOICES.
YOU WEREN'T EXACTLY KEEPING IT DOWN.
ARE YOU SERIOUS?
YEAH.
I'M NOT ENOUGH OF A DEVIL TO KEEP OBJECTING AFTER SEEING THAT.

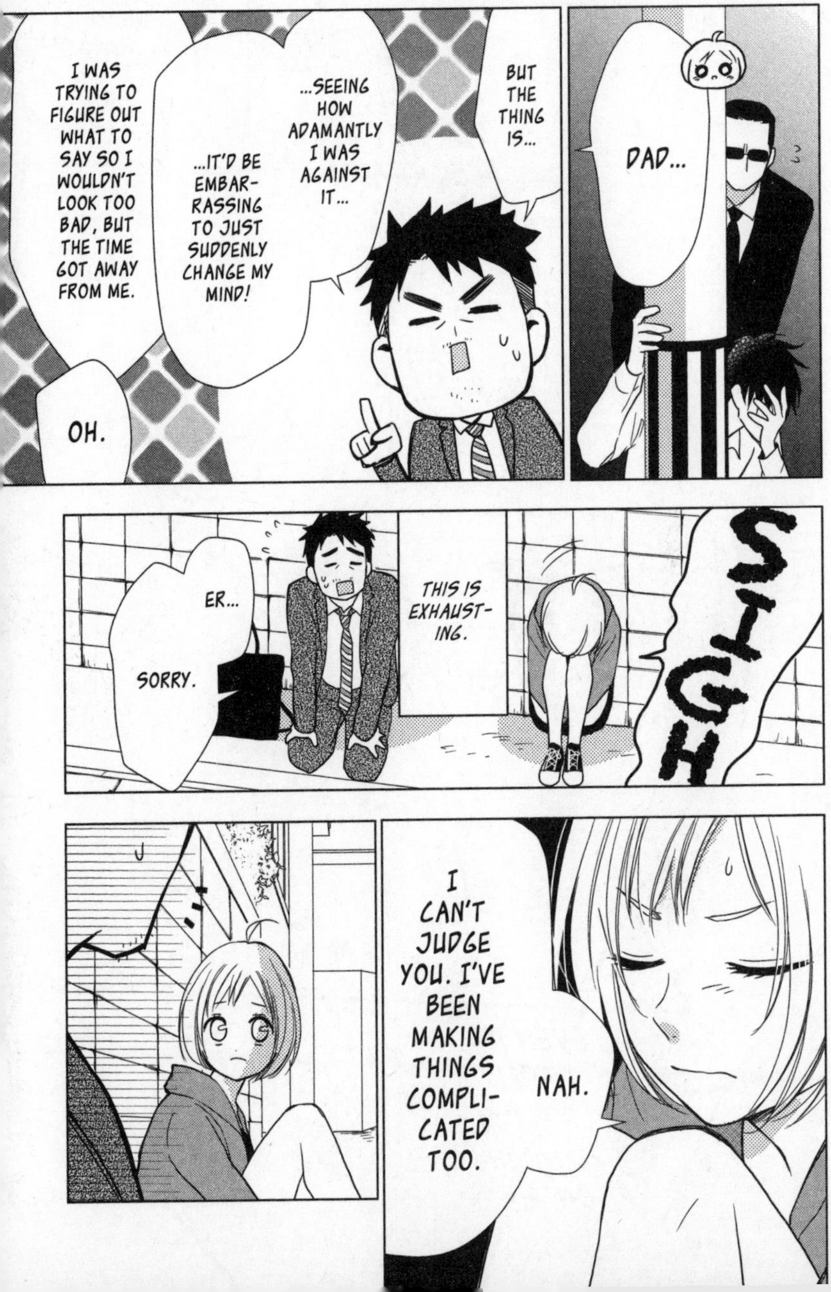
DAD...
BUT THE THING IS...
...SEEING HOW ADAMANTLY I WAS AGAINST IT...
...IT'D BE EMBARRASSING TO JUST SUDDENLY CHANGE MY MIND!
I WAS TRYING TO FIGURE OUT WHAT TO SAY SO I WOULDN'T LOOK TOO BAD, BUT THE TIME GOT AWAY FROM ME.
OH.
SIGH
THIS IS EXHAUSTING.
ER...
SORRY.
NAH.
I CAN'T JUDGE YOU. I'VE BEEN MAKING THINGS COMPLICATED TOO.

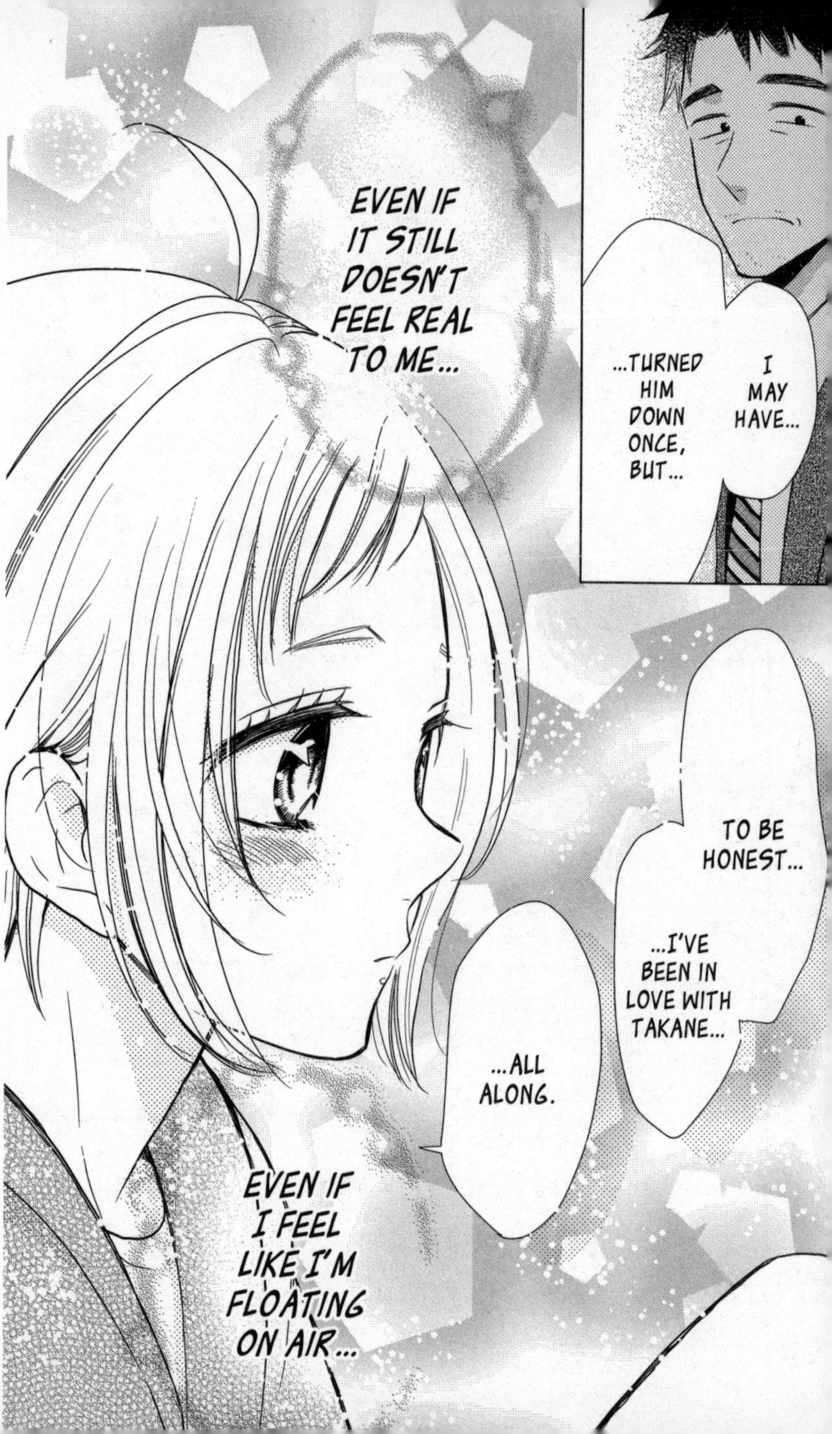
I MAY HAVE...
...TURNED HIM DOWN ONCE, BUT...
EVEN IF IT STILL DOESN'T FEEL REAL TO ME...
TO BE HONEST...
...I'VE BEEN IN LOVE WITH TAKANE...
...ALL ALONG.
EVEN IF I FEEL LIKE I'M FLOATING ON AIR...

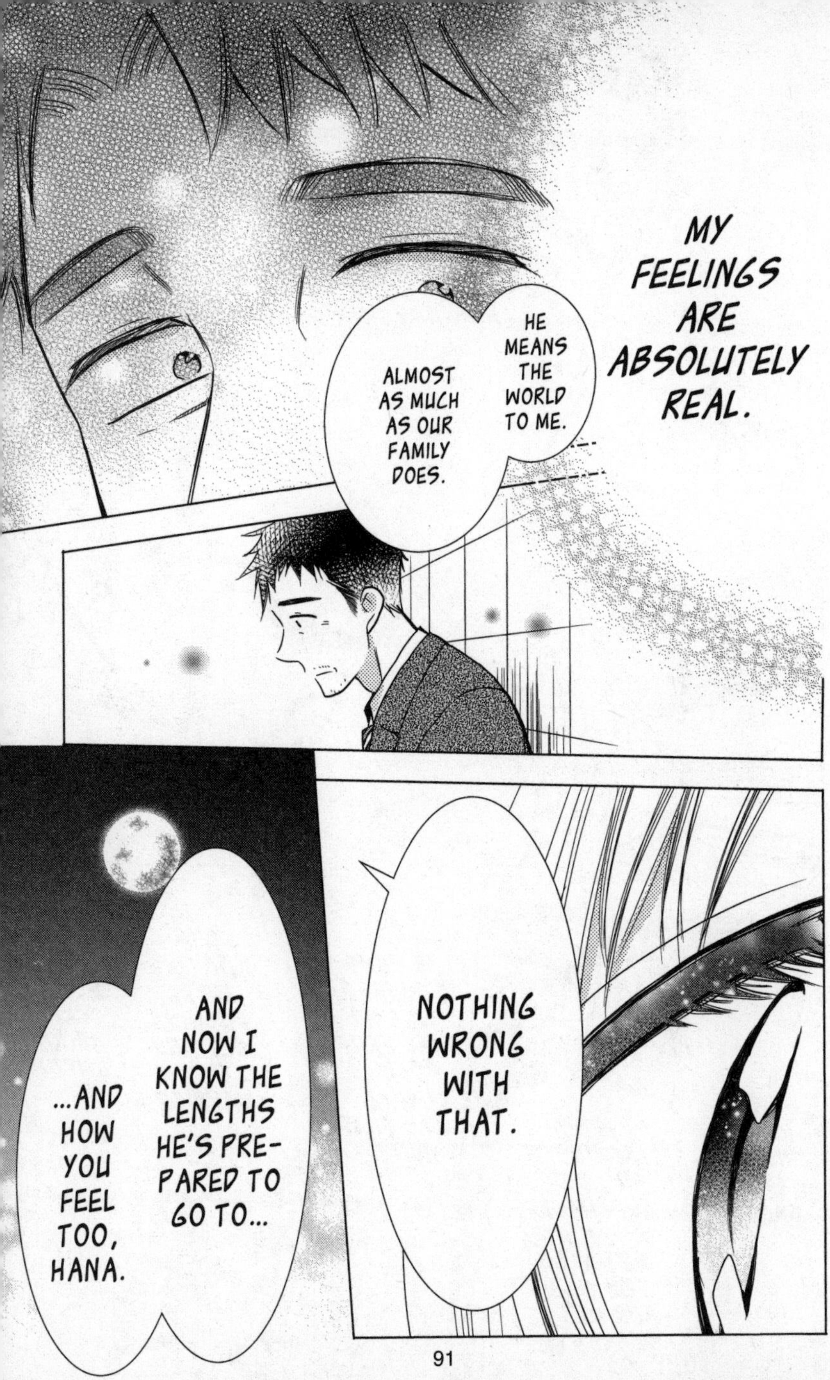
MY FEELINGS ARE ABSOLUTELY REAL.
HE MEANS THE WORLD TO ME.
ALMOST AS MUCH AS OUR FAMILY DOES.
NOTHING WRONG WITH THAT.
AND NOW I KNOW THE LENGTHS HE'S PRE-PARED TO GO TO...
...AND HOW YOU FEEL TOO, HANA.

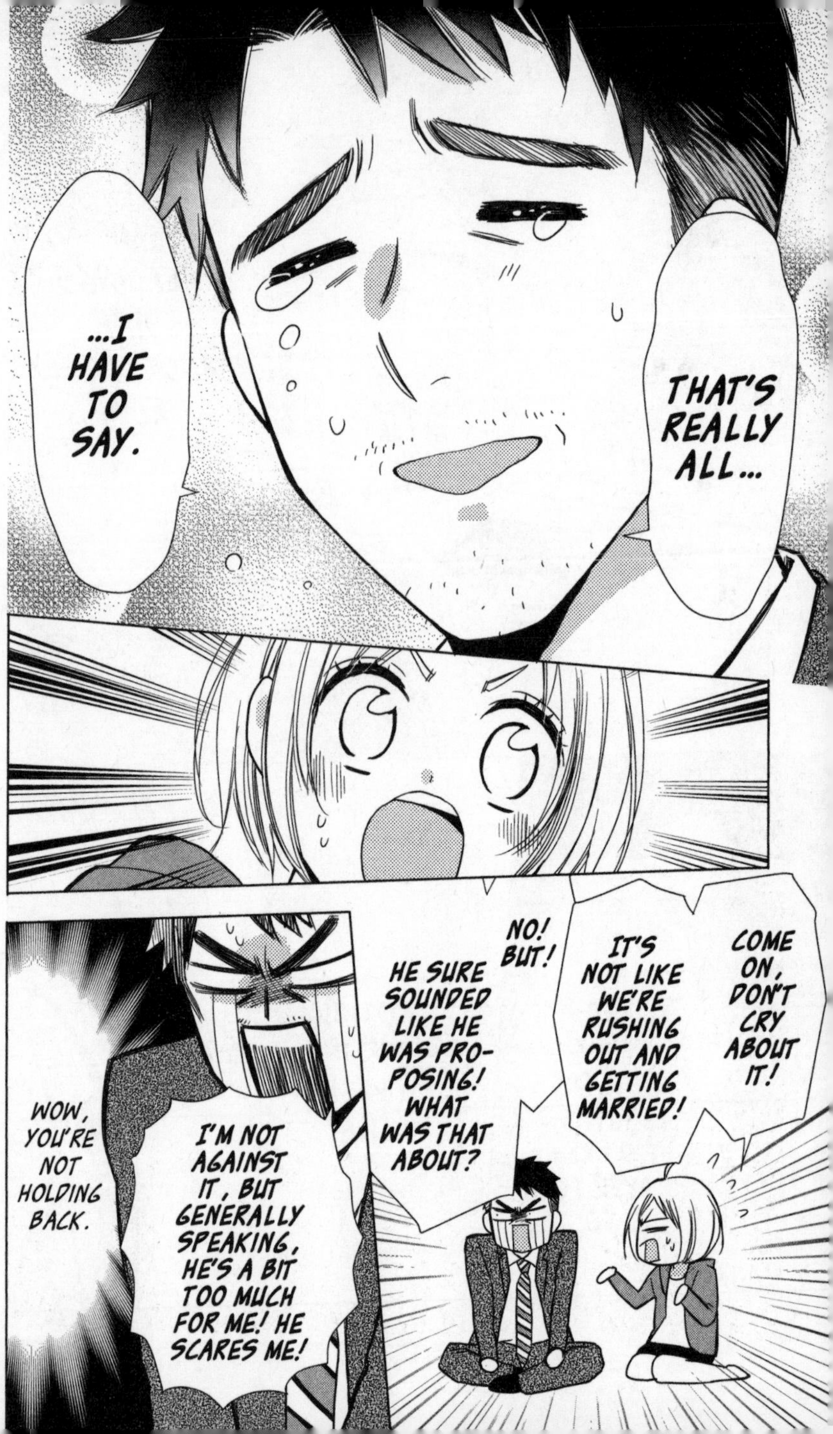
THAT'S REALLY ALL...
...I HAVE TO SAY.
COME ON, DON'T CRY ABOUT IT!
IT'S NOT LIKE WE'RE RUSHING OUT AND GETTING MARRIED!
NO! BUT!
HE SURE SOUNDED LIKE HE WAS PRO-POSING! WHAT WAS THAT ABOUT?
I'M NOT AGAINST IT, BUT GENERALLY SPEAKING, HE'S A BIT TOO MUCH FOR ME! HE SCARES ME!
WOW, YOU'RE NOT HOLDING BACK.

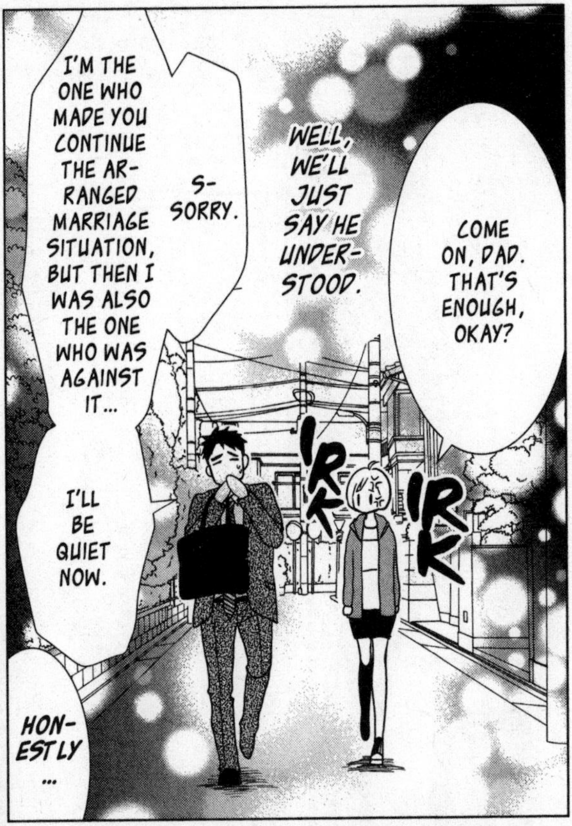
COME ON, DAD. THAT'S ENOUGH, OKAY?
WELL, WE'LL JUST SAY HE UNDERSTOOD.
I'M THE ONE WHO MADE YOU CONTINUE THE ARRANGED MARRIAGE SITUATION, BUT THEN I WAS ALSO THE ONE WHO WAS AGAINST IT...
S-SORRY.
IRK
IRK
I'LL BE QUIET NOW.
HONESTLY...

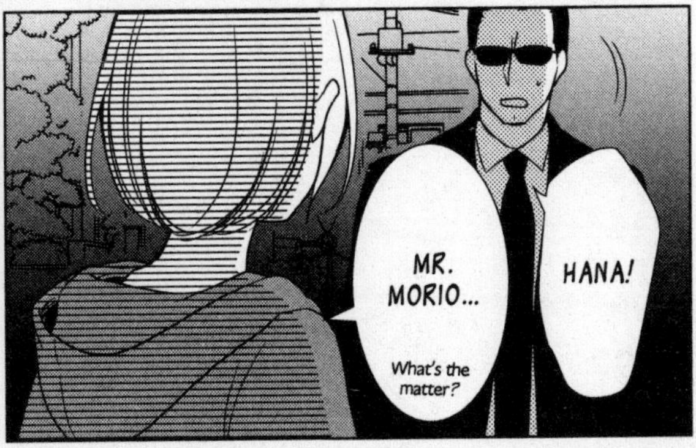
HANA!
MR. MORIO...
What's the matter?

• Yakumo Takaba •

A storm cloud that suddenly cast its shadow over a peaceful world... It's everybody's favorite character, Yakumo! In contrast to Takane, who's a fastidious perfectionist, Yakumo is shameless and doesn't care what others think of him. In a sense, he has the potential to accomplish things that Takane would shy away from. Since he hasn't been ousted from Takaba, he must have produced some results for the company.

But regardless, there's no doubt that he's a perverted psychopath.

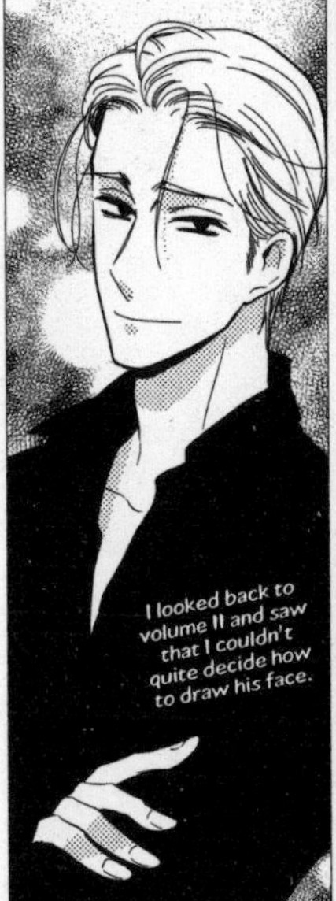
I looked back to volume 11 and saw that I couldn't quite decide how to draw his face.

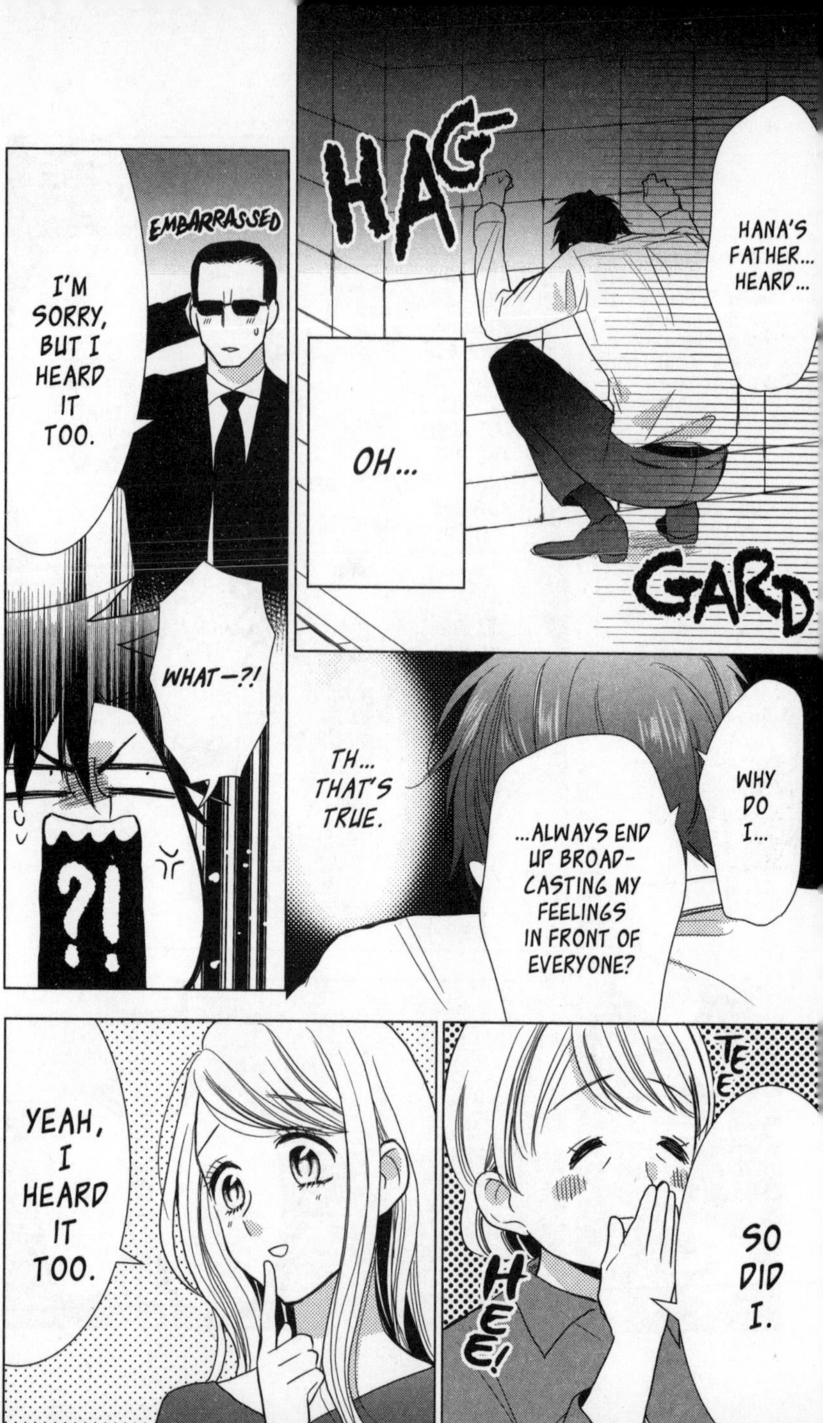
HAG-
GARD
HANA'S FATHER... HEARD...
OH...
WHY DO I...
...ALWAYS END UP BROAD-CASTING MY FEELINGS IN FRONT OF EVERYONE?
TH... THAT'S TRUE.
EMBARRASSED
I'M SORRY, BUT I HEARD IT TOO.
WHAT—?!
?!
TEE
HEE!
SO DID I.
YEAH, I HEARD IT TOO.

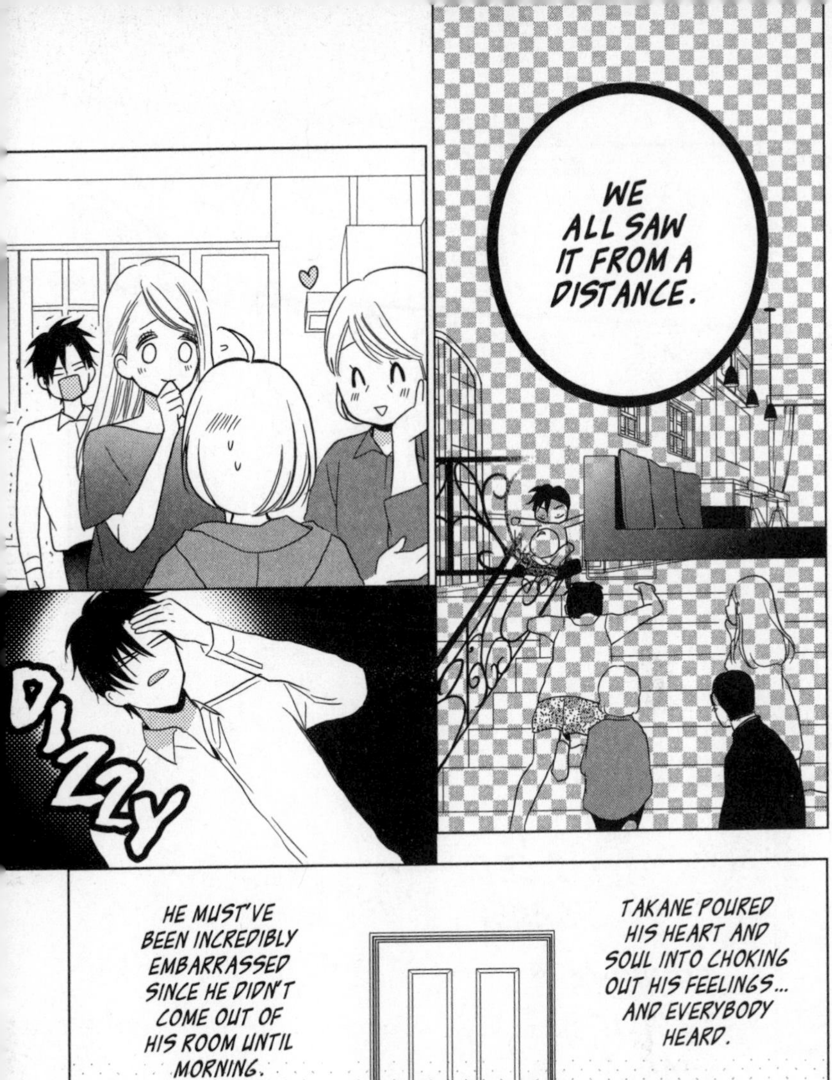
WE ALL SAW IT FROM A DISTANCE.
DIZZY
TAKANE POURED HIS HEART AND SOUL INTO CHOKING OUT HIS FEELINGS... AND EVERYBODY HEARD.
HE MUST'VE BEEN INCREDIBLY EMBARRASSED SINCE HE DIDN'T COME OUT OF HIS ROOM UNTIL MORNING.

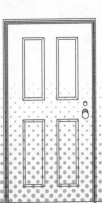

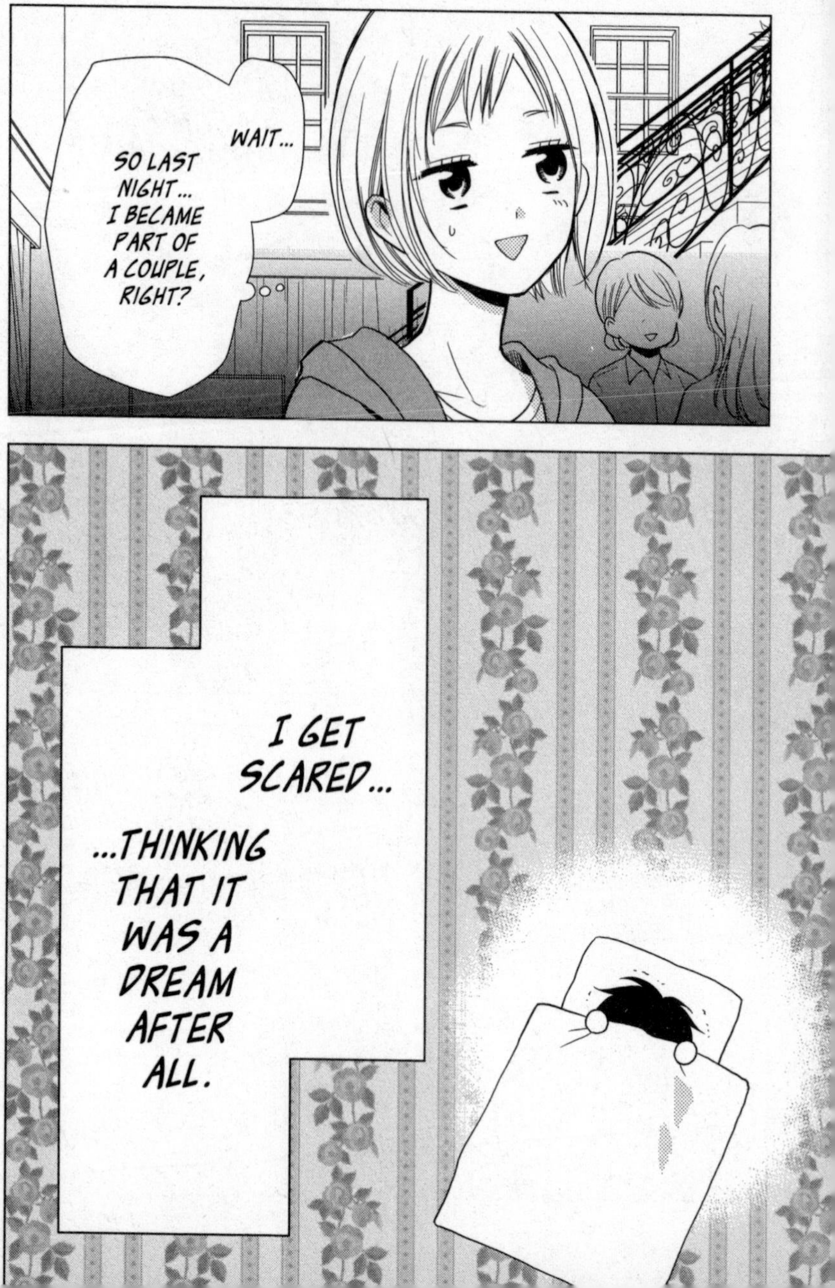
WAIT... SO LAST NIGHT... I BECAME PART OF A COUPLE, RIGHT?
I GET SCARED...
...THINKING THAT IT WAS A DREAM AFTER ALL.

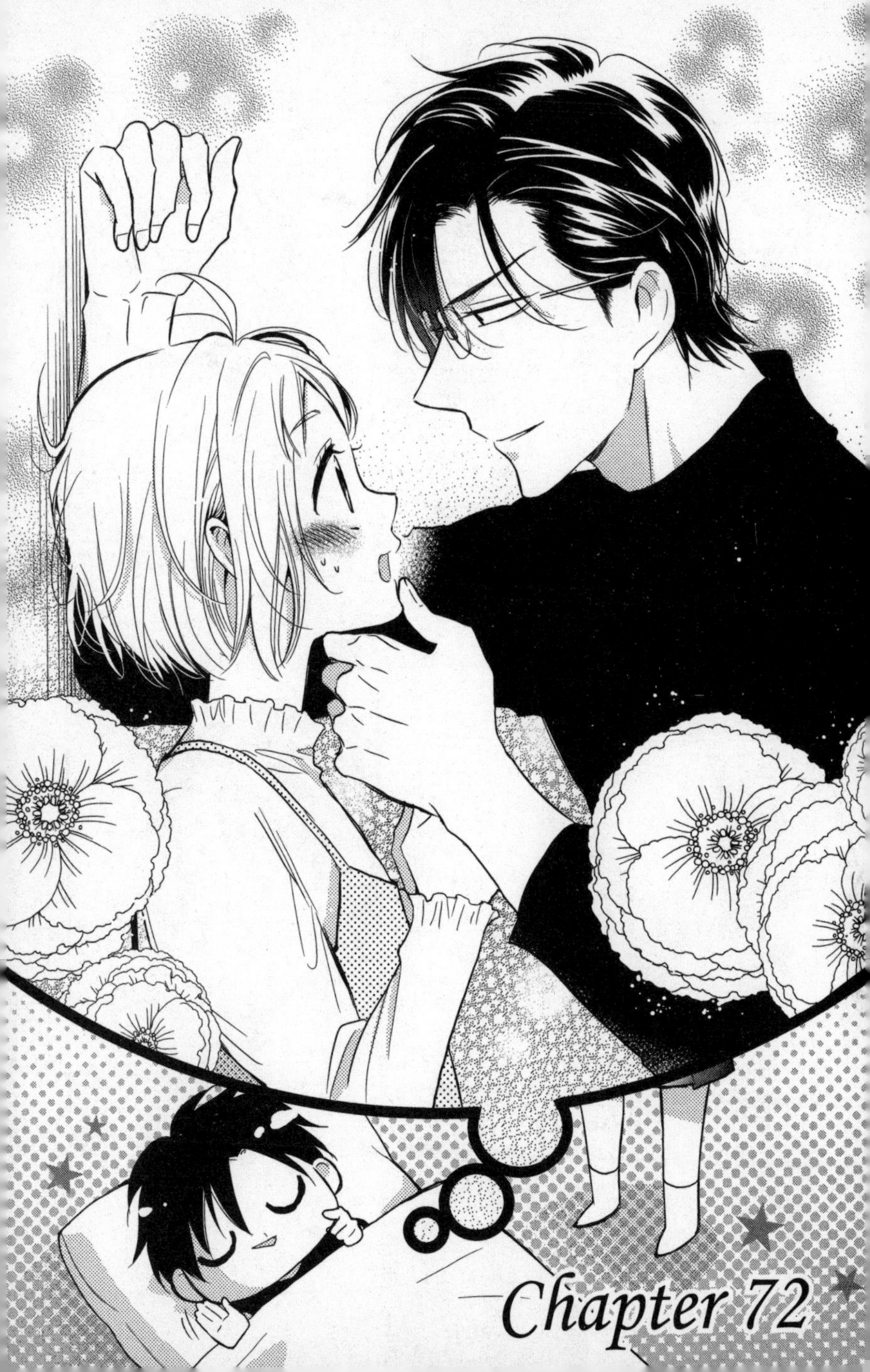
Chapter 72

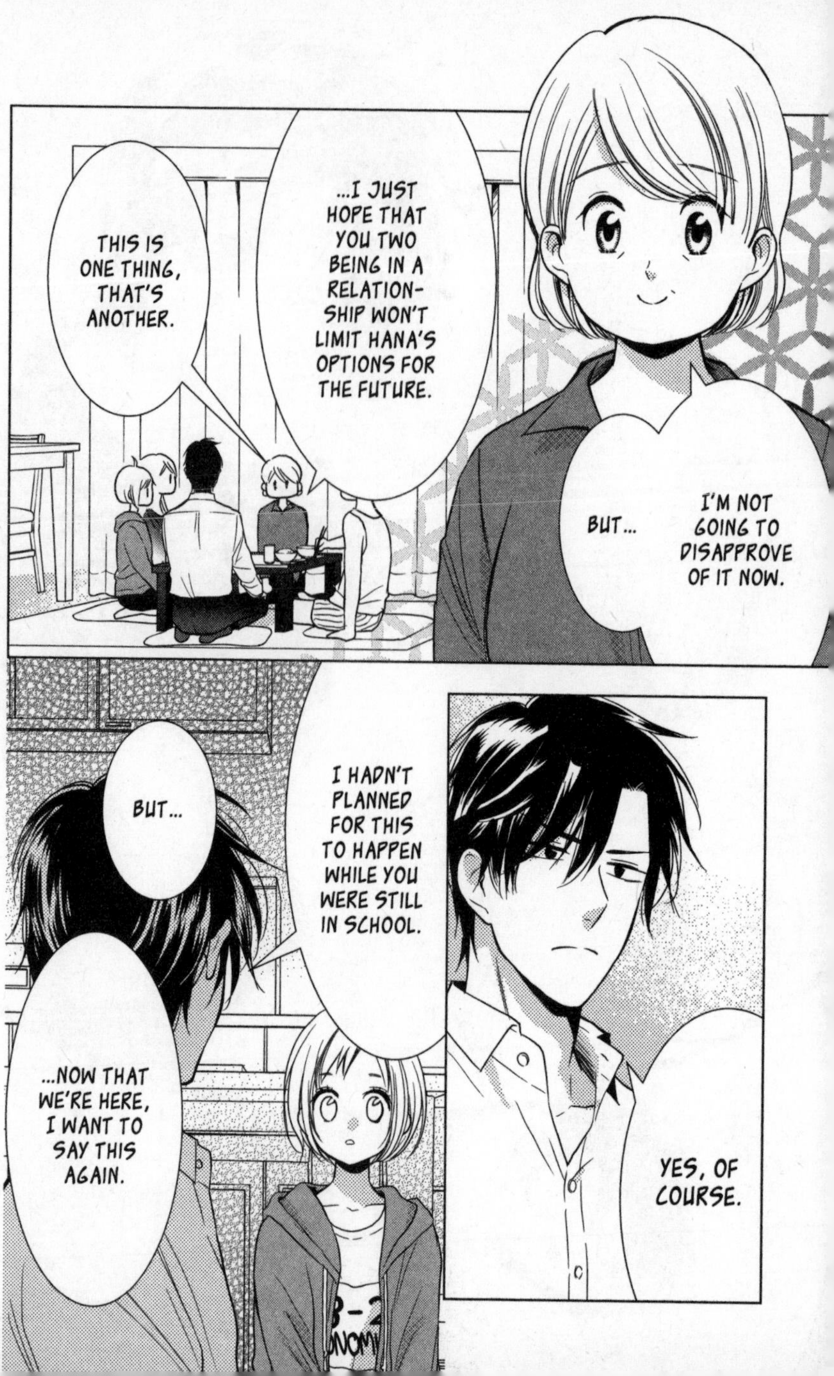
I'M NOT GOING TO DISAPPROVE OF IT NOW.
BUT...
...I JUST HOPE THAT YOU TWO BEING IN A RELATION-SHIP WON'T LIMIT HANA'S OPTIONS FOR THE FUTURE.
THIS IS ONE THING, THAT'S ANOTHER.
YES, OF COURSE.
I HADN'T PLANNED FOR THIS TO HAPPEN WHILE YOU WERE STILL IN SCHOOL.
BUT...
...NOW THAT WE'RE HERE, I WANT TO SAY THIS AGAIN.

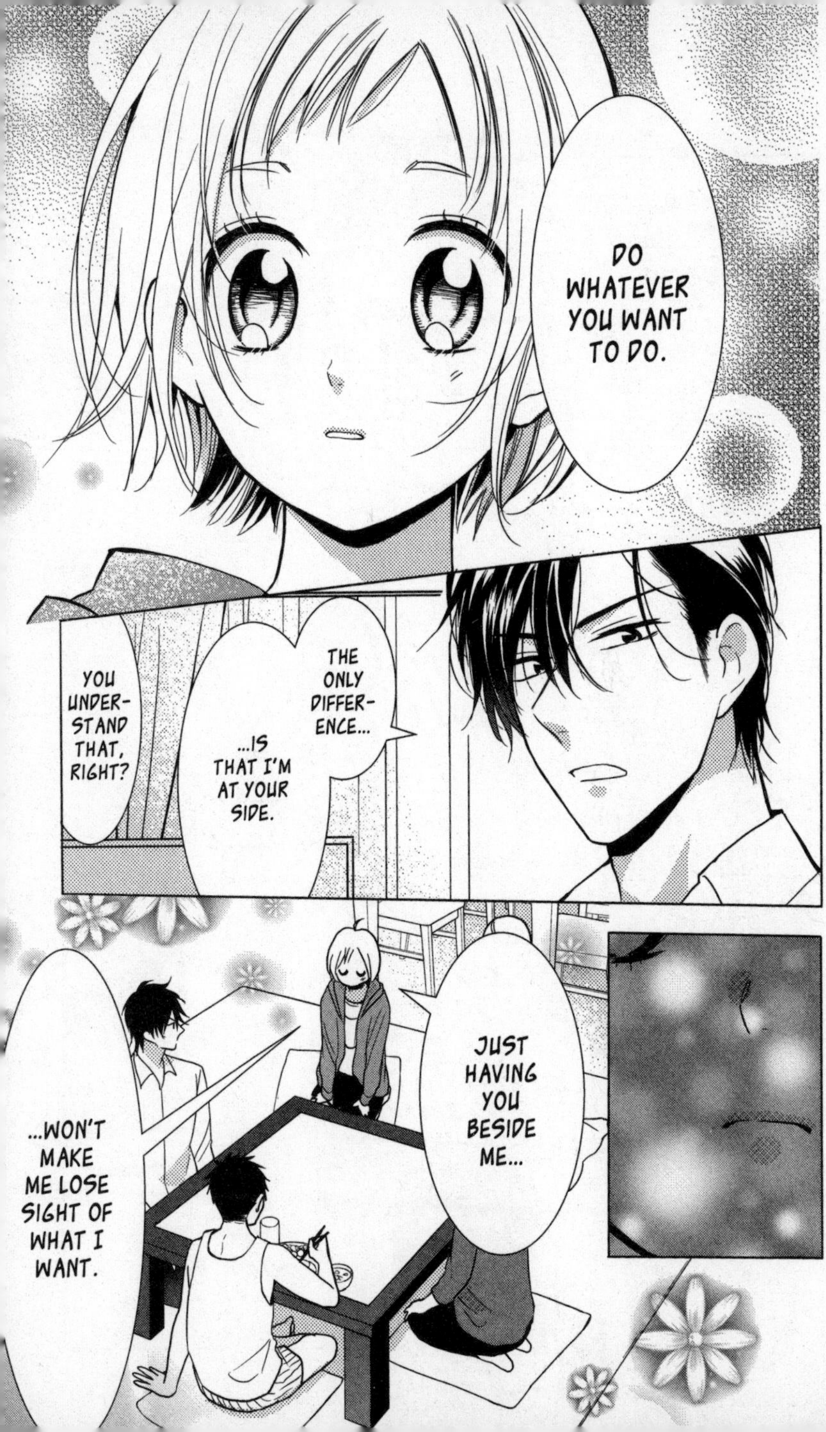
DO WHATEVER YOU WANT TO DO.
THE ONLY DIFFERENCE...
...IS THAT I'M AT YOUR SIDE.
YOU UNDERSTAND THAT, RIGHT?
JUST HAVING YOU BESIDE ME...
...WON'T MAKE ME LOSE SIGHT OF WHAT I WANT.

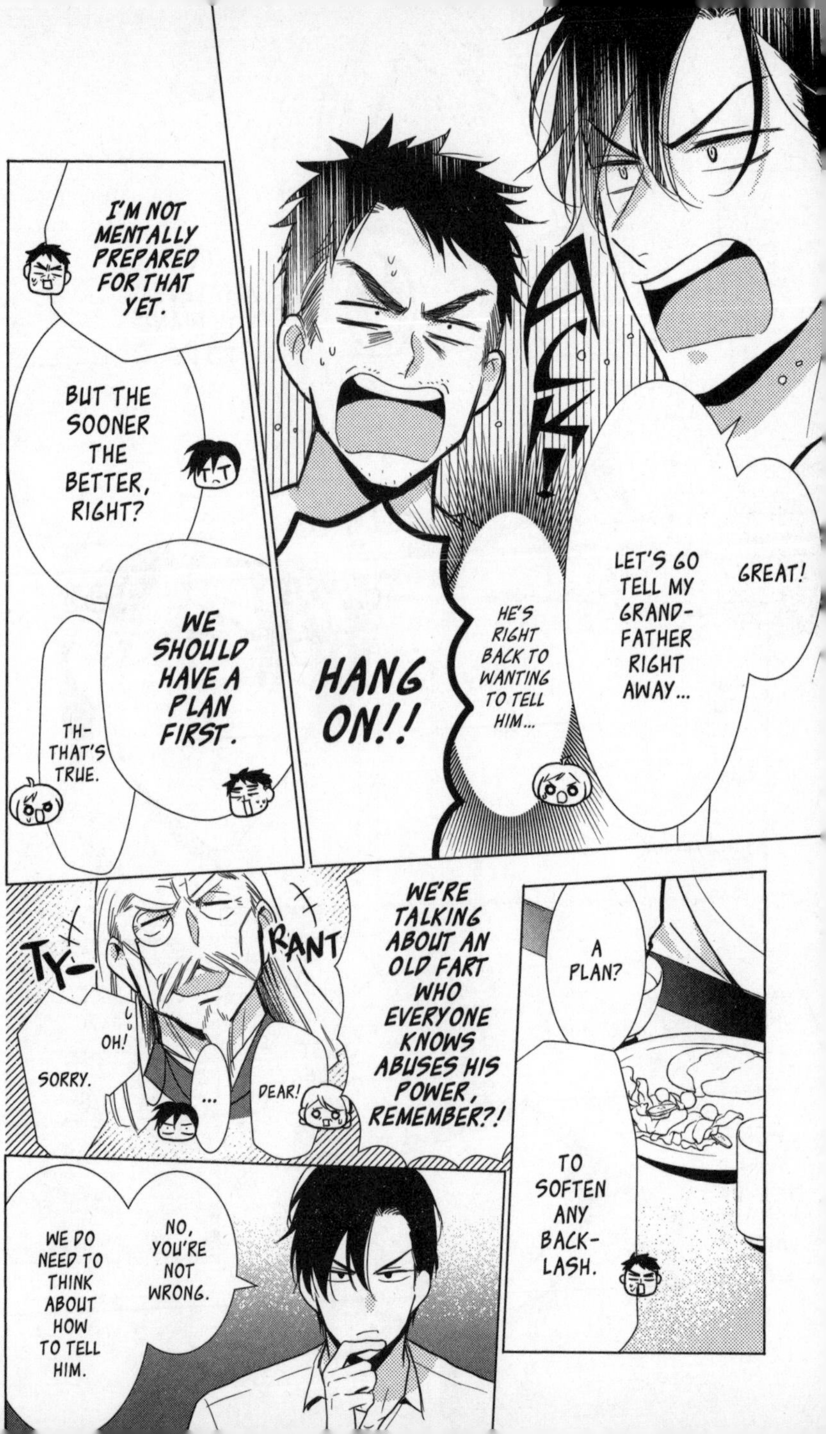
GREAT!
LET'S GO TELL MY GRAND-FATHER RIGHT AWAY...
ACK!
HE'S RIGHT BACK TO WANTING TO TELL HIM...
HANG ON!!
I'M NOT MENTALLY PREPARED FOR THAT YET.
BUT THE SOONER THE BETTER, RIGHT?
WE SHOULD HAVE A PLAN FIRST.
TH-THAT'S TRUE.
A PLAN?
TO SOFTEN ANY BACK-LASH.
WE'RE TALKING ABOUT AN OLD FART WHO EVERYONE KNOWS ABUSES HIS POWER, REMEMBER?!
RANT
TY-
DEAR!
...
OH!
SORRY.
NO, YOU'RE NOT WRONG.
WE DO NEED TO THINK ABOUT HOW TO TELL HIM.

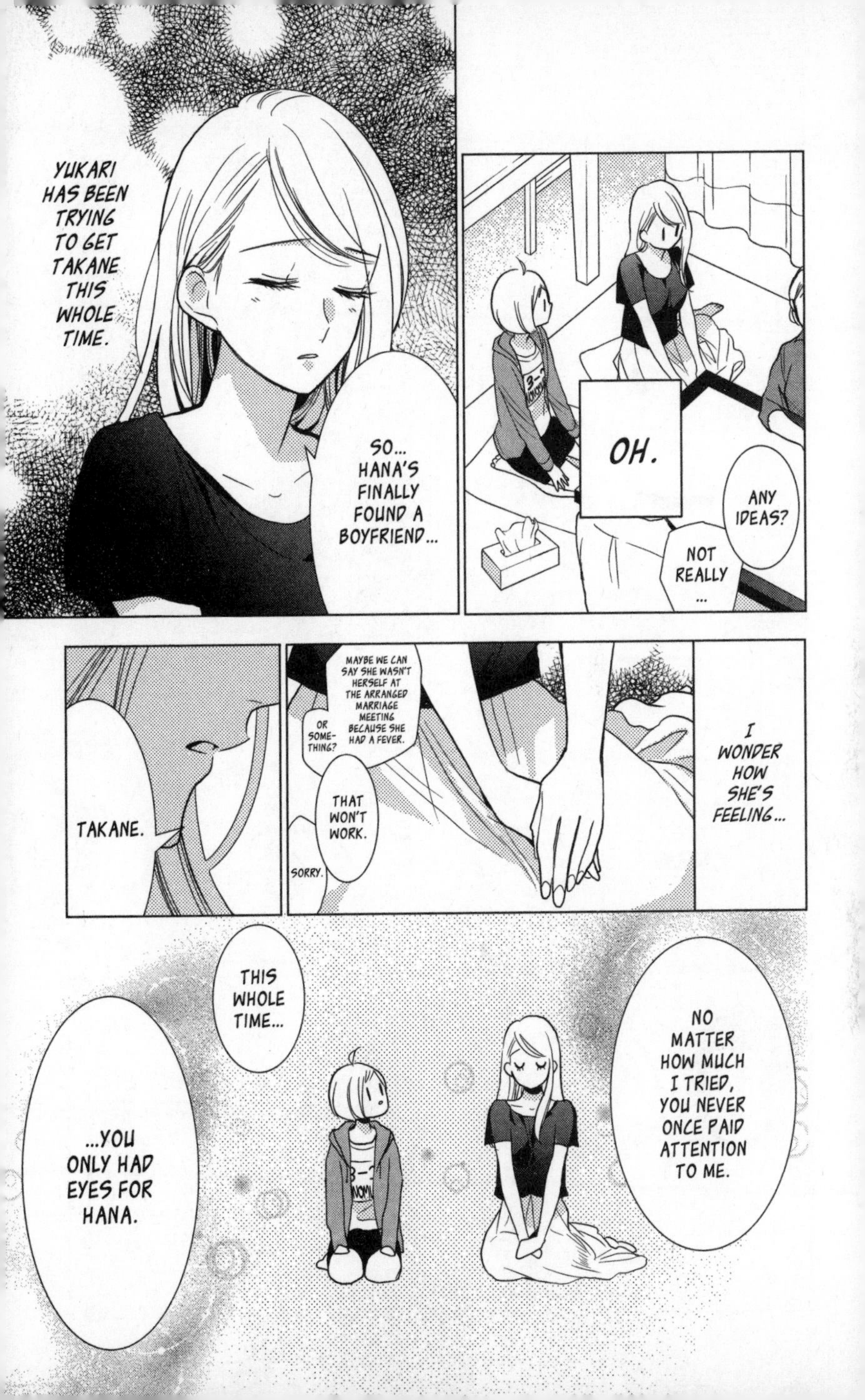
ANY IDEAS?
NOT REALLY...
OH.
SO... HANA'S FINALLY FOUND A BOYFRIEND...
YUKARI HAS BEEN TRYING TO GET TAKANE THIS WHOLE TIME.
I WONDER HOW SHE'S FEELING...
MAYBE WE CAN SAY SHE WASN'T HERSELF AT THE ARRANGED MARRIAGE MEETING BECAUSE SHE HAD A FEVER.
OR SOME-THING?
THAT WON'T WORK.
SORRY.
TAKANE.
NO MATTER HOW MUCH I TRIED, YOU NEVER ONCE PAID ATTENTION TO ME.
THIS WHOLE TIME...
...YOU ONLY HAD EYES FOR HANA.

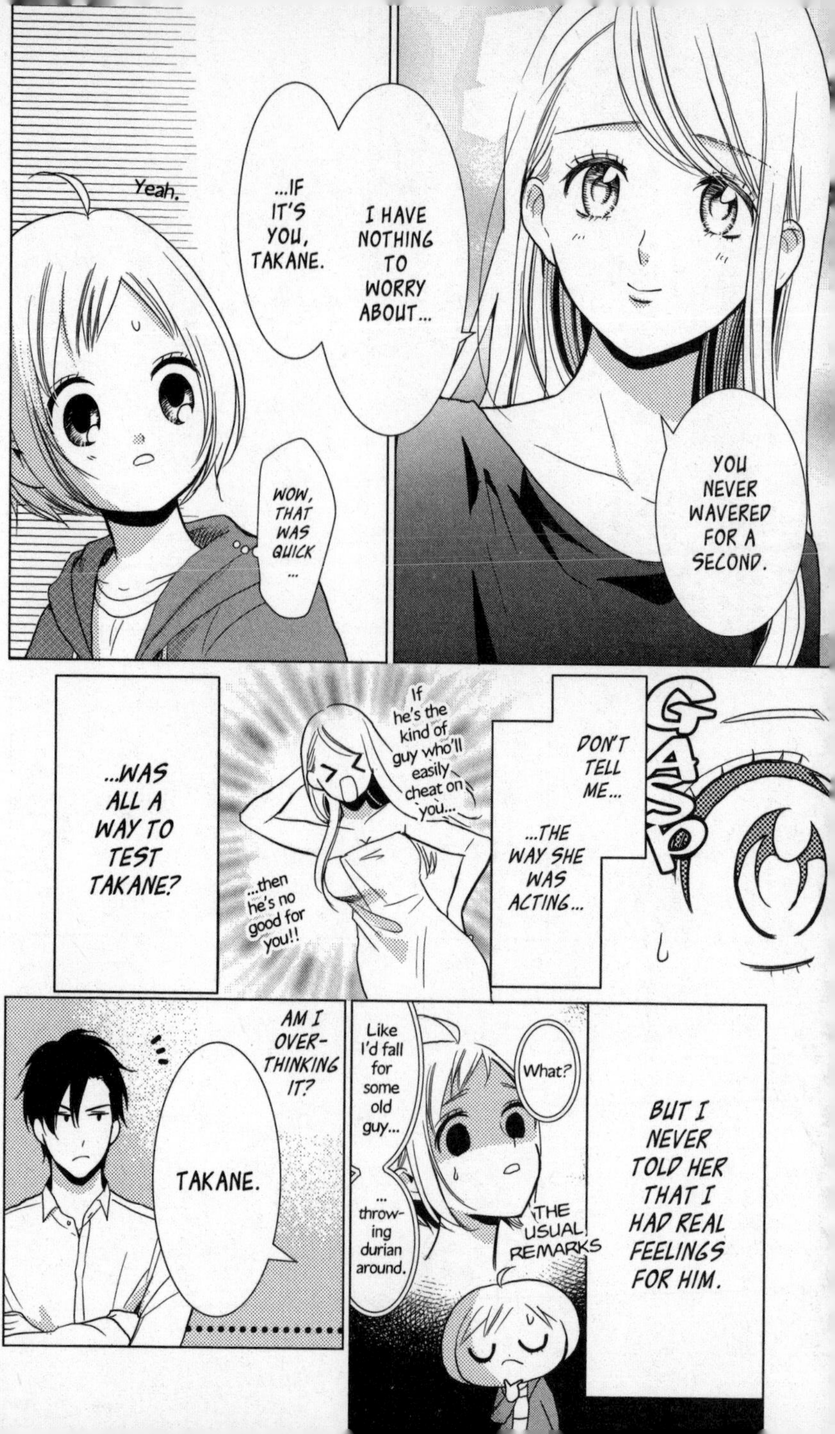
YOU NEVER WAVERED FOR A SECOND.
I HAVE NOTHING TO WORRY ABOUT...
...IF IT'S YOU, TAKANE.
Yeah.
WOW, THAT WAS QUICK...
GASP
DON'T TELL ME...
...THE WAY SHE WAS ACTING...
If he's the kind of guy who'll easily cheat on you...
...then he's no good for you!!
...WAS ALL A WAY TO TEST TAKANE?
BUT I NEVER TOLD HER THAT I HAD REAL FEELINGS FOR HIM.
What?
Like I'd fall for some old guy...
...throwing durian around.
THE USUAL REMARKS
AM I OVER-THINKING IT?
TAKANE.

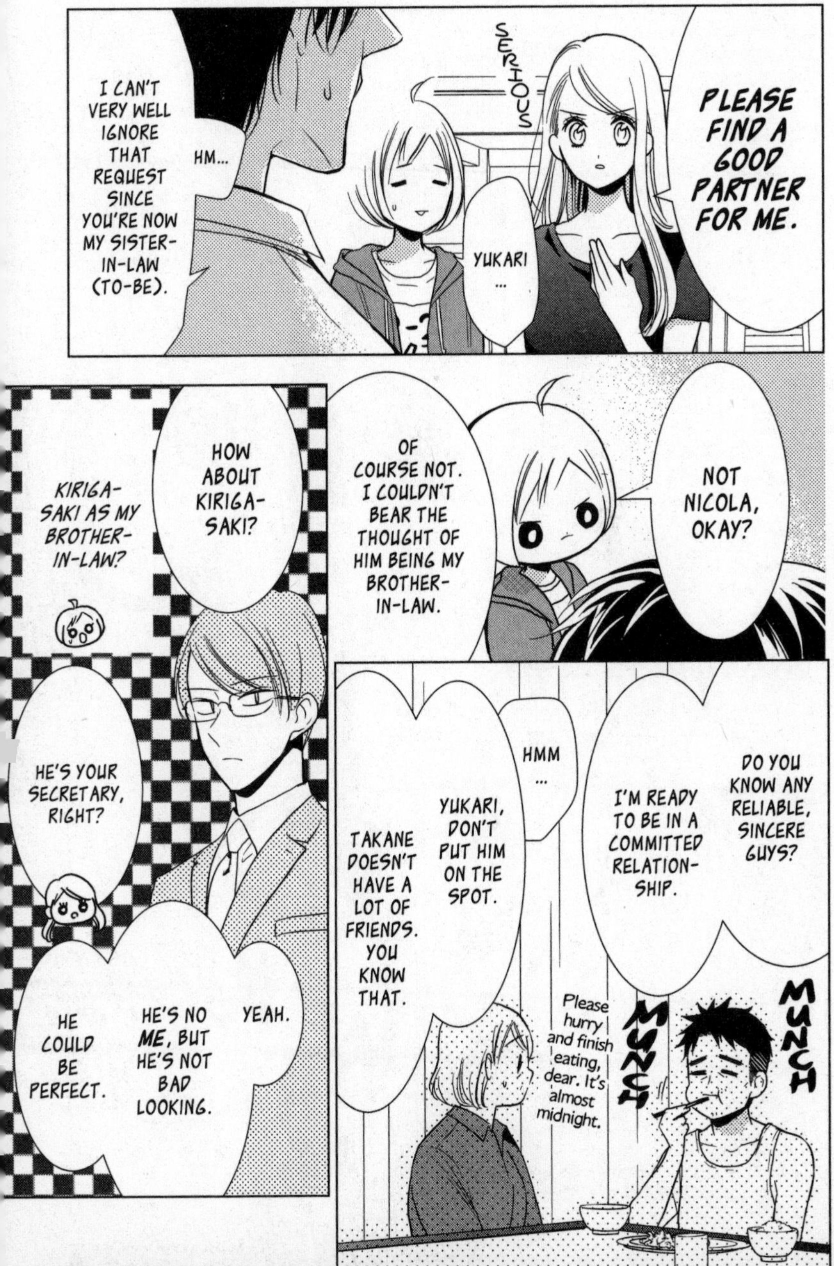
PLEASE FIND A GOOD PARTNER FOR ME.
SERIOUS
YUKARI ...
HM...
I CAN'T VERY WELL IGNORE THAT REQUEST SINCE YOU'RE NOW MY SISTER-IN-LAW (TO-BE).
NOT NICOLA, OKAY?
OF COURSE NOT. I COULDN'T BEAR THE THOUGHT OF HIM BEING MY BROTHER-IN-LAW.
DO YOU KNOW ANY RELIABLE, SINCERE GUYS?
I'M READY TO BE IN A COMMITTED RELATION-SHIP.
HMM ...
YUKARI, DON'T PUT HIM ON THE SPOT.
TAKANE DOESN'T HAVE A LOT OF FRIENDS. YOU KNOW THAT.
MUNCH
MUNCH
Please hurry and finish eating, dear. It's almost midnight.
HOW ABOUT KIRIGA-SAKI?
KIRIGA-SAKI AS MY BROTHER-IN-LAW?
HE'S YOUR SECRETARY, RIGHT?
YEAH.
HE'S NO ME, BUT HE'S NOT BAD LOOKING.
HE COULD BE PERFECT.

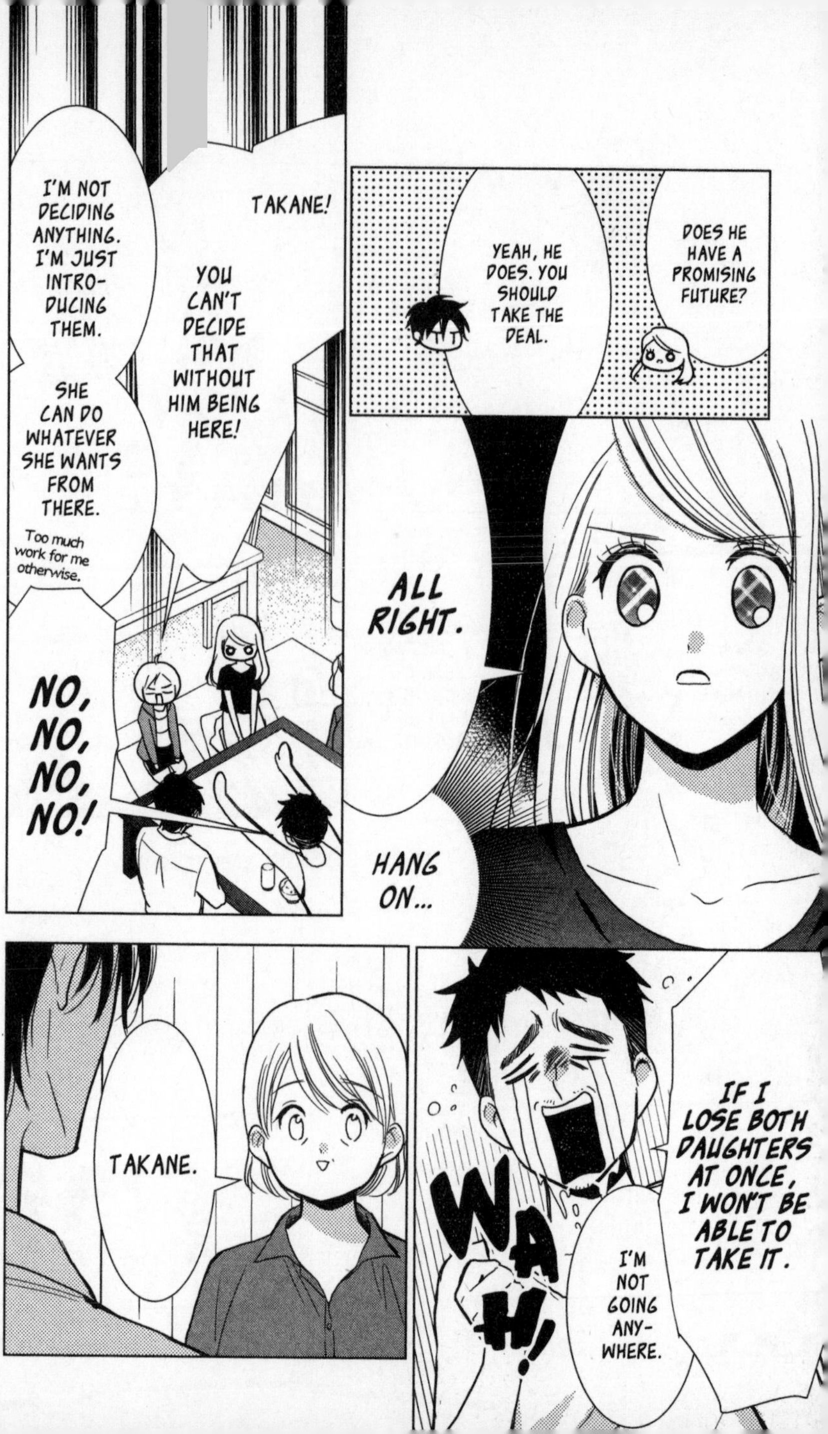
DOES HE HAVE A PROMISING FUTURE?
YEAH, HE DOES. YOU SHOULD TAKE THE DEAL.
ALL RIGHT.
HANG ON...
TAKANE!
YOU CAN'T DECIDE THAT WITHOUT HIM BEING HERE!
I'M NOT DECIDING ANYTHING. I'M JUST INTRO-DUCING THEM.
SHE CAN DO WHATEVER SHE WANTS FROM THERE.
Too much work for me otherwise.
NO, NO, NO, NO!
IF I LOSE BOTH DAUGHTERS AT ONCE, I WON'T BE ABLE TO TAKE IT.
WAH!
I'M NOT GOING ANYWHERE.
TAKANE.

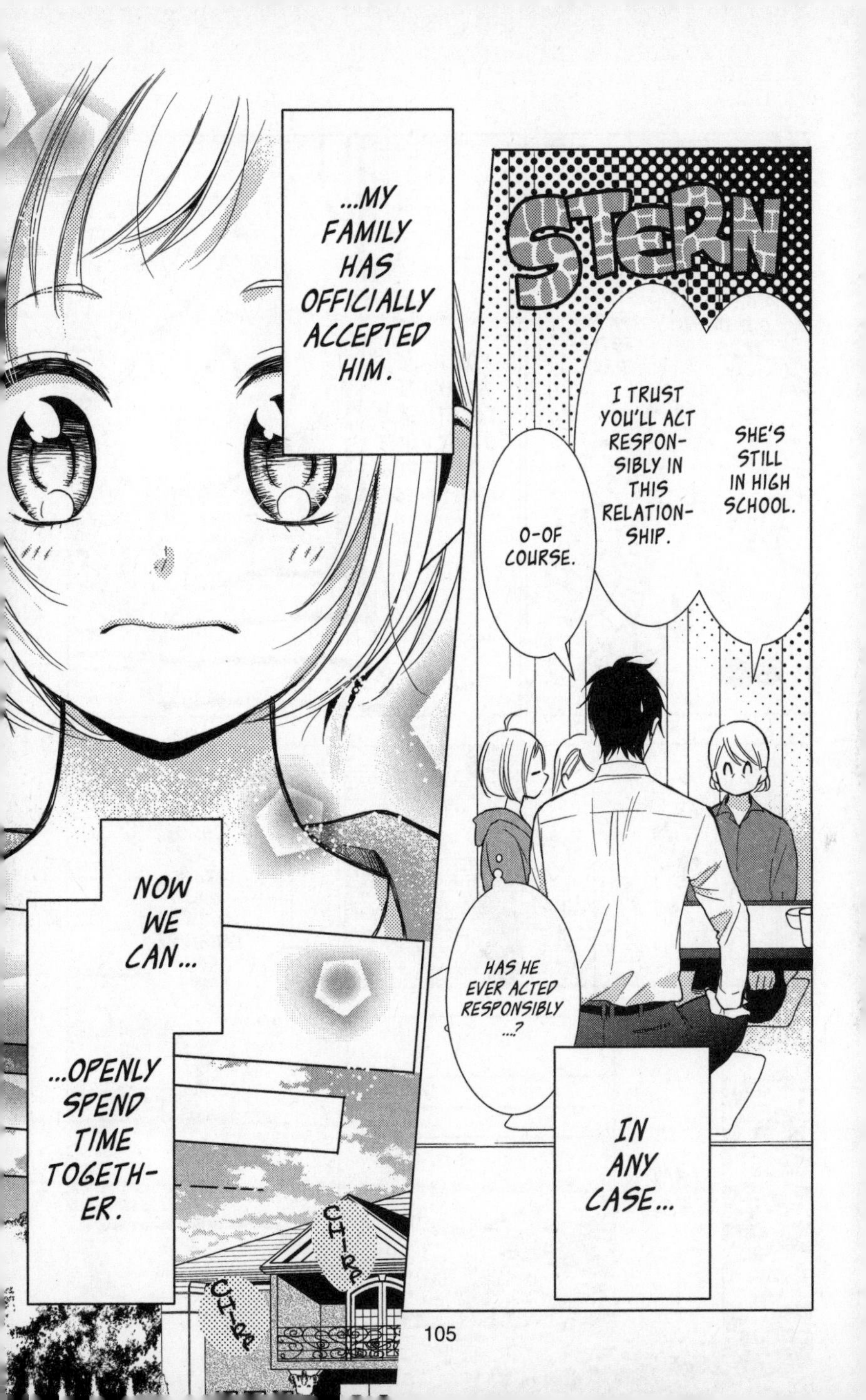
STERN
SHE'S STILL IN HIGH SCHOOL.
I TRUST YOU'LL ACT RESPON-SIBLY IN THIS RELATION-SHIP.
O-OF COURSE.
HAS HE EVER ACTED RESPONSIBLY ...?
IN ANY CASE...
...MY FAMILY HAS OFFICIALLY ACCEPTED HIM.
NOW WE CAN...
...OPENLY SPEND TIME TOGETH-ER.
CHIRP
CHIRP

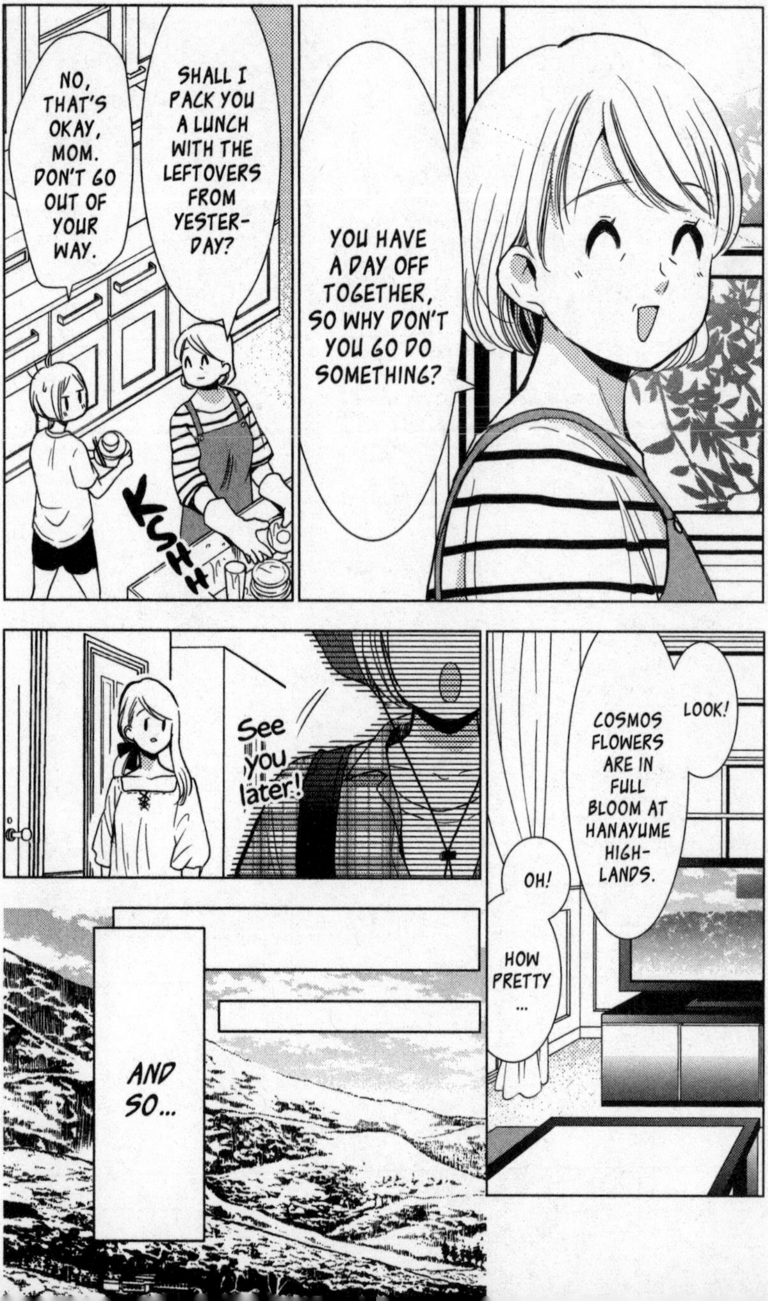
YOU HAVE A DAY OFF TOGETHER, SO WHY DON'T YOU GO DO SOMETHING?
SHALL I PACK YOU A LUNCH WITH THE LEFTOVERS FROM YESTER-DAY?
NO, THAT'S OKAY, MOM. DON'T GO OUT OF YOUR WAY.
KSHH
LOOK!
COSMOS FLOWERS ARE IN FULL BLOOM AT HANAYUME HIGH-LANDS.
OH!
HOW PRETTY ...
See you later!
AND SO...

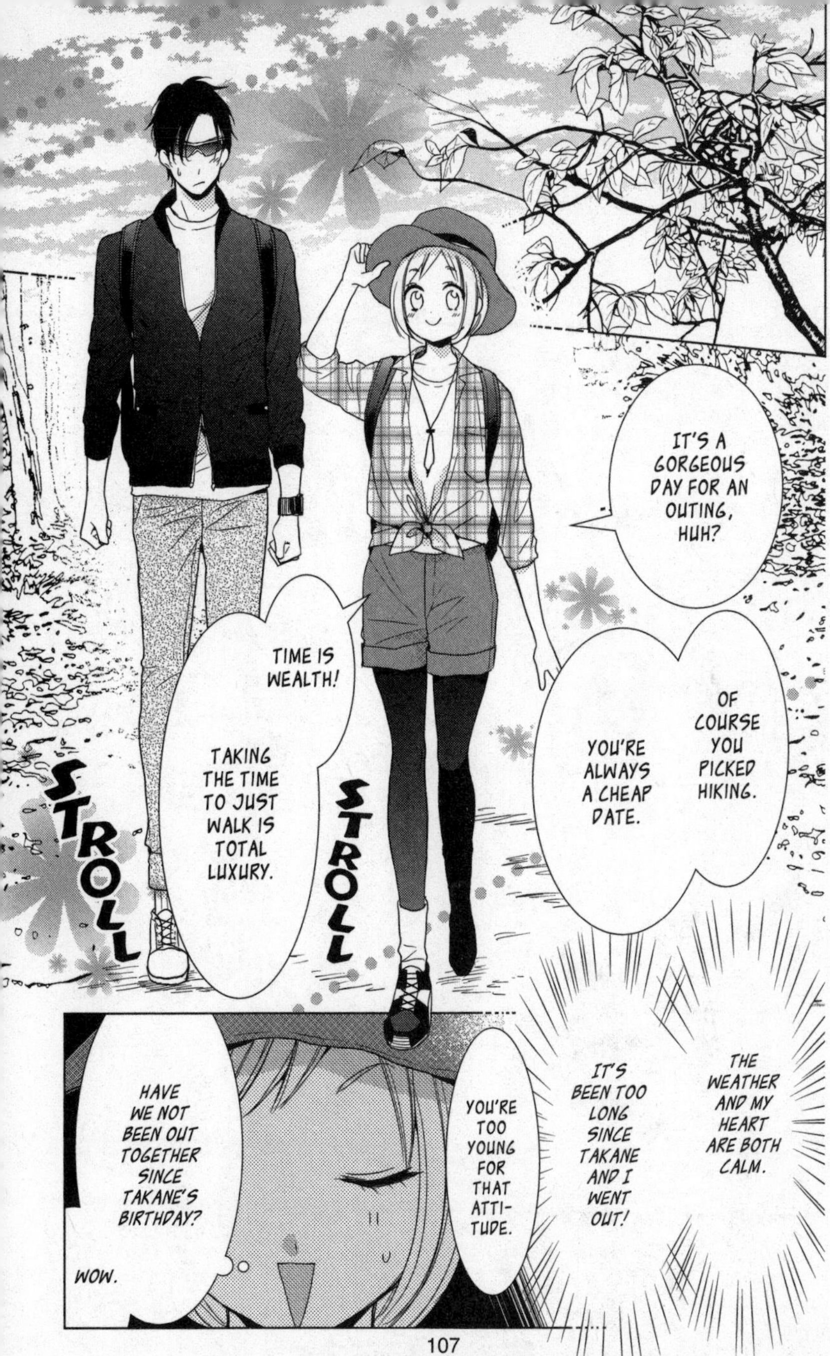
IT'S A GORGEOUS DAY FOR AN OUTING, HUH?
OF COURSE YOU PICKED HIKING.
YOU'RE ALWAYS A CHEAP DATE.
TIME IS WEALTH!
TAKING THE TIME TO JUST WALK IS TOTAL LUXURY.
STROLL
STROLL
THE WEATHER AND MY HEART ARE BOTH CALM.
IT'S BEEN TOO LONG SINCE TAKANE AND I WENT OUT!
YOU'RE TOO YOUNG FOR THAT ATTI-TUDE.
HAVE WE NOT BEEN OUT TOGETHER SINCE TAKANE'S BIRTHDAY?
WOW.

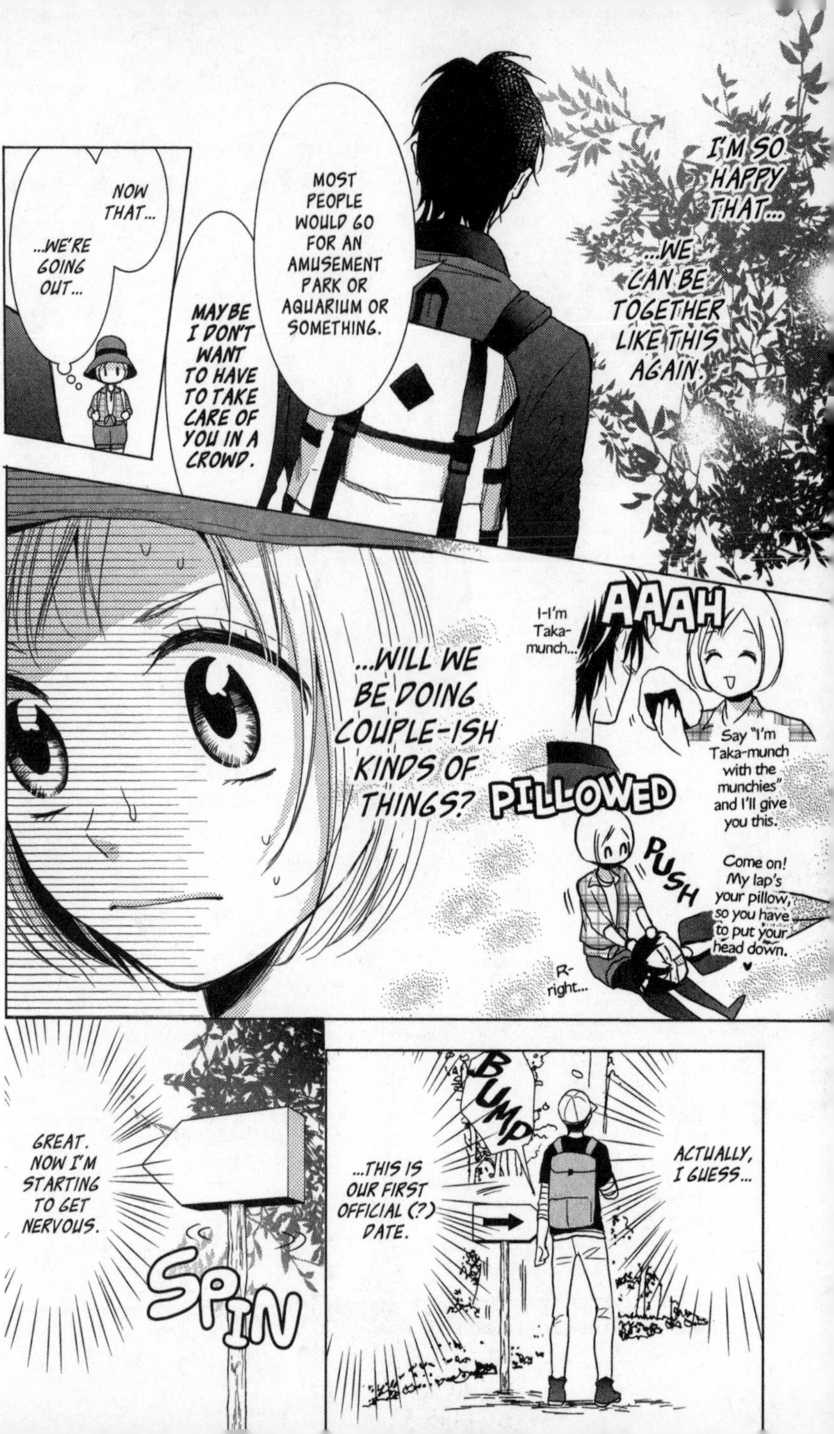
I'M SO HAPPY THAT...
...WE CAN BE TOGETHER LIKE THIS AGAIN.
MOST PEOPLE WOULD GO FOR AN AMUSEMENT PARK OR AQUARIUM OR SOMETHING.
MAYBE I DON'T WANT TO HAVE TO TAKE CARE OF YOU IN A CROWD.
NOW THAT...
...WE'RE GOING OUT...
Say "I'm Taka-munch with the munchies" and I'll give you this.
AAAH
I-I'm Taka-munch...
PILLOWED
PUSH
Come on! My lap's your pillow, so you have to put your head down.
R-right...
...WILL WE BE DOING COUPLE-ISH KINDS OF THINGS?
ACTUALLY, I GUESS...
BUMP
...THIS IS OUR FIRST OFFICIAL (?) DATE.
GREAT. NOW I'M STARTING TO GET NERVOUS.
SPIN

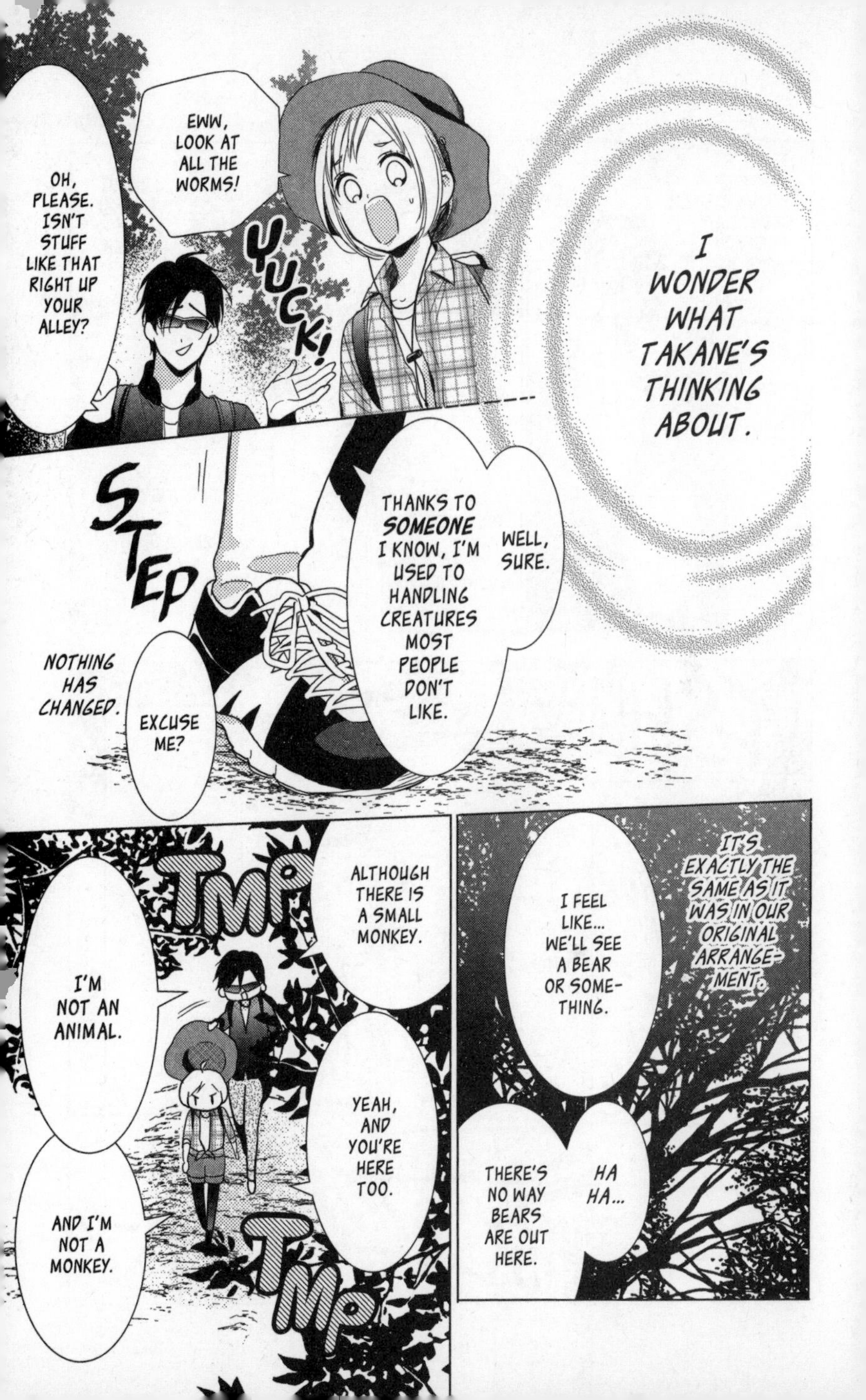
I WONDER WHAT TAKANE'S THINKING ABOUT.
EWW, LOOK AT ALL THE WORMS!
YUCK!
OH, PLEASE. ISN'T STUFF LIKE THAT RIGHT UP YOUR ALLEY?
WELL, SURE.
THANKS TO SOMEONE I KNOW, I'M USED TO HANDLING CREATURES MOST PEOPLE DON'T LIKE.
STEP
EXCUSE ME?
NOTHING HAS CHANGED.
IT'S EXACTLY THE SAME AS IT WAS IN OUR ORIGINAL ARRANGE-MENT.
I FEEL LIKE... WE'LL SEE A BEAR OR SOME-THING.
HA HA...
THERE'S NO WAY BEARS ARE OUT HERE.
TMP
ALTHOUGH THERE IS A SMALL MONKEY.
I'M NOT AN ANIMAL.
YEAH, AND YOU'RE HERE TOO.
AND I'M NOT A MONKEY.
TMP

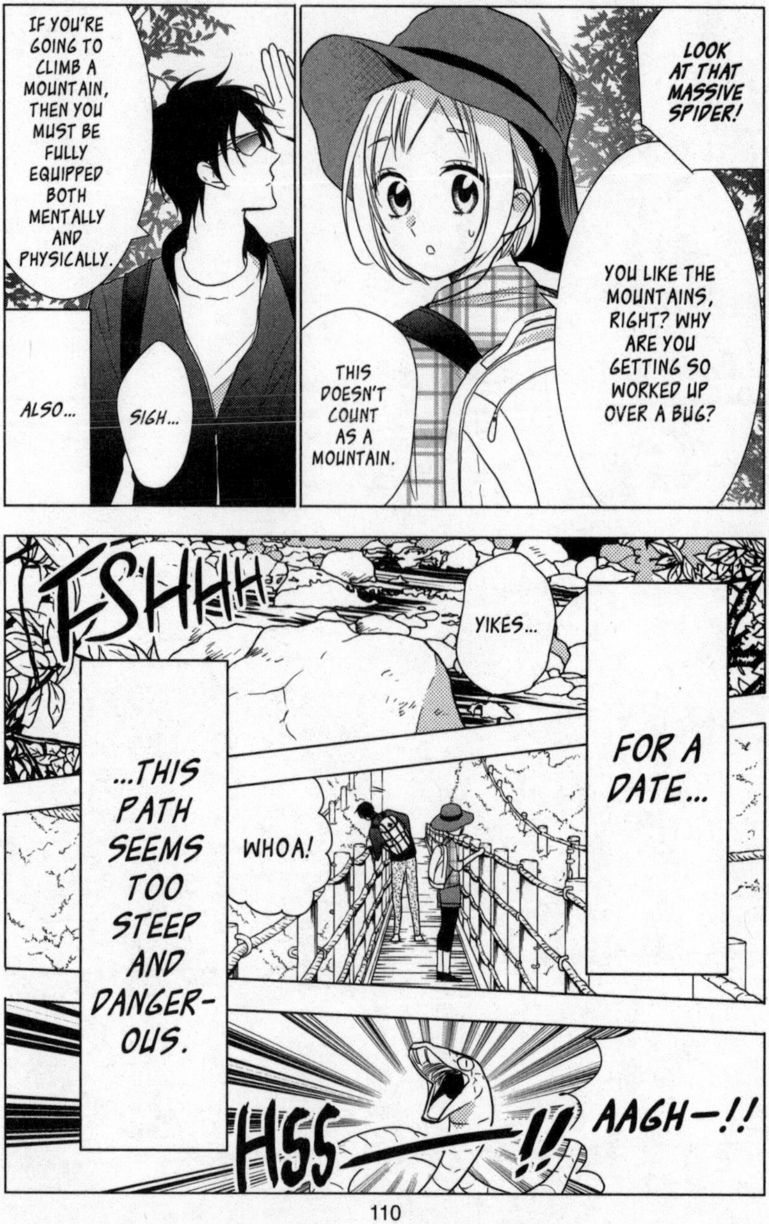
LOOK AT THAT MASSIVE SPIDER!
YOU LIKE THE MOUNTAINS, RIGHT? WHY ARE YOU GETTING SO WORKED UP OVER A BUG?
THIS DOESN'T COUNT AS A MOUNTAIN.
IF YOU'RE GOING TO CLIMB A MOUNTAIN, THEN YOU MUST BE FULLY EQUIPPED BOTH MENTALLY AND PHYSICALLY.
SIGH...
ALSO...
YIKES...
FSHHH
FOR A DATE...
...THIS PATH SEEMS TOO STEEP AND DANGER-OUS.
WHOA!
AAGH—!!
HSS——!!

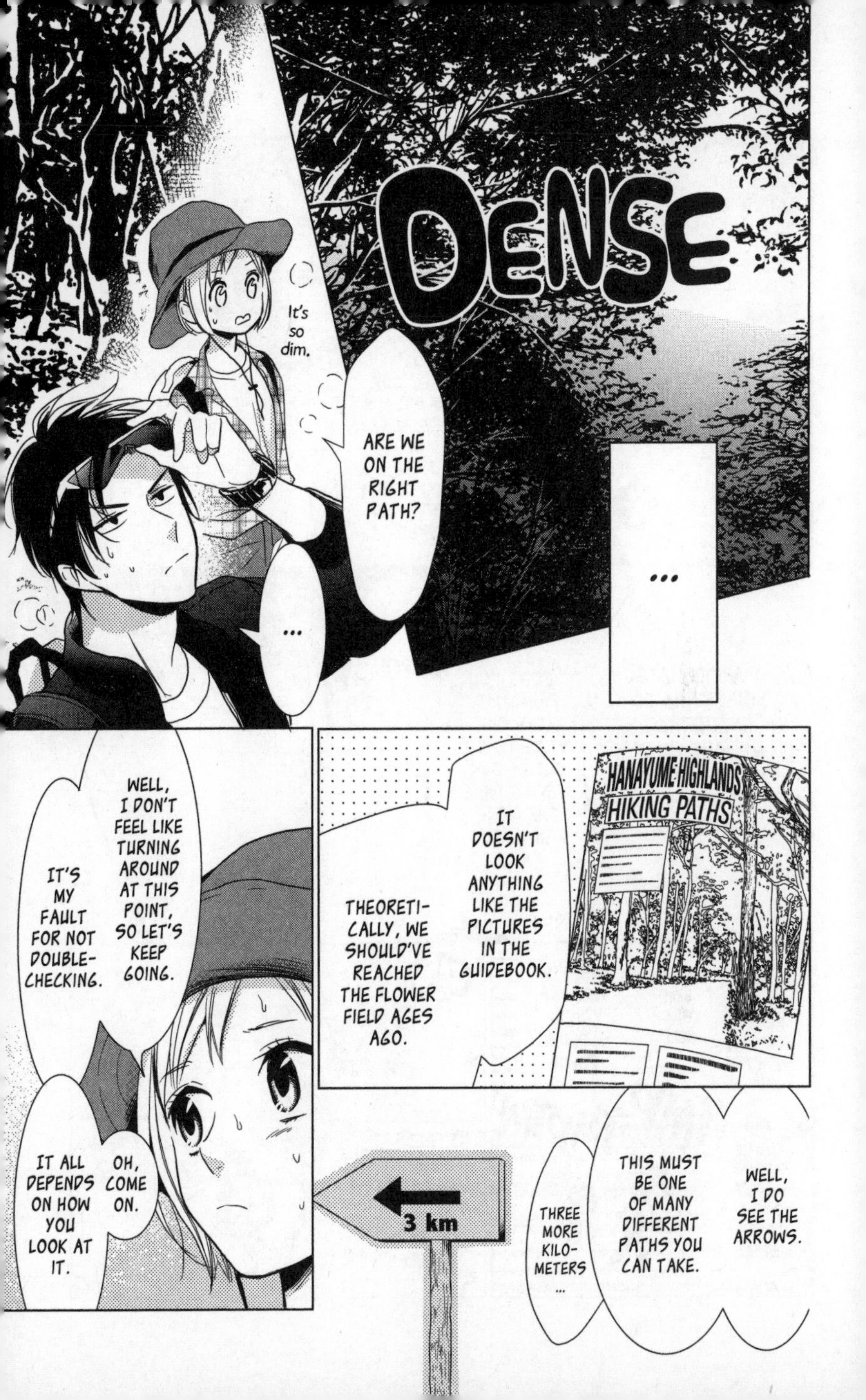
DENSE
It's so dim.
ARE WE ON THE RIGHT PATH?
...
...
HANAYUME HIGHLANDS
HIKING PATHS
IT DOESN'T LOOK ANYTHING LIKE THE PICTURES IN THE GUIDEBOOK.
THEORETI-CALLY, WE SHOULD'VE REACHED THE FLOWER FIELD AGES AGO.
WELL, I DO SEE THE ARROWS.
THIS MUST BE ONE OF MANY DIFFERENT PATHS YOU CAN TAKE.
THREE MORE KILO-METERS ...
3 km
WELL, I DON'T FEEL LIKE TURNING AROUND AT THIS POINT, SO LET'S KEEP GOING.
IT'S MY FAULT FOR NOT DOUBLE-CHECKING.
OH, COME ON.
IT ALL DEPENDS ON HOW YOU LOOK AT IT.

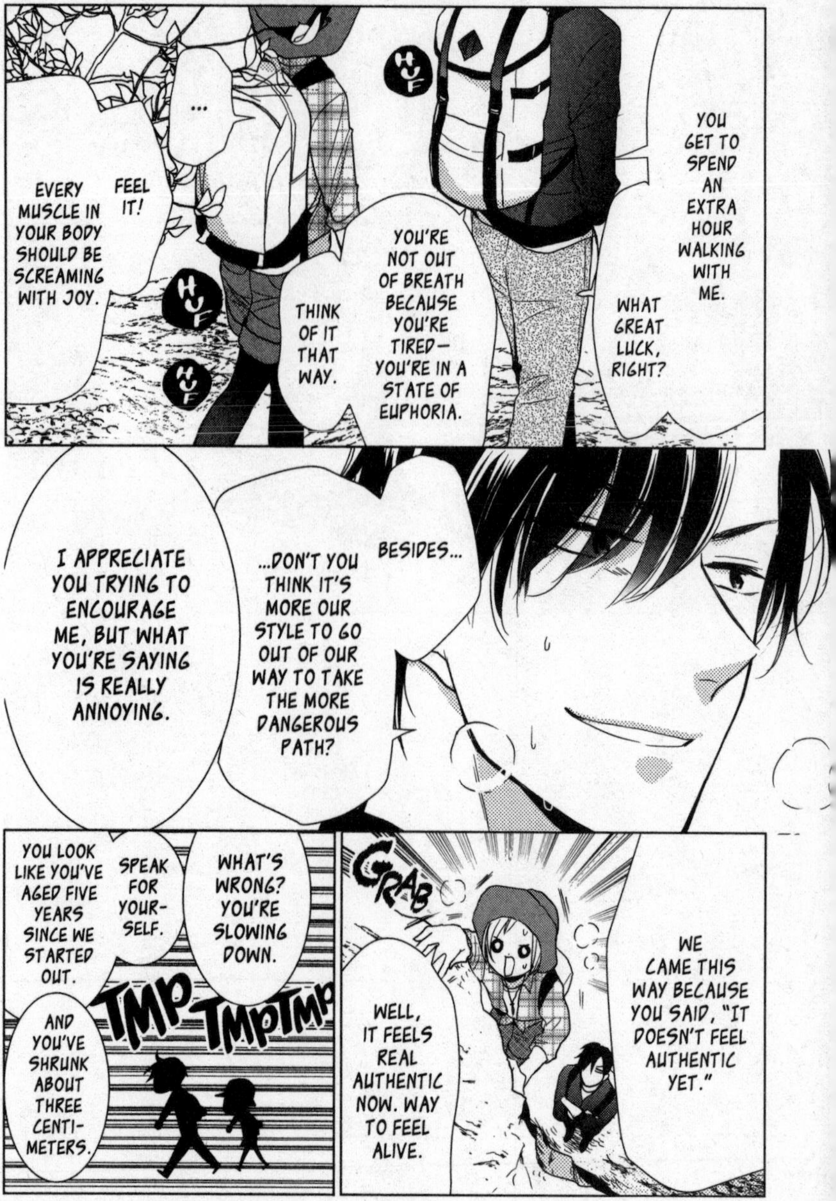
HUF
YOU GET TO SPEND AN EXTRA HOUR WALKING WITH ME.
WHAT GREAT LUCK, RIGHT?
YOU'RE NOT OUT OF BREATH BECAUSE YOU'RE TIRED—YOU'RE IN A STATE OF EUPHORIA.
THINK OF IT THAT WAY.
...
FEEL IT!
EVERY MUSCLE IN YOUR BODY SHOULD BE SCREAMING WITH JOY.
HUF
HUF
BESIDES...
...DON'T YOU THINK IT'S MORE OUR STYLE TO GO OUT OF OUR WAY TO TAKE THE MORE DANGEROUS PATH?
I APPRECIATE YOU TRYING TO ENCOURAGE ME, BUT WHAT YOU'RE SAYING IS REALLY ANNOYING.
WE CAME THIS WAY BECAUSE YOU SAID, "IT DOESN'T FEEL AUTHENTIC YET."
GRAB
WELL, IT FEELS REAL AUTHENTIC NOW. WAY TO FEEL ALIVE.
WHAT'S WRONG? YOU'RE SLOWING DOWN.
SPEAK FOR YOUR-SELF.
YOU LOOK LIKE YOU'VE AGED FIVE YEARS SINCE WE STARTED OUT.
TMP TMPTMP
AND YOU'VE SHRUNK ABOUT THREE CENTI-METERS.

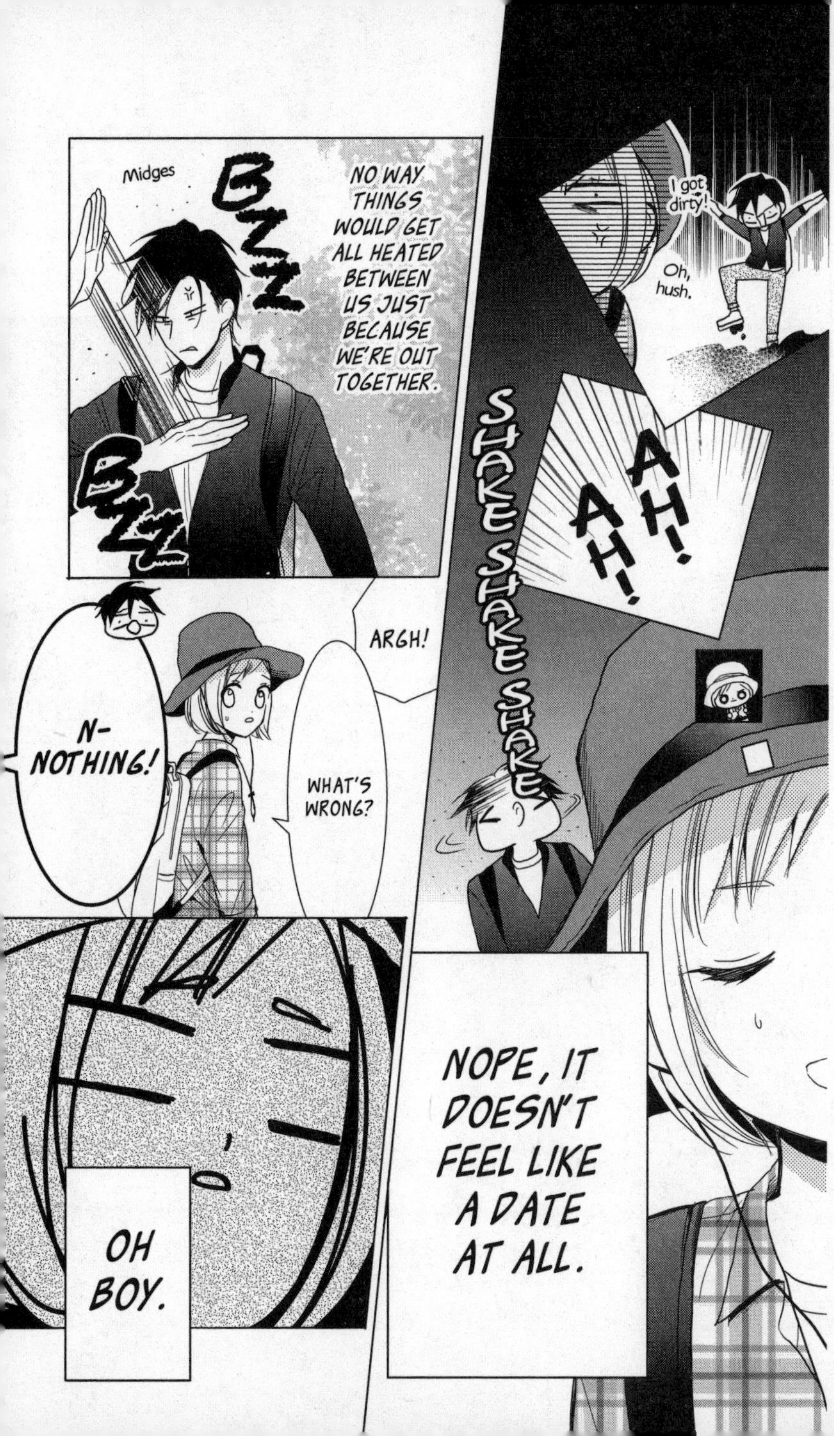
I got dirty!
Oh, hush.
Midges
BZZ
NO WAY THINGS WOULD GET ALL HEATED BETWEEN US JUST BECAUSE WE'RE OUT TOGETHER.
BZZ
AH! AH!
SHAKE SHAKE SHAKE
ARGH!
WHAT'S WRONG?
N-NOTHING!
NOPE, IT DOESN'T FEEL LIKE A DATE AT ALL.
OH BOY.

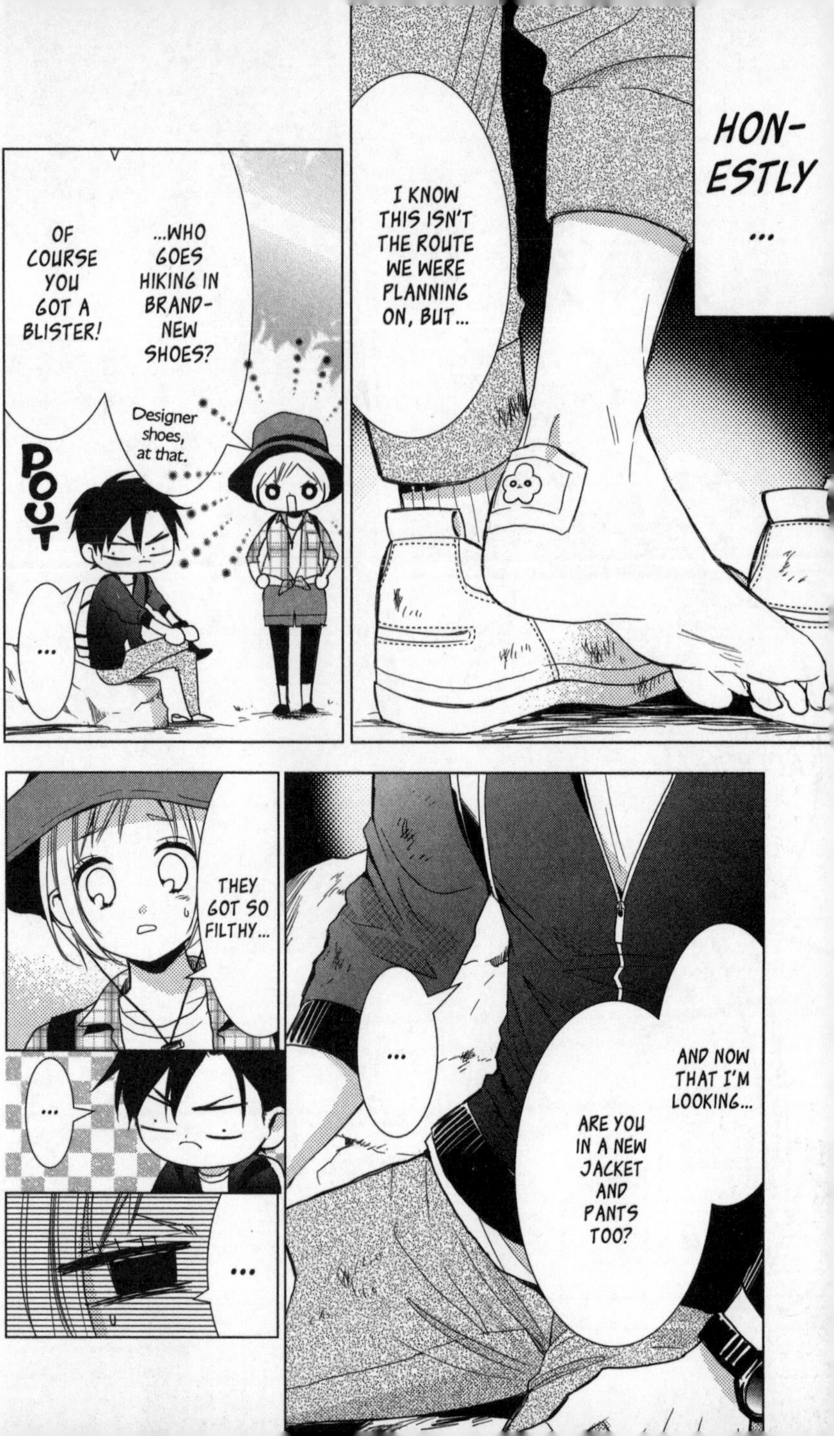
HON-
ESTLY
...
I KNOW THIS ISN'T THE ROUTE WE WERE PLANNING ON, BUT...
...WHO GOES HIKING IN BRAND-NEW SHOES?
OF COURSE YOU GOT A BLISTER!
Designer shoes, at that.
POUT
...
AND NOW THAT I'M LOOKING...
ARE YOU IN A NEW JACKET AND PANTS TOO?
...
THEY GOT SO FILTHY...
...
...

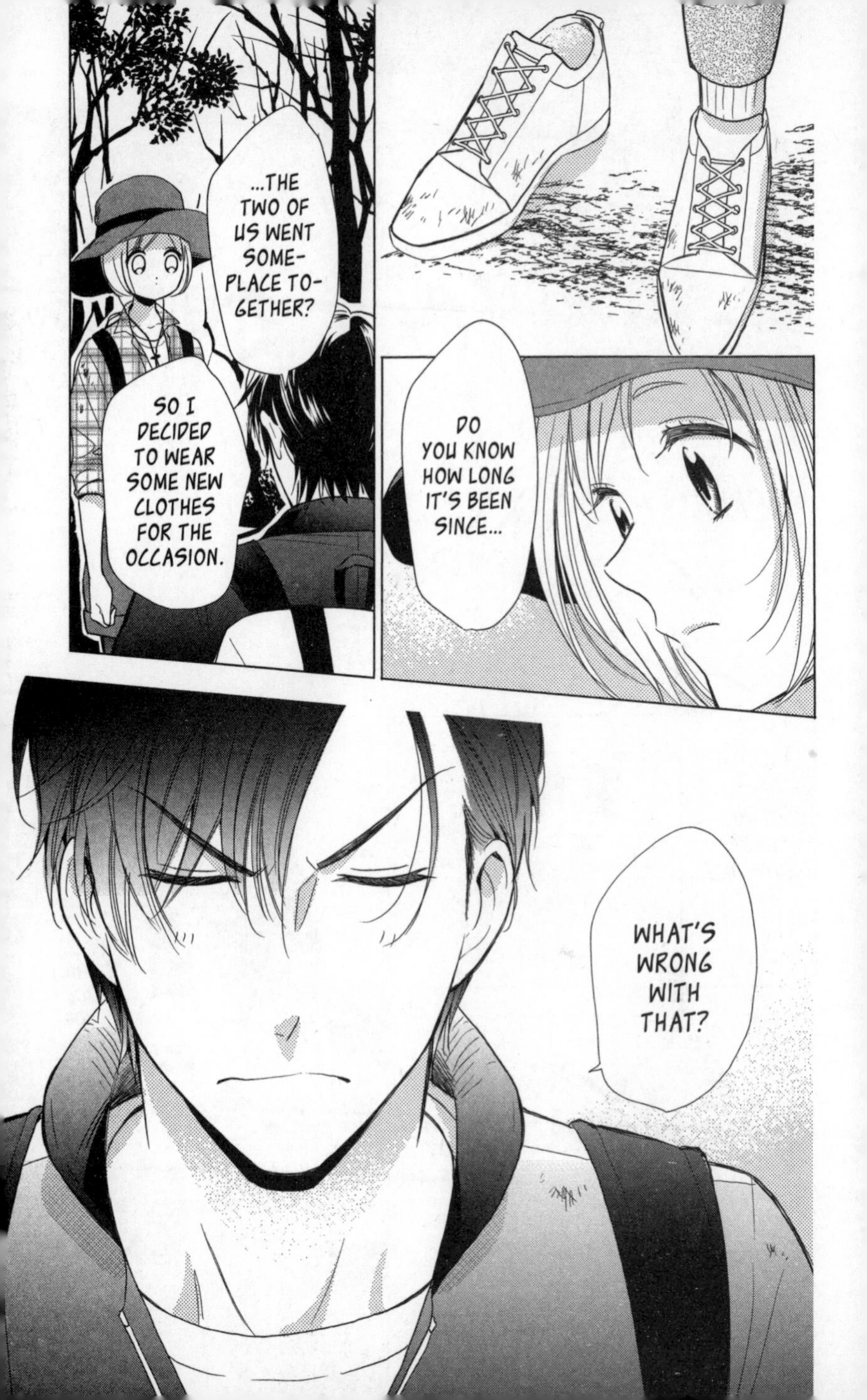
DO YOU KNOW HOW LONG IT'S BEEN SINCE...
...THE TWO OF US WENT SOME-PLACE TO-GETHER?
SO I DECIDED TO WEAR SOME NEW CLOTHES FOR THE OCCASION.
WHAT'S WRONG WITH THAT?

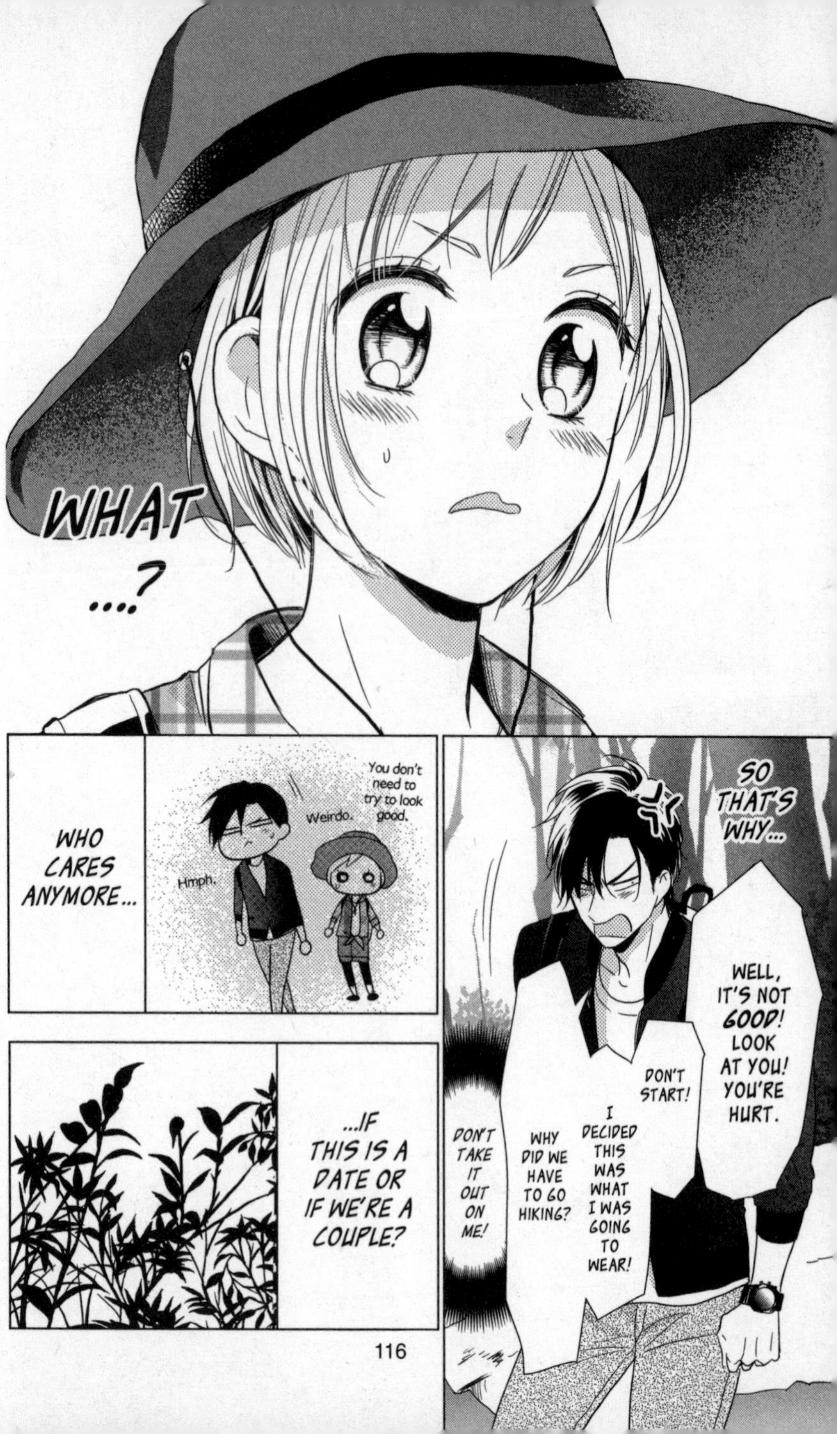
WHAT ...?
SO THAT'S WHY...
WELL, IT'S NOT GOOD! LOOK AT YOU! YOU'RE HURT.
DON'T START!
I DECIDED THIS WAS WHAT I WAS GOING TO WEAR!
WHY DID WE HAVE TO GO HIKING?
DON'T TAKE IT OUT ON ME!
You don't need to try to look good.
Weirdo.
Hmph.
WHO CARES ANYMORE...
...IF THIS IS A DATE OR IF WE'RE A COUPLE?

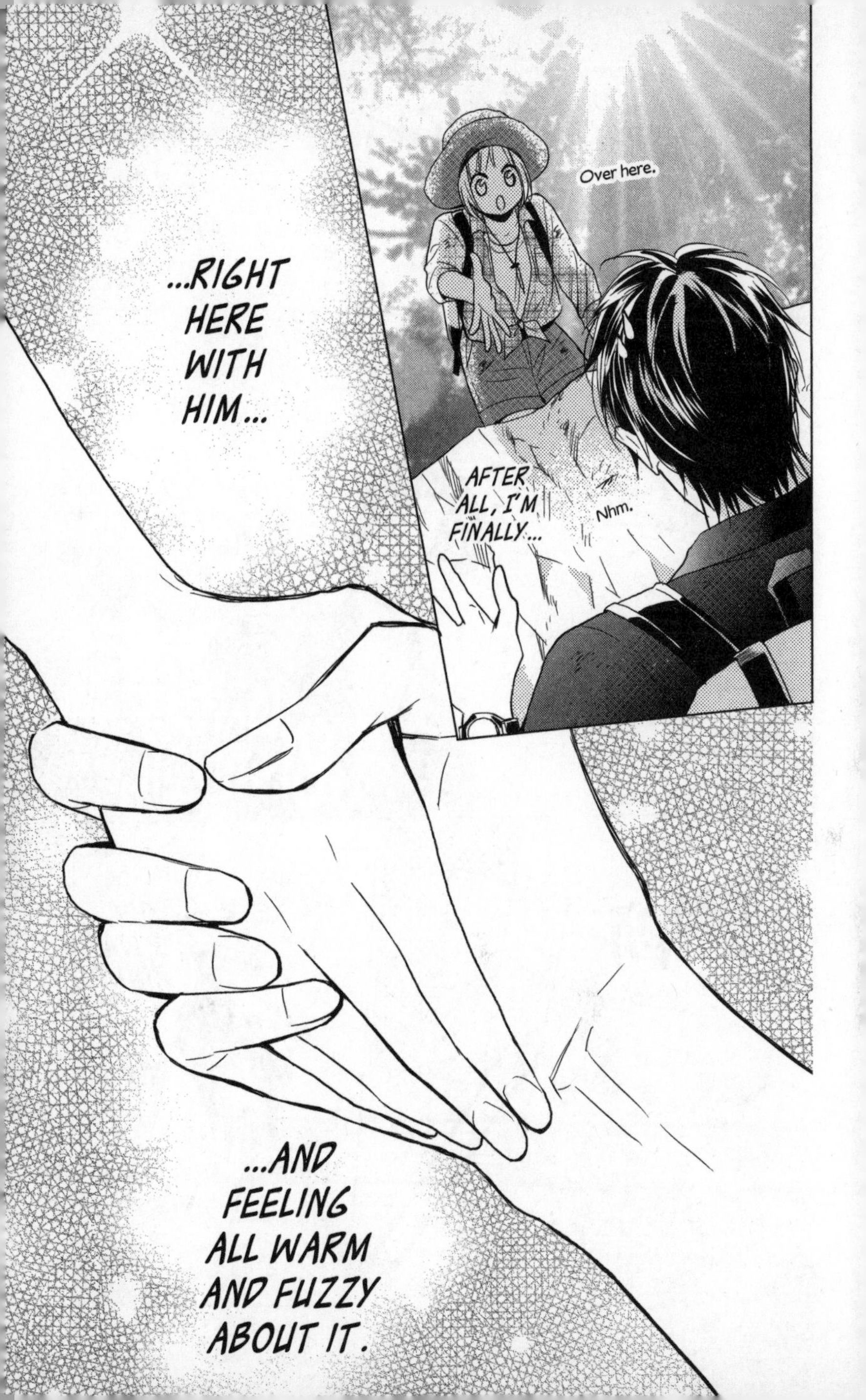
Over here.
Nhm.
AFTER ALL, I'M FINALLY...
...RIGHT HERE WITH HIM...
...AND FEELING ALL WARM AND FUZZY ABOUT IT.

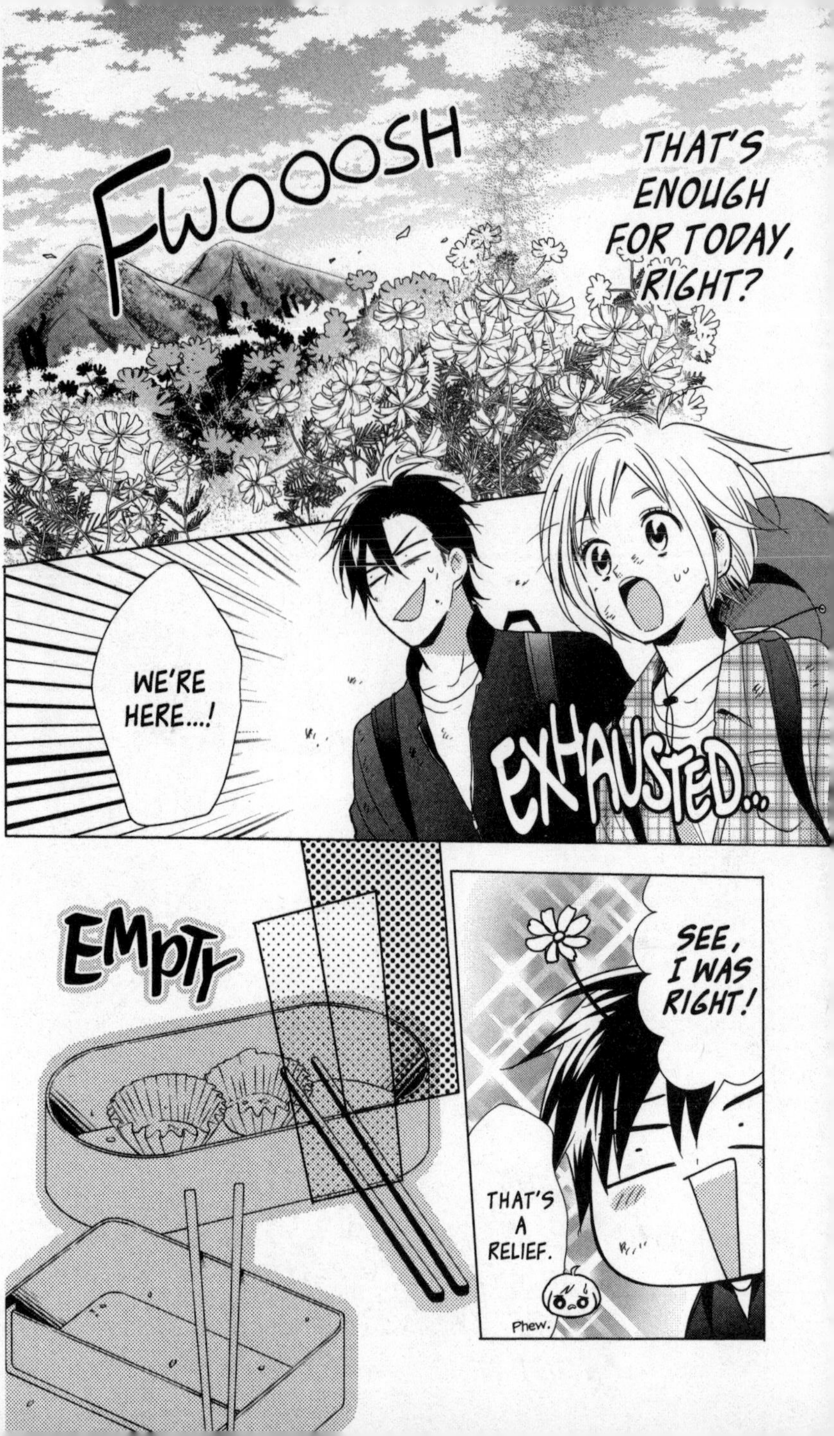
THAT'S ENOUGH FOR TODAY, RIGHT?
FWOOOSH
EXHAUSTED..
WE'RE HERE...!
SEE, I WAS RIGHT!
THAT'S A RELIEF.
Phew.
EMPTY

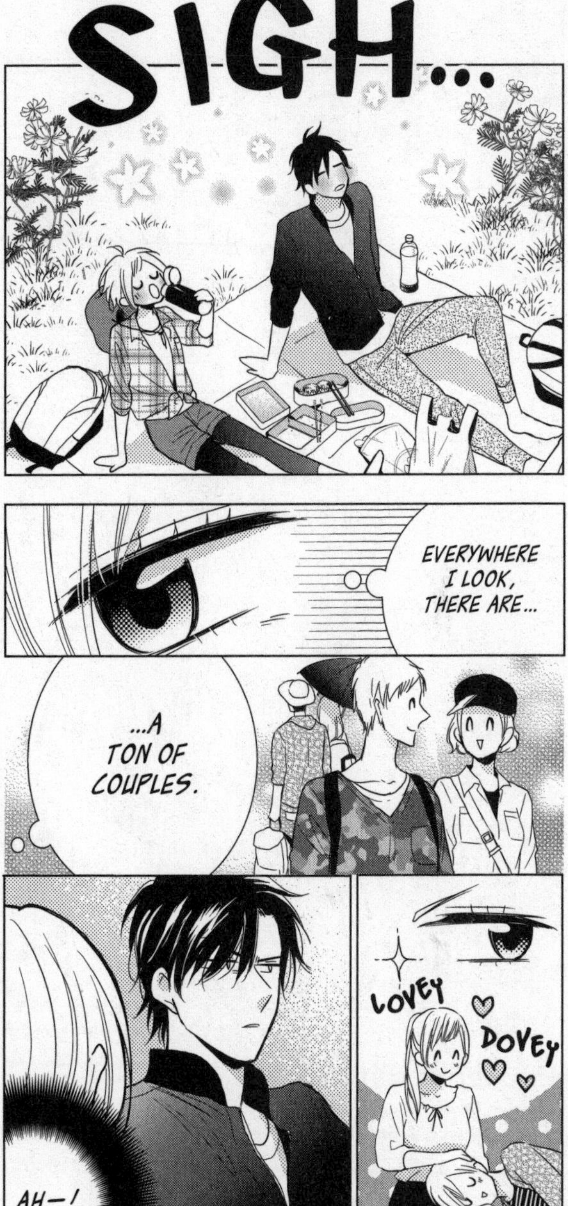
SIGH...
EVERYWHERE I LOOK, THERE ARE...
...A TON OF COUPLES.
LOVEY
DOVEY
AH—!

• We've finally • made it this far!

Takane & Hana has finally become Takane's Hana—I mean, Hana's Takane.

Ultimately, this is a comedy, but when it came to their true feelings, I tried to be more serious. Portraying their feelings for each other was tricky business, and to get to this point was a painstaking process. Not to mention the pain from Takane's broken shins!

What Takane said that settled Hana's heart was "Just trust me. Be with me."

No matter how childish he is, Takane still has ten years on Hana. I thought it was important to show his maturity at a critical moment like this, so that's why I chose to have him say that.

I hope you can see from this that *Takane & Hana* is genuinely a story about age difference.

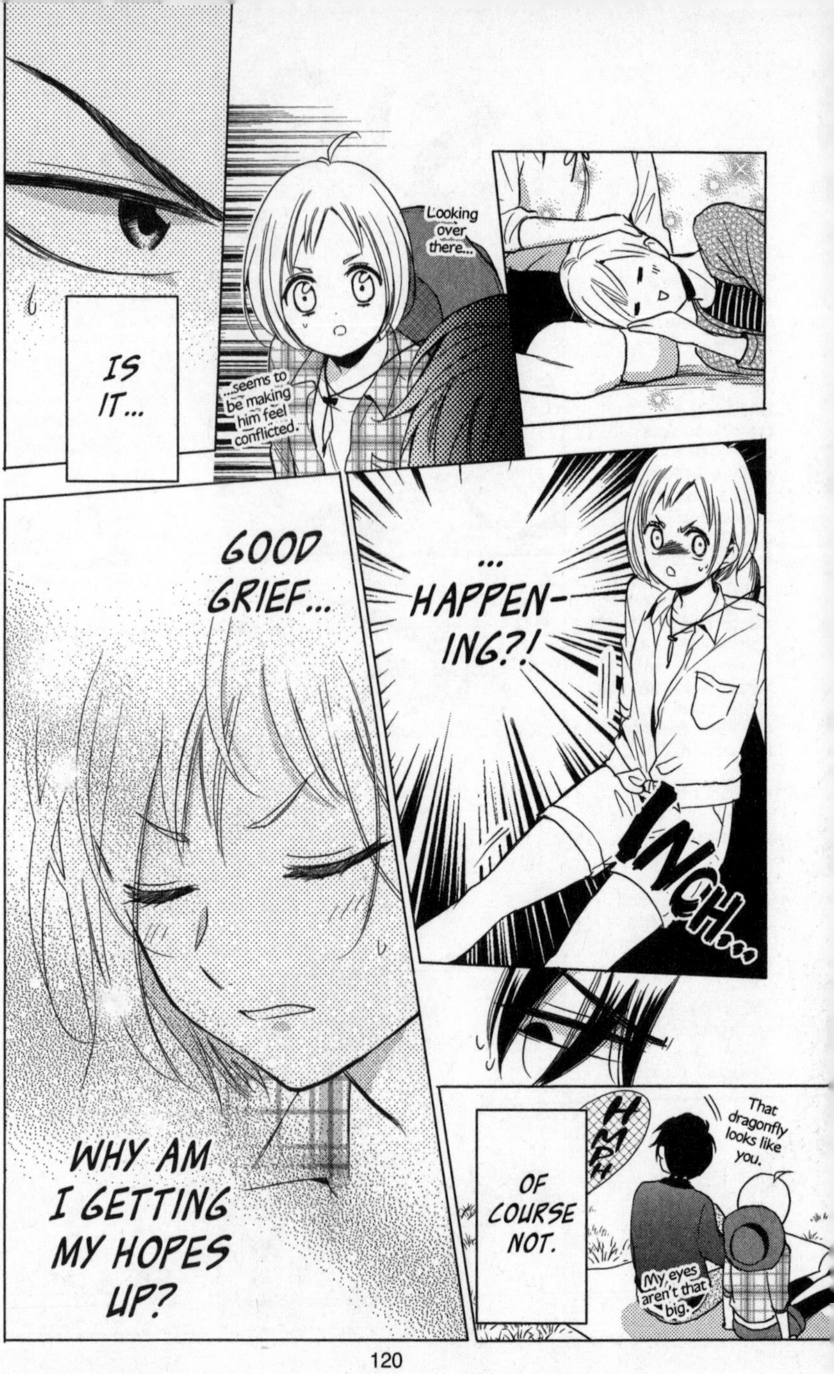
Looking over there...
...seems to be making him feel conflicted.
IS IT...
...HAPPEN-ING?!
INCH...
That dragonfly looks like you.
HMPH
My eyes aren't that big.
OF COURSE NOT.
GOOD GRIEF...
WHY AM I GETTING MY HOPES UP?

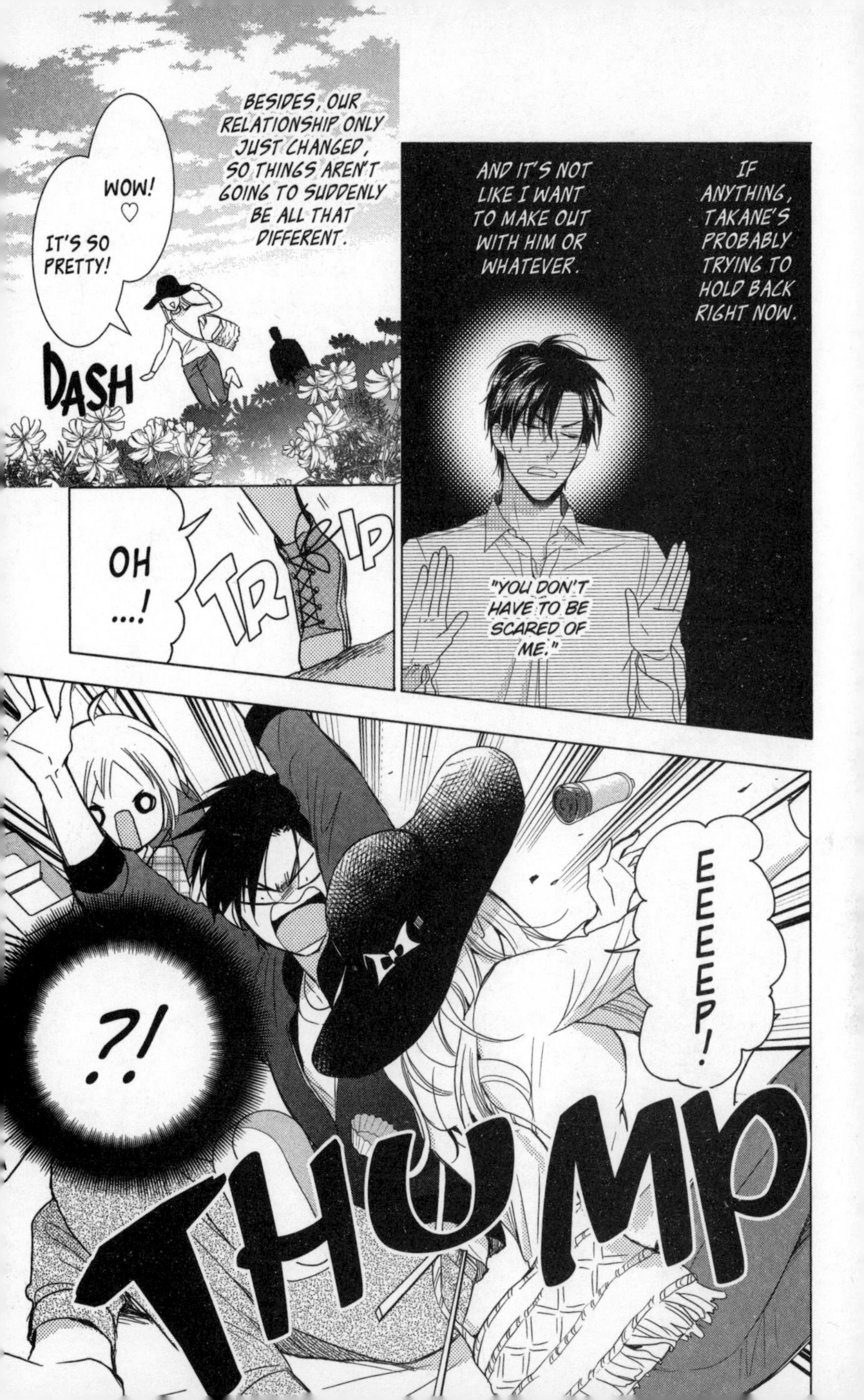
IF ANYTHING, TAKANE'S PROBABLY TRYING TO HOLD BACK RIGHT NOW.
AND IT'S NOT LIKE I WANT TO MAKE OUT WITH HIM OR WHATEVER.
"YOU DON'T HAVE TO BE SCARED OF ME."
BESIDES, OUR RELATIONSHIP ONLY JUST CHANGED, SO THINGS AREN'T GOING TO SUDDENLY BE ALL THAT DIFFERENT.
WOW! ♡ IT'S SO PRETTY!
DASH
TRIP
OH ...!
EEEEP!
?!
THUMP

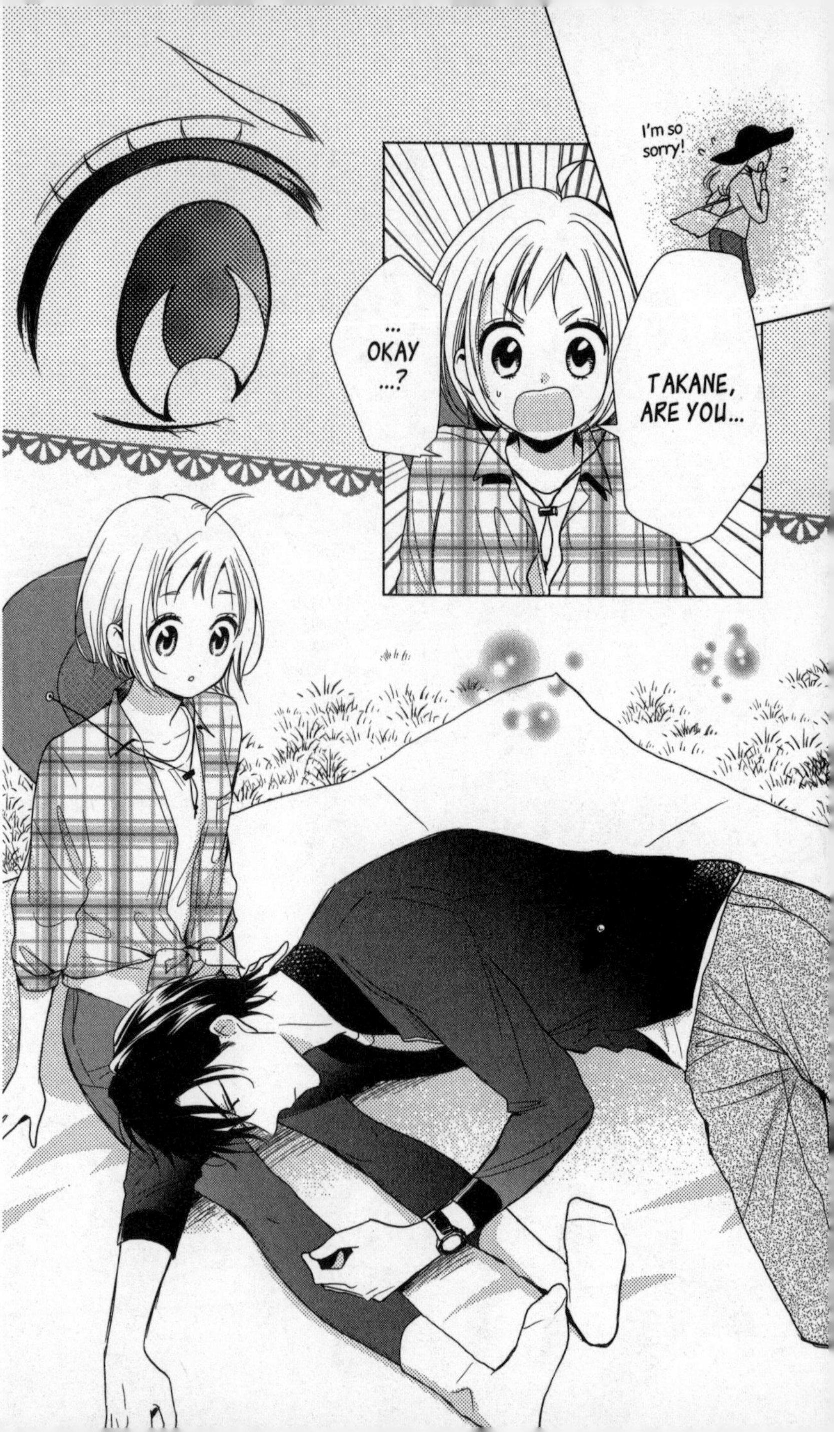
I'm so sorry!
TAKANE, ARE YOU...
... OKAY ...?

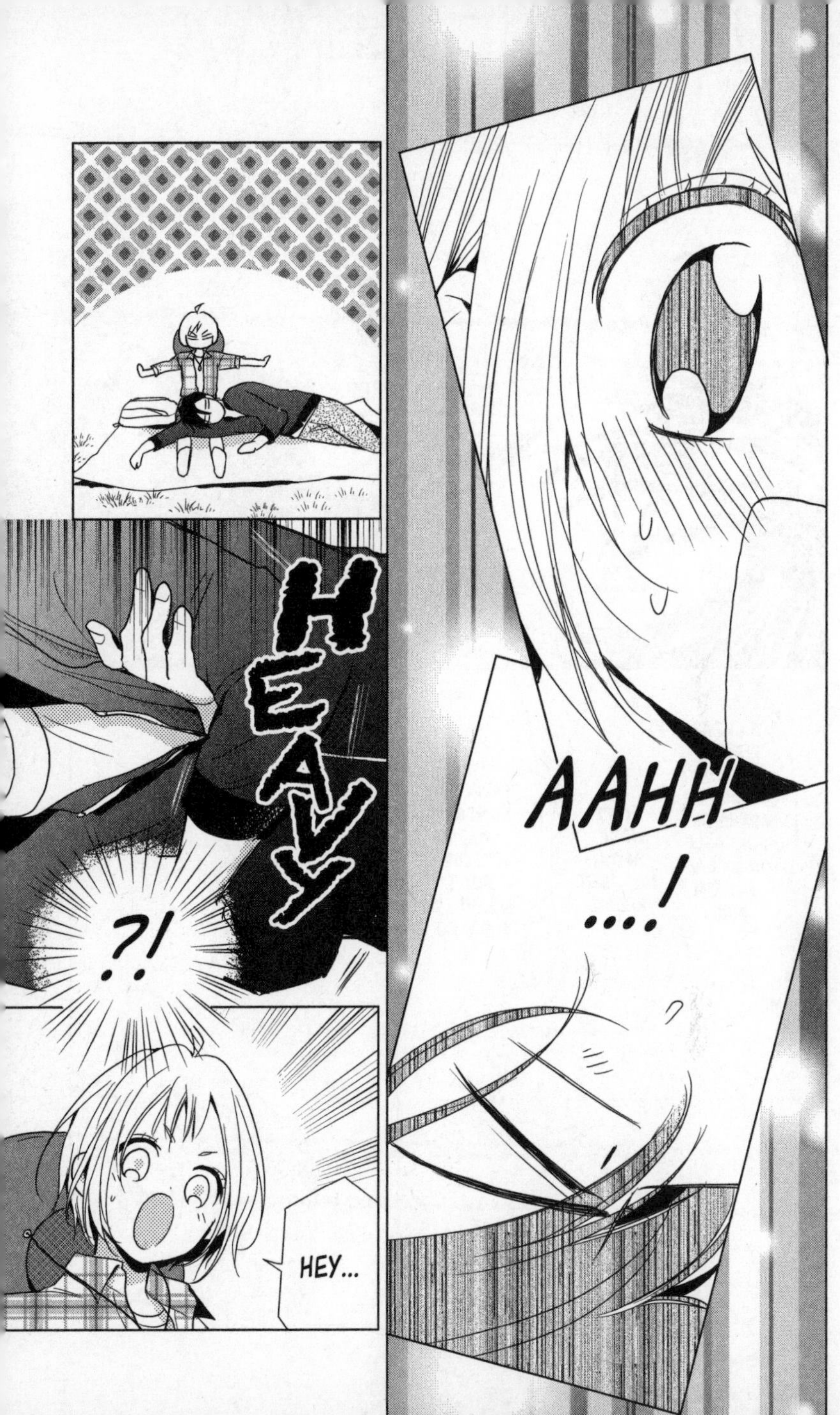
AAHH ...!
HEAVY
?!
HEY...

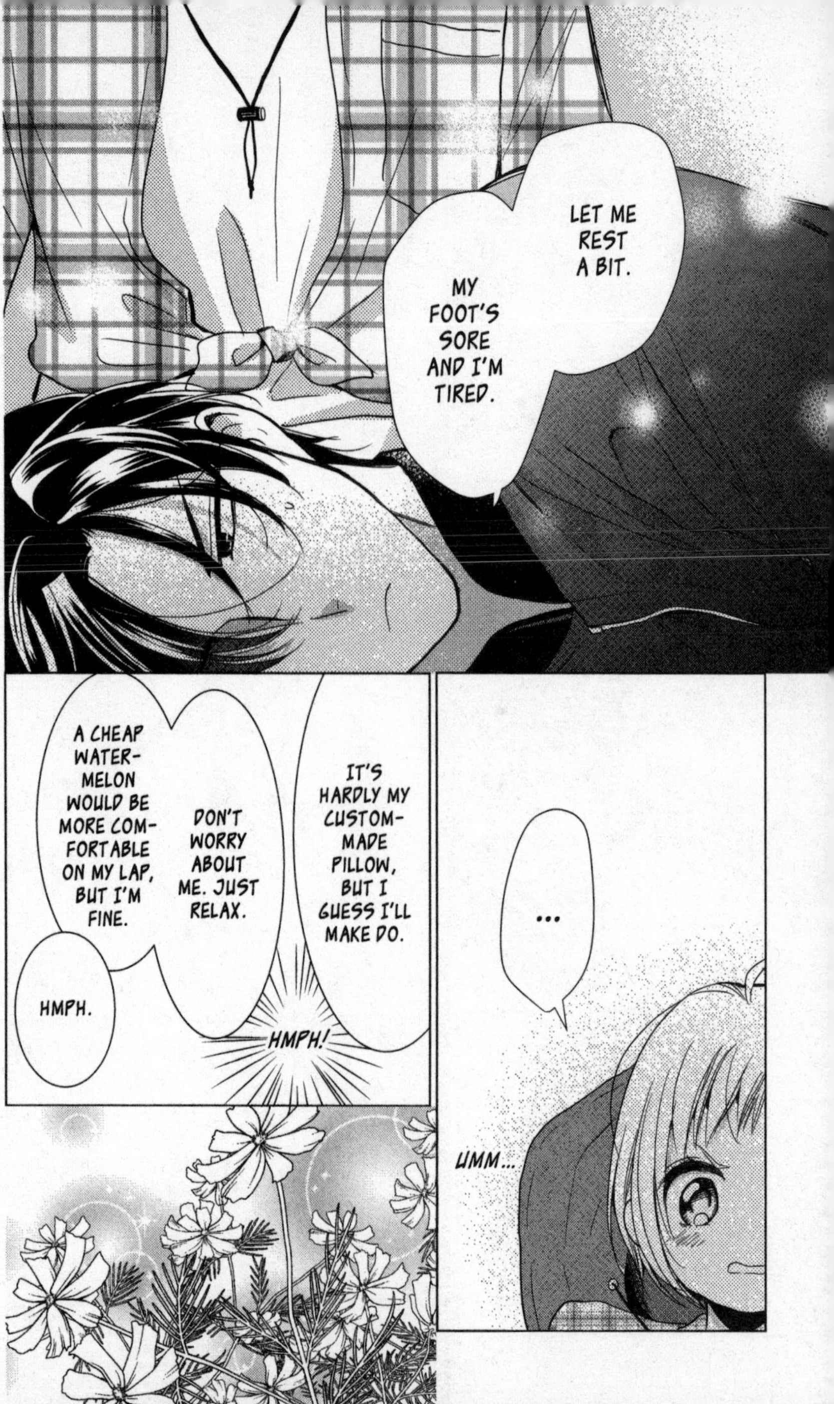
LET ME REST A BIT.
MY FOOT'S SORE AND I'M TIRED.
...
UMM...
IT'S HARDLY MY CUSTOM-MADE PILLOW, BUT I GUESS I'LL MAKE DO.
DON'T WORRY ABOUT ME. JUST RELAX.
A CHEAP WATER-MELON WOULD BE MORE COM-FORTABLE ON MY LAP, BUT I'M FINE.
HMPH!
HMPH.

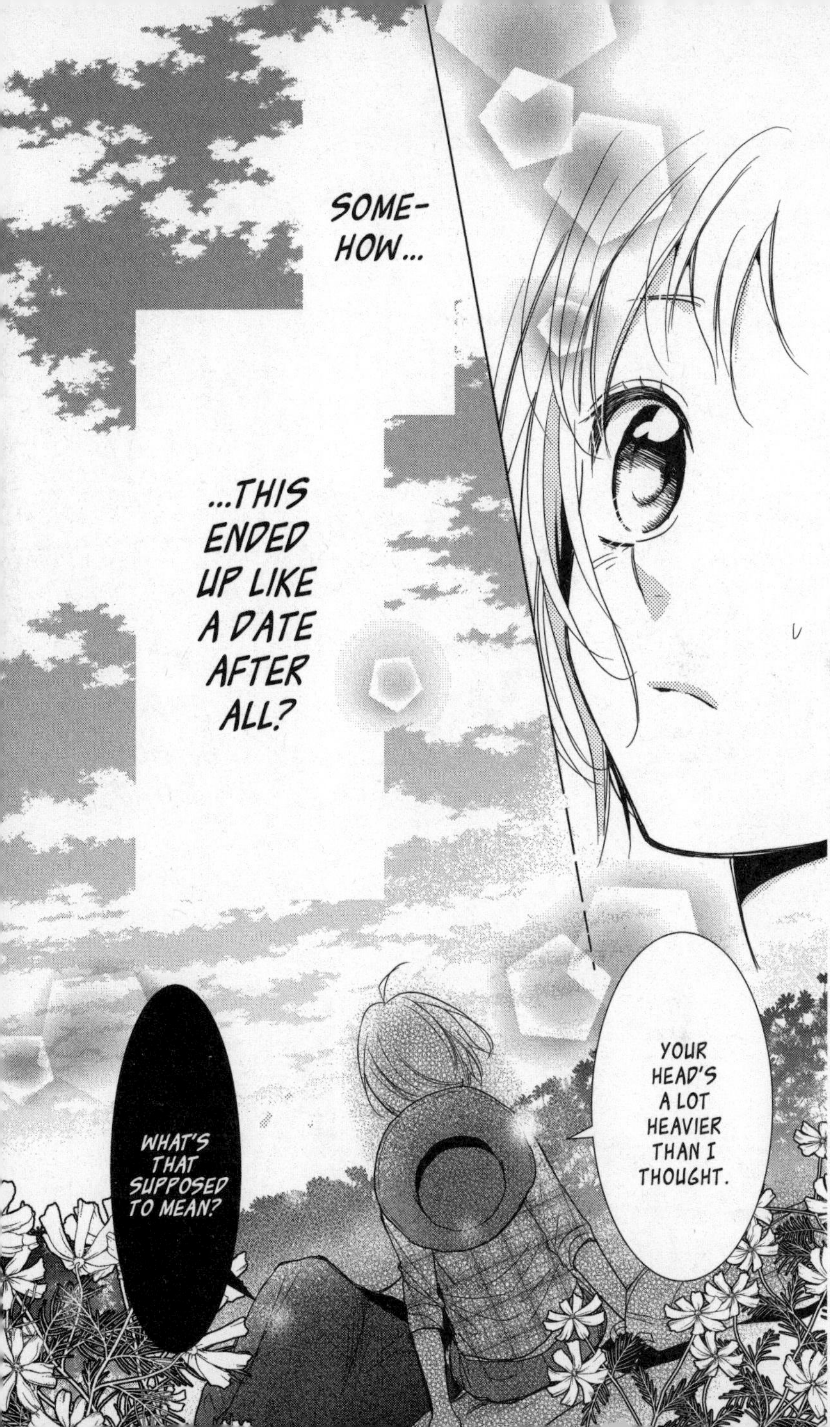
SOME-HOW...
...THIS ENDED UP LIKE A DATE AFTER ALL?
YOUR HEAD'S A LOT HEAVIER THAN I THOUGHT.
WHAT'S THAT SUPPOSED TO MEAN?

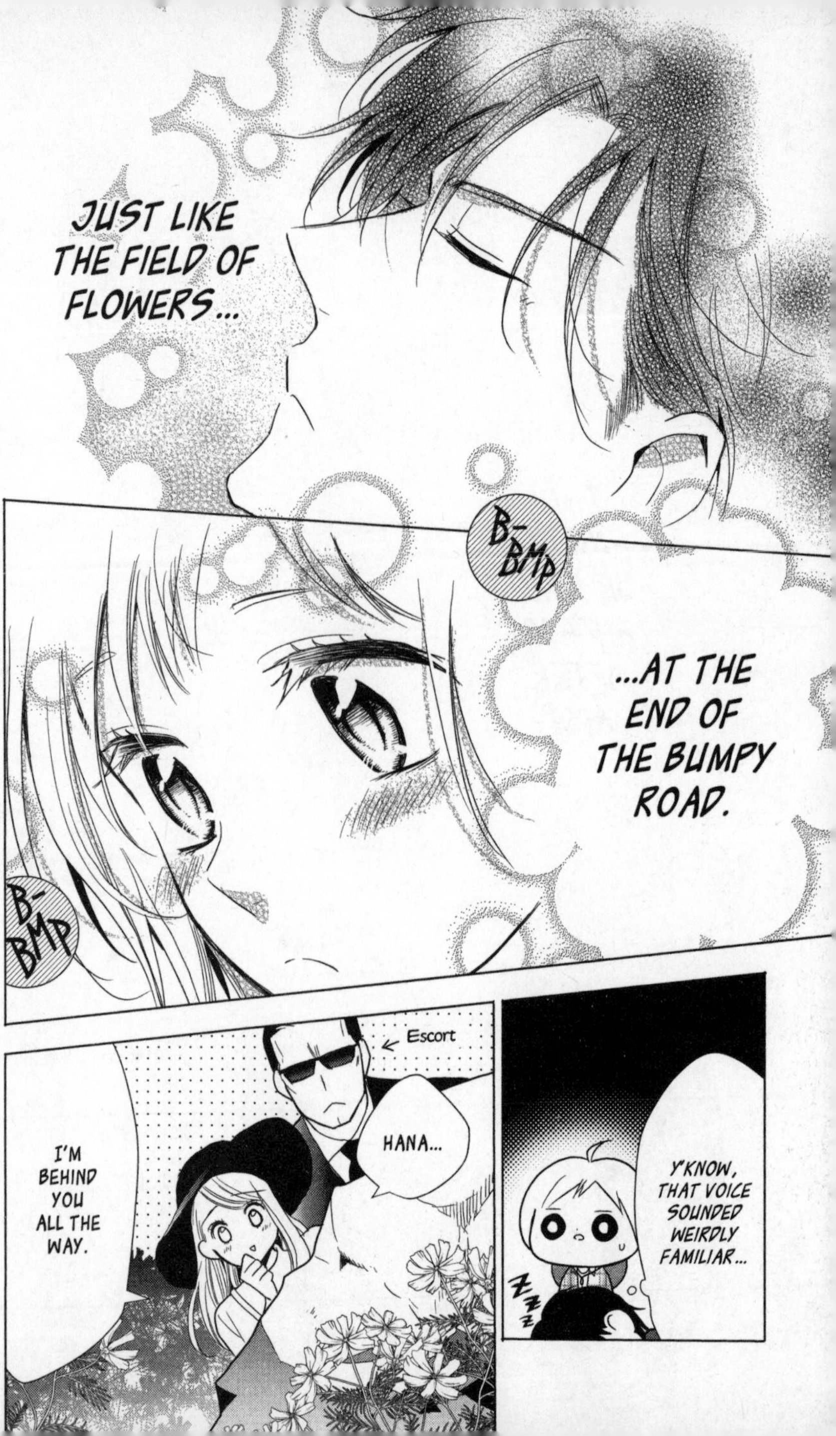
JUST LIKE THE FIELD OF FLOWERS...
B-BMP
...AT THE END OF THE BUMPY ROAD.
B-BMP
Y'KNOW, THAT VOICE SOUNDED WEIRDLY FAMILIAR...
ZZZ
Escort
HANA...
I'M BEHIND YOU ALL THE WAY.

Chapter 73

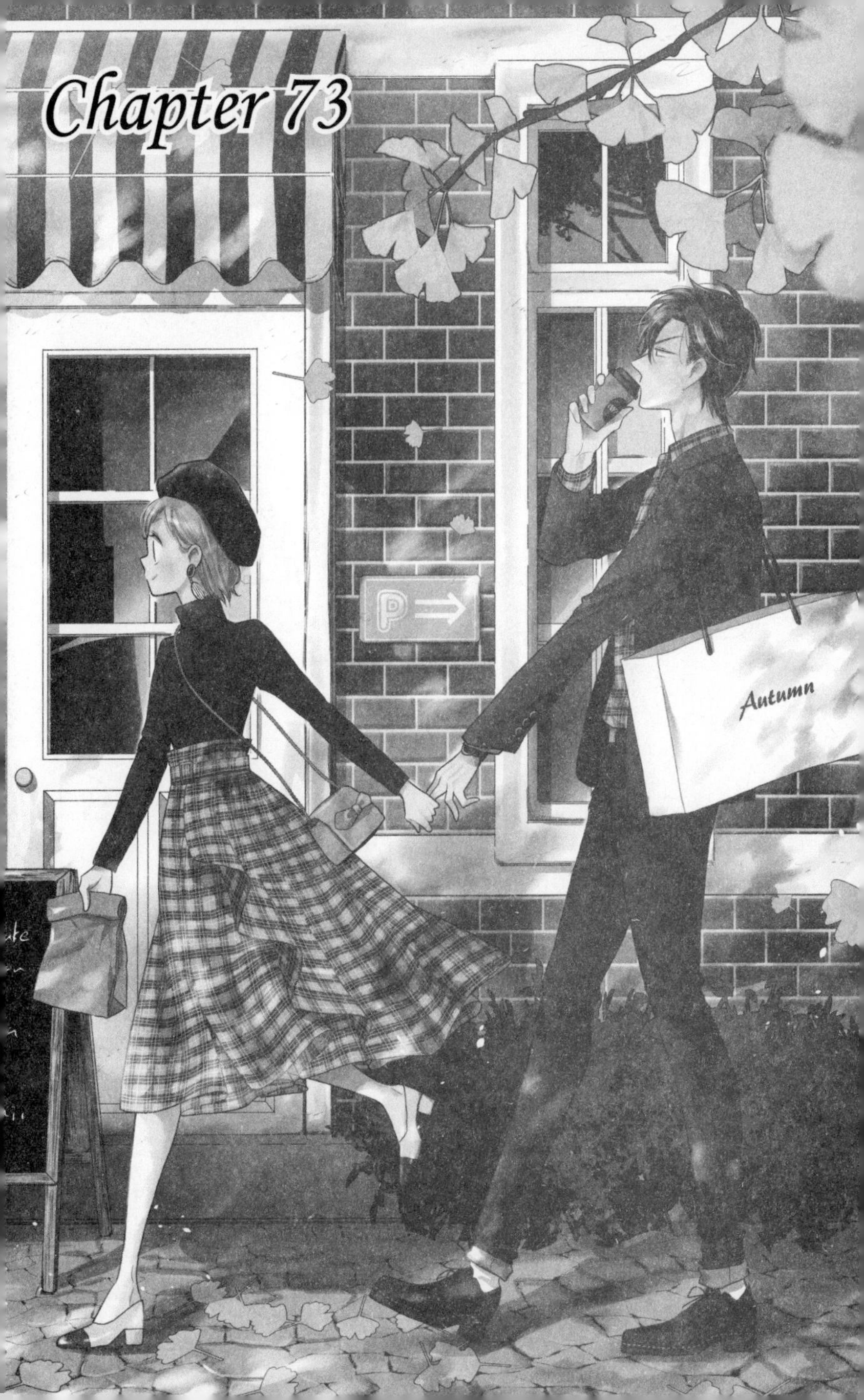
Autumn

An Enthusiastic Sister

I'M GOING TO GO CHECK ON HANA, GUYS!
YES-!
I WONDER IF THEY'RE DOING COUPLE STUFF.
I'D BETTER HURRY AND CATCH UP TO THEM.
AT THAT MOMENT ...
Top of the mountain
THEY'RE LATE!
How come?

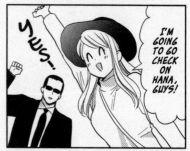

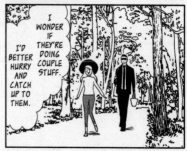

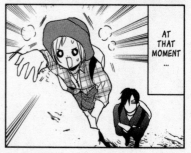

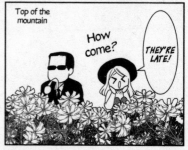

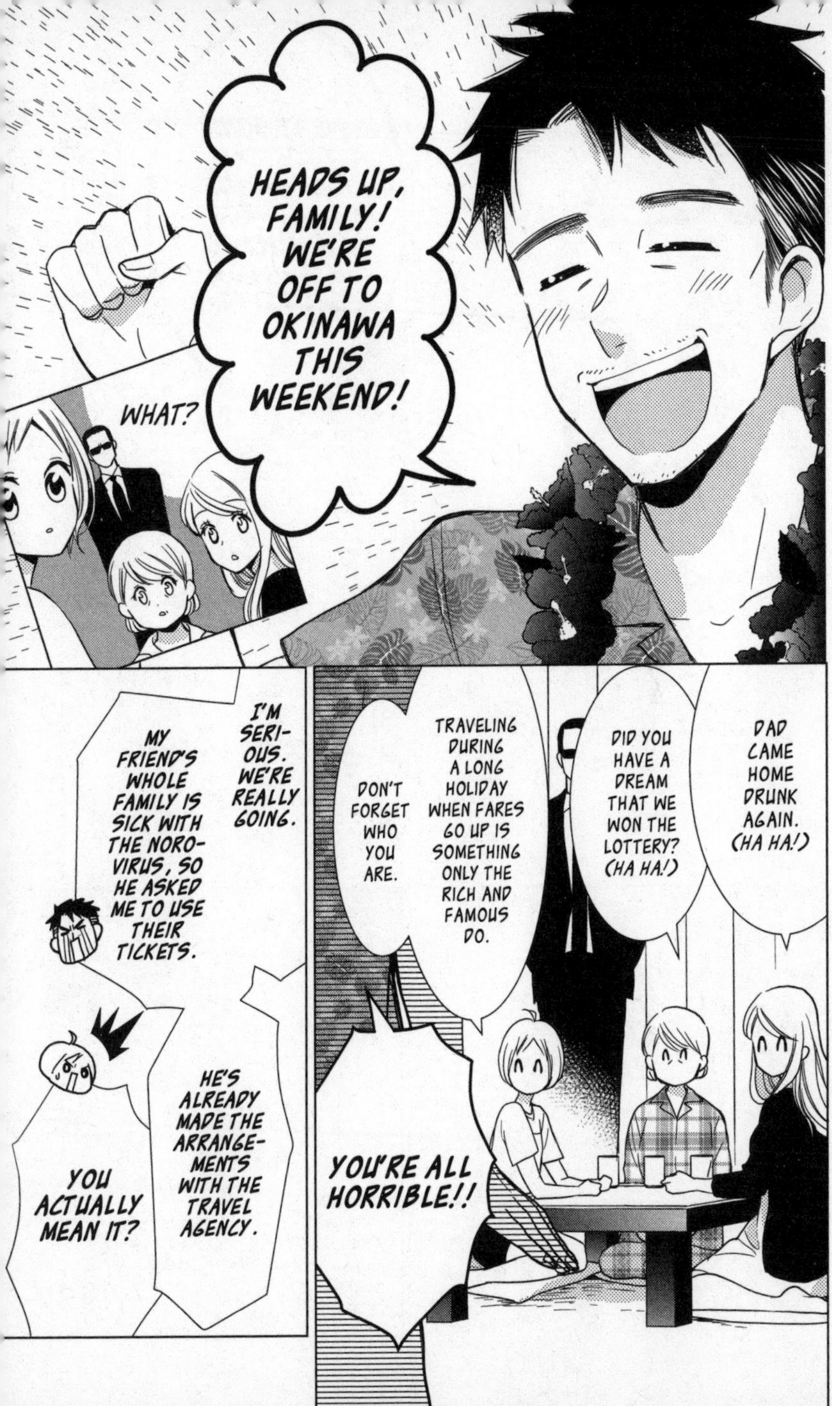
HEADS UP, FAMILY! WE'RE OFF TO OKINAWA THIS WEEKEND!
WHAT?
DAD CAME HOME DRUNK AGAIN. (HA HA!)
DID YOU HAVE A DREAM THAT WE WON THE LOTTERY? (HA HA!)
TRAVELING DURING A LONG HOLIDAY WHEN FARES GO UP IS SOMETHING ONLY THE RICH AND FAMOUS DO.
DON'T FORGET WHO YOU ARE.
YOU'RE ALL HORRIBLE!!
I'M SERIOUS. WE'RE REALLY GOING.
MY FRIEND'S WHOLE FAMILY IS SICK WITH THE NOROVIRUS, SO HE ASKED ME TO USE THEIR TICKETS.
HE'S ALREADY MADE THE ARRANGEMENTS WITH THE TRAVEL AGENCY.
YOU ACTUALLY MEAN IT?

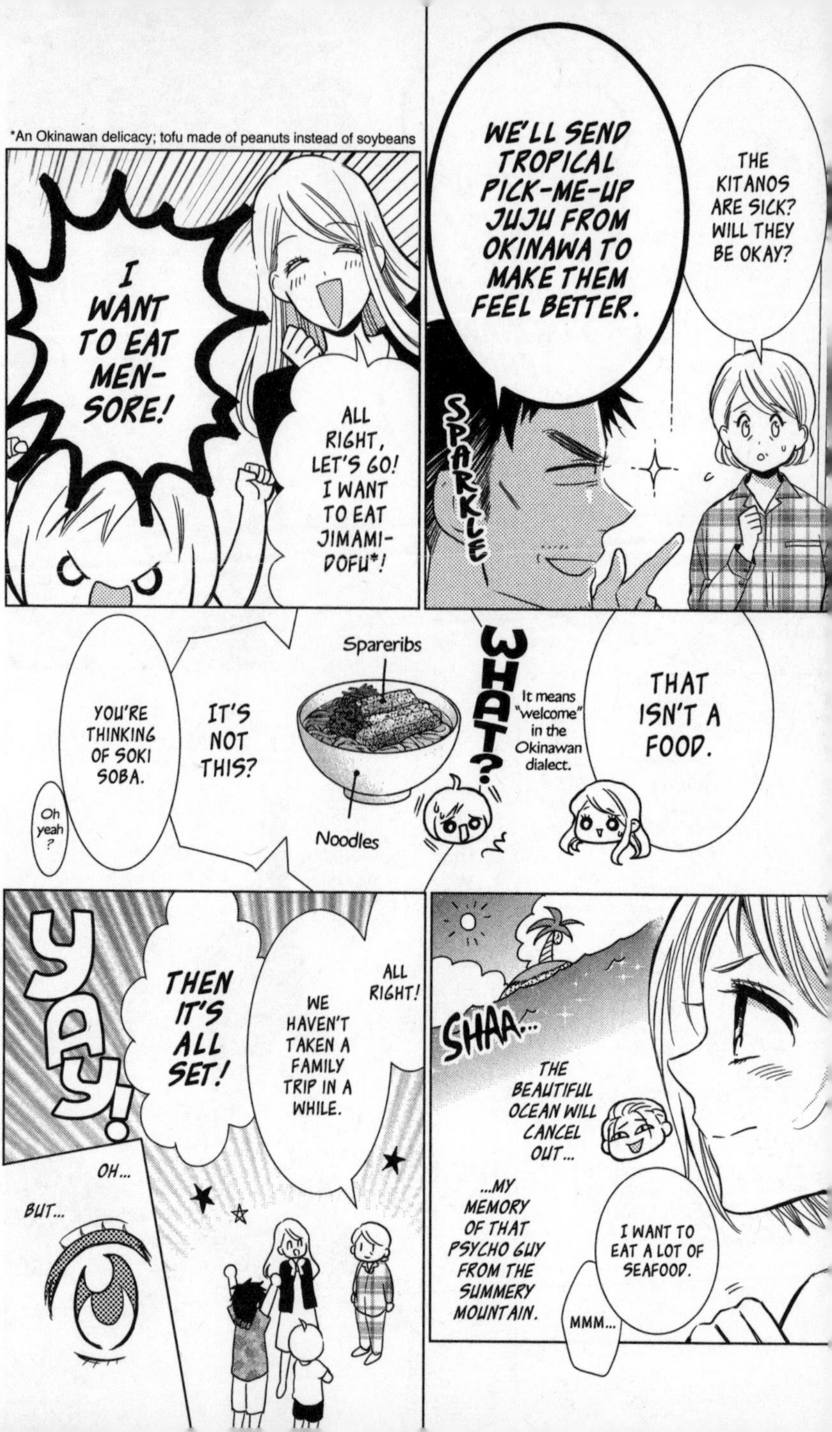
THE KITANOS ARE SICK? WILL THEY BE OKAY?
WE'LL SEND TROPICAL PICK-ME-UP JUJU FROM OKINAWA TO MAKE THEM FEEL BETTER.
SPARKLE
I WANT TO EAT MEN-SORE!
ALL RIGHT, LET'S GO! I WANT TO EAT JIMAMI-DOFU*!
THAT ISN'T A FOOD.
It means "welcome" in the Okinawan dialect.
WHAT?
Spareribs
Noodles
IT'S NOT THIS?
YOU'RE THINKING OF SOKI SOBA.
Oh yeah?
SHAA...
THE BEAUTIFUL OCEAN WILL CANCEL OUT...
...MY MEMORY OF THAT PSYCHO GUY FROM THE SUMMERY MOUNTAIN.
I WANT TO EAT A LOT OF SEAFOOD.
MMM...
ALL RIGHT!
WE HAVEN'T TAKEN A FAMILY TRIP IN A WHILE.
THEN IT'S ALL SET!
YAY!
OH...
BUT...

*An Okinawan delicacy; tofu made of peanuts instead of soybeans

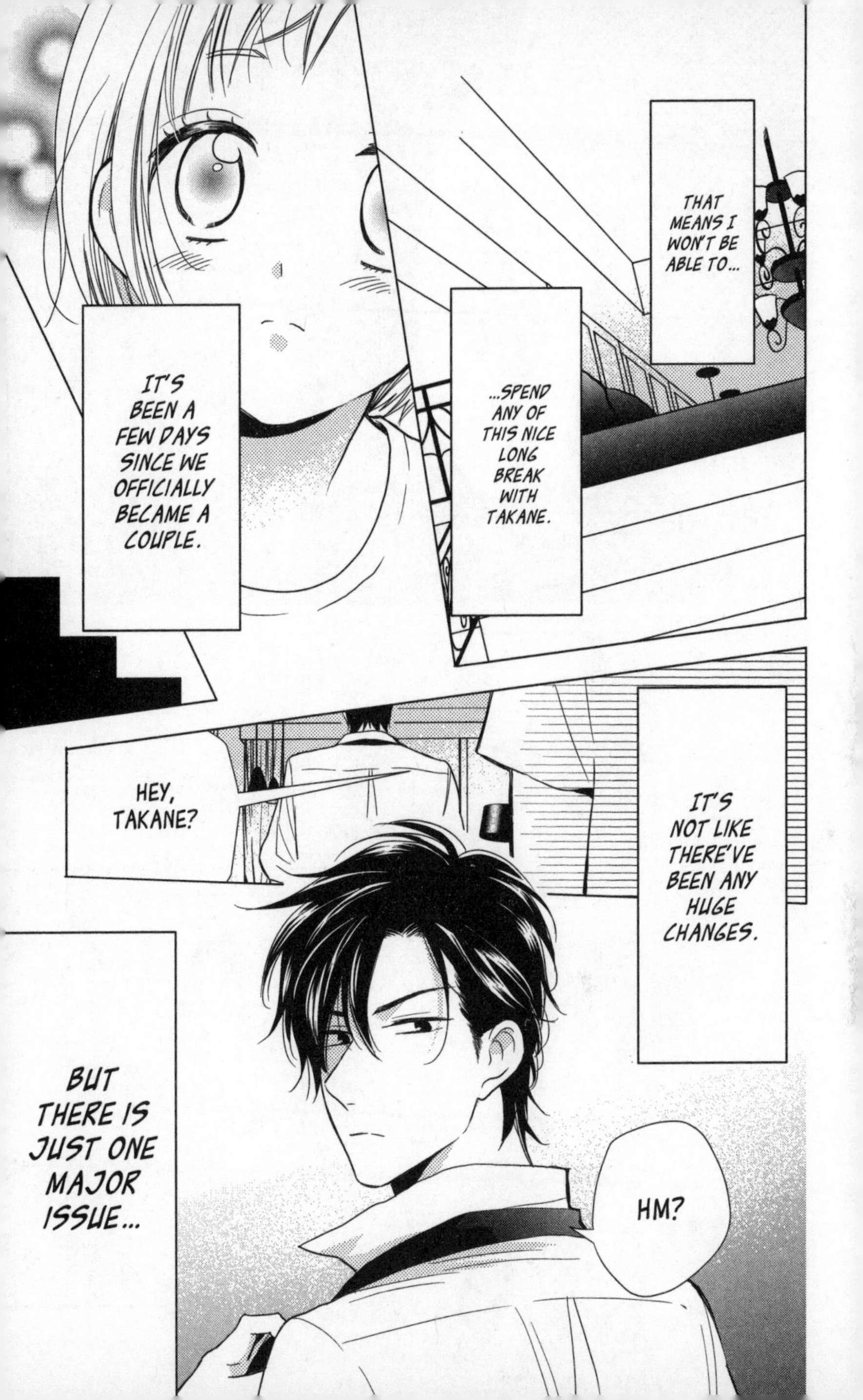
THAT MEANS I WON'T BE ABLE TO...
...SPEND ANY OF THIS NICE LONG BREAK WITH TAKANE.
IT'S BEEN A FEW DAYS SINCE WE OFFICIALLY BECAME A COUPLE.
IT'S NOT LIKE THERE'VE BEEN ANY HUGE CHANGES.
HEY, TAKANE?
HM?
BUT THERE IS JUST ONE MAJOR ISSUE...

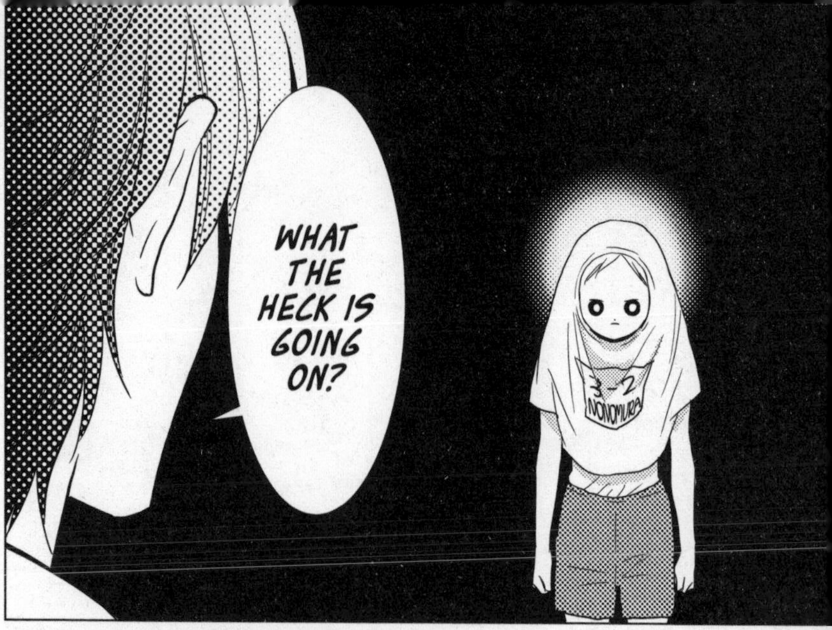
WHAT THE HECK IS GOING ON?
3-2 NONOMURA

*A string of consecutive holidays in September

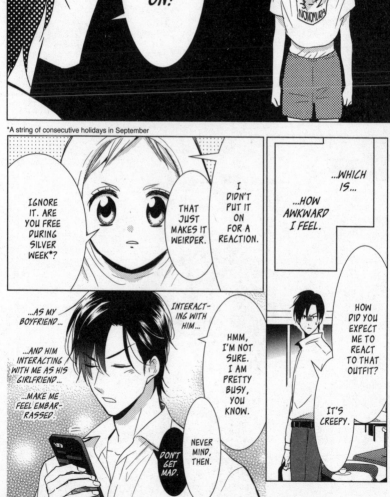

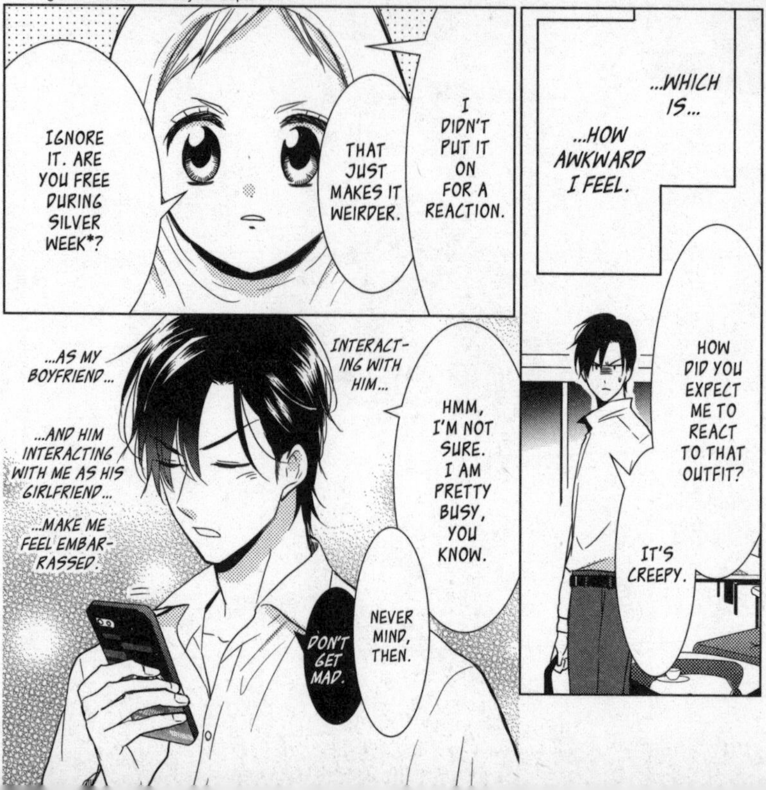
...WHICH IS...
...HOW AWKWARD I FEEL.
I DIDN'T PUT IT ON FOR A REACTION.
THAT JUST MAKES IT WEIRDER.
IGNORE IT. ARE YOU FREE DURING SILVER WEEK*?
HOW DID YOU EXPECT ME TO REACT TO THAT OUTFIT?
IT'S CREEPY.
INTERACTING WITH HIM...
HMM, I'M NOT SURE. I AM PRETTY BUSY, YOU KNOW.
NEVER MIND, THEN.
DON'T GET MAD.
...AS MY BOYFRIEND...
...AND HIM INTERACTING WITH ME AS HIS GIRLFRIEND...
...MAKE ME FEEL EMBARRASSED.

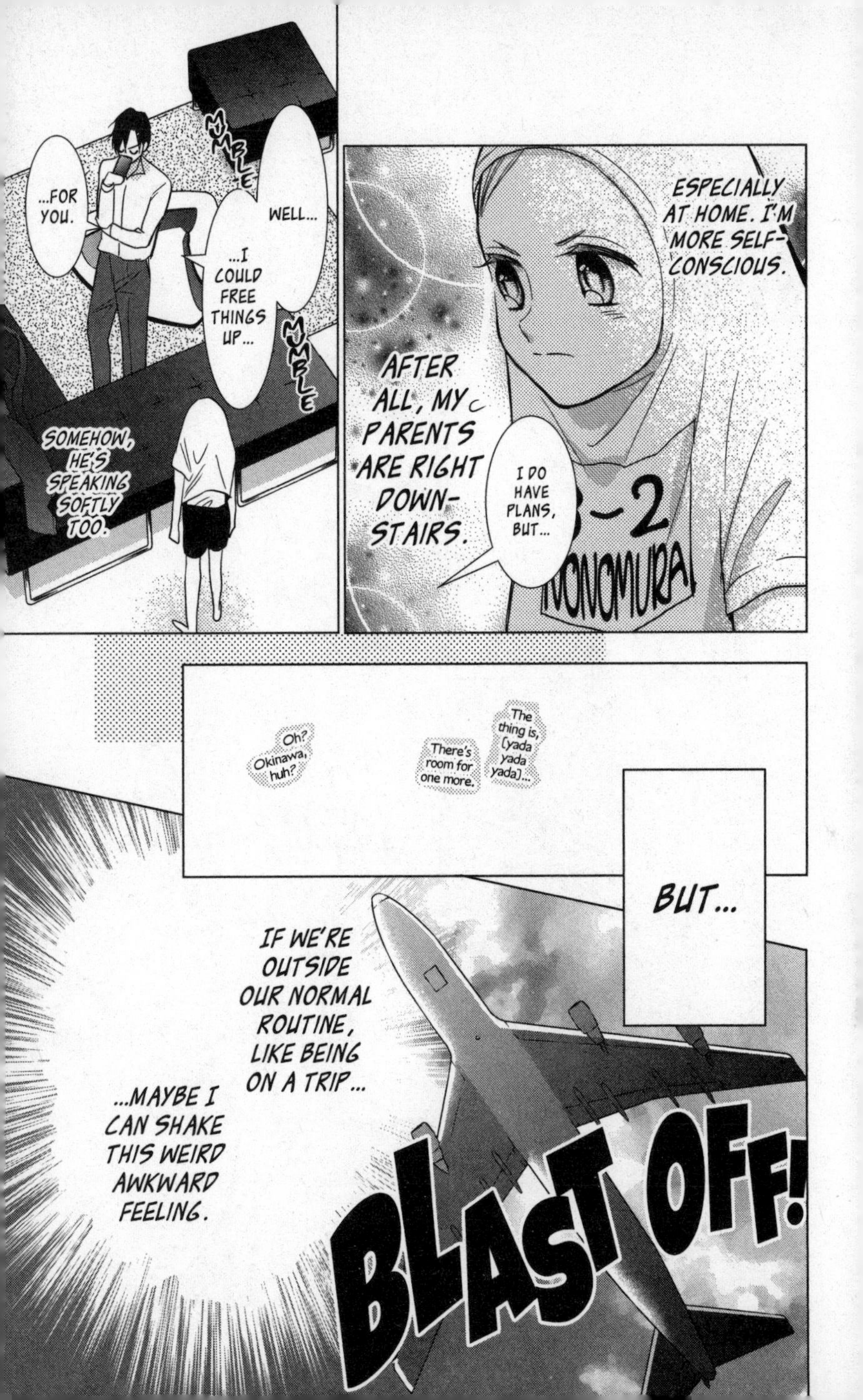
ESPECIALLY AT HOME. I'M MORE SELF-CONSCIOUS.
AFTER ALL, MY PARENTS ARE RIGHT DOWN-STAIRS.
I DO HAVE PLANS, BUT...
MUMBLE
WELL...
...I COULD FREE THINGS UP...
MUMBLE
...FOR YOU.
SOMEHOW, HE'S SPEAKING SOFTLY TOO.
The thing is, (yada yada yada)...
There's room for one more.
Oh? Okinawa, huh?
BUT...
IF WE'RE OUTSIDE OUR NORMAL ROUTINE, LIKE BEING ON A TRIP...
...MAYBE I CAN SHAKE THIS WEIRD AWKWARD FEELING.
BLAST OFF!

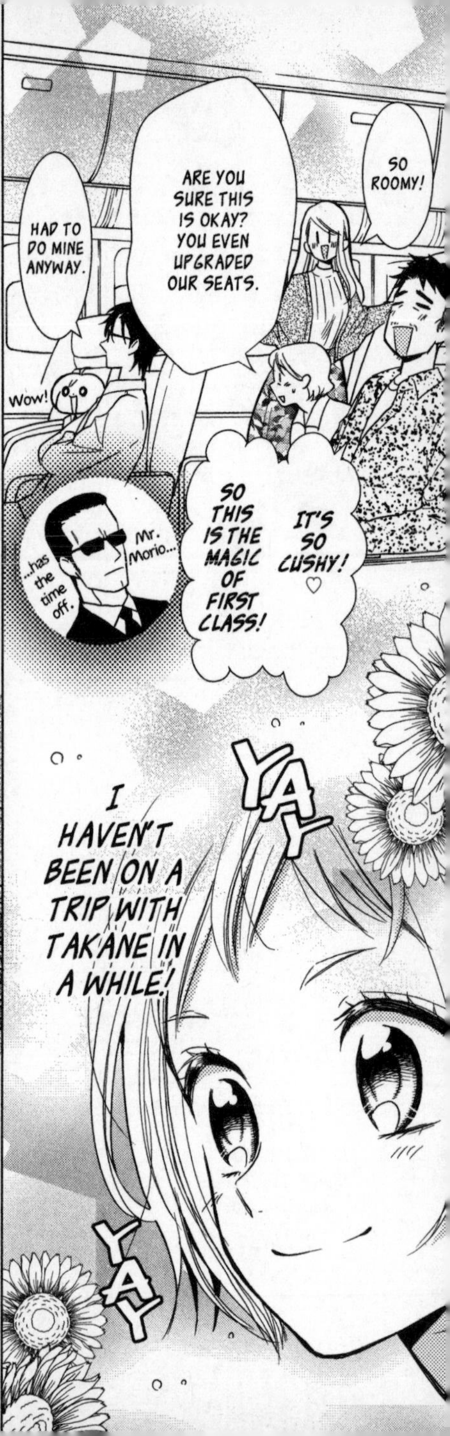
SO ROOMY!
ARE YOU SURE THIS IS OKAY? YOU EVEN UPGRADED OUR SEATS.
HAD TO DO MINE ANYWAY.
Wow!
IT'S SO CUSHY! ♡
SO THIS IS THE MAGIC OF FIRST CLASS!
Mr. Morio...
...has the time off.
YAY
I HAVEN'T BEEN ON A TRIP WITH TAKANE IN A WHILE!
YAY
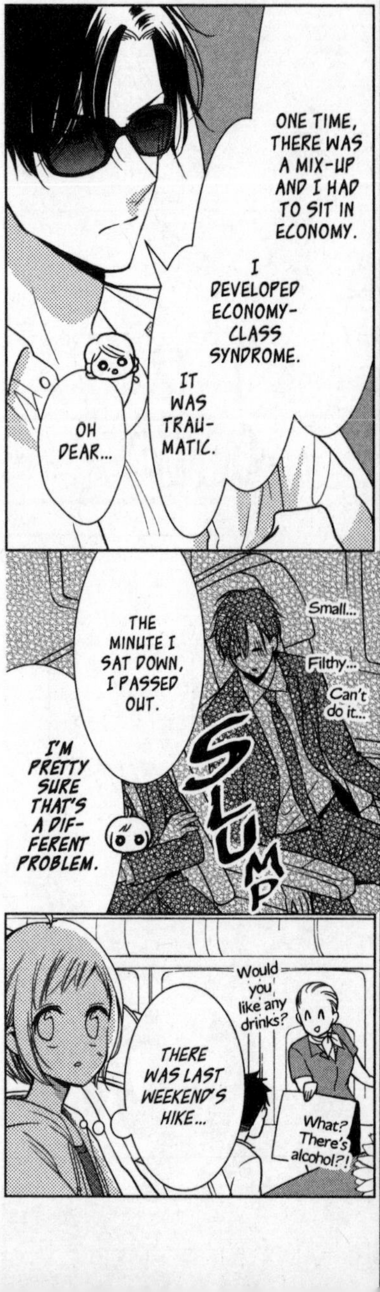
ONE TIME, THERE WAS A MIX-UP AND I HAD TO SIT IN ECONOMY.
I DEVELOPED ECONOMY-CLASS SYNDROME.
IT WAS TRAUMATIC.
OH DEAR...
THE MINUTE I SAT DOWN, I PASSED OUT.
Small...
Filthy...
Can't do it...
SLUMP
I'M PRETTY SURE THAT'S A DIFFERENT PROBLEM.
Would you like any drinks?
What? There's alcohol?!
THERE WAS LAST WEEKEND'S HIKE...

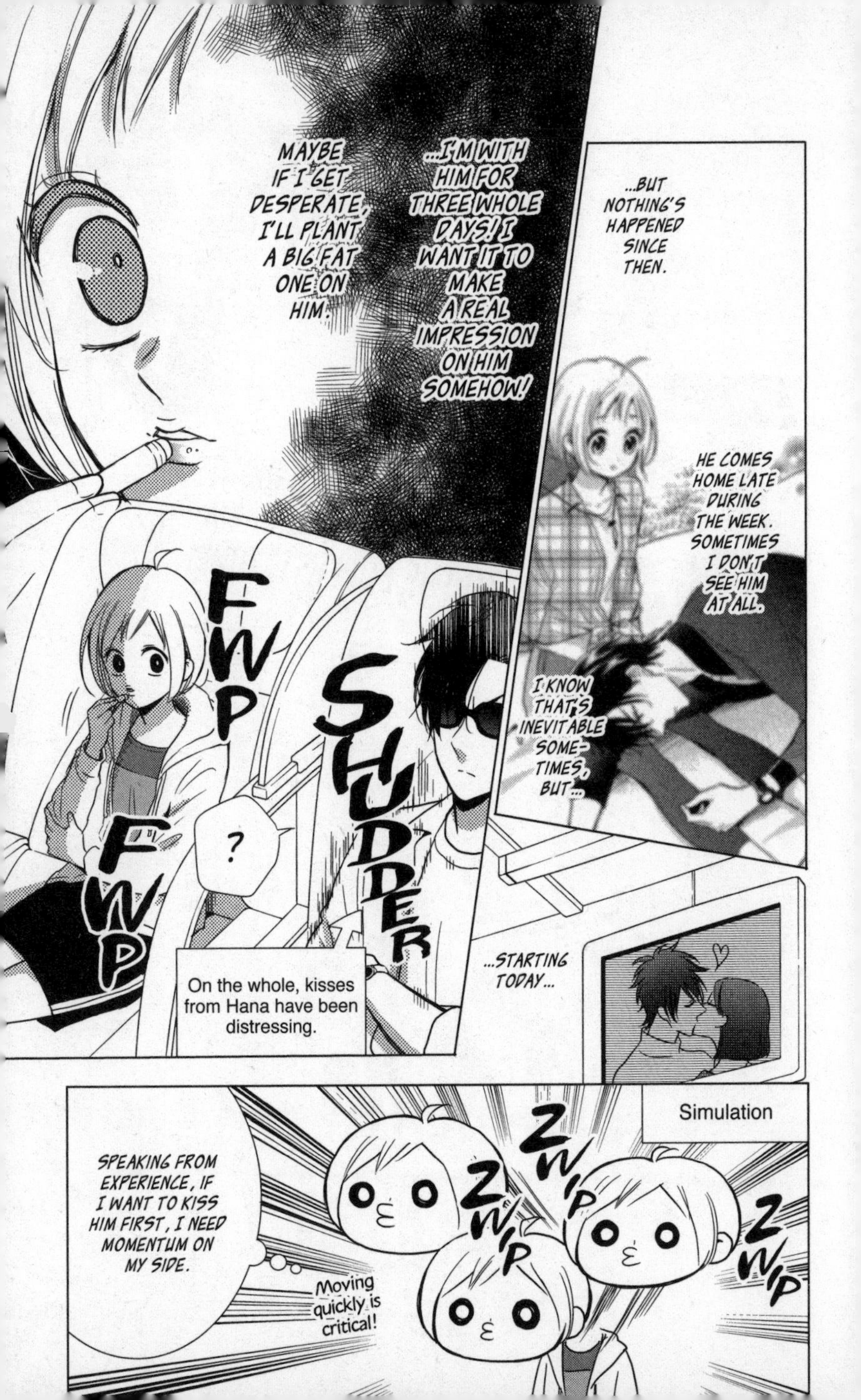
...BUT NOTHING'S HAPPENED SINCE THEN.
HE COMES HOME LATE DURING THE WEEK. SOMETIMES I DON'T SEE HIM AT ALL.
I KNOW THAT'S INEVITABLE SOME-TIMES, BUT...
...STARTING TODAY...
...I'M WITH HIM FOR THREE WHOLE DAYS! I WANT IT TO MAKE A REAL IMPRESSION ON HIM SOMEHOW!
MAYBE IF I GET DESPERATE, I'LL PLANT A BIG FAT ONE ON HIM.
SHUDDER
FWP
FWP
?
On the whole, kisses from Hana have been distressing.
Simulation
ZWIP
ZWIP
ZWIP
SPEAKING FROM EXPERIENCE, IF I WANT TO KISS HIM FIRST, I NEED MOMENTUM ON MY SIDE.
Moving quickly is critical!

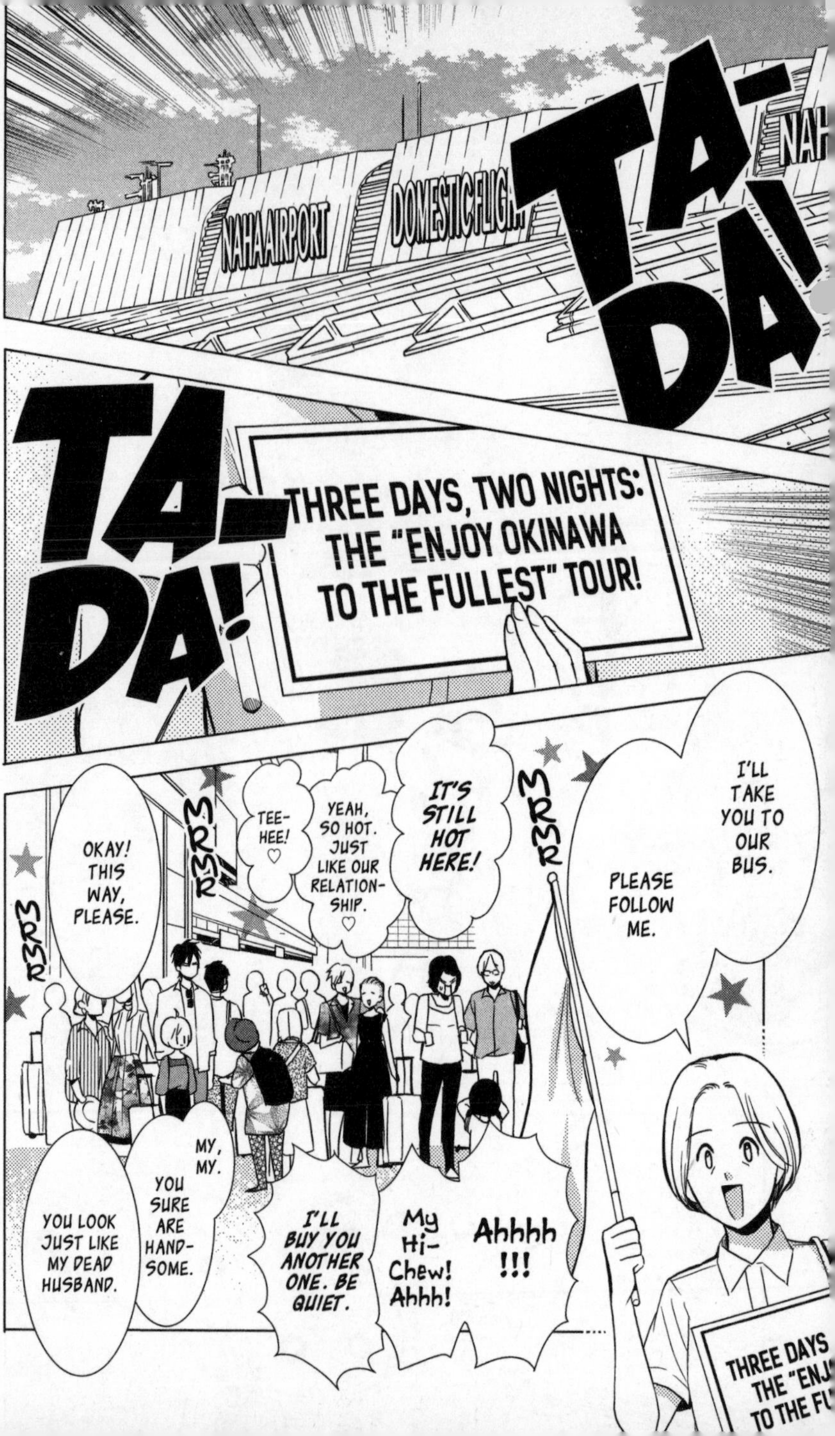
NAHA AIRPORT
DOMESTIC FLIGH...
TA-DA!
TA-DA!
THREE DAYS, TWO NIGHTS: THE "ENJOY OKINAWA TO THE FULLEST" TOUR!
I'LL TAKE YOU TO OUR BUS.
PLEASE FOLLOW ME.
MRMR
IT'S STILL HOT HERE!
YEAH, SO HOT. JUST LIKE OUR RELATIONSHIP. ♡
TEE-HEE! ♡
MRMR
OKAY! THIS WAY, PLEASE.
MRMR
Ahhhh!!!
My Hi-Chew! Ahhh!
I'LL BUY YOU ANOTHER ONE. BE QUIET.
MY, MY.
YOU SURE ARE HANDSOME.
YOU LOOK JUST LIKE MY DEAD HUSBAND.

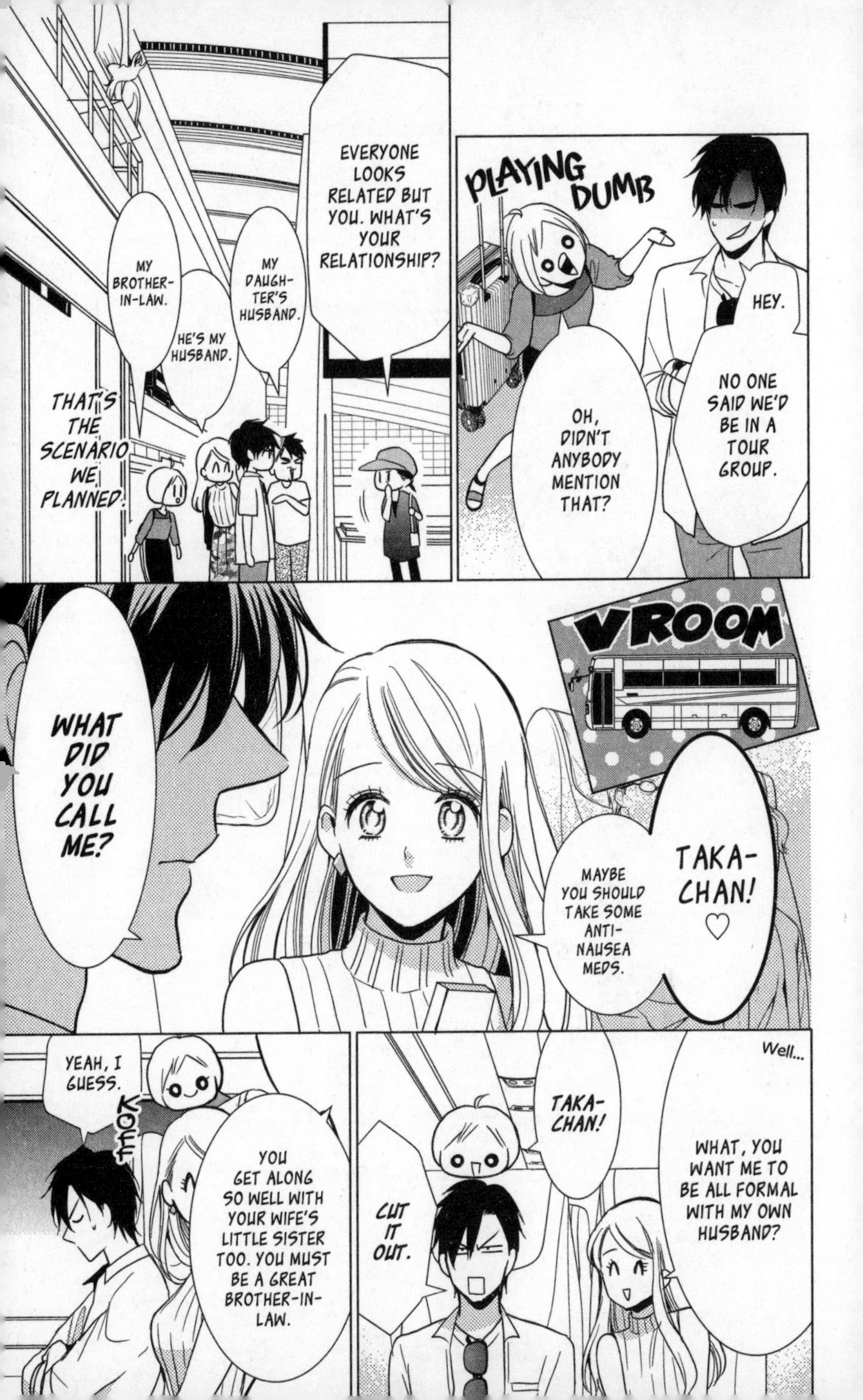
PLAYING DUMB
HEY.
NO ONE SAID WE'D BE IN A TOUR GROUP.
OH, DIDN'T ANYBODY MENTION THAT?
EVERYONE LOOKS RELATED BUT YOU. WHAT'S YOUR RELATIONSHIP?
MY DAUGHTER'S HUSBAND.
HE'S MY HUSBAND.
MY BROTHER-IN-LAW.
THAT'S THE SCENARIO WE PLANNED.
VROOM
TAKA-CHAN! ♡
MAYBE YOU SHOULD TAKE SOME ANTI-NAUSEA MEDS.
WHAT DID YOU CALL ME?
Well...
WHAT, YOU WANT ME TO BE ALL FORMAL WITH MY OWN HUSBAND?
TAKA-CHAN!
CUT IT OUT.
YOU GET ALONG SO WELL WITH YOUR WIFE'S LITTLE SISTER TOO. YOU MUST BE A GREAT BROTHER-IN-LAW.
KOFF
YEAH, I GUESS.

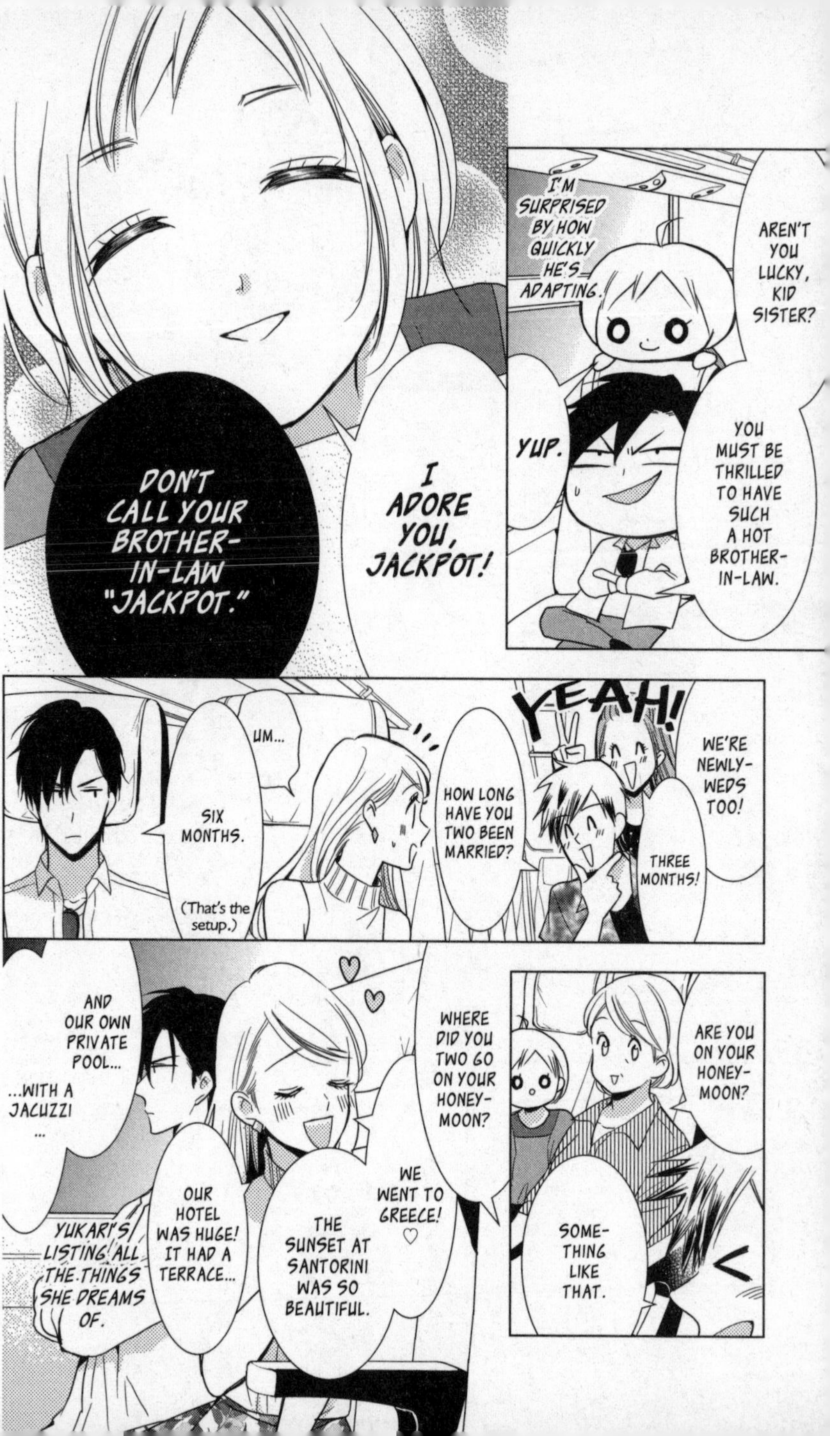
ARE YOU LUCKY, KID SISTER?
I'M SURPRISED BY HOW QUICKLY HE'S ADAPTING.
YOU MUST BE THRILLED TO HAVE SUCH A HOT BROTHER-IN-LAW.
YUP.
I ADORE YOU, JACKPOT!
DON'T CALL YOUR BROTHER-IN-LAW "JACKPOT."
WE'RE NEWLY-WEDS TOO!
YEAH!
THREE MONTHS!
HOW LONG HAVE YOU TWO BEEN MARRIED?
UM...
SIX MONTHS.
(That's the setup.)
ARE YOU ON YOUR HONEY-MOON?
SOME-THING LIKE THAT.
WHERE DID YOU TWO GO ON YOUR HONEY-MOON?
WE WENT TO GREECE! ♡
THE SUNSET AT SANTORINI WAS SO BEAUTIFUL.
OUR HOTEL WAS HUGE! IT HAD A TERRACE...
AND OUR OWN PRIVATE POOL...
...WITH A JACUZZI ...
YUKARI'S LISTING ALL THE THINGS SHE DREAMS OF.

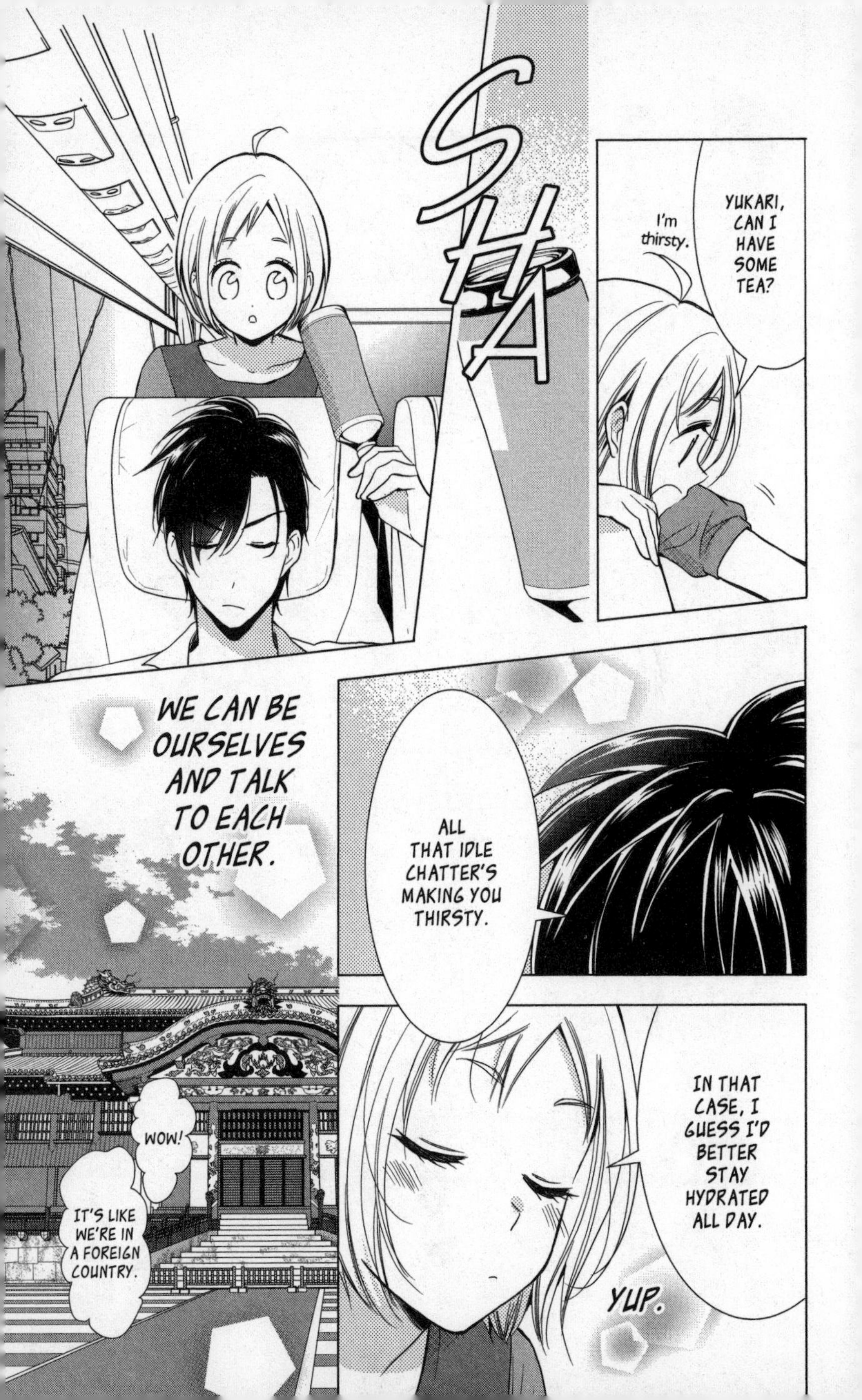
YUKARI, CAN I HAVE SOME TEA?
I'm thirsty.
SHA
ALL THAT IDLE CHATTER'S MAKING YOU THIRSTY.
IN THAT CASE, I GUESS I'D BETTER STAY HYDRATED ALL DAY.
YUP.
WE CAN BE OURSELVES AND TALK TO EACH OTHER.
WOW!
IT'S LIKE WE'RE IN A FOREIGN COUNTRY.

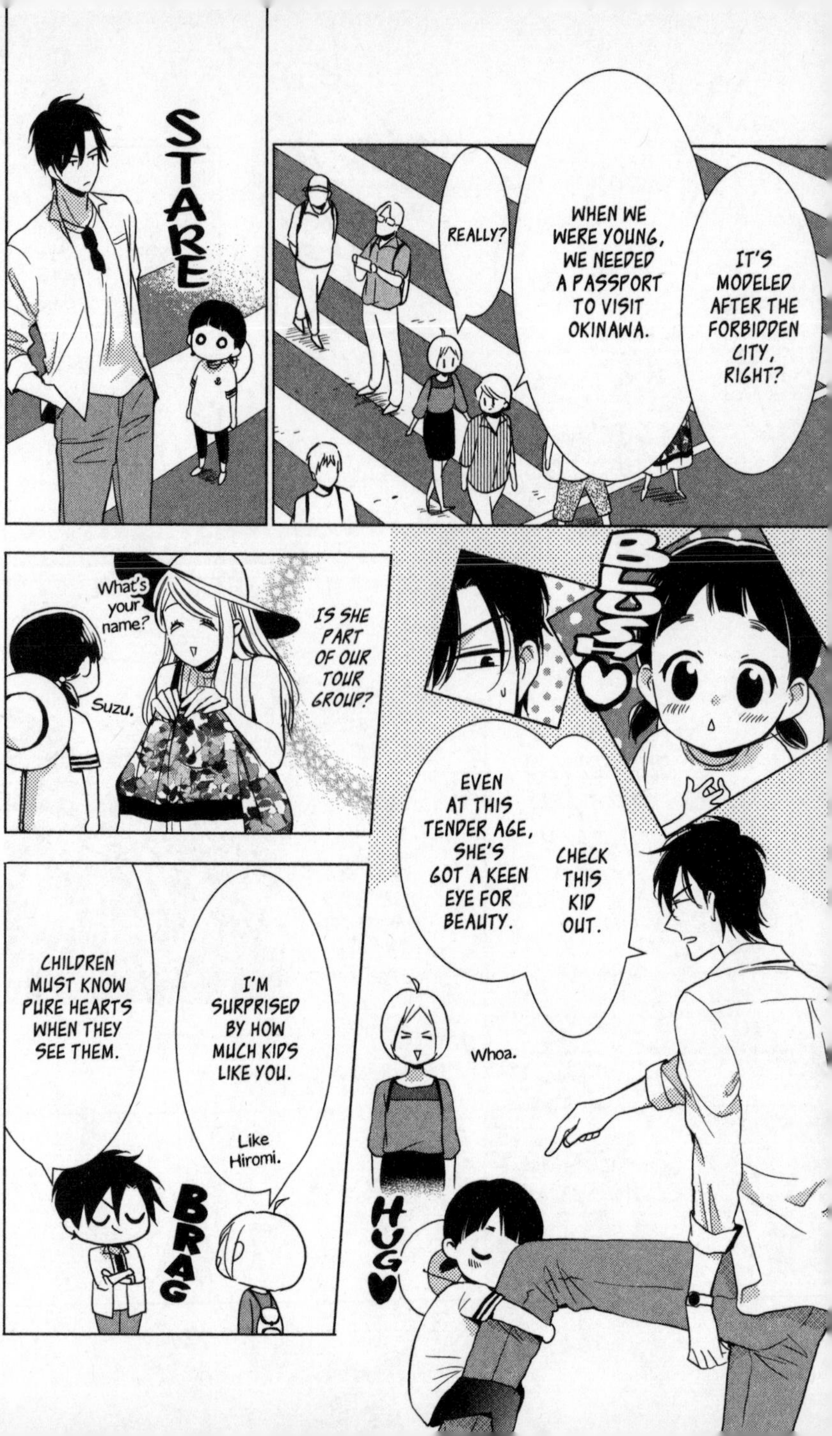
IT'S MODELED AFTER THE FORBIDDEN CITY, RIGHT?
WHEN WE WERE YOUNG, WE NEEDED A PASSPORT TO VISIT OKINAWA.
REALLY?
STARE
BLUSH
CHECK THIS KID OUT.
EVEN AT THIS TENDER AGE, SHE'S GOT A KEEN EYE FOR BEAUTY.
Whoa.
HUG♥
IS SHE PART OF OUR TOUR GROUP?
What's your name?
Suzu.
I'M SURPRISED BY HOW MUCH KIDS LIKE YOU.
Like Hiromi.
CHILDREN MUST KNOW PURE HEARTS WHEN THEY SEE THEM.
BRAG

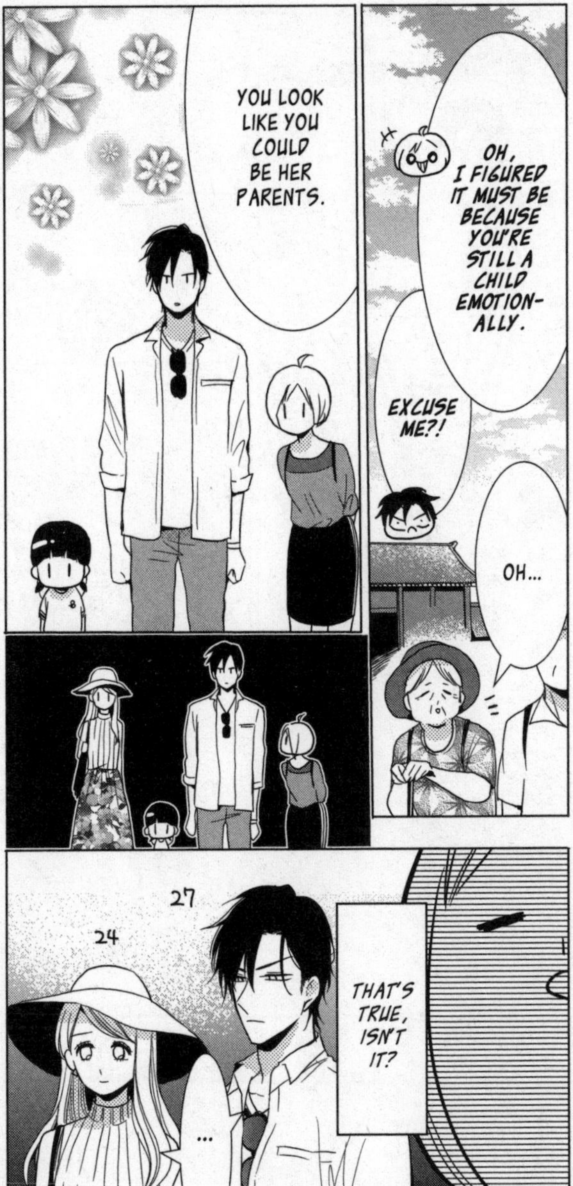
OH, I FIGURED IT MUST BE BECAUSE YOU'RE STILL A CHILD EMOTION-ALLY.
EXCUSE ME?!
OH...
YOU LOOK LIKE YOU COULD BE HER PARENTS.
27
24
THAT'S TRUE, ISN'T IT?
...

• Okinawa Chapter •

We're now starting the Okinawa chapter as a reward for Takane and Hana overcoming adversity to become a couple!

To write this arc, I looked through pictures of Okinawa from when I visited three years ago and checked ●*rubu* magazine, which also put me in a complete Okinawa mood.

I had a strong urge to eat sea grapes while writing this chapter. I'd initially planned just a normal family trip for them, but I thought it would be more interesting if I threw Takane into a tour group, and thus this scenario was born.

• The Table Tennis Scene •

I was unaware that in table tennis doubles, you alternate hits. Since I didn't know that, I just kinda went with the flow to write that scene.

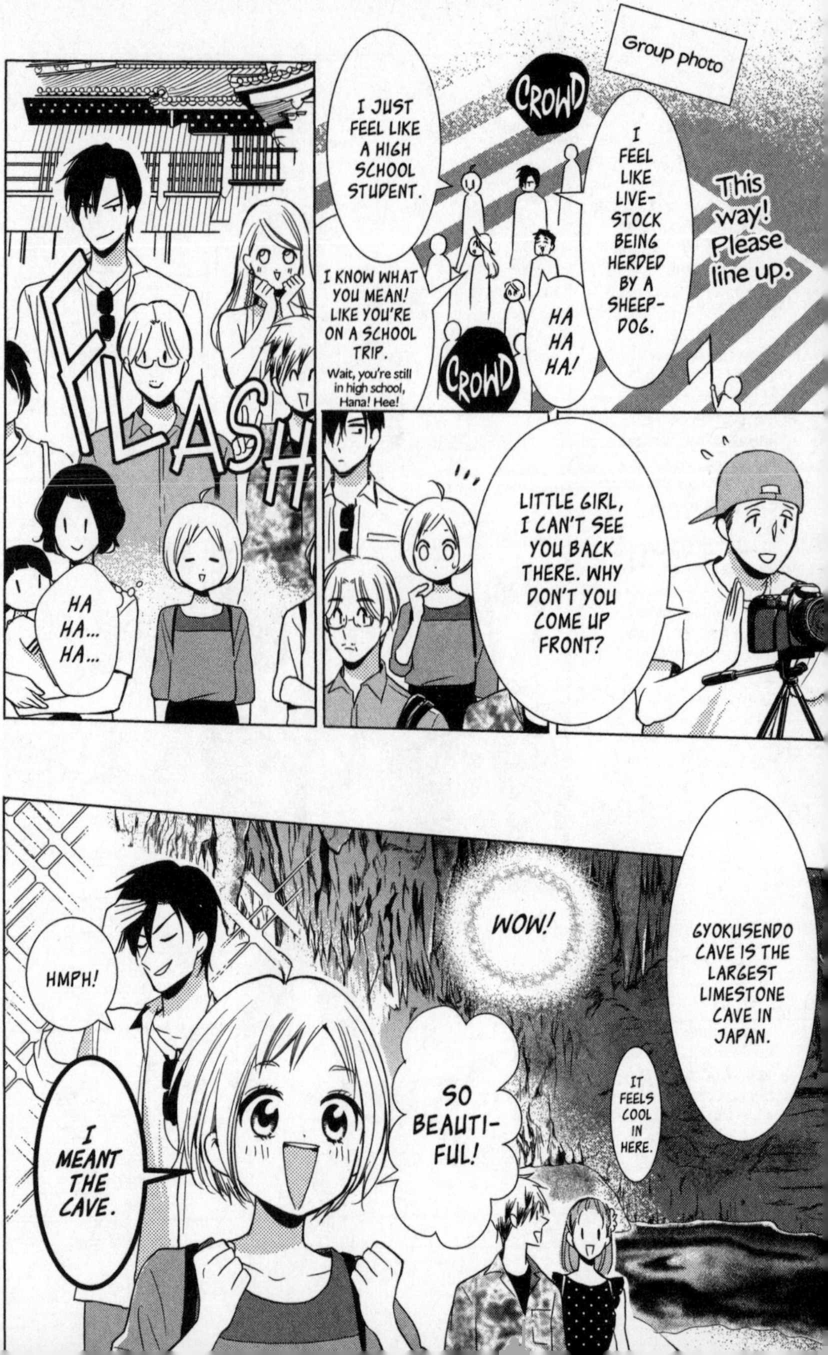

Group photo
This way! Please line up.
CROWD
I FEEL LIKE LIVE-STOCK BEING HERDED BY A SHEEP-DOG.
I JUST FEEL LIKE A HIGH SCHOOL STUDENT.
HA HA HA!
I KNOW WHAT YOU MEAN! LIKE YOU'RE ON A SCHOOL TRIP.
Wait, you're still in high school, Hana! Hee!
CROWD
LITTLE GIRL, I CAN'T SEE YOU BACK THERE. WHY DON'T YOU COME UP FRONT?
FLASH
HA HA... HA...
GYOKUSENDO CAVE IS THE LARGEST LIMESTONE CAVE IN JAPAN.
WOW!
IT FEELS COOL IN HERE.
SO BEAUTI-FUL!
HMPH!
I MEANT THE CAVE.

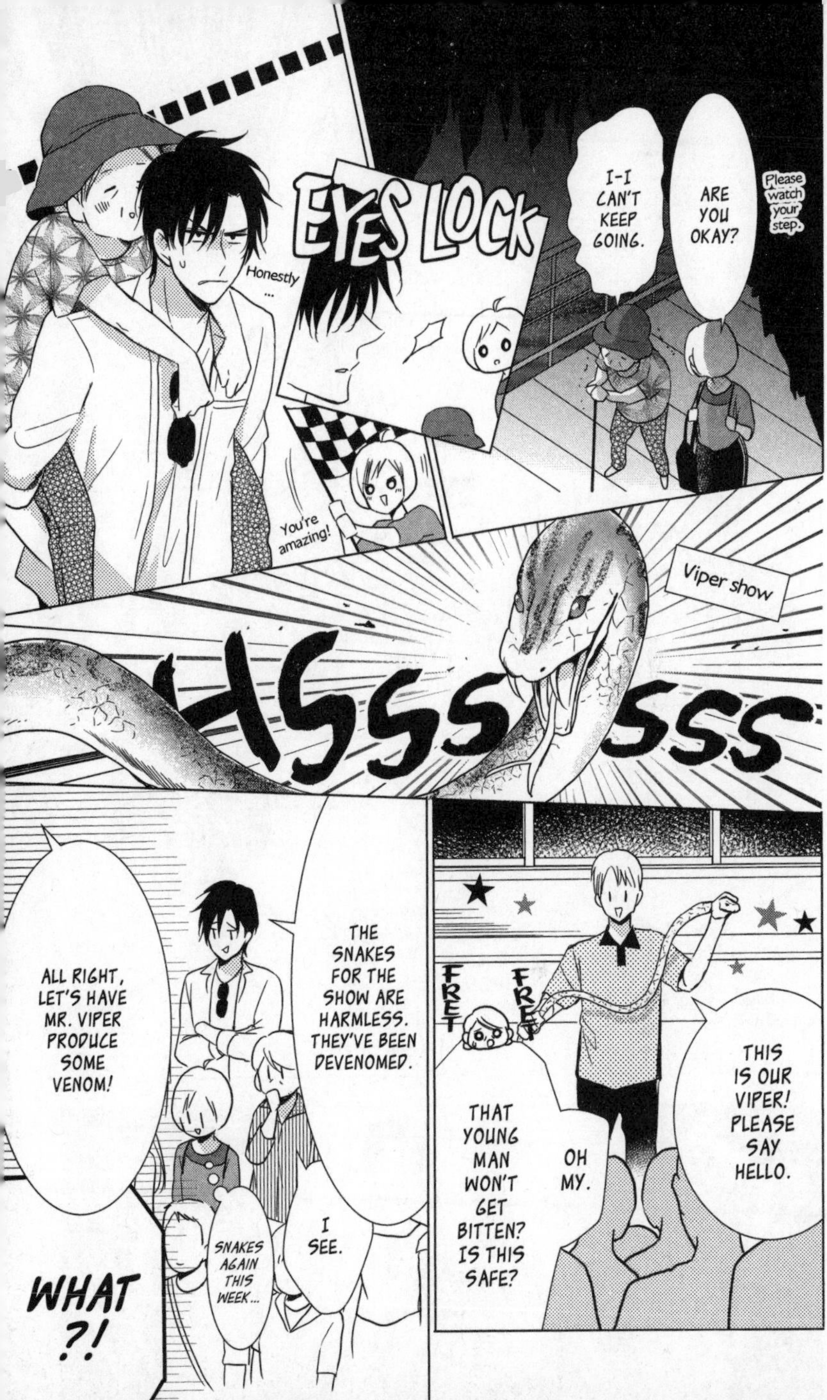
Please watch your step.
ARE YOU OKAY?
I-I CAN'T KEEP GOING.
EYES LOCK
You're amazing!
Honestly...
Viper show
HSSSSSSS
THIS IS OUR VIPER! PLEASE SAY HELLO.
FRET FRET
OH MY.
THAT YOUNG MAN WON'T GET BITTEN? IS THIS SAFE?
THE SNAKES FOR THE SHOW ARE HARMLESS. THEY'VE BEEN DEVENOMED.
ALL RIGHT, LET'S HAVE MR. VIPER PRODUCE SOME VENOM!
I SEE.
SNAKES AGAIN THIS WEEK...
WHAT?!

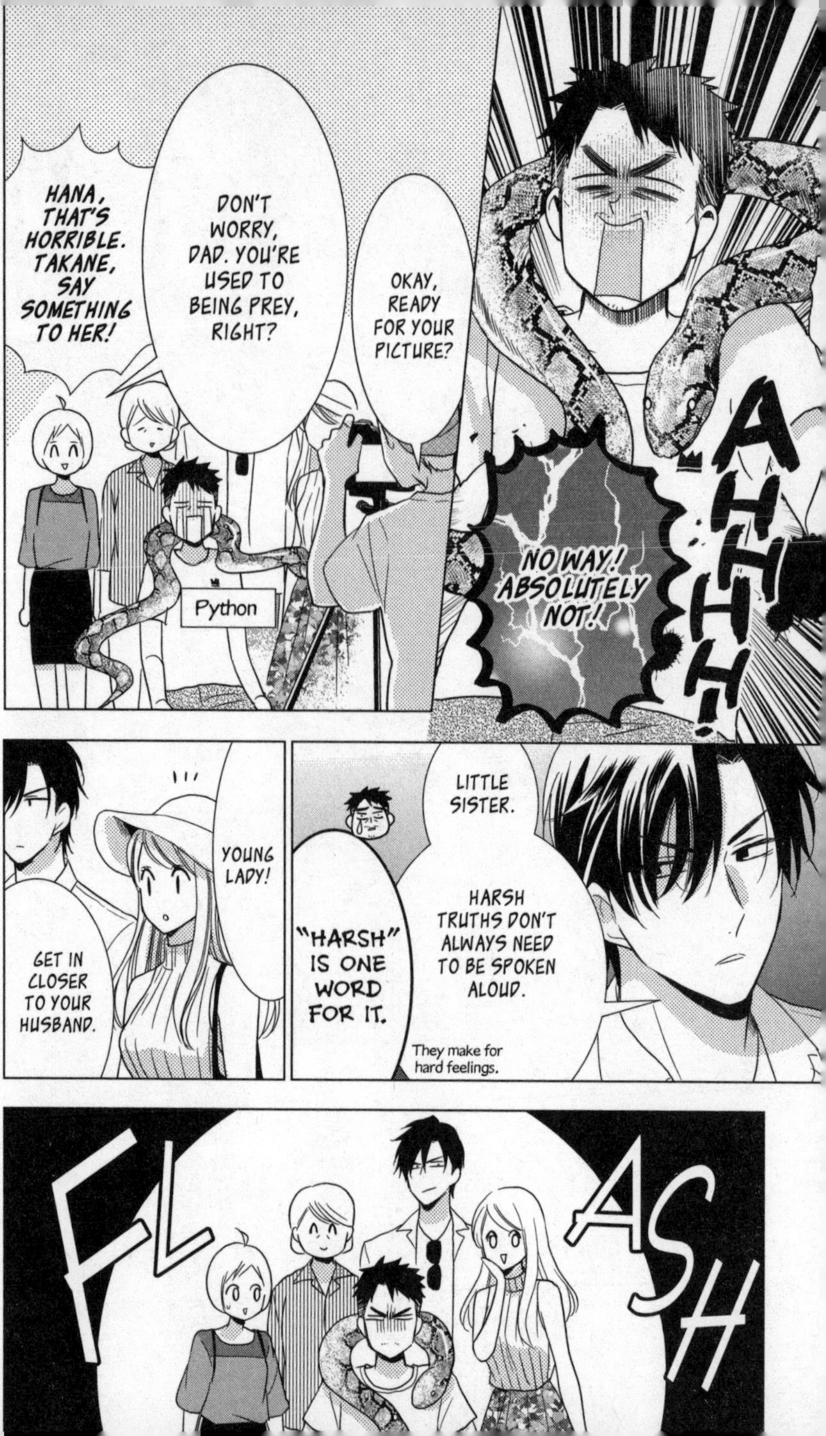
AHHHH!
NO WAY! ABSOLUTELY NOT!
OKAY, READY FOR YOUR PICTURE?
DON'T WORRY, DAD. YOU'RE USED TO BEING PREY, RIGHT?
HANA, THAT'S HORRIBLE. TAKANE, SAY SOMETHING TO HER!
Python
LITTLE SISTER.
HARSH TRUTHS DON'T ALWAYS NEED TO BE SPOKEN ALOUD.
"HARSH" IS ONE WORD FOR IT.
They make for hard feelings.
YOUNG LADY!
GET IN CLOSER TO YOUR HUSBAND.
FLASH

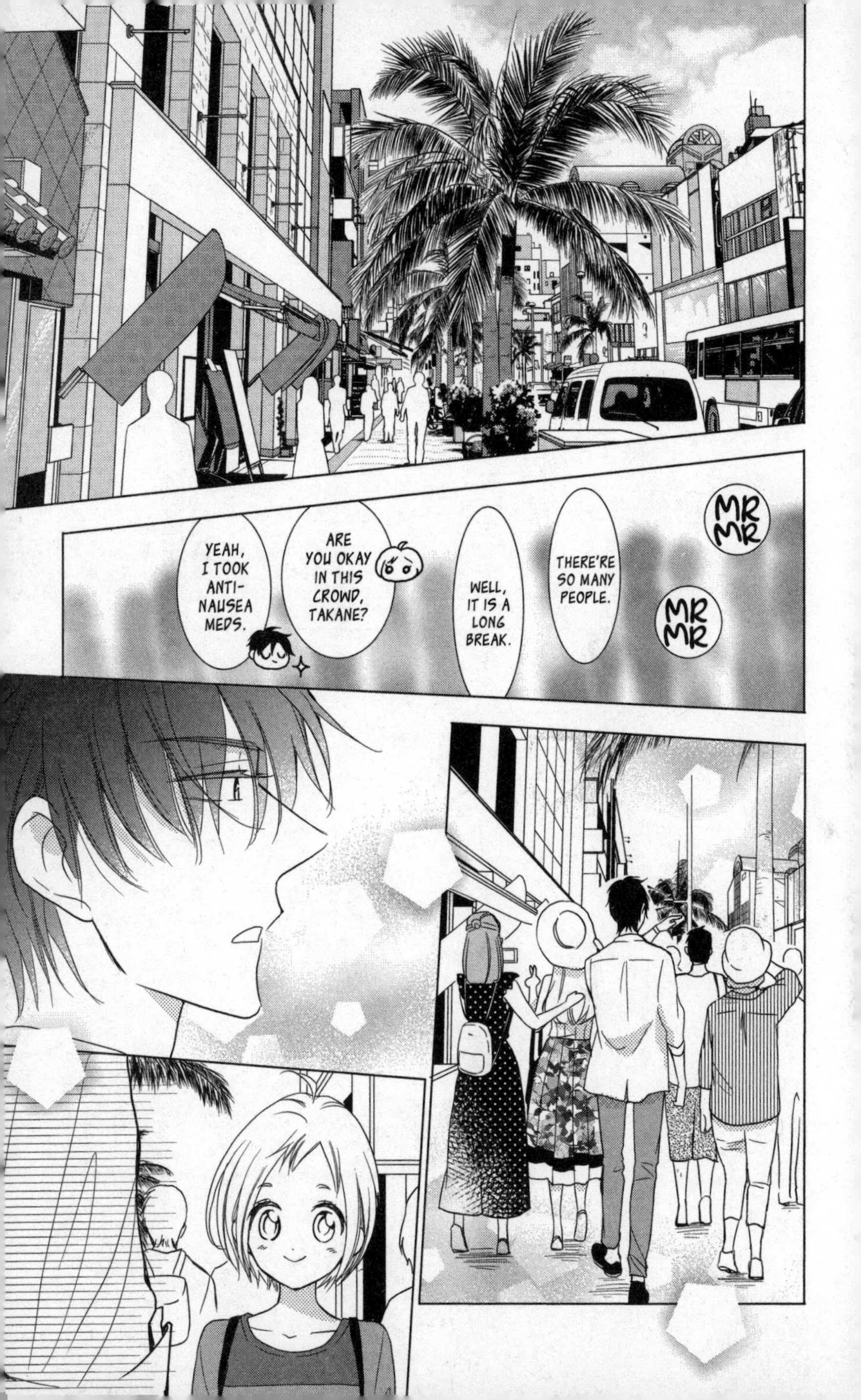
MR MR
MR MR
THERE'RE SO MANY PEOPLE.
WELL, IT IS A LONG BREAK.
ARE YOU OKAY IN THIS CROWD, TAKANE?
YEAH, I TOOK ANTI-NAUSEA MEDS.

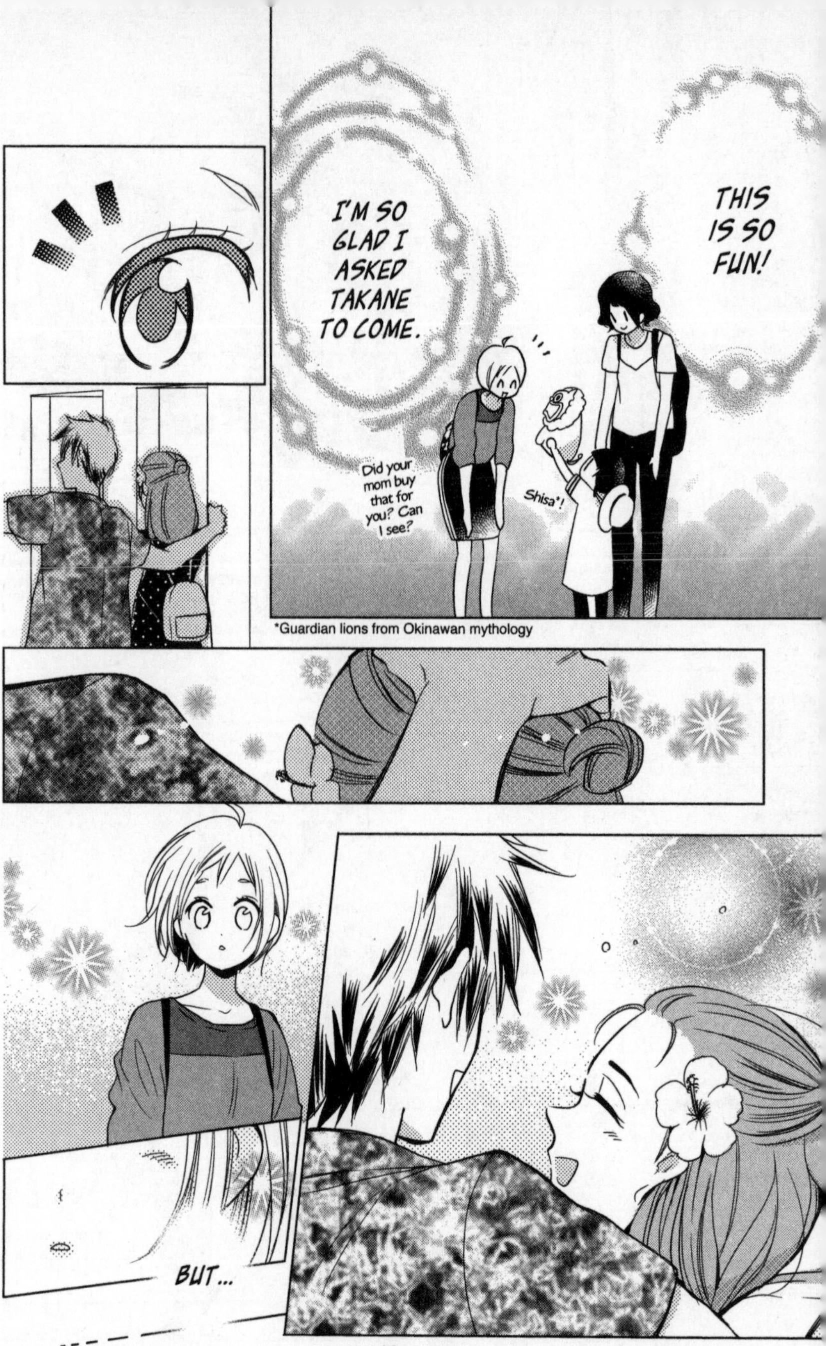
THIS IS SO FUN!
I'M SO GLAD I ASKED TAKANE TO COME.
Shisa*!
Did your mom buy that for you? Can I see?
BUT...
*Guardian lions from Okinawan mythology

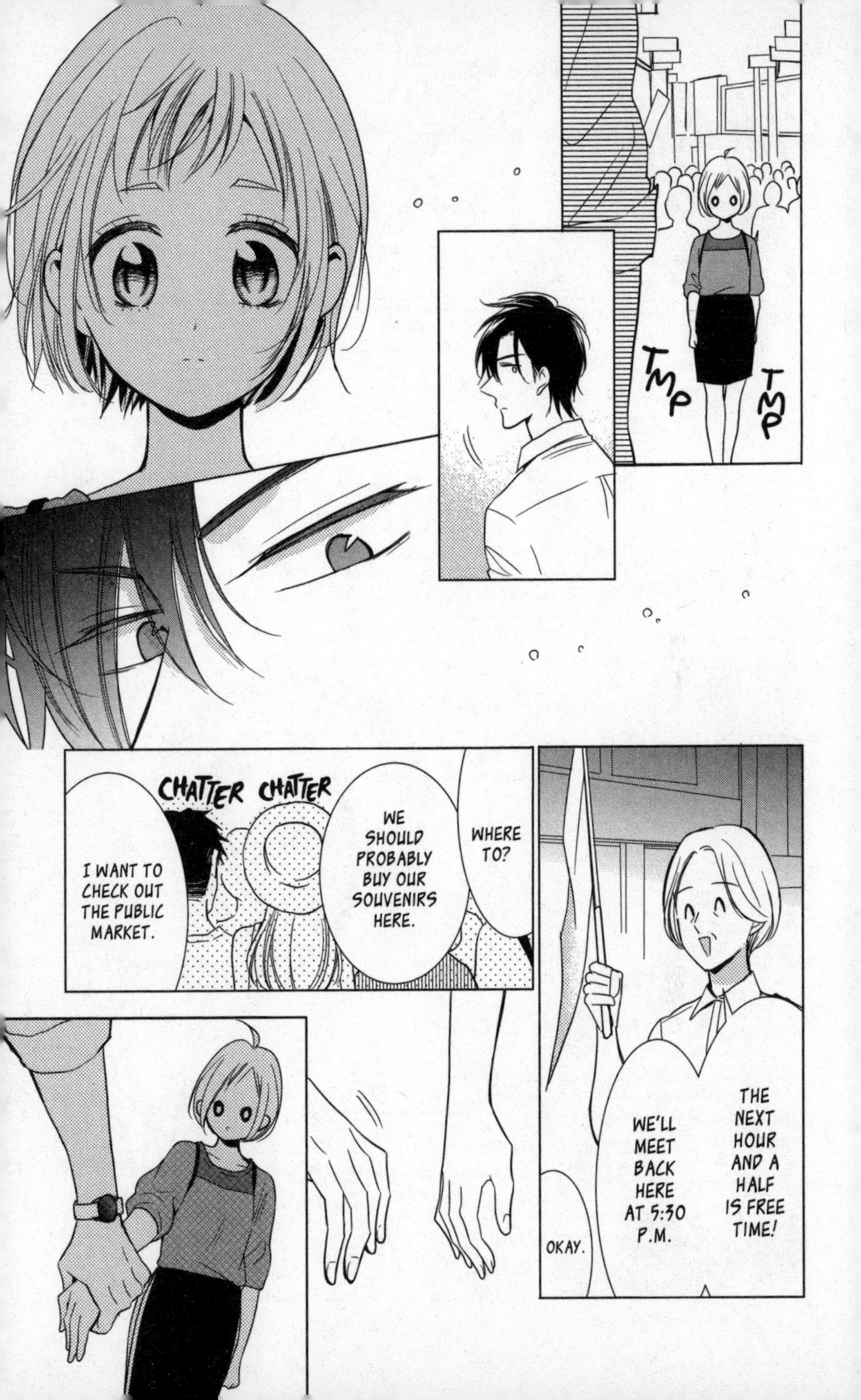
TMP
TMP
THE NEXT HOUR AND A HALF IS FREE TIME!
WE'LL MEET BACK HERE AT 5:30 P.M.
OKAY.
WHERE TO?
WE SHOULD PROBABLY BUY OUR SOUVENIRS HERE.
CHATTER CHATTER
I WANT TO CHECK OUT THE PUBLIC MARKET.

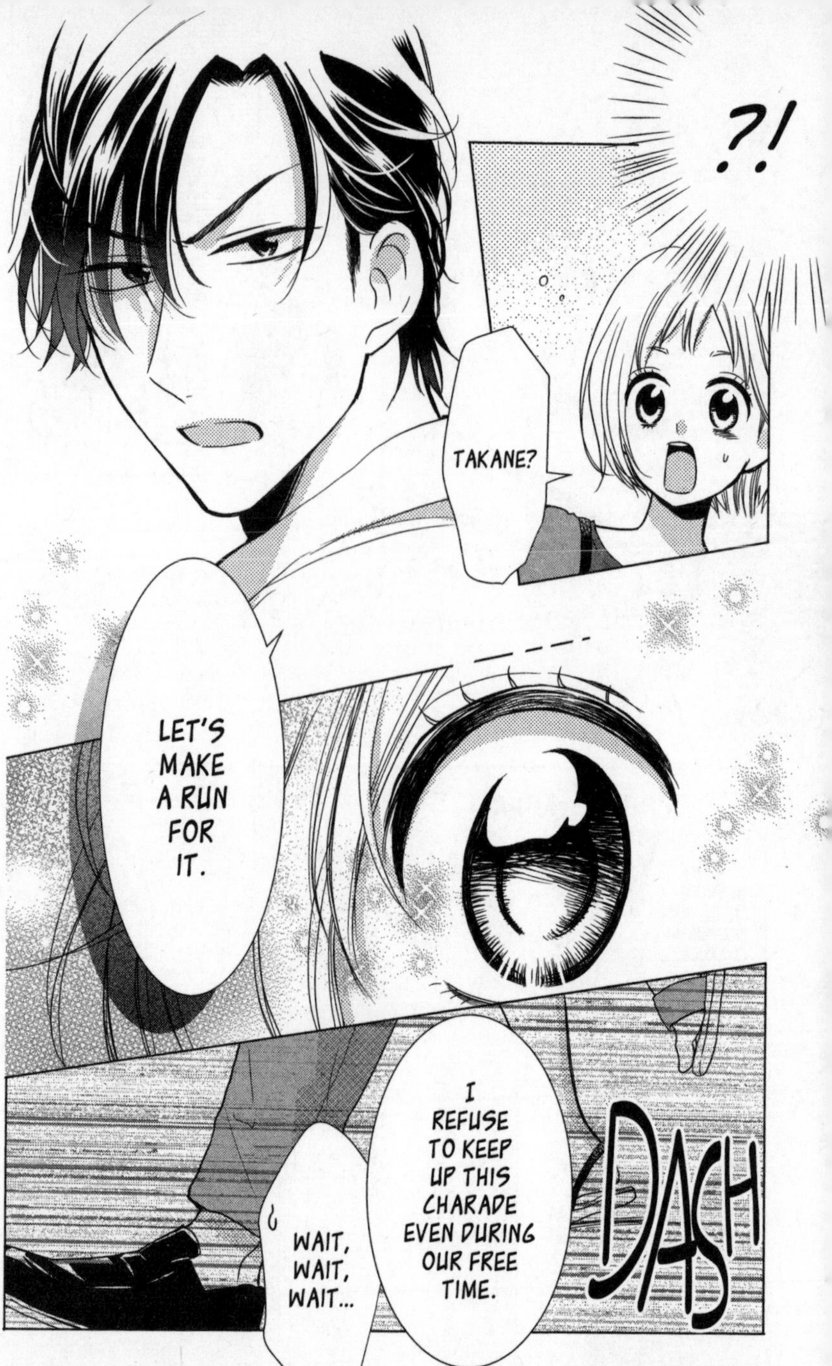
?!
TAKANE?
LET'S MAKE A RUN FOR IT.
DASH
I REFUSE TO KEEP UP THIS CHARADE EVEN DURING OUR FREE TIME.
WAIT, WAIT, WAIT...

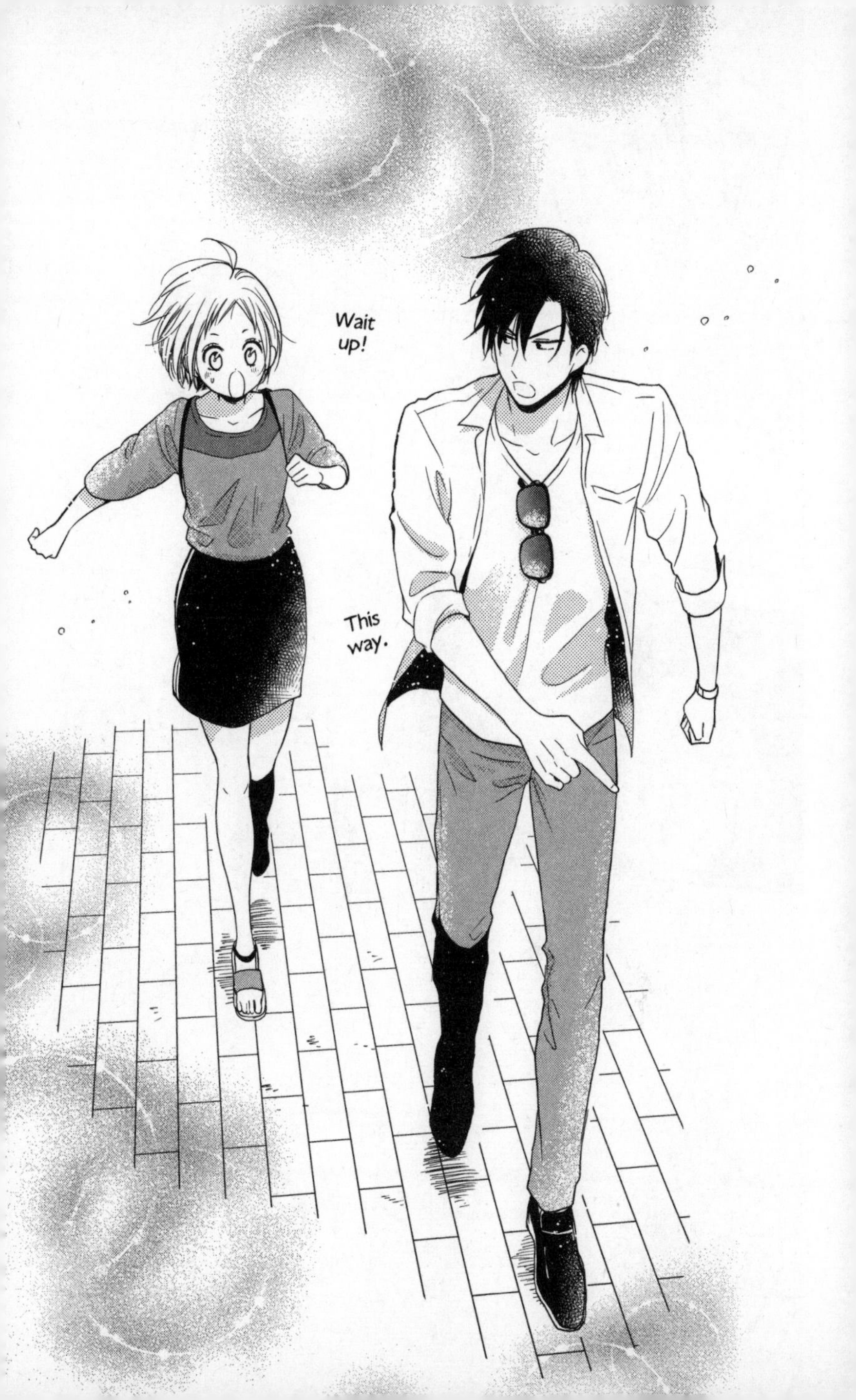
Wait up!
This way.

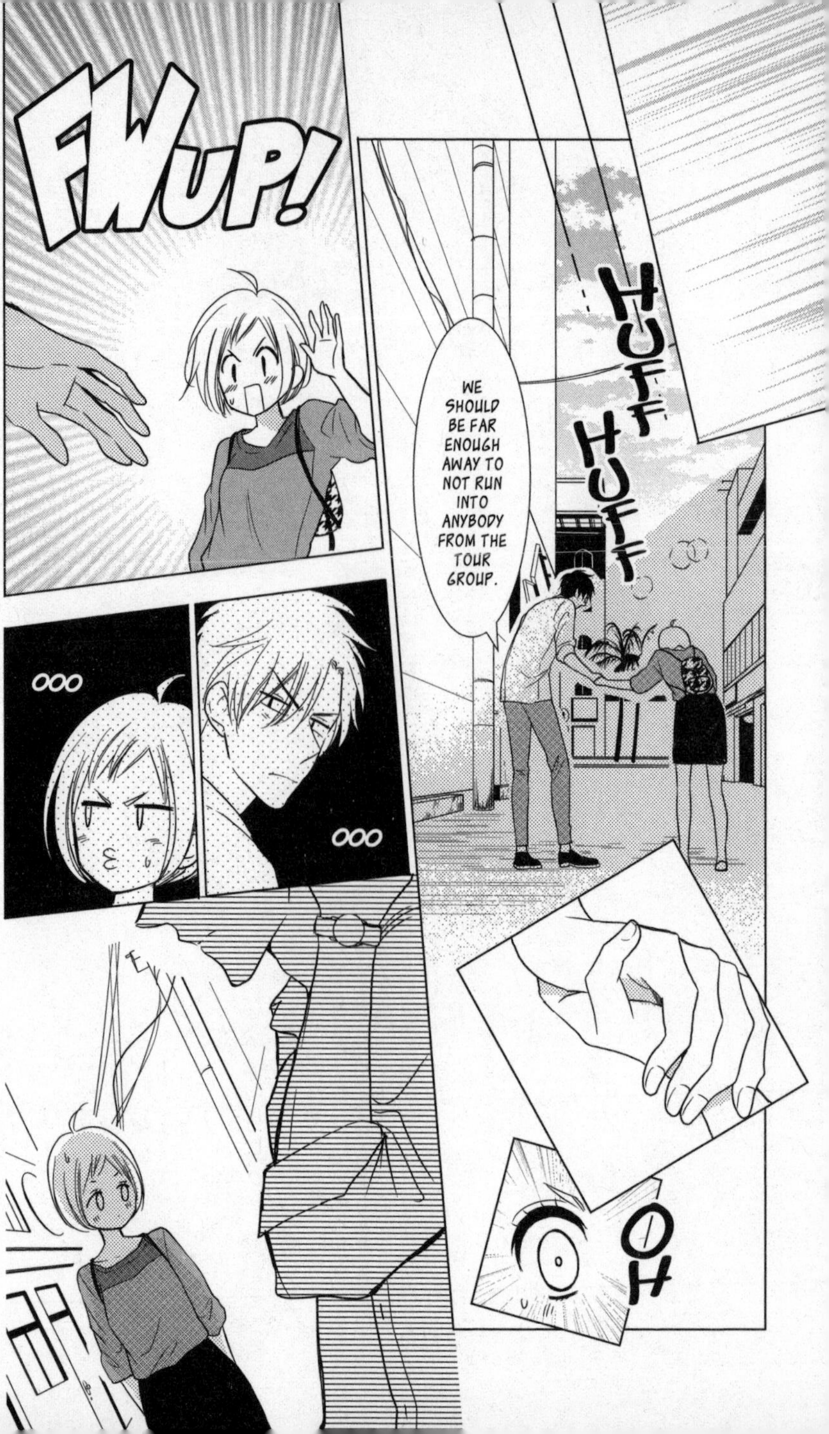
HUFF HUFF
WE SHOULD BE FAR ENOUGH AWAY TO NOT RUN INTO ANYBODY FROM THE TOUR GROUP.
OH
FWUP!
ooo
ooo

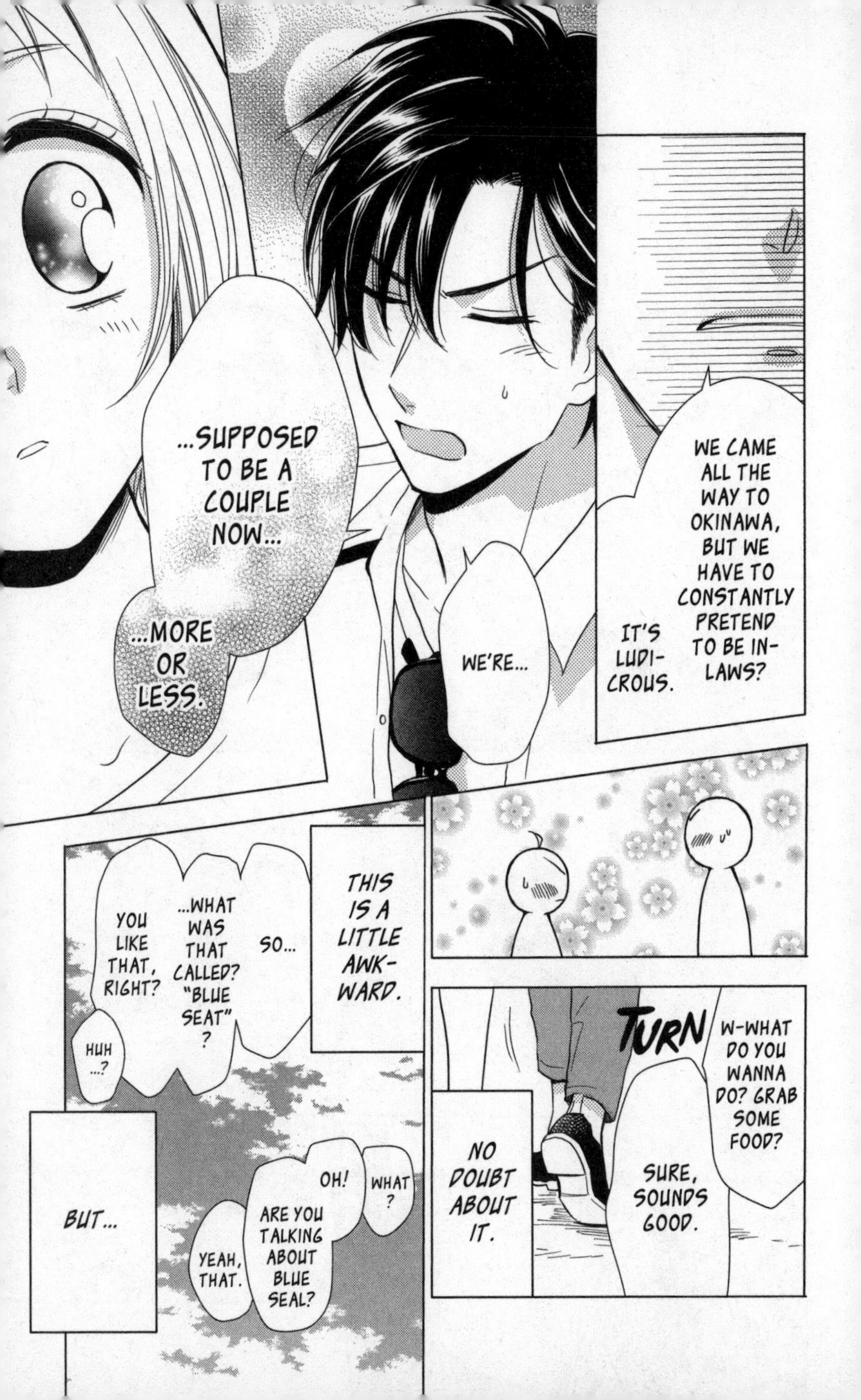
WE CAME ALL THE WAY TO OKINAWA, BUT WE HAVE TO CONSTANTLY PRETEND TO BE IN-LAWS?
IT'S LUDICROUS.
WE'RE...
...SUPPOSED TO BE A COUPLE NOW...
...MORE OR LESS.
TURN
W-WHAT DO YOU WANNA DO? GRAB SOME FOOD?
SURE, SOUNDS GOOD.
NO DOUBT ABOUT IT.
THIS IS A LITTLE AWKWARD.
SO...
...WHAT WAS THAT CALLED? "BLUE SEAT"?
YOU LIKE THAT, RIGHT?
HUH...?
WHAT?
OH!
ARE YOU TALKING ABOUT BLUE SEAL?
YEAH, THAT.
BUT...

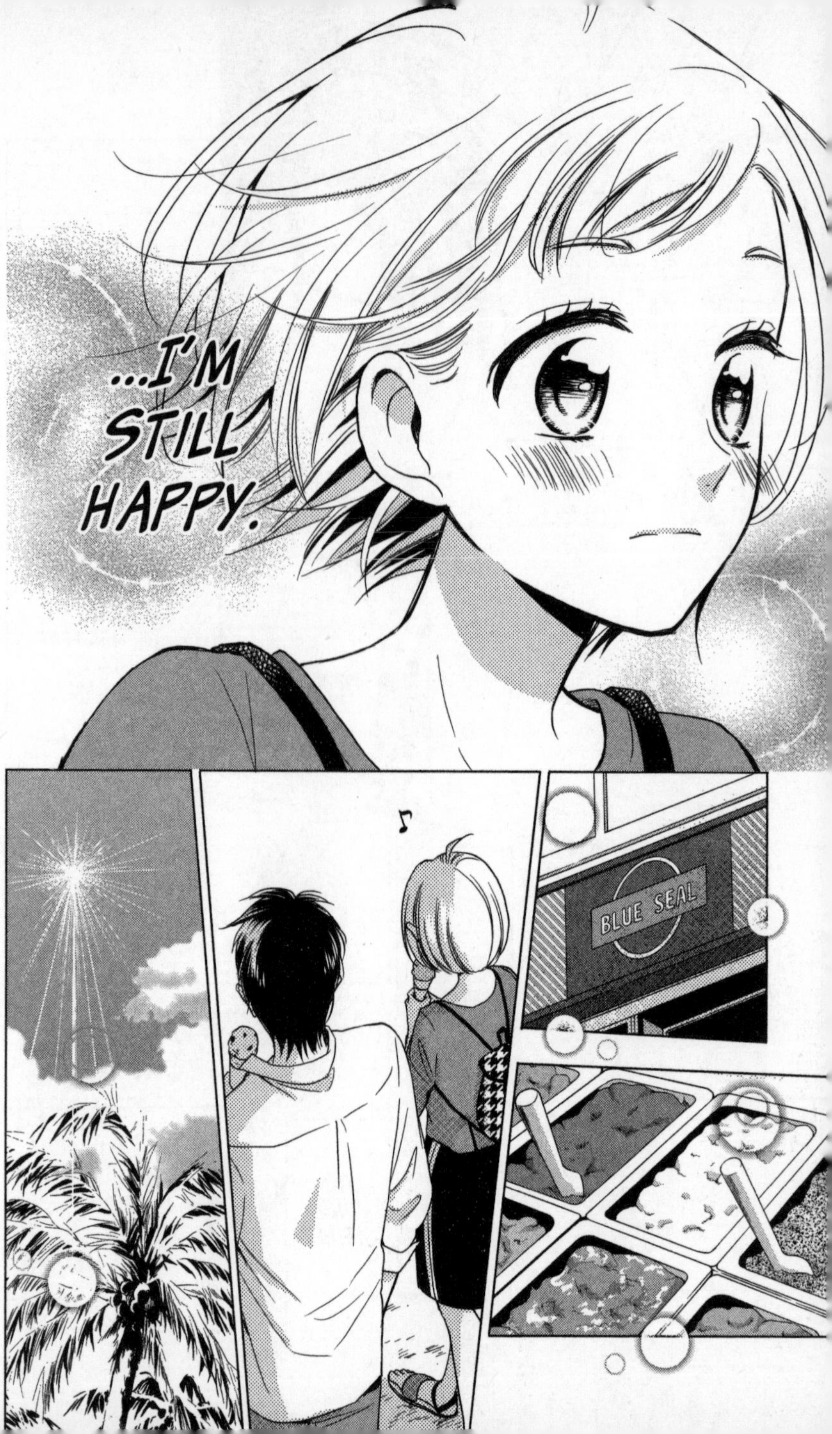

...I'M STILL HAPPY.
♪
BLUE SEAL

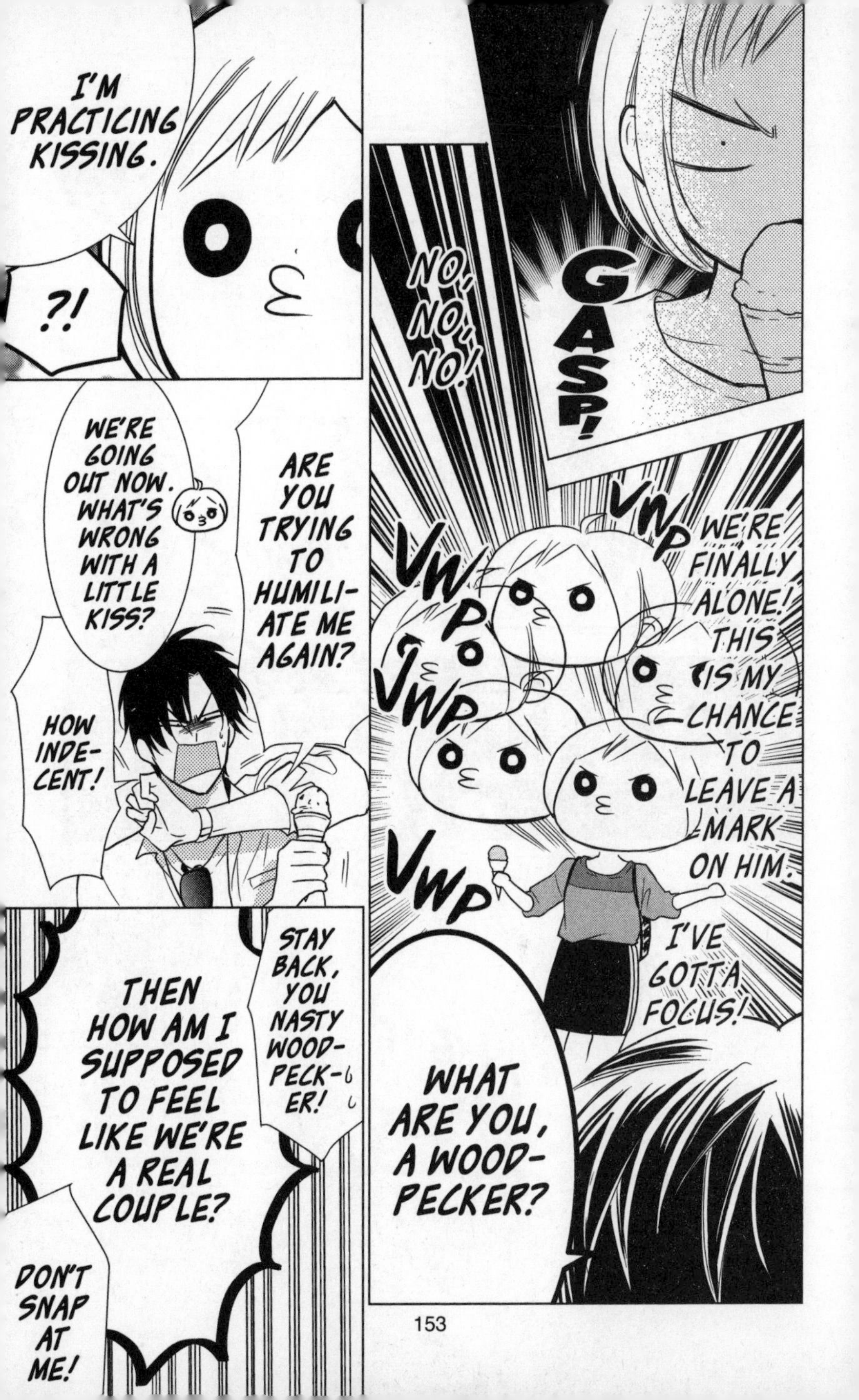
NO, NO, NO!
GASP!
VWP
VWP
VWP
VWP
WE'RE FINALLY ALONE! THIS IS MY CHANCE TO LEAVE A MARK ON HIM.
I'VE GOTTA FOCUS!
WHAT ARE YOU, A WOODPECKER?
I'M PRACTICING KISSING.
?!
ARE YOU TRYING TO HUMILIATE ME AGAIN?
WE'RE GOING OUT NOW. WHAT'S WRONG WITH A LITTLE KISS?
HOW INDECENT!
STAY BACK, YOU NASTY WOODPECKER!
THEN HOW AM I SUPPOSED TO FEEL LIKE WE'RE A REAL COUPLE?
DON'T SNAP AT ME!

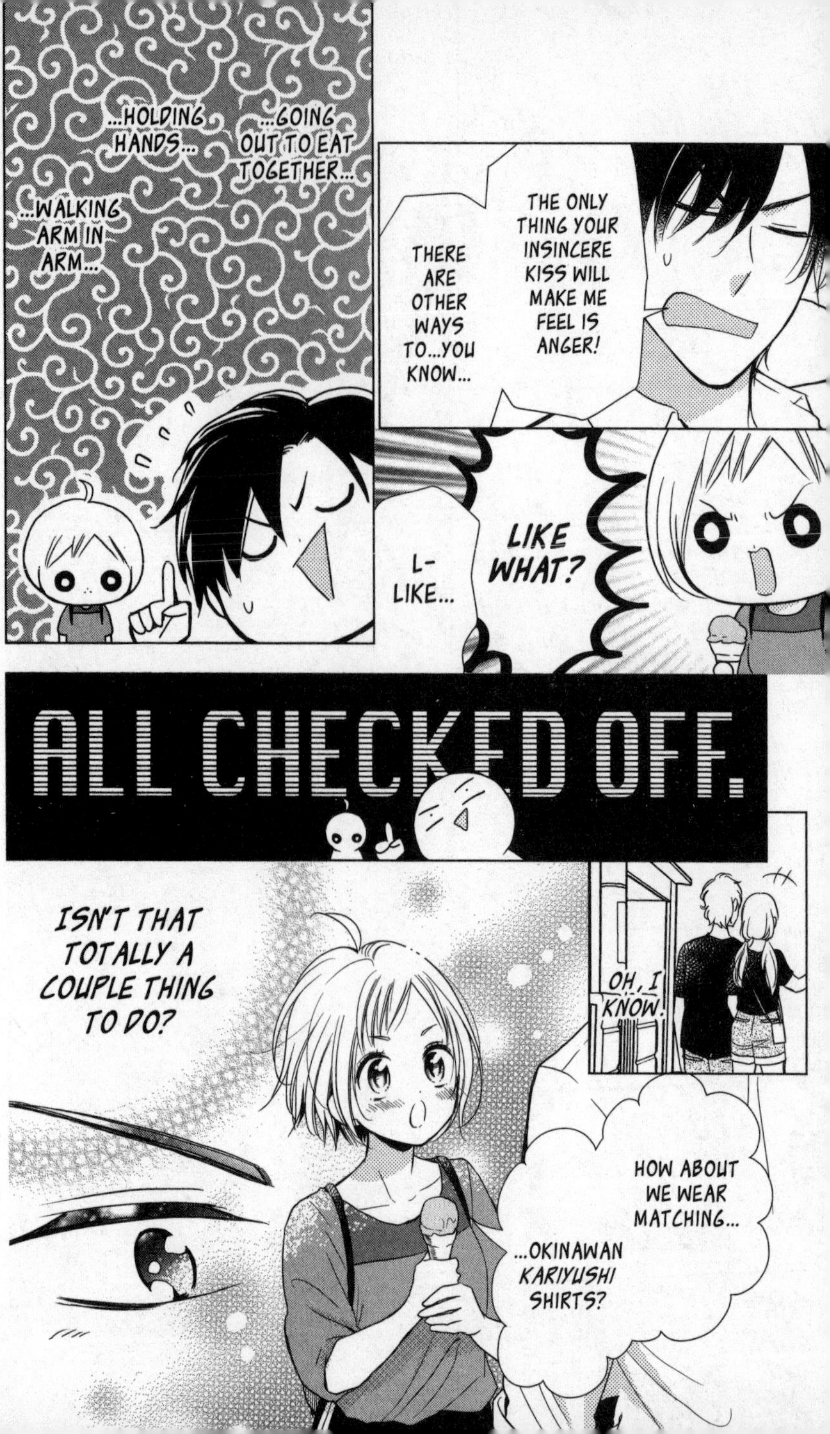
THE ONLY THING YOUR INSINCERE KISS WILL MAKE ME FEEL IS ANGER!
THERE ARE OTHER WAYS TO...YOU KNOW...
LIKE WHAT?
L- LIKE...
...GOING OUT TO EAT TOGETHER...
...HOLDING HANDS...
...WALKING ARM IN ARM...
ALL CHECKED OFF.
OH, I KNOW.
HOW ABOUT WE WEAR MATCHING...
...OKINAWAN KARIYUSHI SHIRTS?
ISN'T THAT TOTALLY A COUPLE THING TO DO?

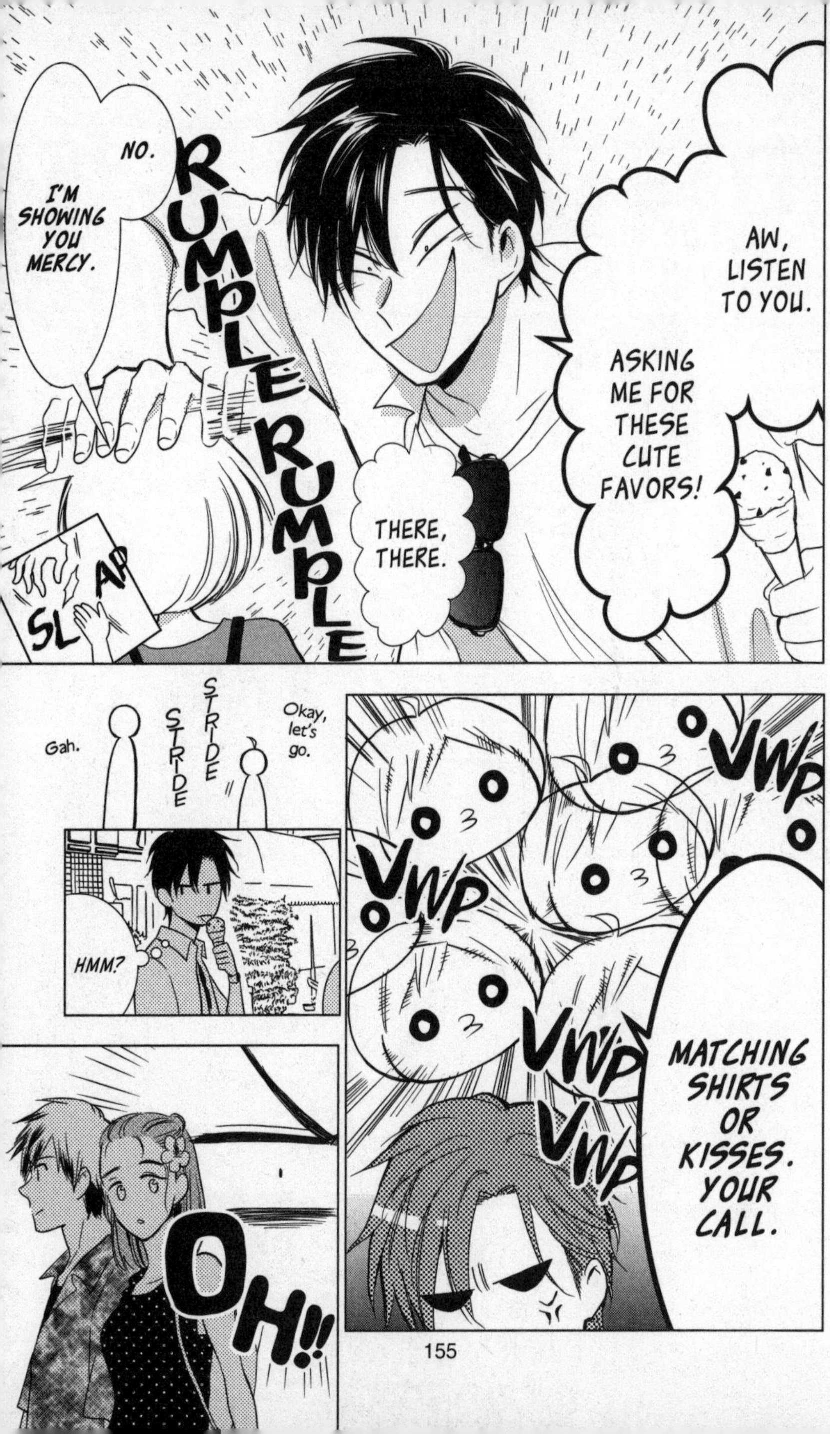
AW, LISTEN TO YOU.
ASKING ME FOR THESE CUTE FAVORS!
THERE, THERE.
RUMPLE RUMPLE
NO.
I'M SHOWING YOU MERCY.
SLAP
VWP
VWP
VWP
VWP
MATCHING SHIRTS OR KISSES. YOUR CALL.
Okay, let's go.
STRIDE STRIDE
Gah.
HMM?
OH!!

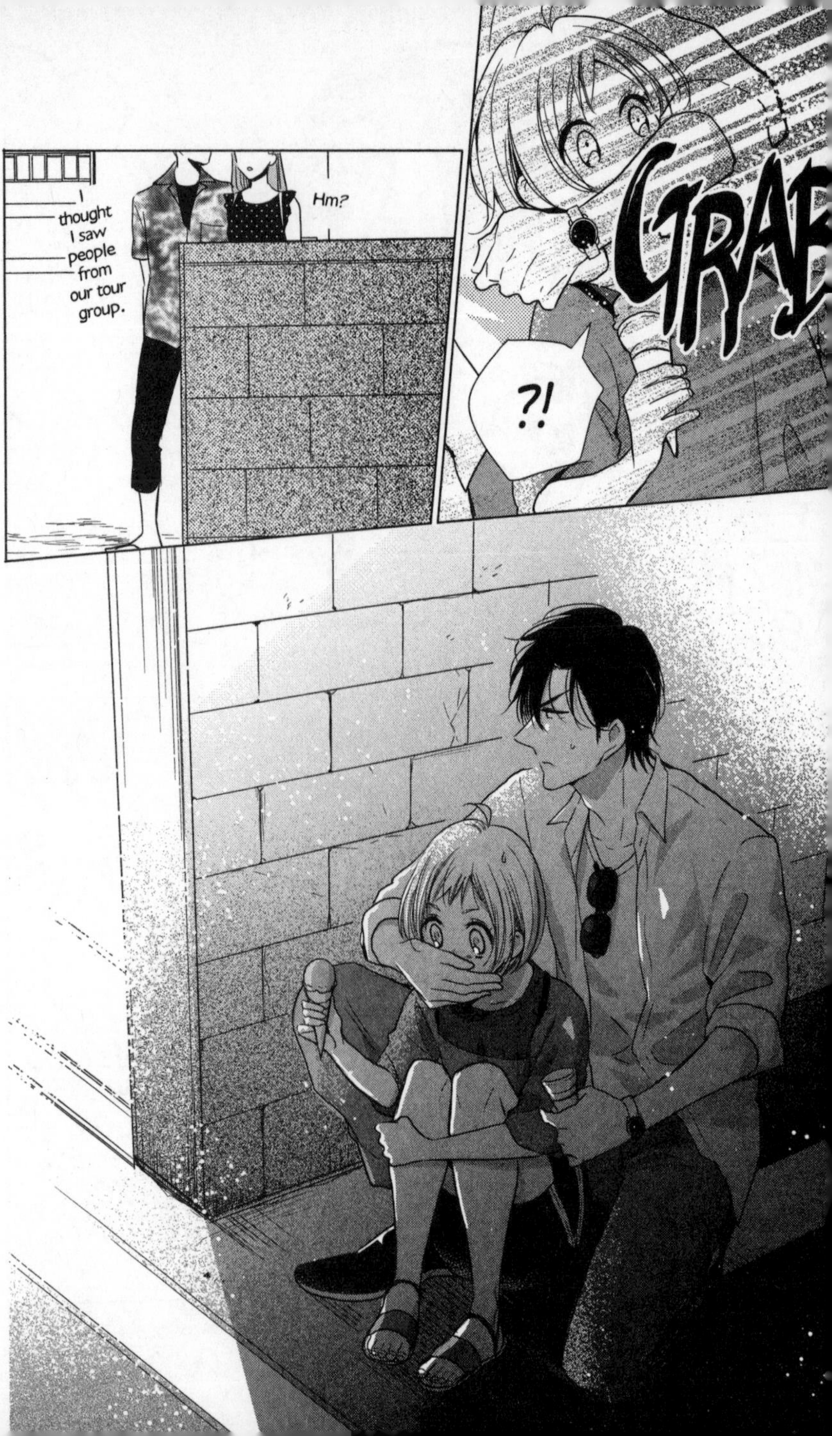
GRAB
?!
Hm?
I thought I saw people from our tour group.

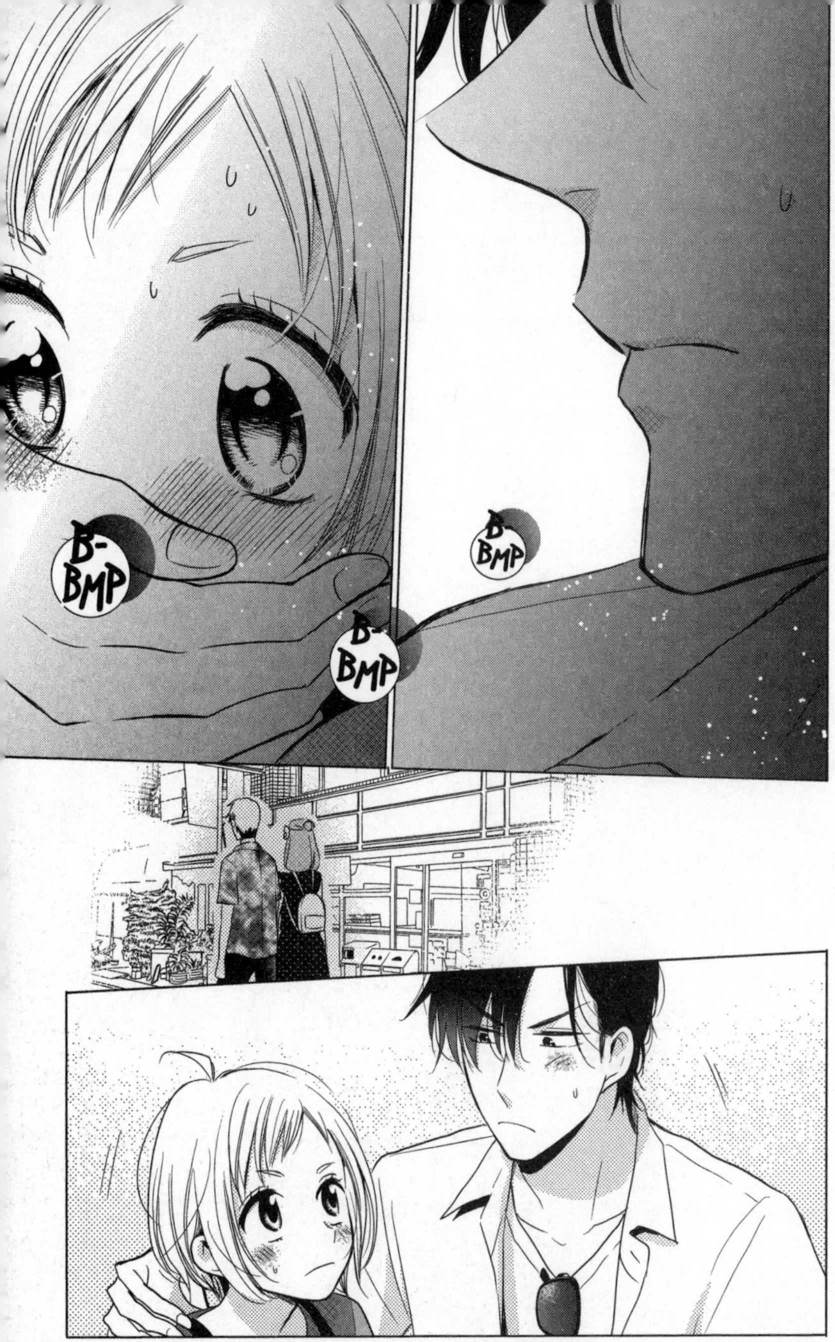
B-BMP
B-BMP
B-BMP

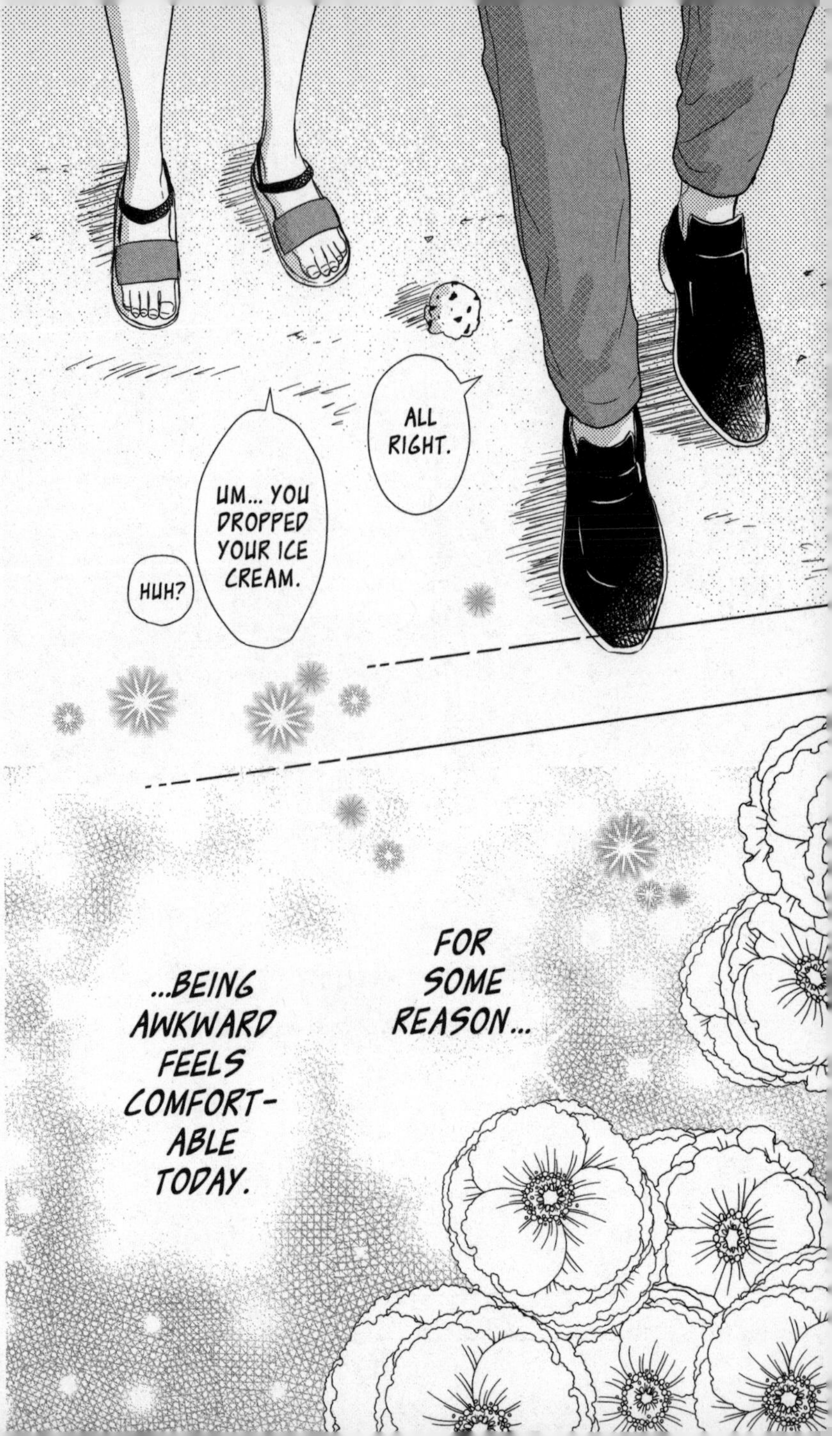
ALL RIGHT.
UM... YOU DROPPED YOUR ICE CREAM.
HUH?
FOR SOME REASON...
...BEING AWKWARD FEELS COMFORT-ABLE TODAY.

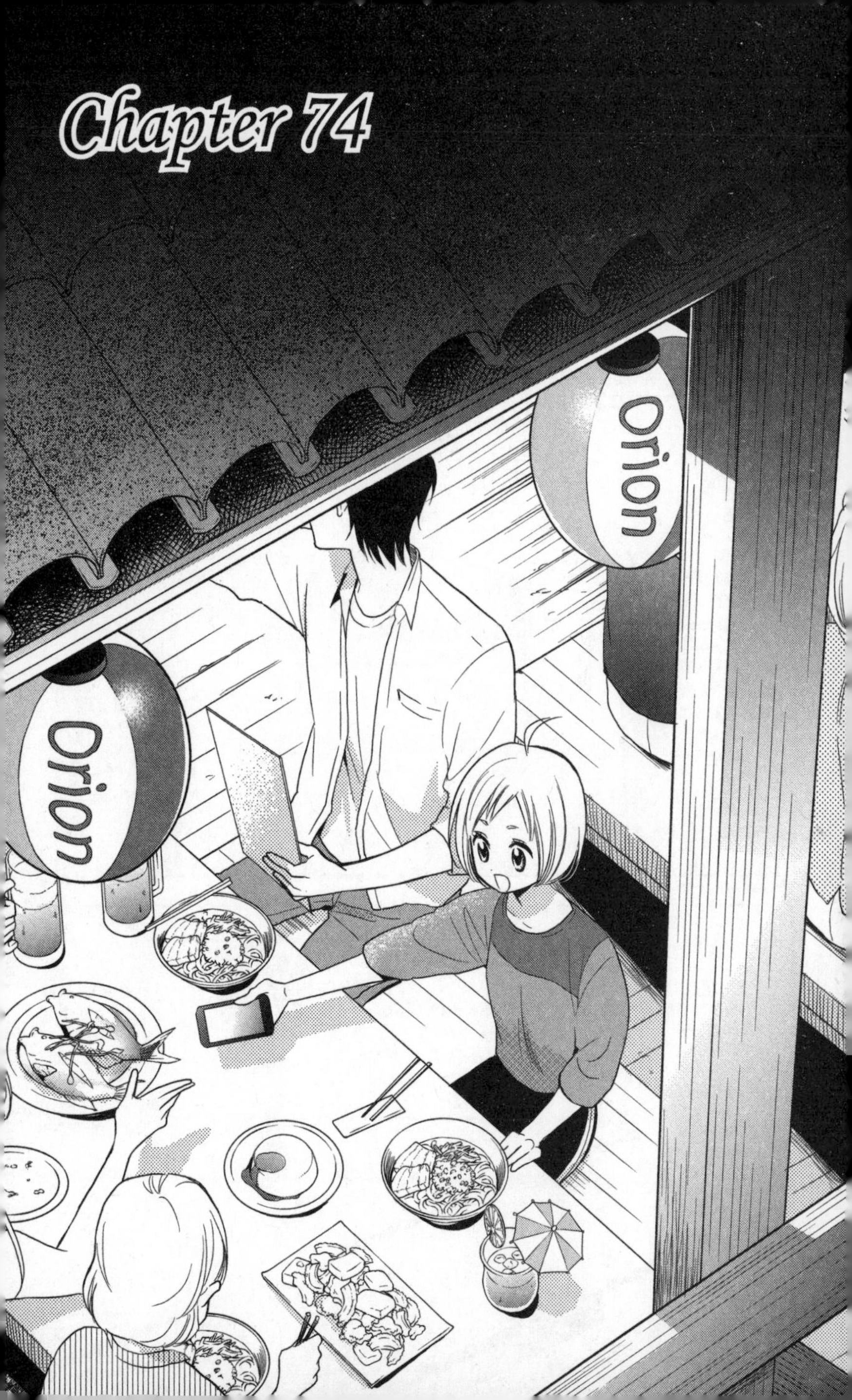
Chapter 74
Orion
Orion

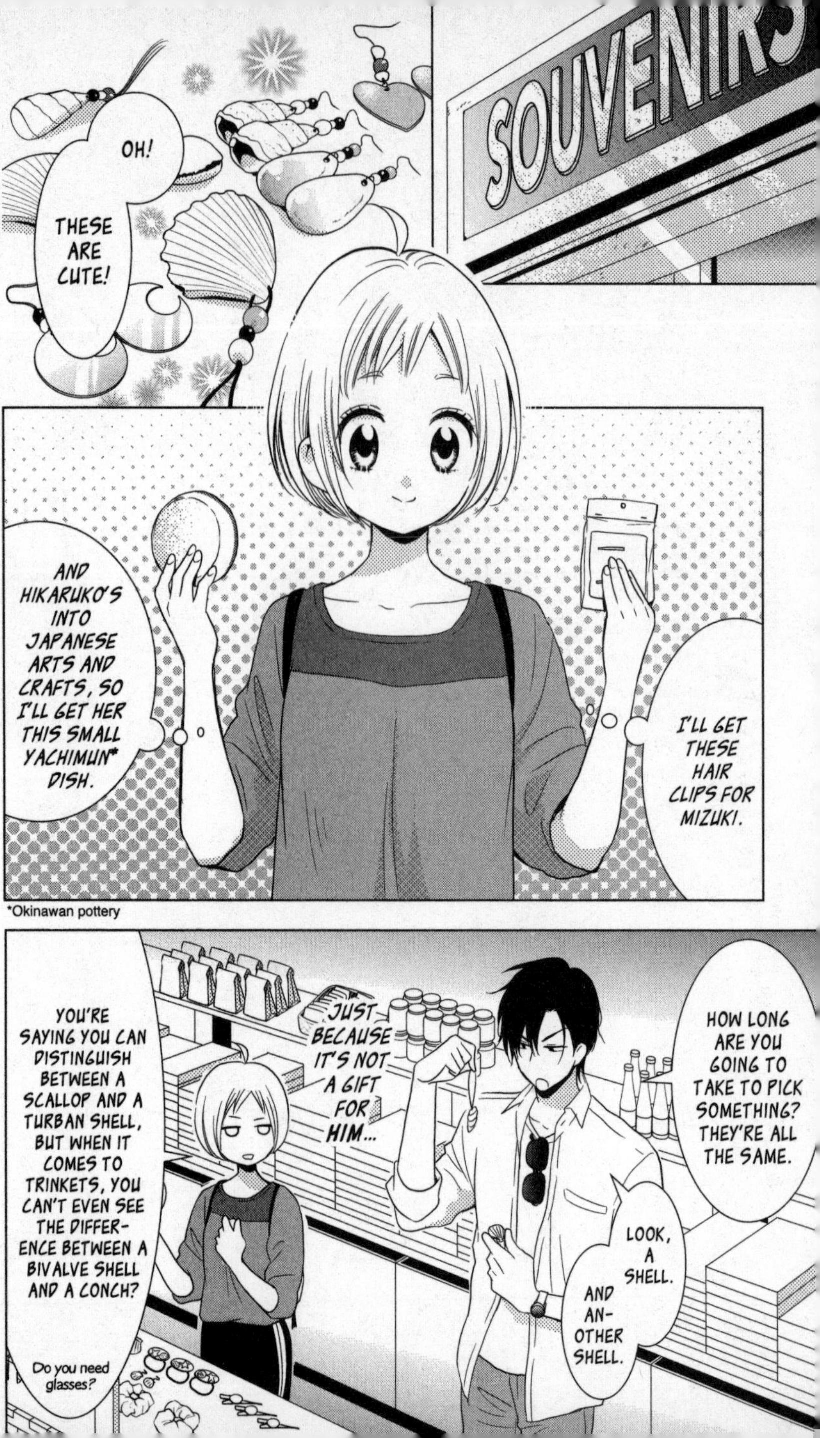
SOUVENIRS
OH! THESE ARE CUTE!
I'LL GET THESE HAIR CLIPS FOR MIZUKI.
AND HIKARUKO'S INTO JAPANESE ARTS AND CRAFTS, SO I'LL GET HER THIS SMALL YACHIMUN* DISH.
HOW LONG ARE YOU GOING TO TAKE TO PICK SOMETHING? THEY'RE ALL THE SAME.
LOOK, A SHELL.
AND ANOTHER SHELL.
JUST BECAUSE IT'S NOT A GIFT FOR HIM...
YOU'RE SAYING YOU CAN DISTINGUISH BETWEEN A SCALLOP AND A TURBAN SHELL, BUT WHEN IT COMES TO TRINKETS, YOU CAN'T EVEN SEE THE DIFFERENCE BETWEEN A BIVALVE SHELL AND A CONCH?
Do you need glasses?

*Okinawan pottery

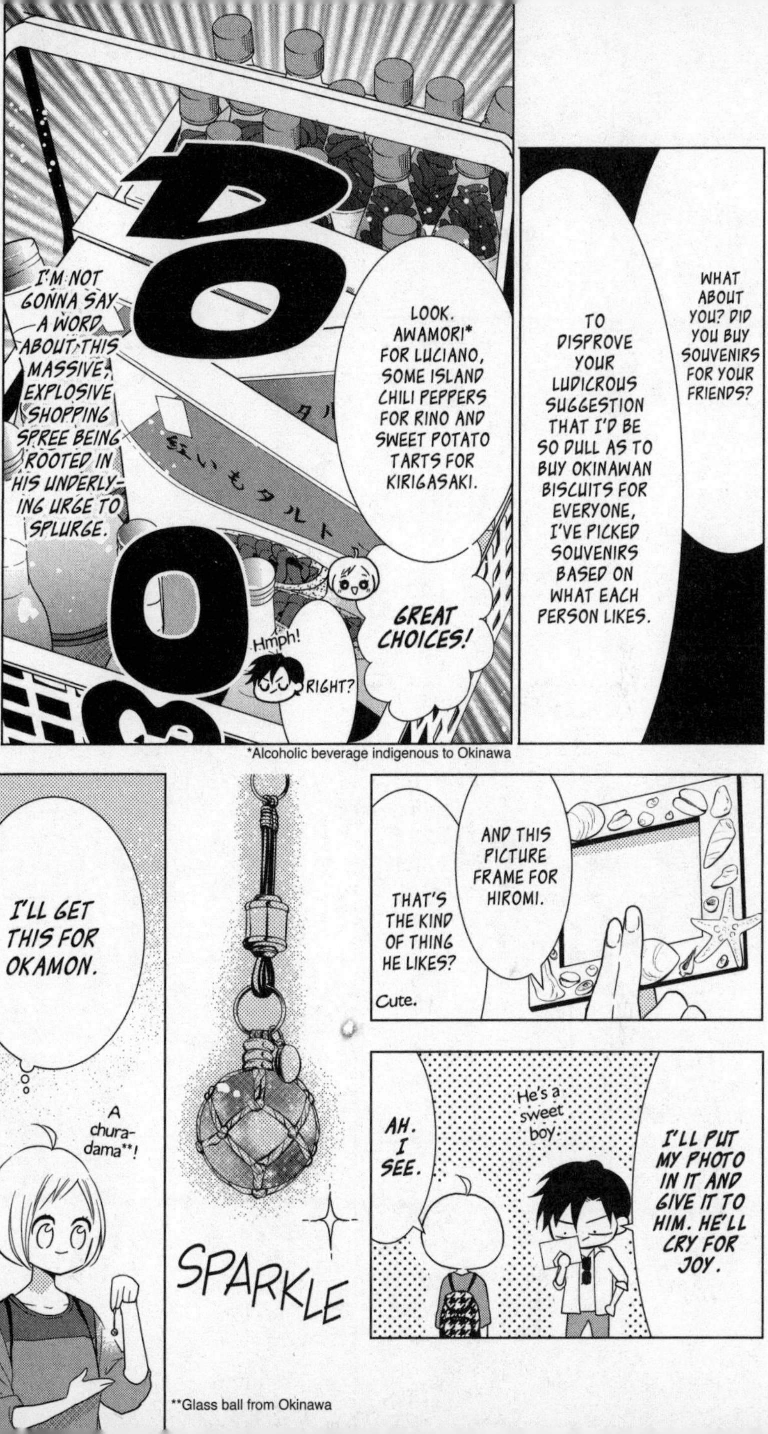
WHAT ABOUT YOU? DID YOU BUY SOUVENIRS FOR YOUR FRIENDS?
TO DISPROVE YOUR LUDICROUS SUGGESTION THAT I'D BE SO DULL AS TO BUY OKINAWAN BISCUITS FOR EVERYONE, I'VE PICKED SOUVENIRS BASED ON WHAT EACH PERSON LIKES.
LOOK. AWAMORI* FOR LUCIANO, SOME ISLAND CHILI PEPPERS FOR RINO AND SWEET POTATO TARTS FOR KIRIGASAKI.
GREAT CHOICES!
RIGHT?
Hmph!
I'M NOT GONNA SAY A WORD ABOUT THIS MASSIVE, EXPLOSIVE SHOPPING SPREE BEING ROOTED IN HIS UNDERLYING URGE TO SPLURGE.
AND THIS PICTURE FRAME FOR HIROMI.
THAT'S THE KIND OF THING HE LIKES?
Cute.
I'LL PUT MY PHOTO IN IT AND GIVE IT TO HIM. HE'LL CRY FOR JOY.
He's a sweet boy.
AH. I SEE.
SPARKLE
I'LL GET THIS FOR OKAMON.
A churadama**!
*Alcoholic beverage indigenous to Okinawa

**Glass ball from Okinawa

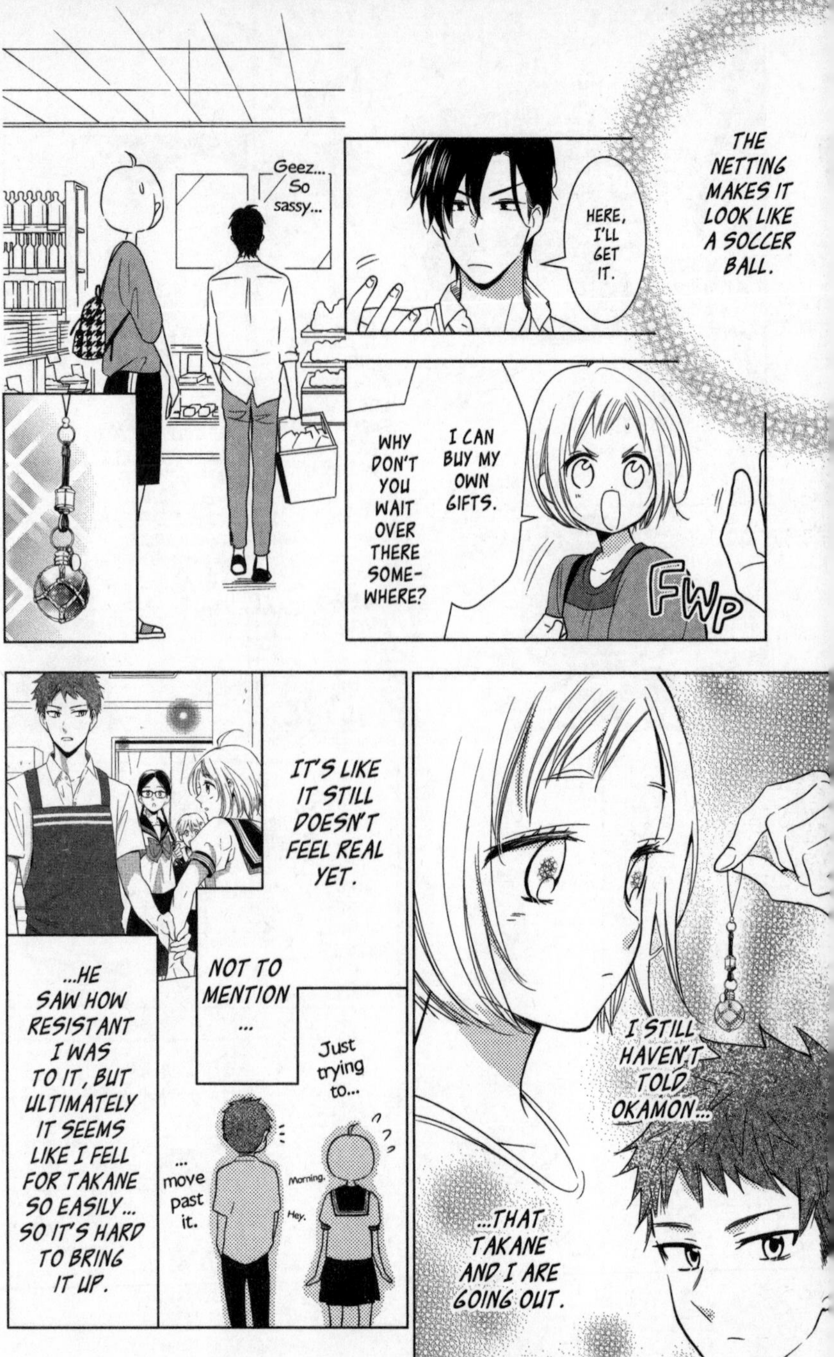
THE NETTING MAKES IT LOOK LIKE A SOCCER BALL.
HERE, I'LL GET IT.
I CAN BUY MY OWN GIFTS.
WHY DON'T YOU WAIT OVER THERE SOME-WHERE?
FWP
Geez... So sassy...
I STILL HAVEN'T TOLD OKAMON...
...THAT TAKANE AND I ARE GOING OUT.
IT'S LIKE IT STILL DOESN'T FEEL REAL YET.
NOT TO MENTION...
...HE SAW HOW RESISTANT I WAS TO IT, BUT ULTIMATELY IT SEEMS LIKE I FELL FOR TAKANE SO EASILY... SO IT'S HARD TO BRING IT UP.
Just trying to...
...move past it.
Morning.
Hey.

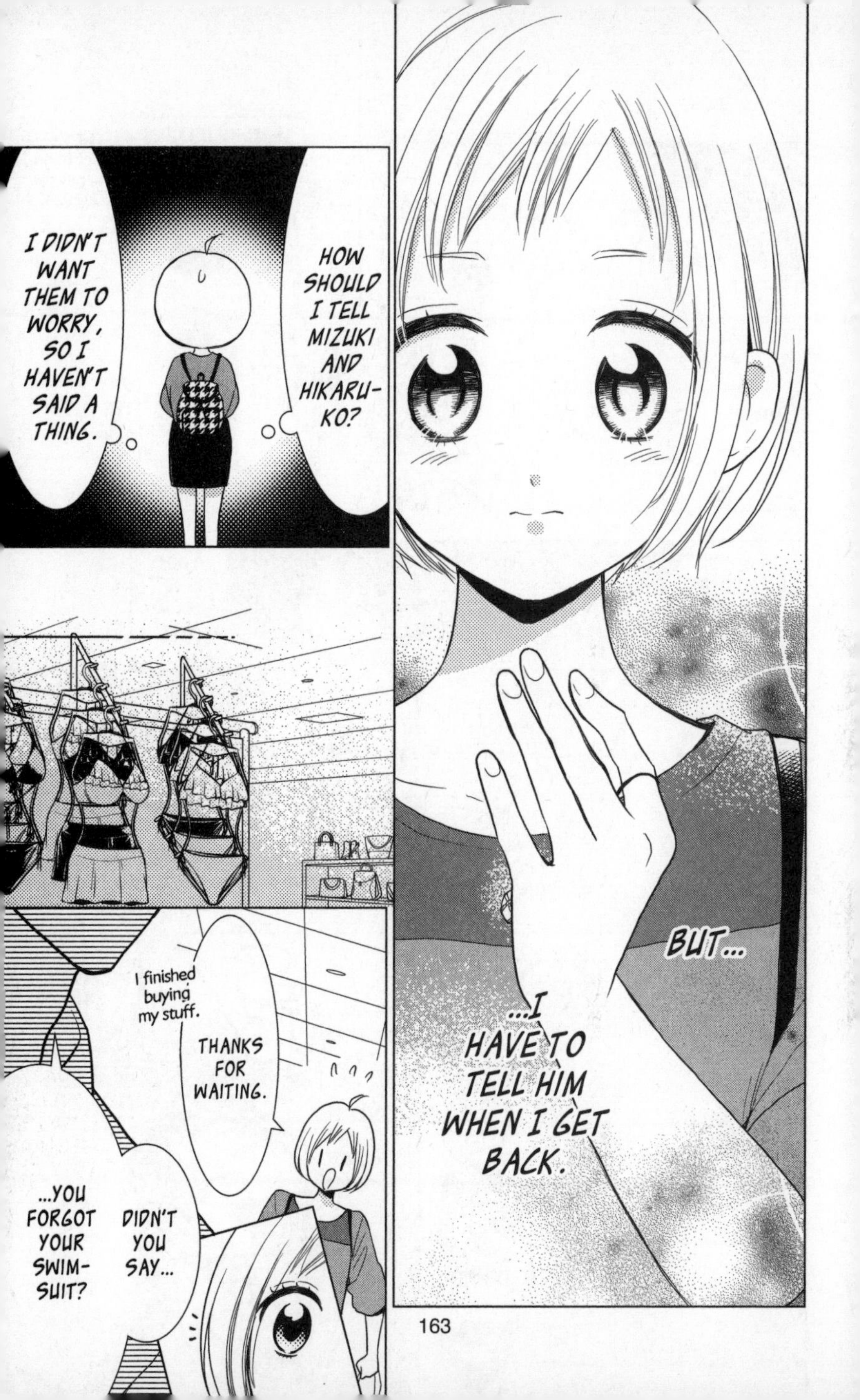
BUT...
...I HAVE TO TELL HIM WHEN I GET BACK.
HOW SHOULD I TELL MIZUKI AND HIKARU-KO?
I DIDN'T WANT THEM TO WORRY, SO I HAVEN'T SAID A THING.
I finished buying my stuff.
THANKS FOR WAITING.
DIDN'T YOU SAY...
...YOU FORGOT YOUR SWIM-SUIT?

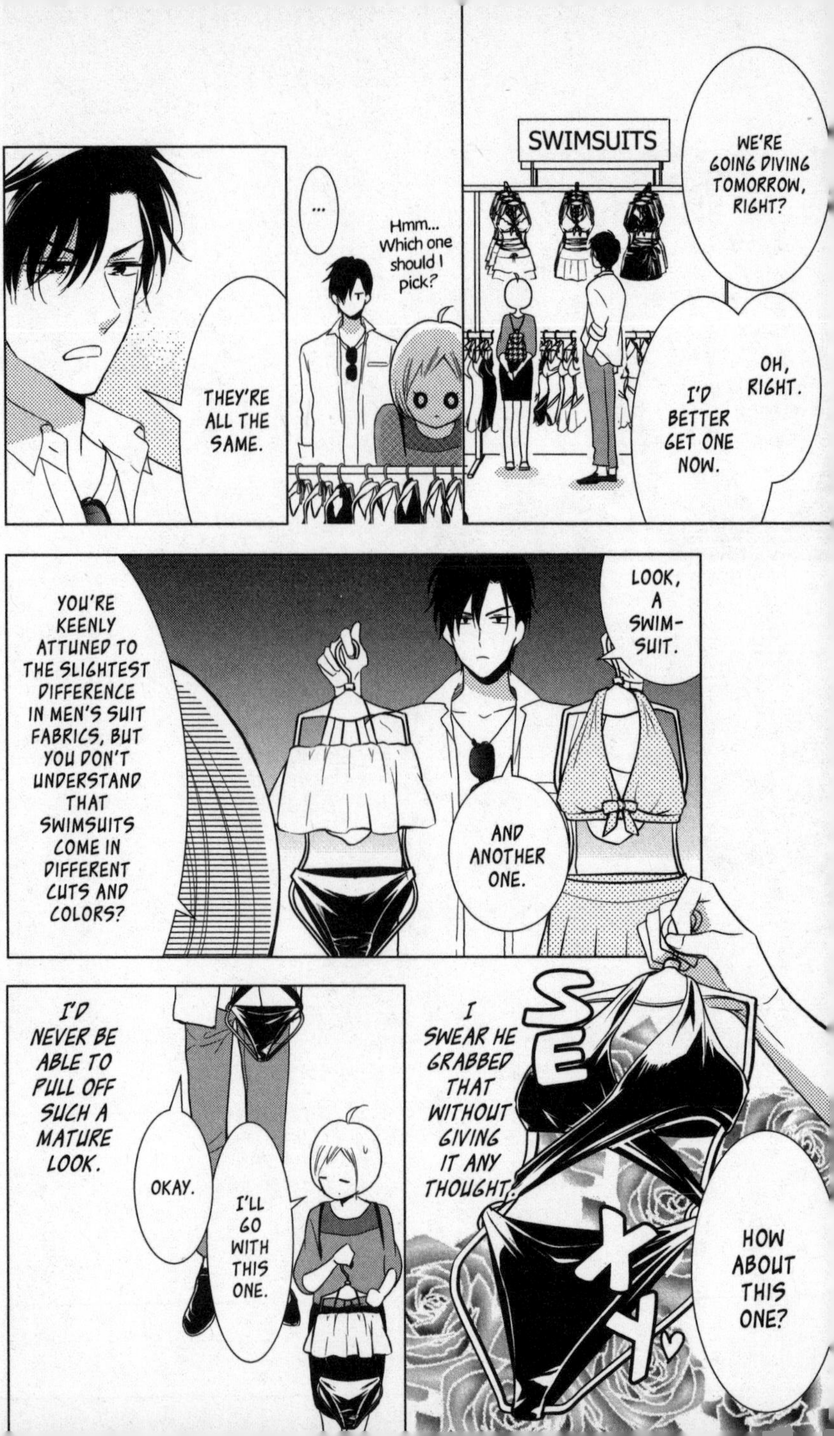
SWIMSUITS
WE'RE GOING DIVING TOMORROW, RIGHT?
OH, RIGHT.
I'D BETTER GET ONE NOW.
...
Hmm... Which one should I pick?
THEY'RE ALL THE SAME.
LOOK, A SWIM-SUIT.
AND ANOTHER ONE.
YOU'RE KEENLY ATTUNED TO THE SLIGHTEST DIFFERENCE IN MEN'S SUIT FABRICS, BUT YOU DON'T UNDERSTAND THAT SWIMSUITS COME IN DIFFERENT CUTS AND COLORS?
HOW ABOUT THIS ONE?
SEXY
I SWEAR HE GRABBED THAT WITHOUT GIVING IT ANY THOUGHT.
I'LL GO WITH THIS ONE.
OKAY.
I'D NEVER BE ABLE TO PULL OFF SUCH A MATURE LOOK.

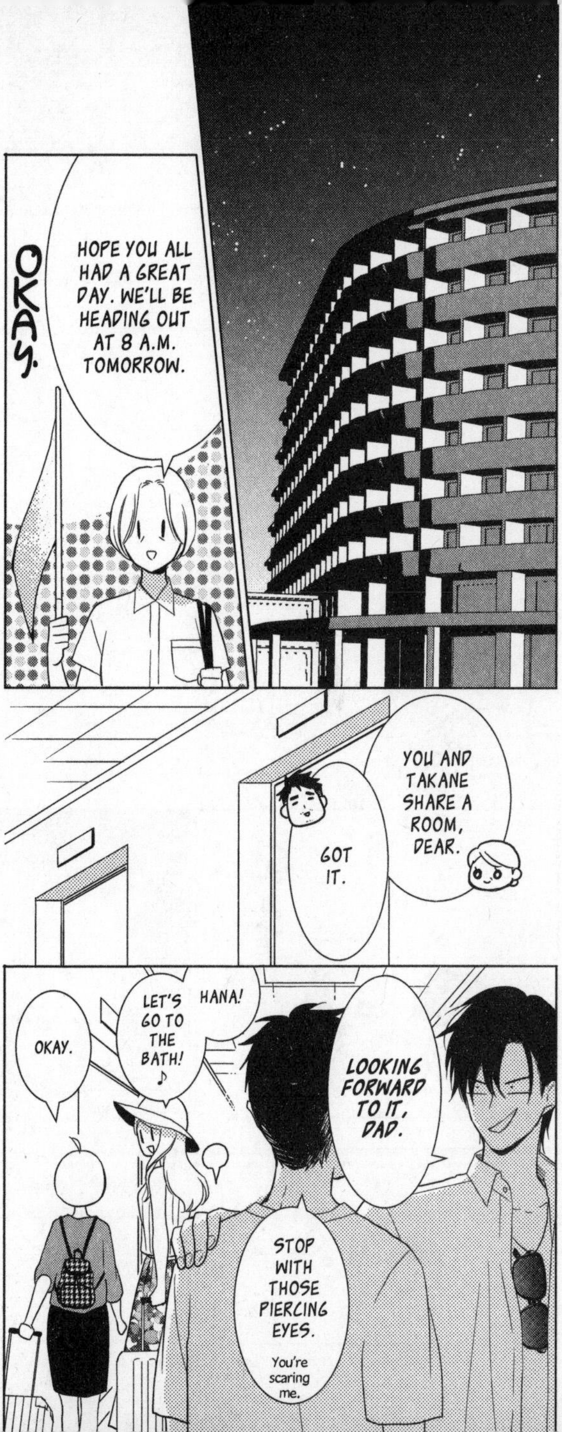
HOPE YOU ALL HAD A GREAT DAY. WE'LL BE HEADING OUT AT 8 A.M. TOMORROW.
OKAY.
YOU AND TAKANE SHARE A ROOM, DEAR.
GOT IT.
LOOKING FORWARD TO IT, DAD.
STOP WITH THOSE PIERCING EYES.
You're scaring me.
HANA!
LET'S GO TO THE BATH! ♪
OKAY.

• Live-Action Drama in the Works! •

This calls for a celebration!

Eeee! I'm so excited! The announcement will probably have been made by the time this volume goes on sale.

Last month (December 2018), I met with the staff involved in creating the live-action drama. I was once again struck by the sheer number of people it takes to create the live-action version of *Takane and Hana*. It humbled me, and at the same time it was tremendously motivating.

Reading the script, I came across scenes that made me think, "Oh, yeah, this is exactly the type of character he/she is..."

It gave me the perfect opportunity to review the story again.

When all is said and done, I walked away feeling more inspired than ever. It made me want to keep working hard to create the very best *Takane and Hana* manga.

I can't wait to see the live-action drama!

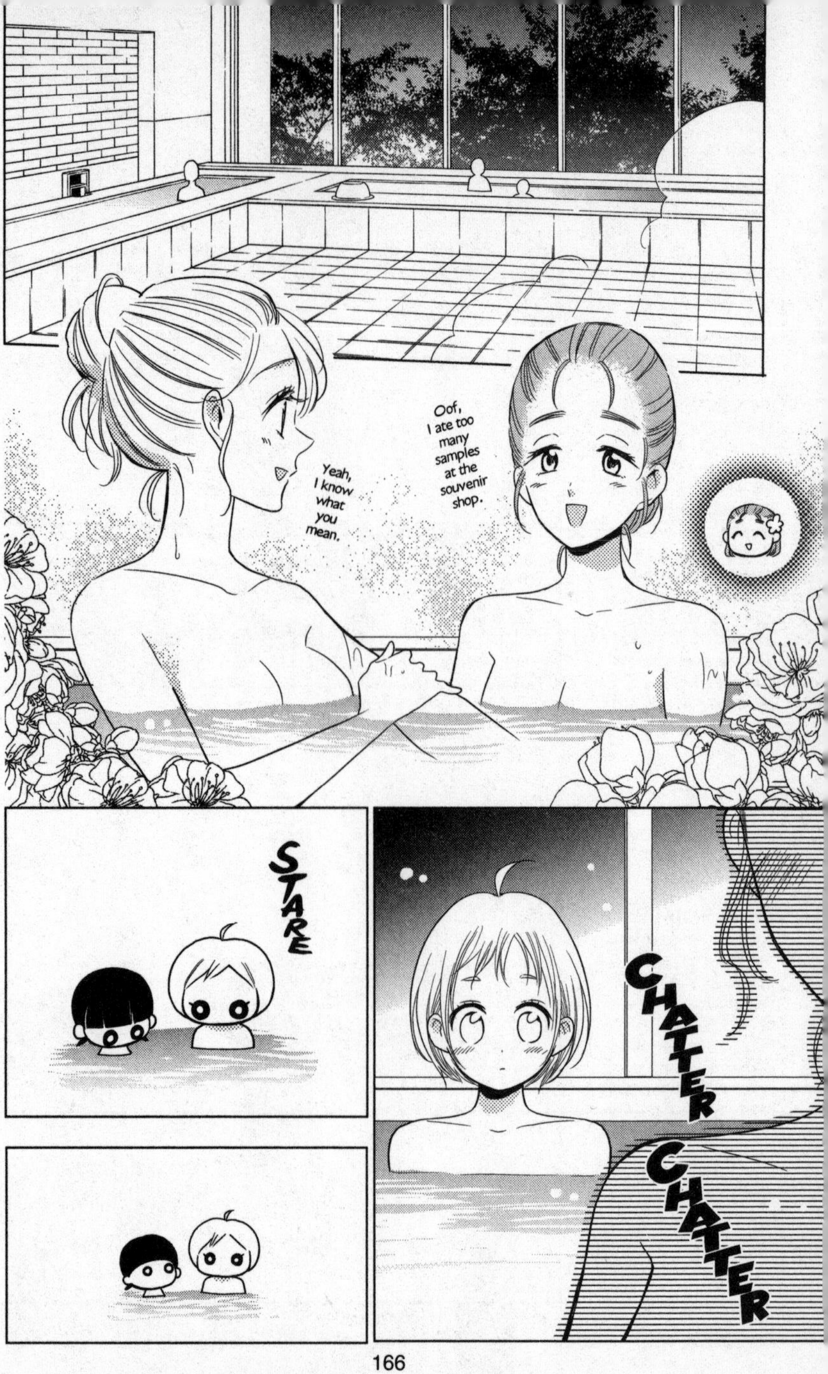
Oof, I ate too many samples at the souvenir shop.
Yeah, I know what you mean.
CHATTER CHATTER
STARE

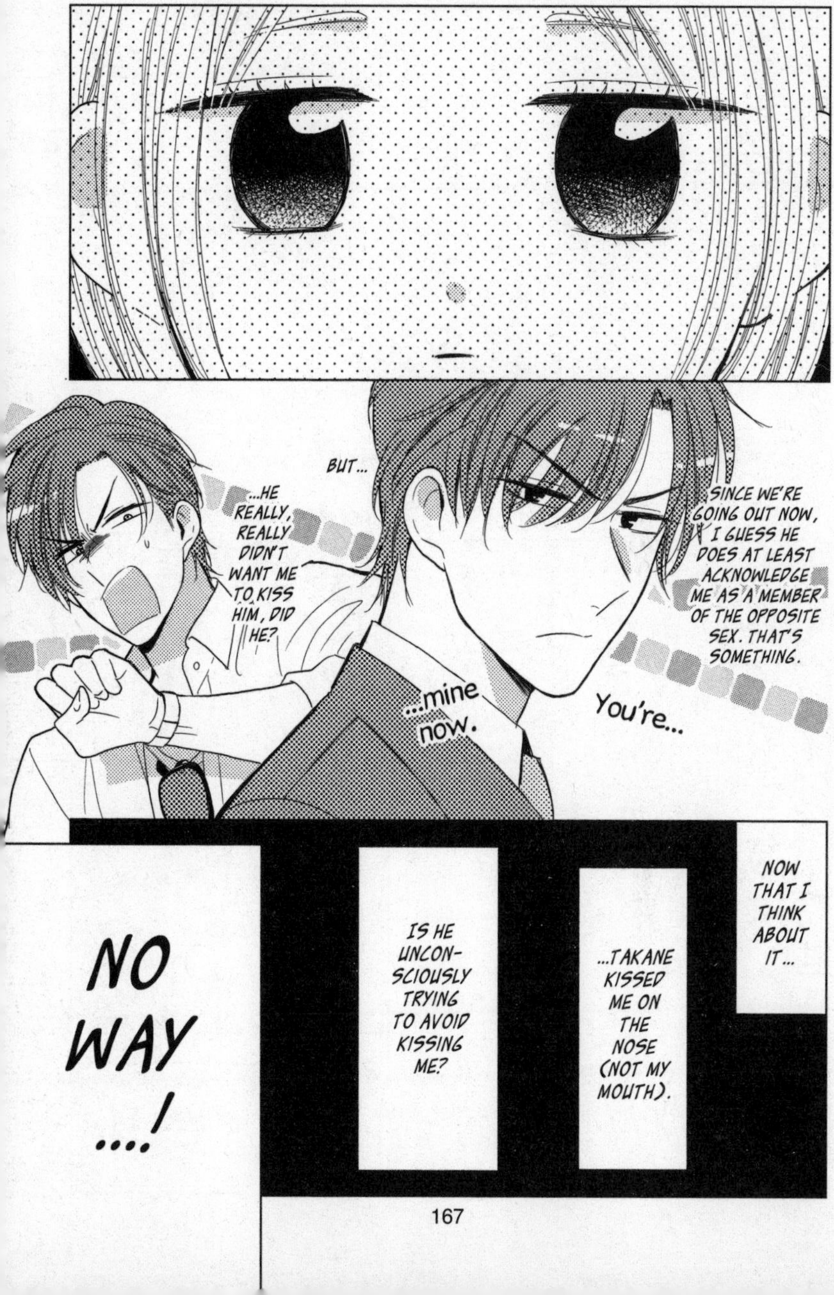
SINCE WE'RE GOING OUT NOW, I GUESS HE DOES AT LEAST ACKNOWLEDGE ME AS A MEMBER OF THE OPPOSITE SEX. THAT'S SOMETHING.
You're...
...mine now.
BUT...
...HE REALLY, REALLY DIDN'T WANT ME TO KISS HIM, DID HE?
NOW THAT I THINK ABOUT IT...
...TAKANE KISSED ME ON THE NOSE (NOT MY MOUTH).
IS HE UNCONSCIOUSLY TRYING TO AVOID KISSING ME?
NO WAY ...!

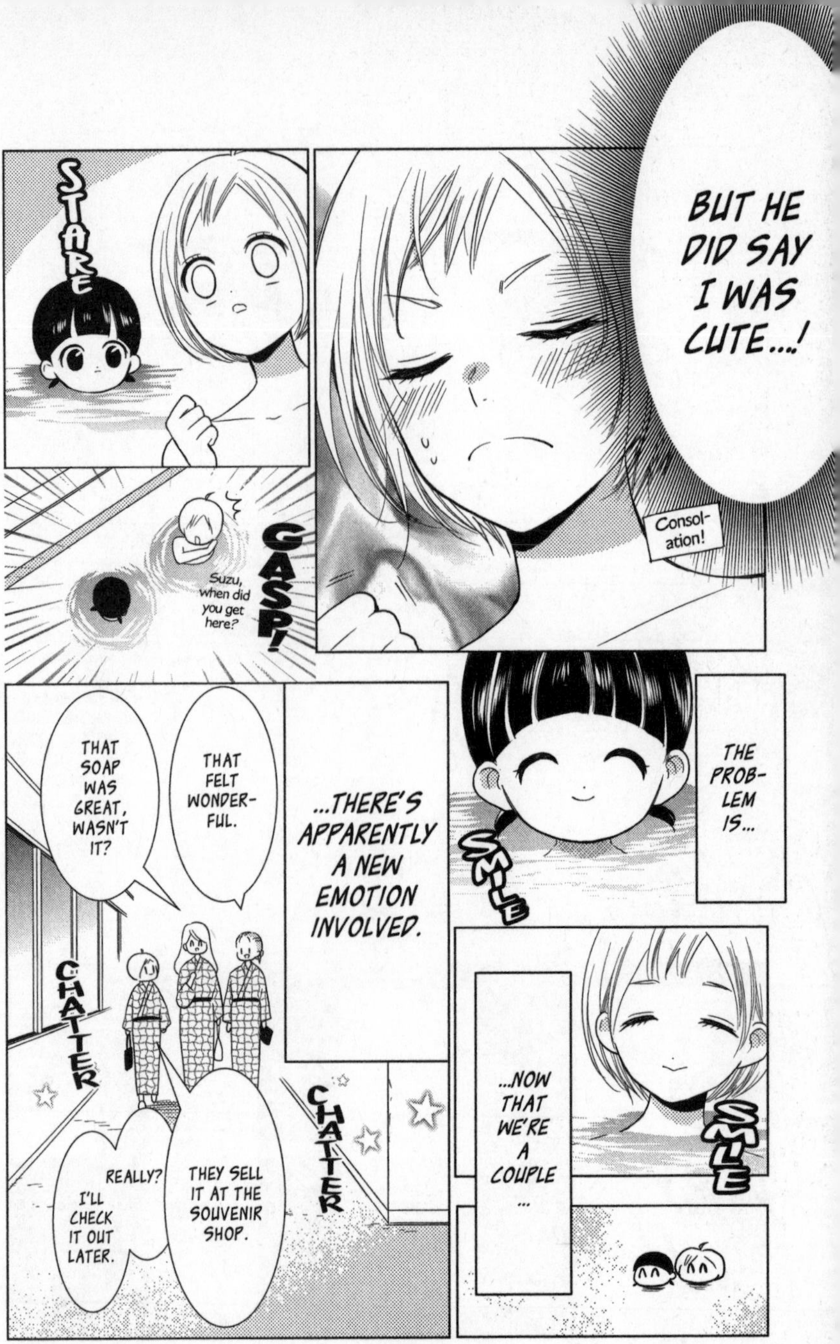
BUT HE DID SAY I WAS CUTE...!
Consol-ation!
STARE
GASP!
Suzu, when did you get here?
THE PROB-LEM IS...
SMILE
...NOW THAT WE'RE A COUPLE ...
SMILE
...THERE'S APPARENTLY A NEW EMOTION INVOLVED.
THAT FELT WONDER-FUL.
THAT SOAP WAS GREAT, WASN'T IT?
CHATTER
THEY SELL IT AT THE SOUVENIR SHOP.
REALLY? I'LL CHECK IT OUT LATER.
CHATTER

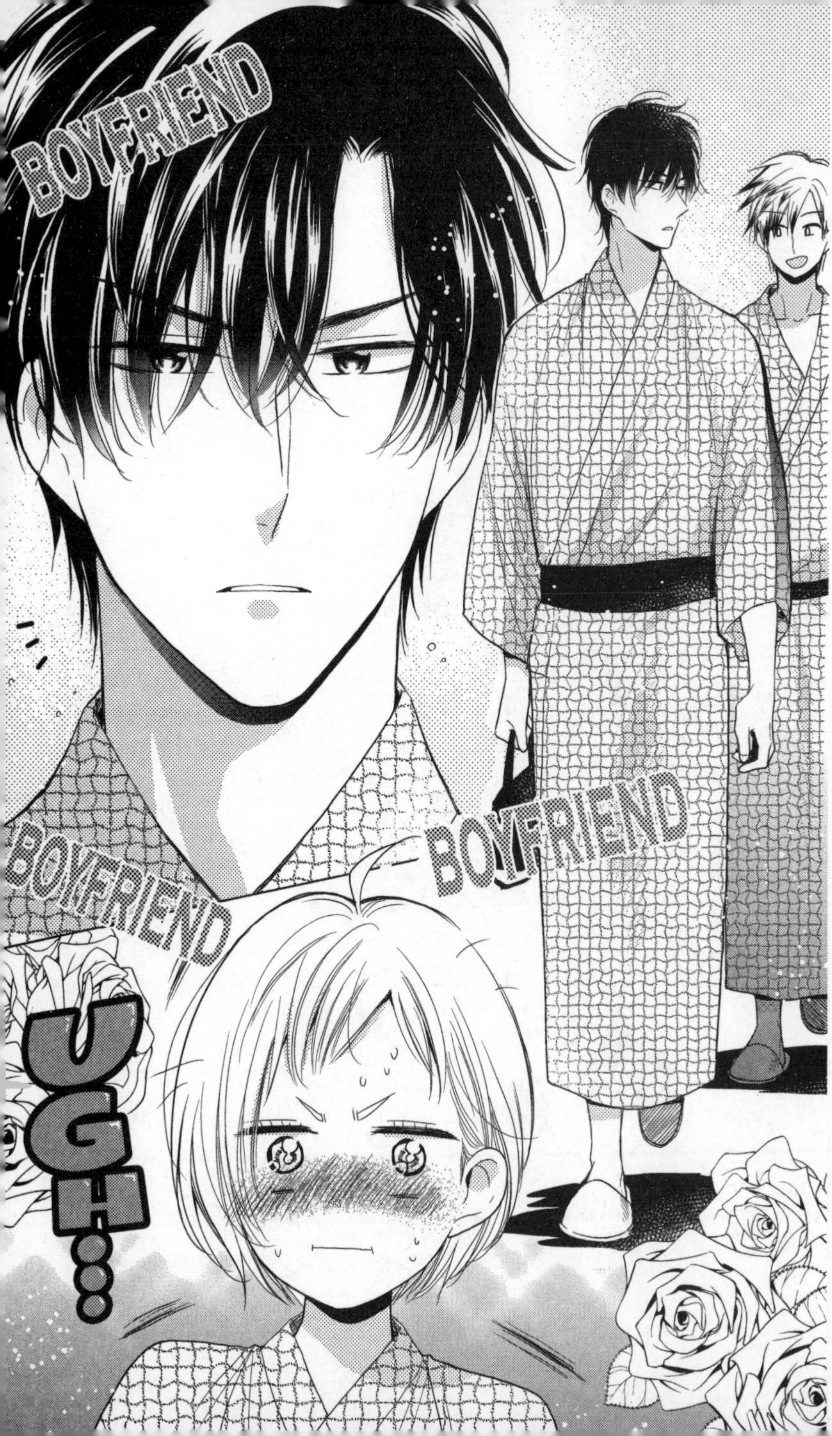
BOYFRIEND
BOYFRIEND
BOYFRIEND
BOYFRIEND
UGH...

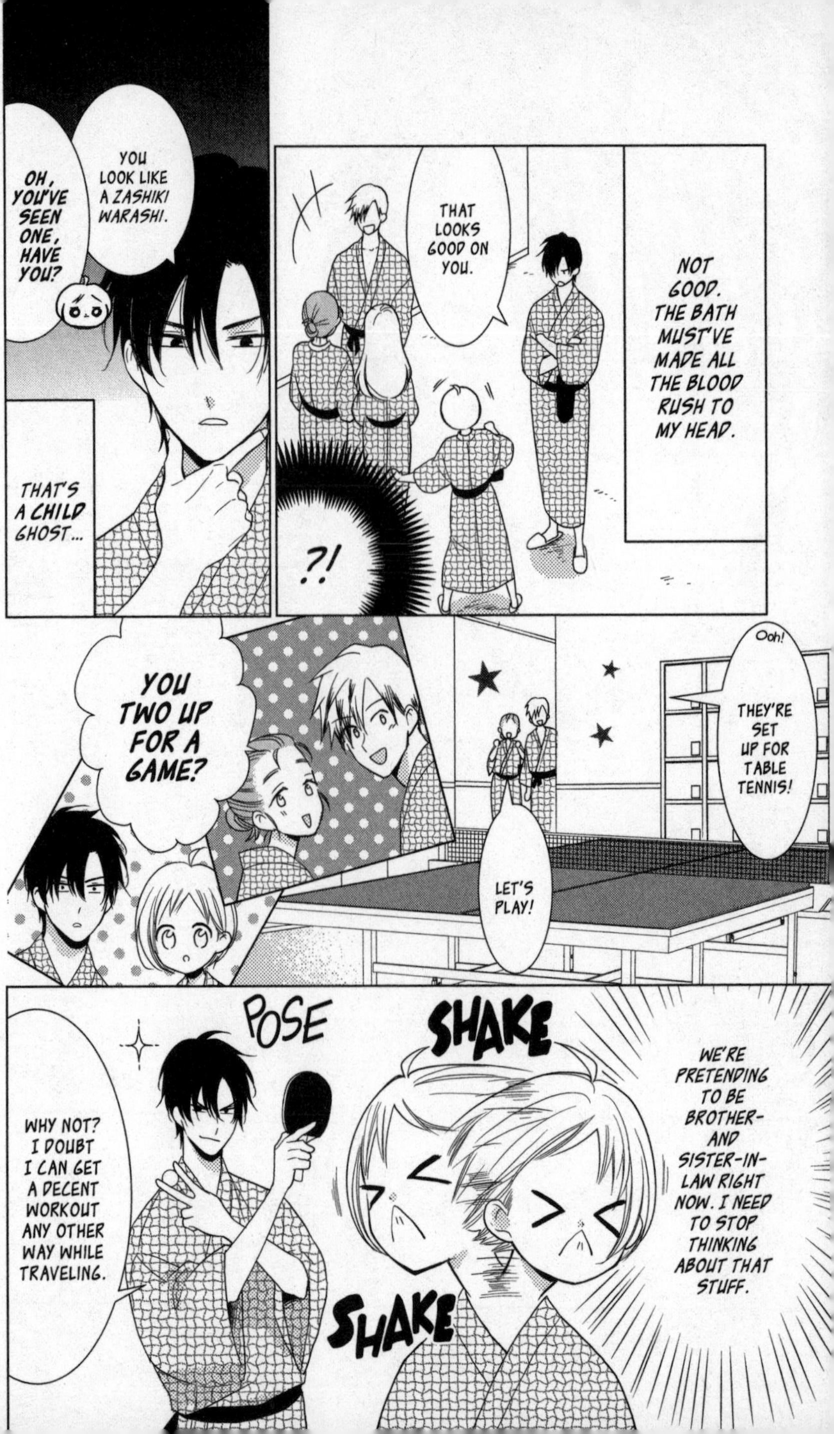
NOT GOOD. THE BATH MUST'VE MADE ALL THE BLOOD RUSH TO MY HEAD.
THAT LOOKS GOOD ON YOU.
?!
YOU LOOK LIKE A ZASHIKI WARASHI.
OH, YOU'VE SEEN ONE, HAVE YOU?
THAT'S A CHILD GHOST...
Ooh!
THEY'RE SET UP FOR TABLE TENNIS!
LET'S PLAY!
YOU TWO UP FOR A GAME?
SHAKE
WE'RE PRETENDING TO BE BROTHER- AND SISTER-IN-LAW RIGHT NOW. I NEED TO STOP THINKING ABOUT THAT STUFF.
SHAKE
POSE
WHY NOT? I DOUBT I CAN GET A DECENT WORKOUT ANY OTHER WAY WHILE TRAVELING.

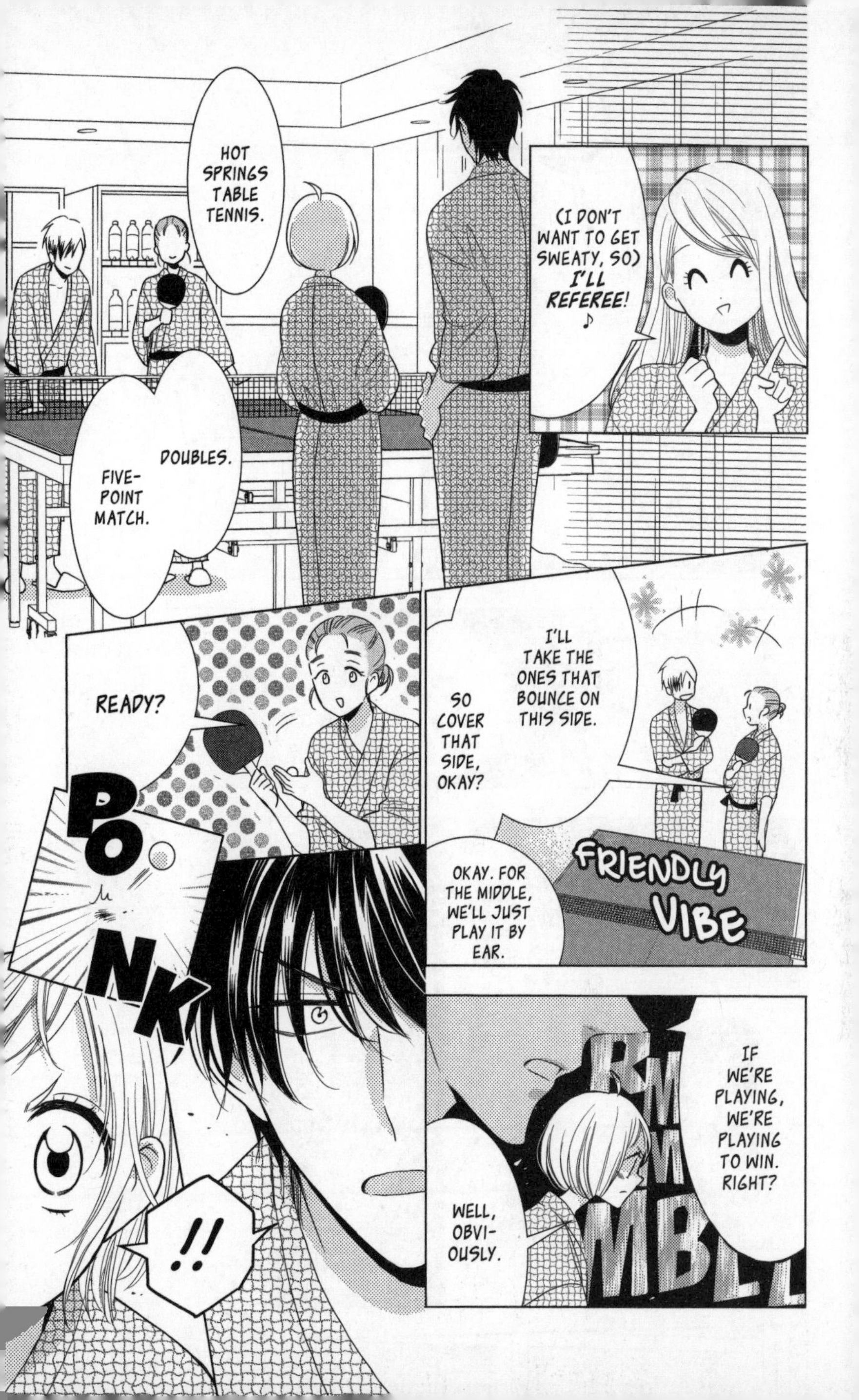
(I DON'T WANT TO GET SWEATY, SO) I'LL REFEREE! ♪
HOT SPRINGS TABLE TENNIS.
DOUBLES.
FIVE-POINT MATCH.
I'LL TAKE THE ONES THAT BOUNCE ON THIS SIDE.
SO COVER THAT SIDE, OKAY?
OKAY. FOR THE MIDDLE, WE'LL JUST PLAY IT BY EAR.
FRIENDLY VIBE
READY?
PONK
IF WE'RE PLAYING, WE'RE PLAYING TO WIN. RIGHT?
WELL, OBVIOUSLY.
RMMMBLL
!!

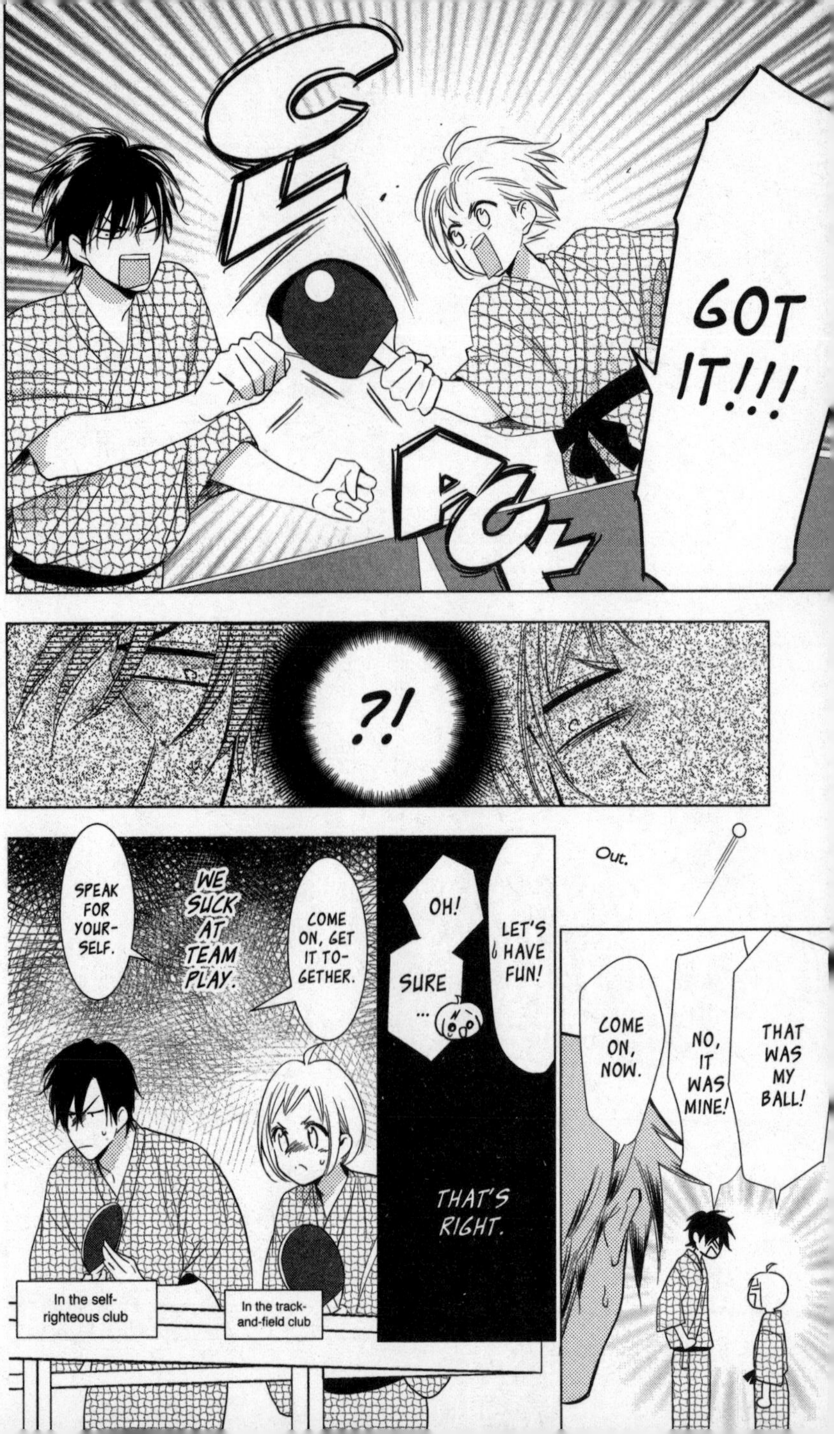
GOT IT!!!!
?!
Out.
THAT WAS MY BALL!
NO, IT WAS MINE!
COME ON, NOW.
LET'S HAVE FUN!
OH!
SURE ...
THAT'S RIGHT.
COME ON, GET IT TO-GETHER.
WE SUCK AT TEAM PLAY.
SPEAK FOR YOUR-SELF.
In the track-and-field club
In the self-righteous club

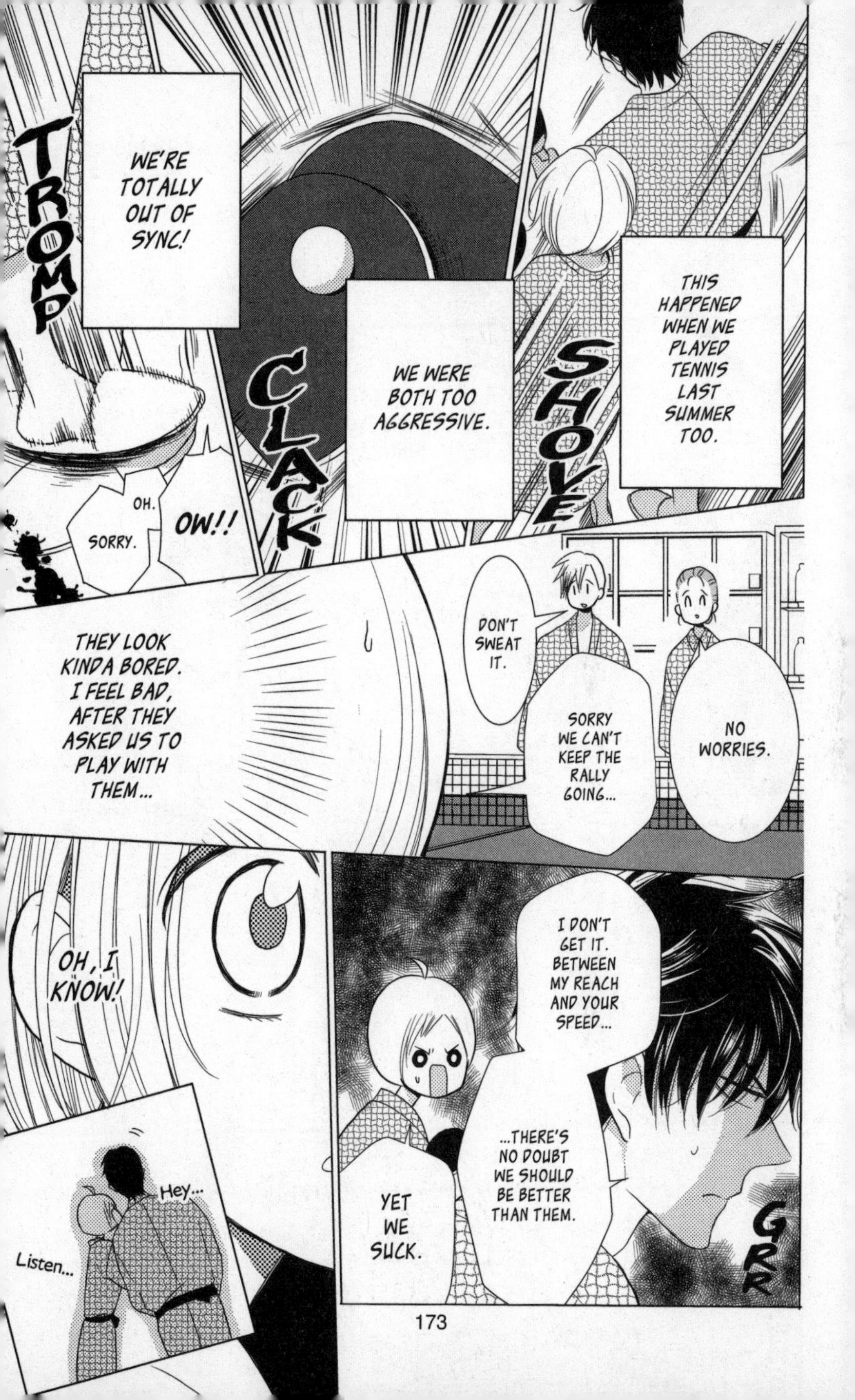
THIS HAPPENED WHEN WE PLAYED TENNIS LAST SUMMER TOO.
SHOVE
WE WERE BOTH TOO AGGRESSIVE.
CLACK
WE'RE TOTALLY OUT OF SYNC!
TROMP
OW!!
OH.
SORRY.
DON'T SWEAT IT.
NO WORRIES.
SORRY WE CAN'T KEEP THE RALLY GOING...
THEY LOOK KINDA BORED. I FEEL BAD, AFTER THEY ASKED US TO PLAY WITH THEM...
I DON'T GET IT. BETWEEN MY REACH AND YOUR SPEED...
GRR
...THERE'S NO DOUBT WE SHOULD BE BETTER THAN THEM.
YET WE SUCK.
OH, I KNOW!
Hey...
Listen...

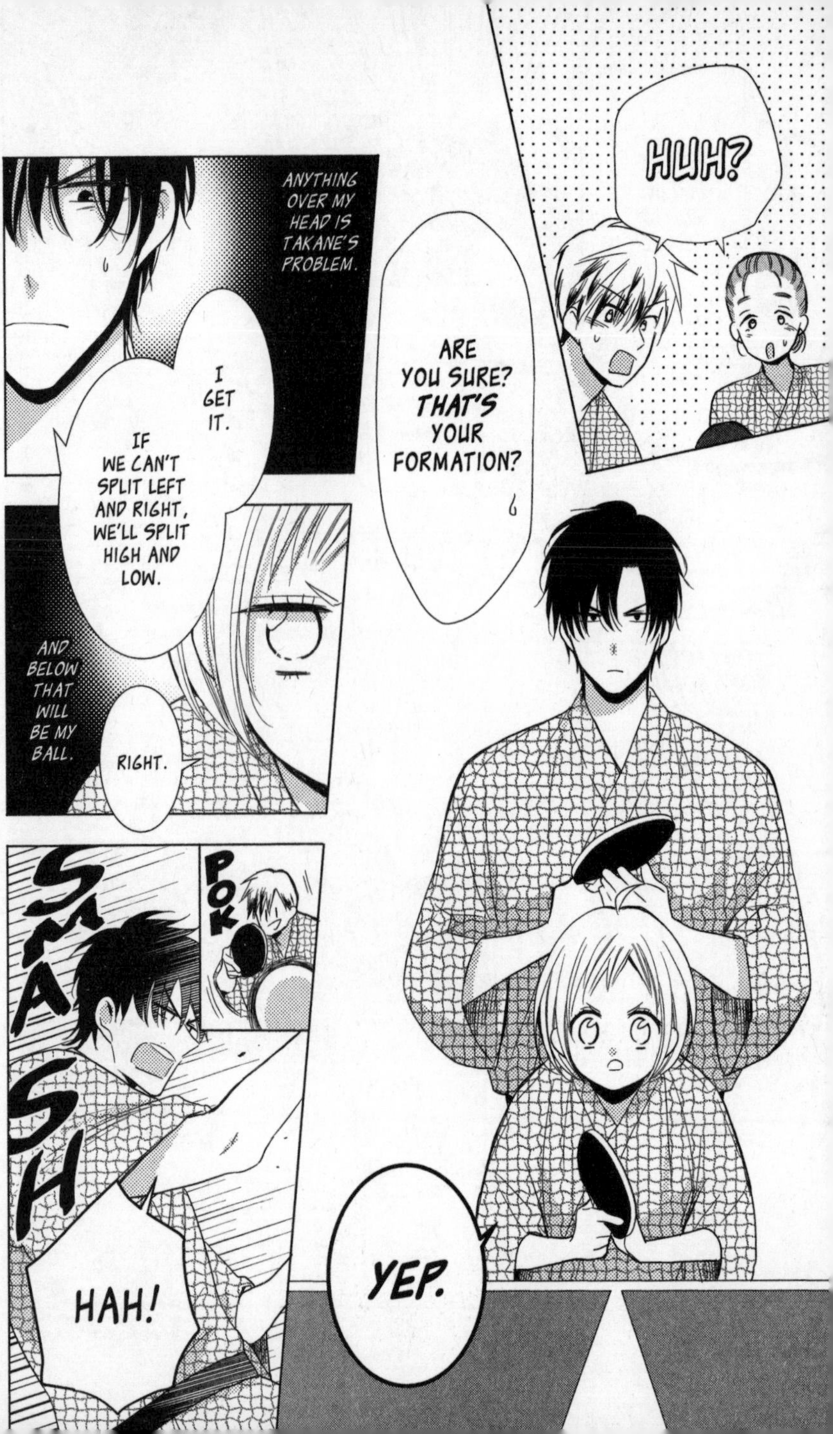
HUH?
ARE YOU SURE? THAT'S YOUR FORMATION?
YEP.
I GET IT.
IF WE CAN'T SPLIT LEFT AND RIGHT, WE'LL SPLIT HIGH AND LOW.
ANYTHING OVER MY HEAD IS TAKANE'S PROBLEM.
RIGHT.
AND BELOW THAT WILL BE MY BALL.
POK
SMASH
HAH!

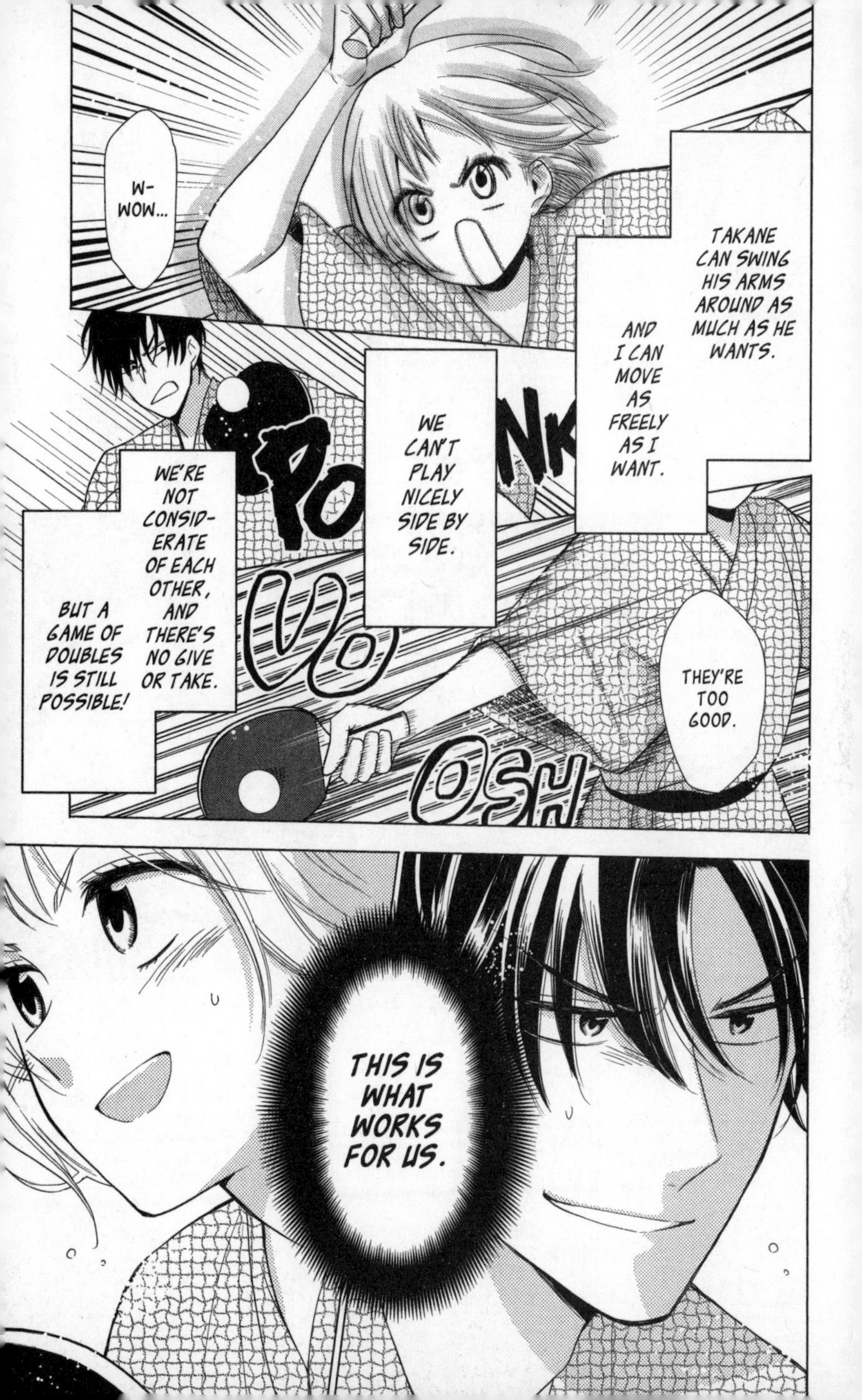
W-WOW...
TAKANE CAN SWING HIS ARMS AROUND AS MUCH AS HE WANTS.
AND I CAN MOVE AS FREELY AS I WANT.
WE CAN'T PLAY NICELY SIDE BY SIDE.
WE'RE NOT CONSIDERATE OF EACH OTHER, AND THERE'S NO GIVE OR TAKE.
BUT A GAME OF DOUBLES IS STILL POSSIBLE!
THEY'RE TOO GOOD.
THIS IS WHAT WORKS FOR US.

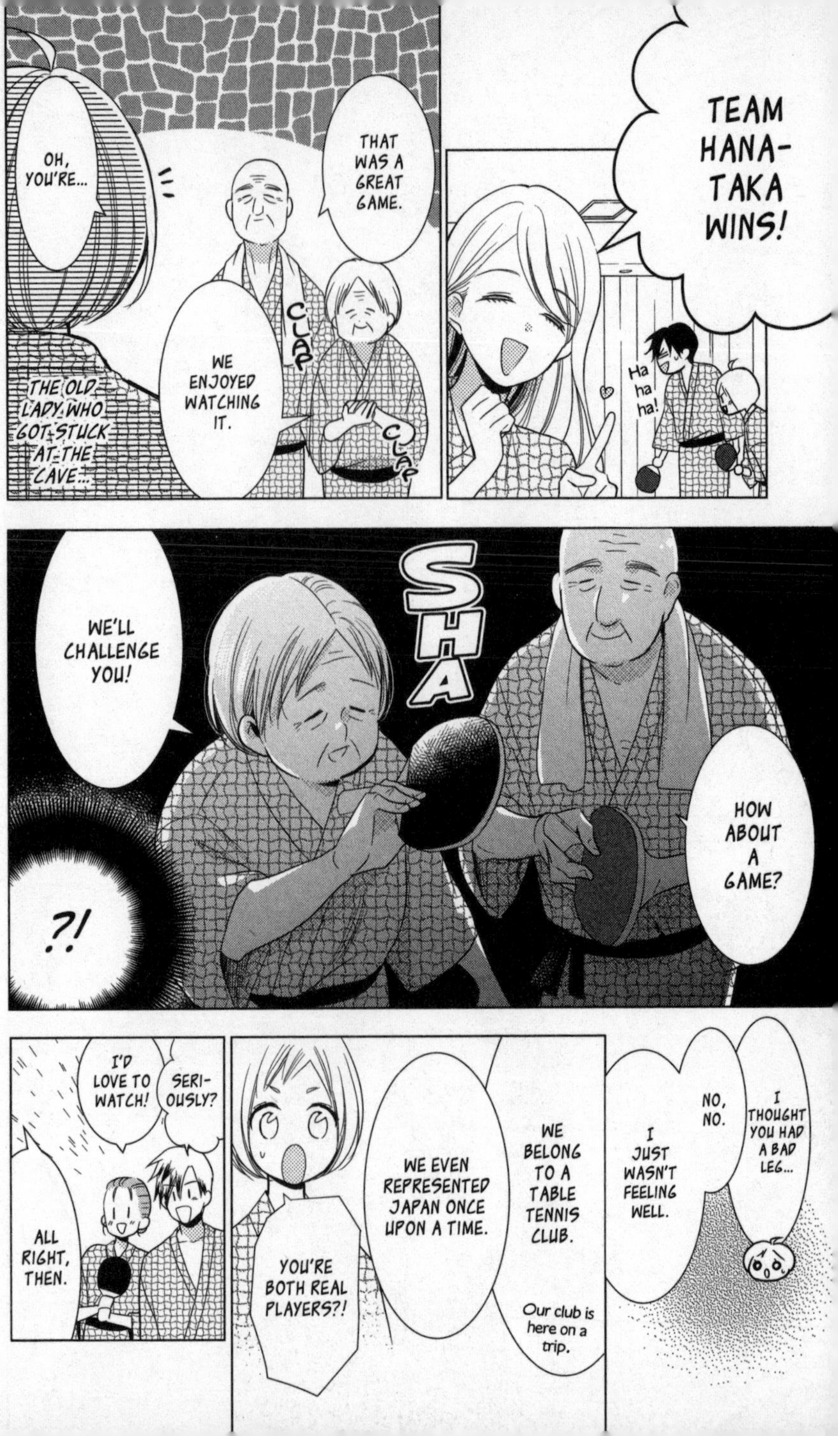
TEAM HANA-TAKA WINS!
Ha ha ha!
THAT WAS A GREAT GAME.
OH, YOU'RE...
CLAP
CLAP
WE ENJOYED WATCHING IT.
THE OLD LADY WHO GOT STUCK AT THE CAVE...
HOW ABOUT A GAME?
SHA
WE'LL CHALLENGE YOU!
?!
I THOUGHT YOU HAD A BAD LEG...
NO, NO.
I JUST WASN'T FEELING WELL.
WE BELONG TO A TABLE TENNIS CLUB.
Our club is here on a trip.
WE EVEN REPRESENTED JAPAN ONCE UPON A TIME.
YOU'RE BOTH REAL PLAYERS?!
SERIOUSLY?
I'D LOVE TO WATCH!
ALL RIGHT, THEN.

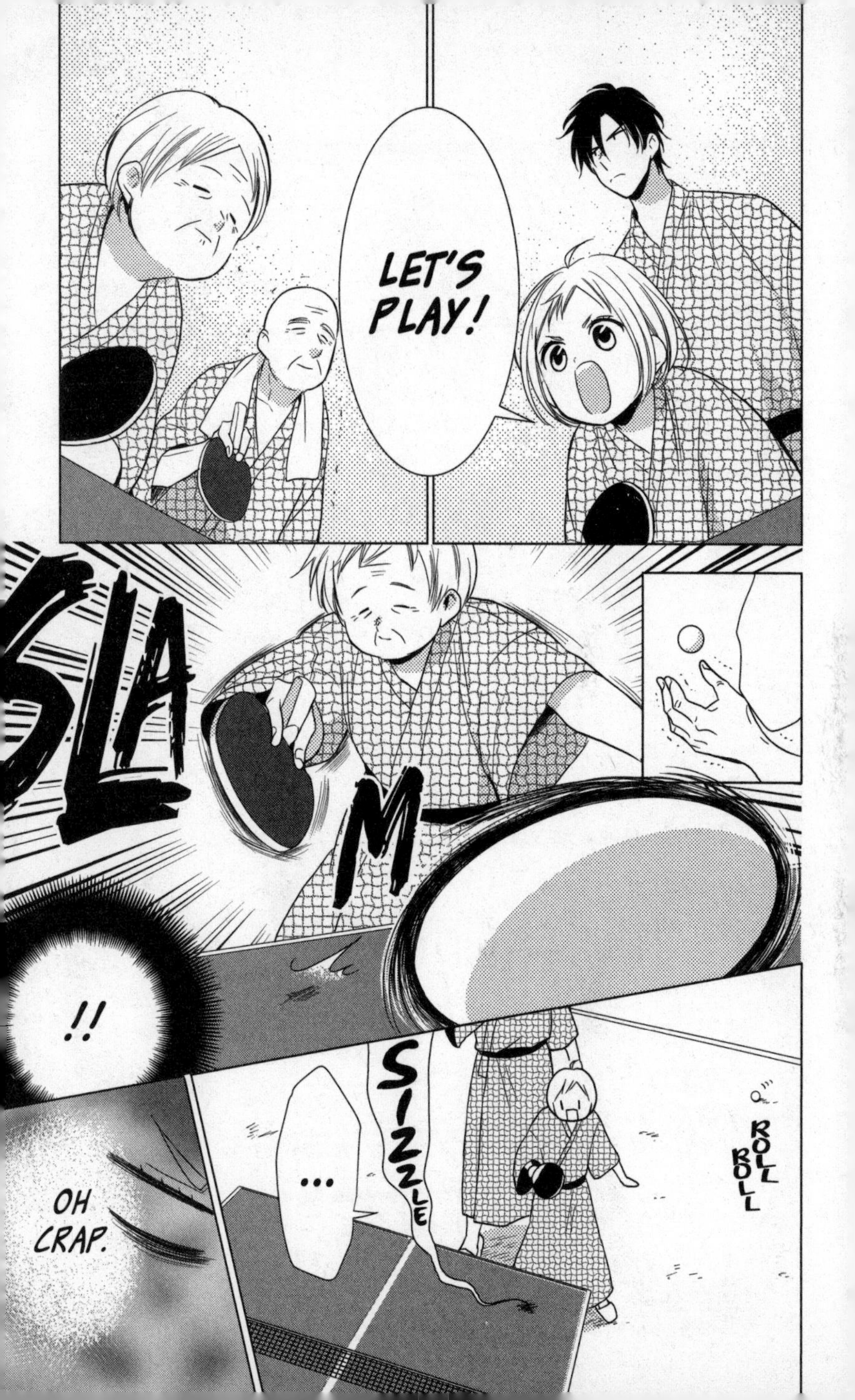
LET'S PLAY!
SLAM
!!
ROLL ROLL
SIZZLE
...
OH CRAP.

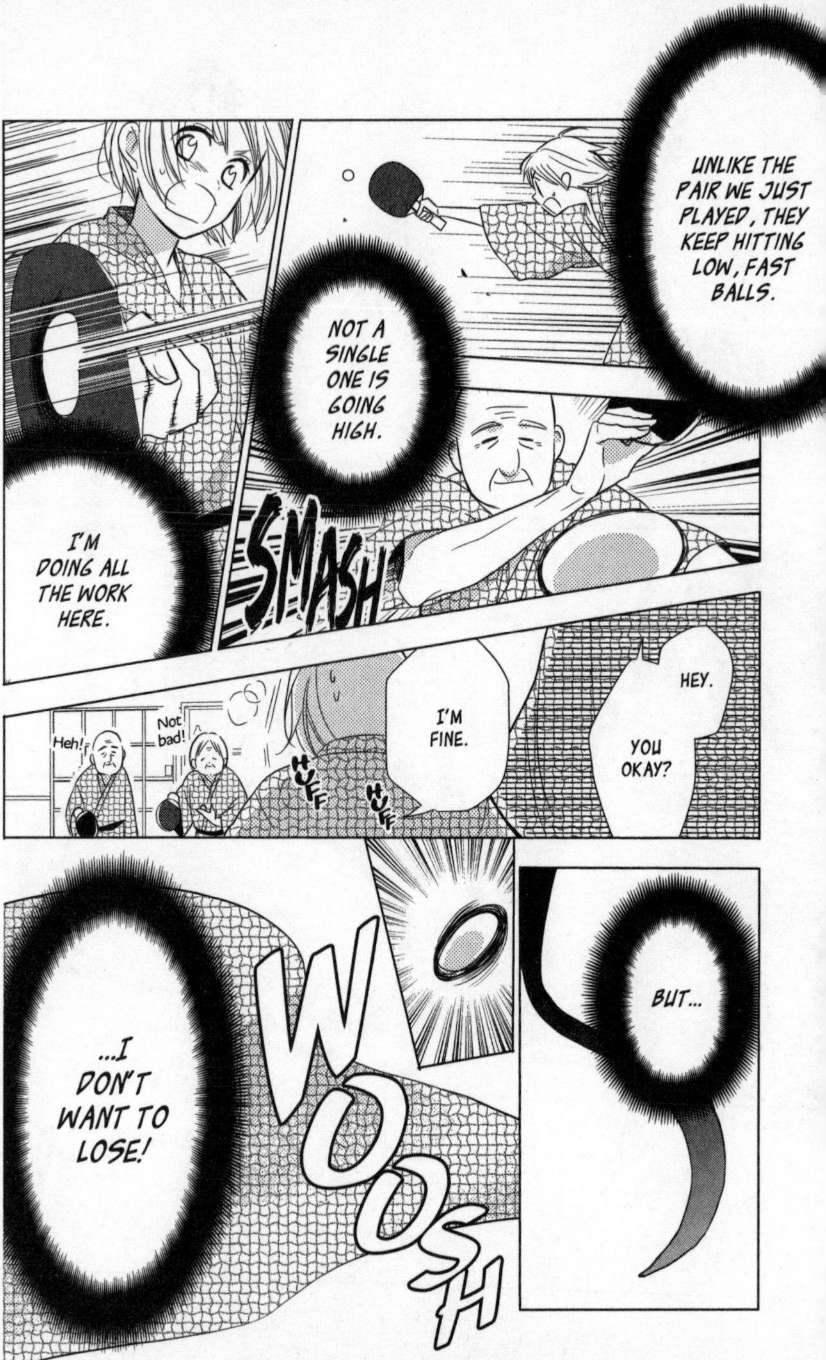
UNLIKE THE PAIR WE JUST PLAYED, THEY KEEP HITTING LOW, FAST BALLS.
NOT A SINGLE ONE IS GOING HIGH.
SMASH
I'M DOING ALL THE WORK HERE.
HEY.
YOU OKAY?
I'M FINE.
HUFF
HUFF
Not bad!
Heh!
BUT...
WOOSH
...I DON'T WANT TO LOSE!

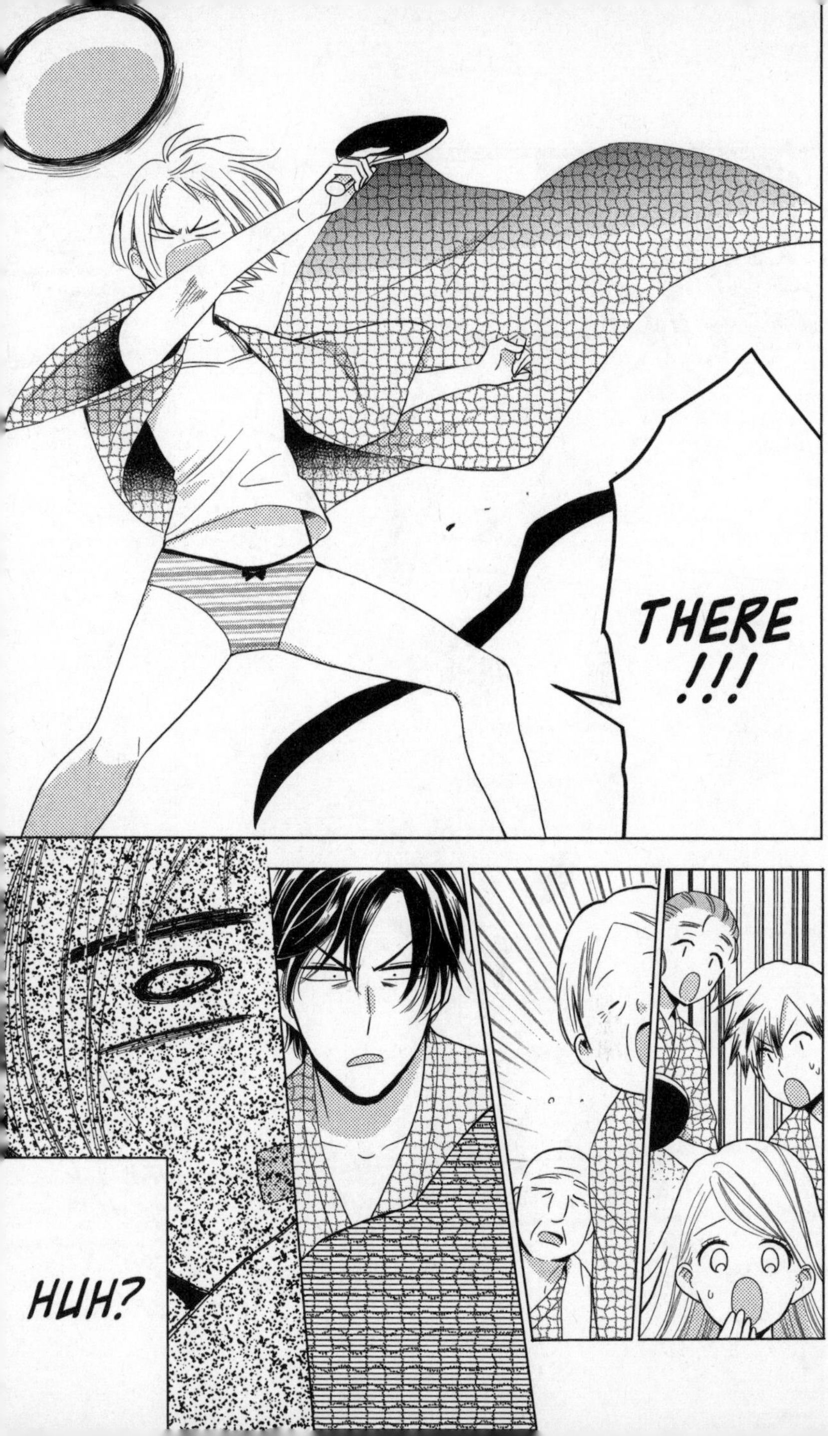
THERE !!!
HUH?

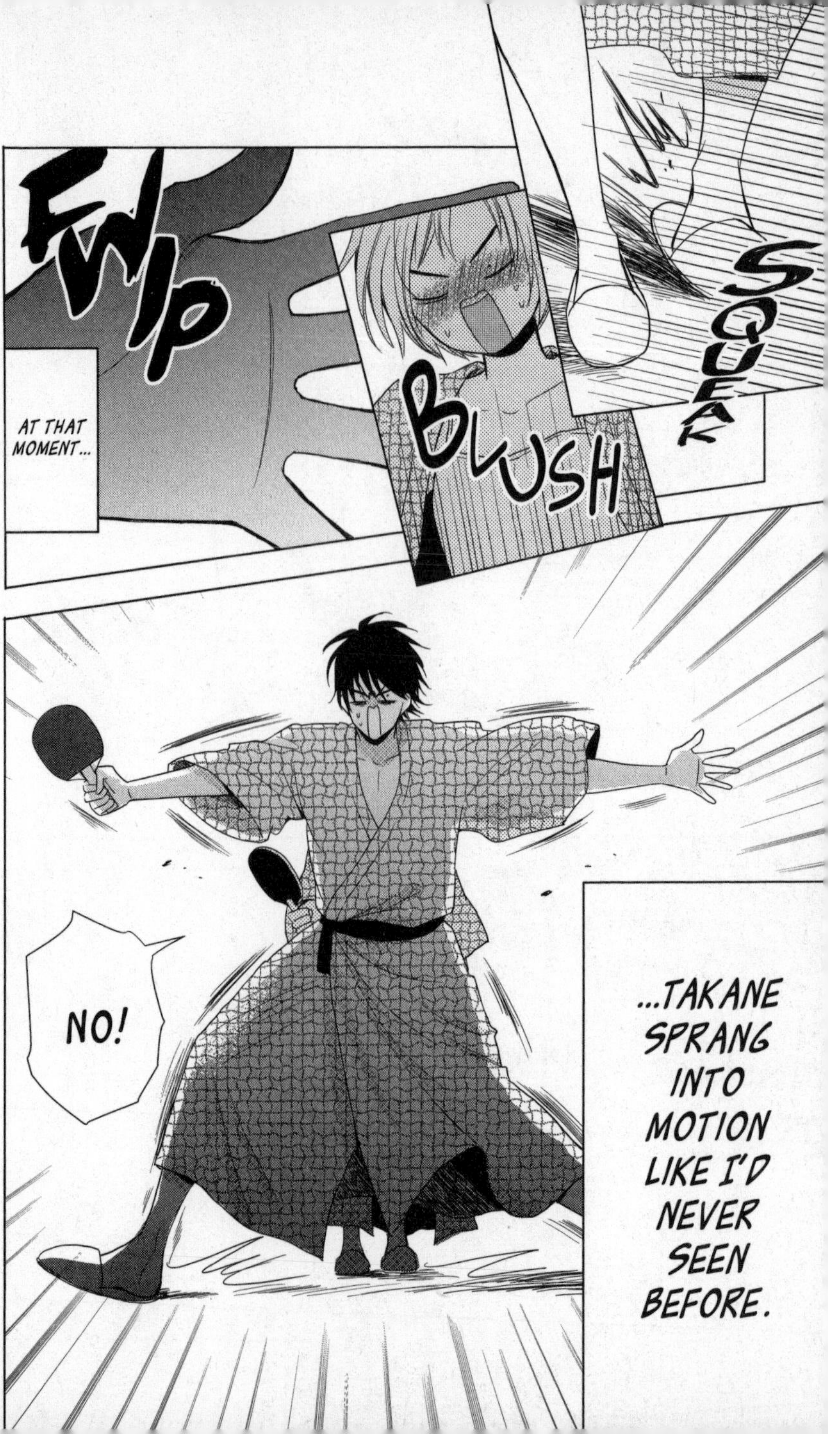
SQUEAK
BLUSH
FWIP
AT THAT MOMENT...
...TAKANE SPRANG INTO MOTION LIKE I'D NEVER SEEN BEFORE.
NO!

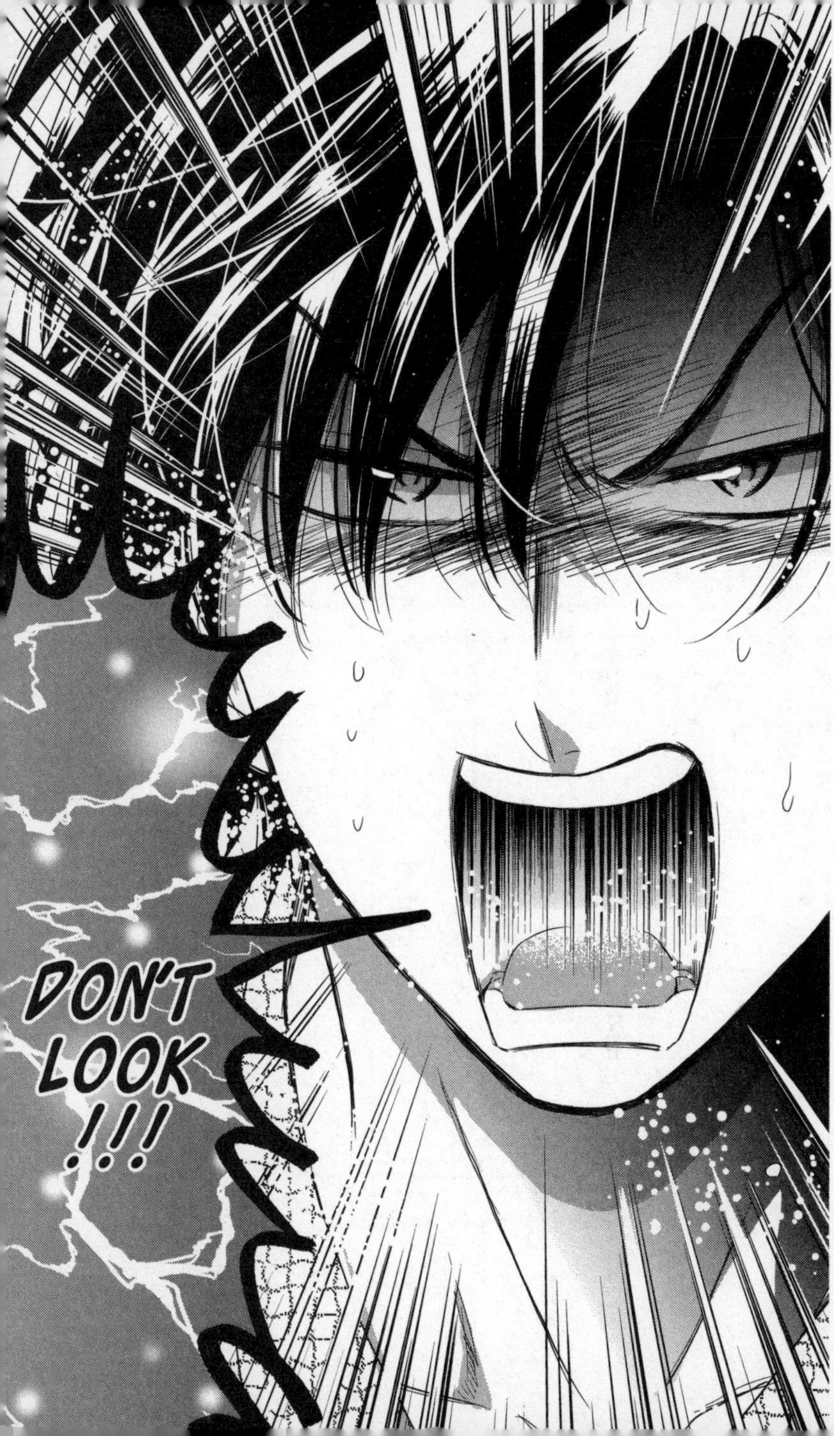
DON'T LOOK !!!

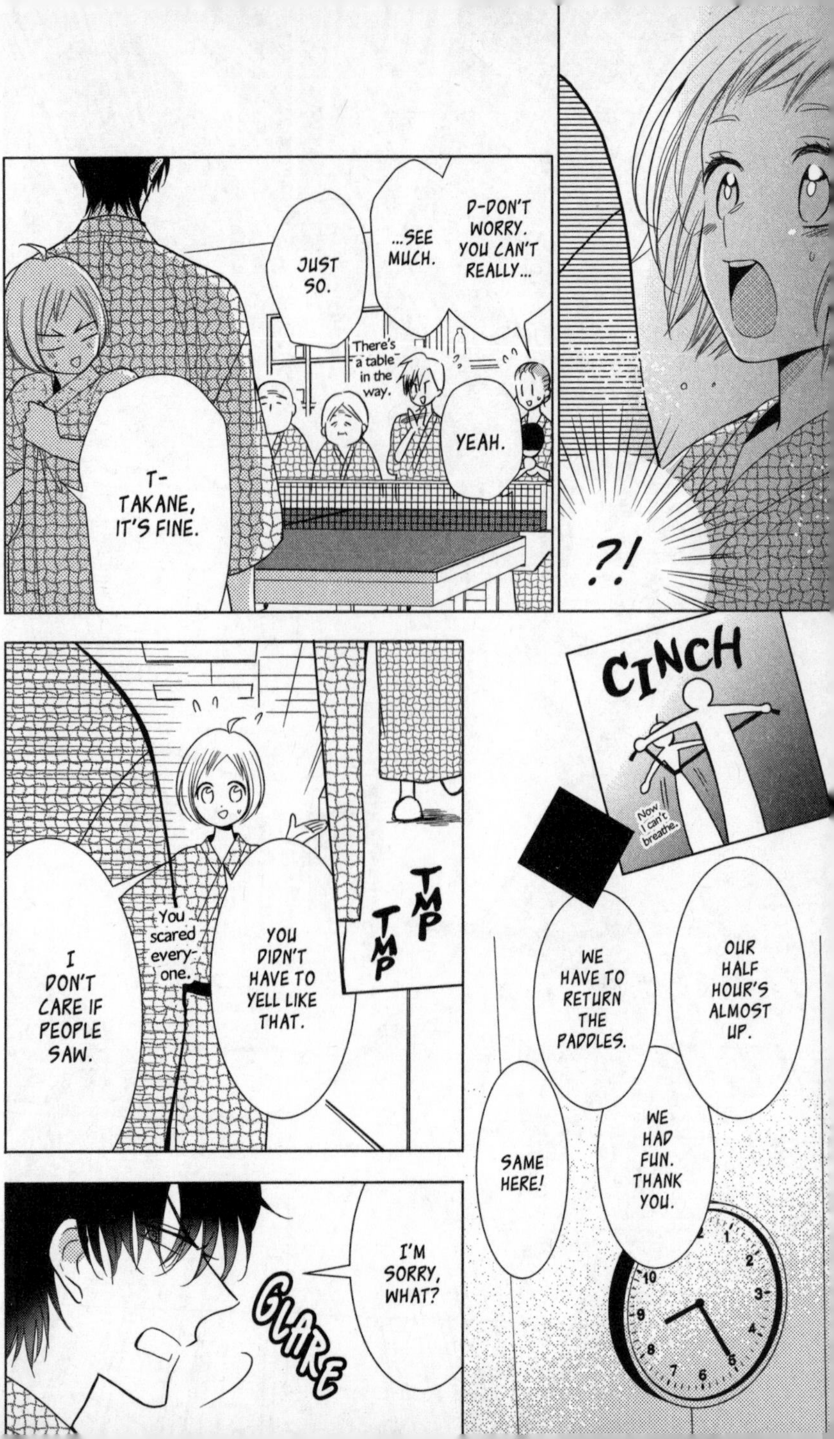
?!
D-DON'T WORRY. YOU CAN'T REALLY...
...SEE MUCH.
JUST SO.
There's a table in the way.
YEAH.
T-TAKANE, IT'S FINE.
CINCH
Now I can't breathe.
OUR HALF HOUR'S ALMOST UP.
WE HAVE TO RETURN THE PADDLES.
WE HAD FUN. THANK YOU.
SAME HERE!
TMP TMP
YOU DIDN'T HAVE TO YELL LIKE THAT.
You scared every-one.
I DON'T CARE IF PEOPLE SAW.
I'M SORRY, WHAT?
GLARE

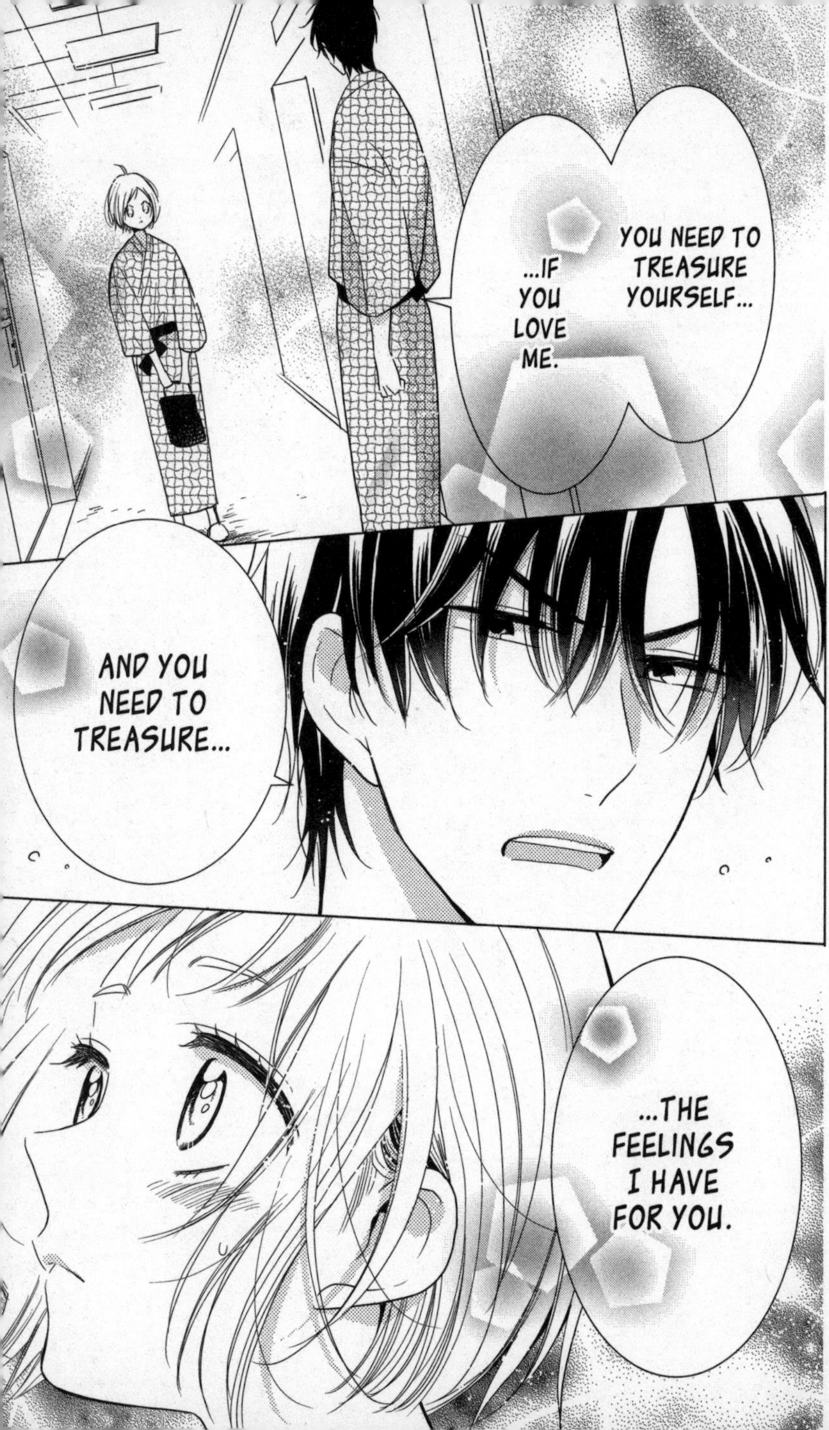

YOU NEED TO TREASURE YOURSELF...
...IF YOU LOVE ME.
AND YOU NEED TO TREASURE...
...THE FEELINGS I HAVE FOR YOU.

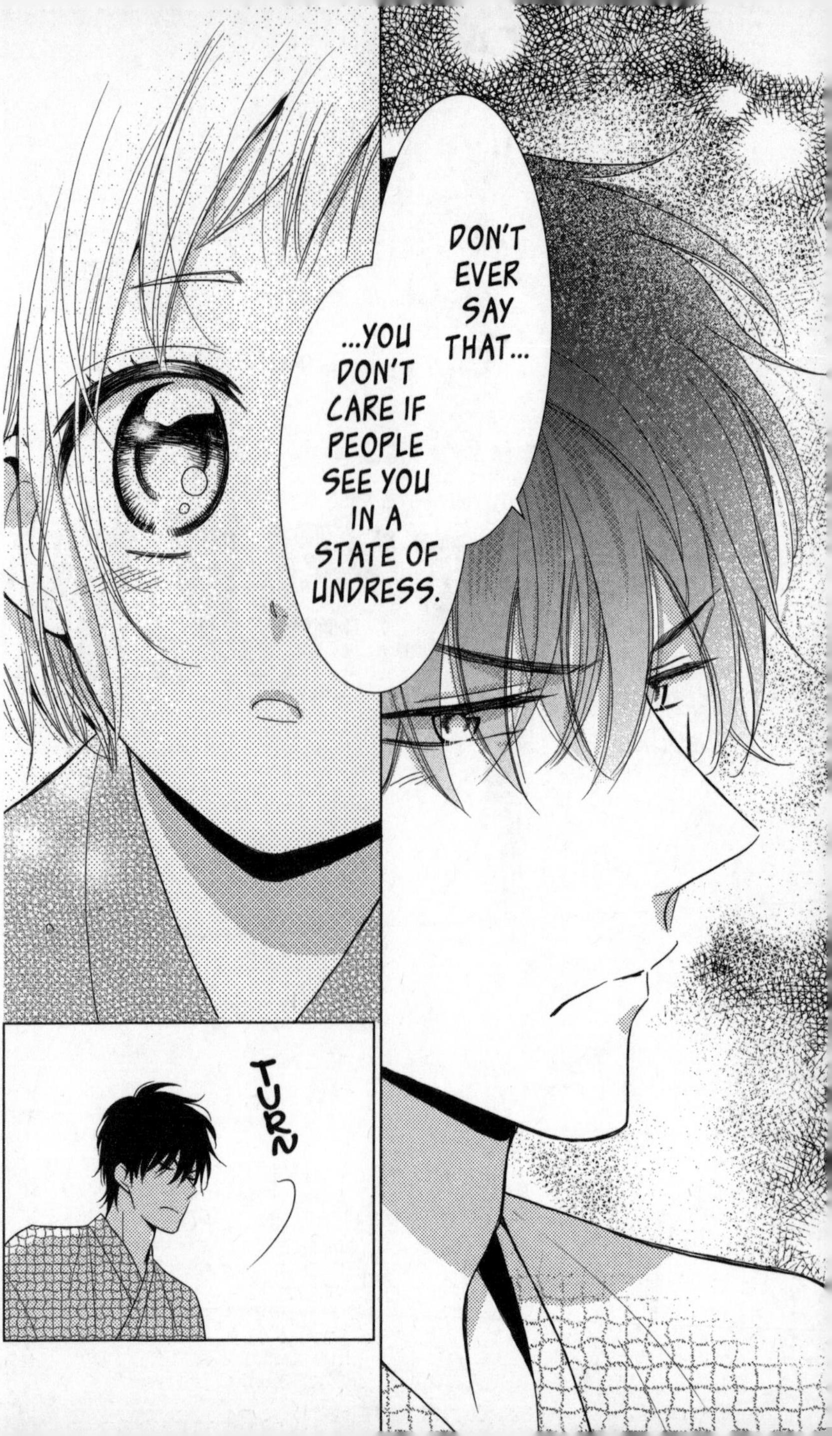
DON'T EVER SAY THAT...
...YOU DON'T CARE IF PEOPLE SEE YOU IN A STATE OF UNDRESS.
TURN

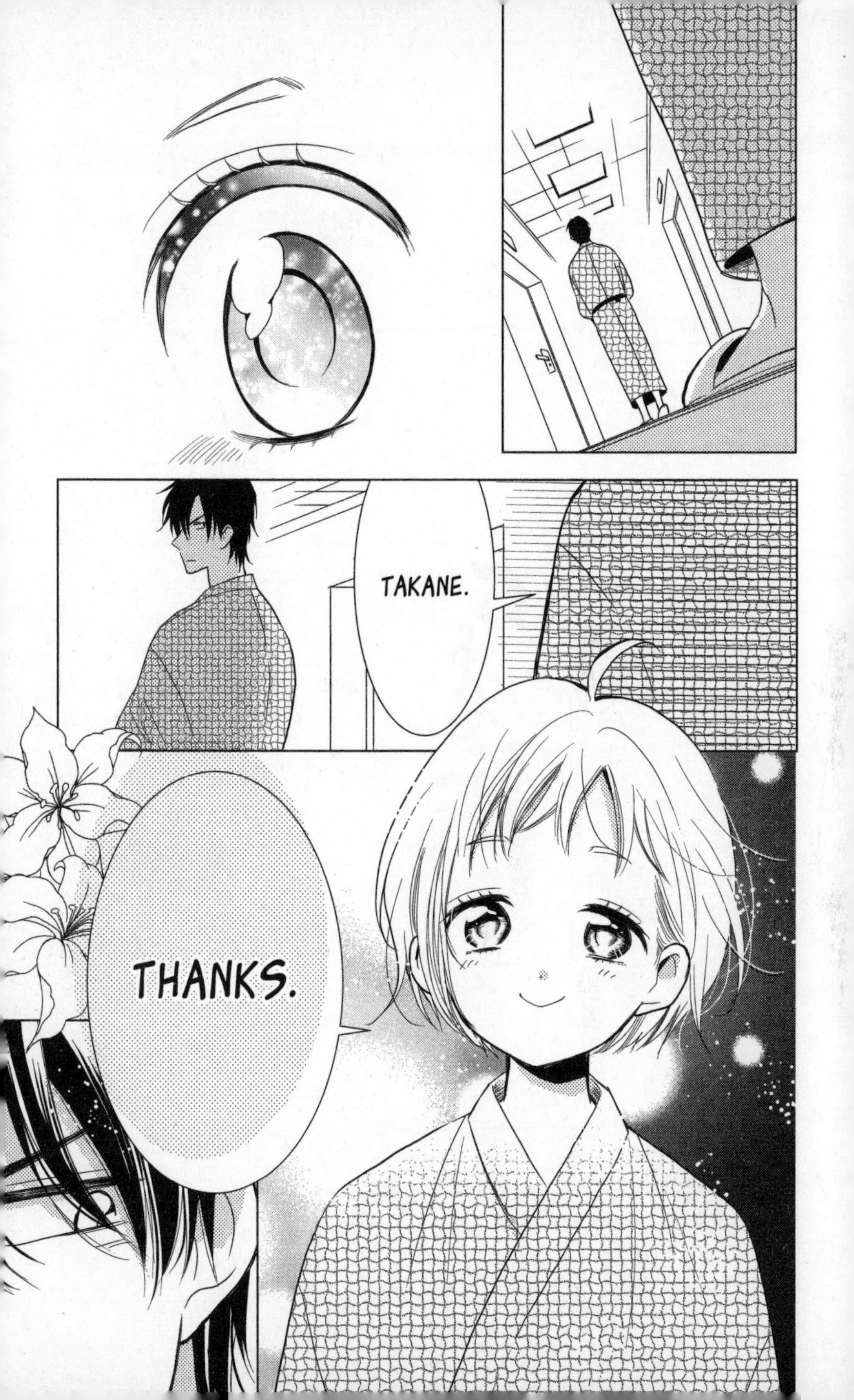
TAKANE.
THANKS.

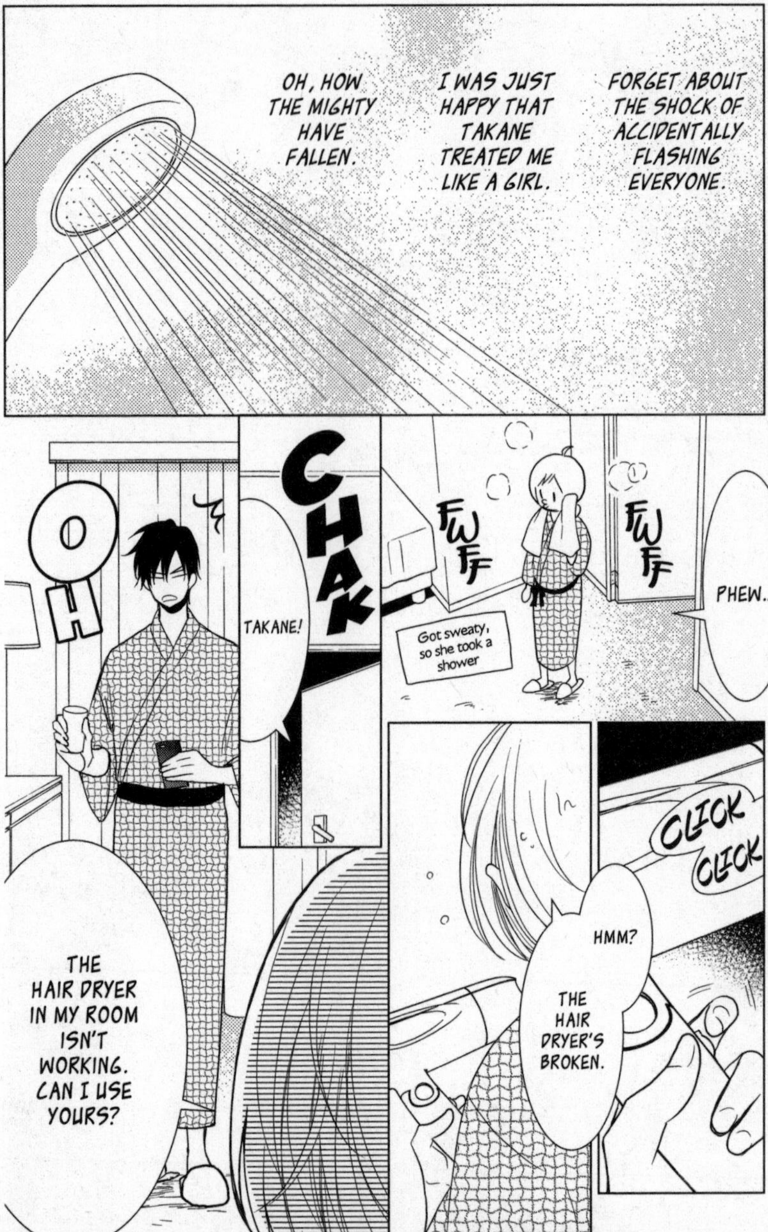
FORGET ABOUT THE SHOCK OF ACCIDENTALLY FLASHING EVERYONE.
I WAS JUST HAPPY THAT TAKANE TREATED ME LIKE A GIRL.
OH, HOW THE MIGHTY HAVE FALLEN.
PHEW...
FWFF
FWFF
Got sweaty, so she took a shower
CHAK
TAKANE!
CLICK
CLICK
HMM?
THE HAIR DRYER'S BROKEN.
OH
THE HAIR DRYER IN MY ROOM ISN'T WORKING. CAN I USE YOURS?

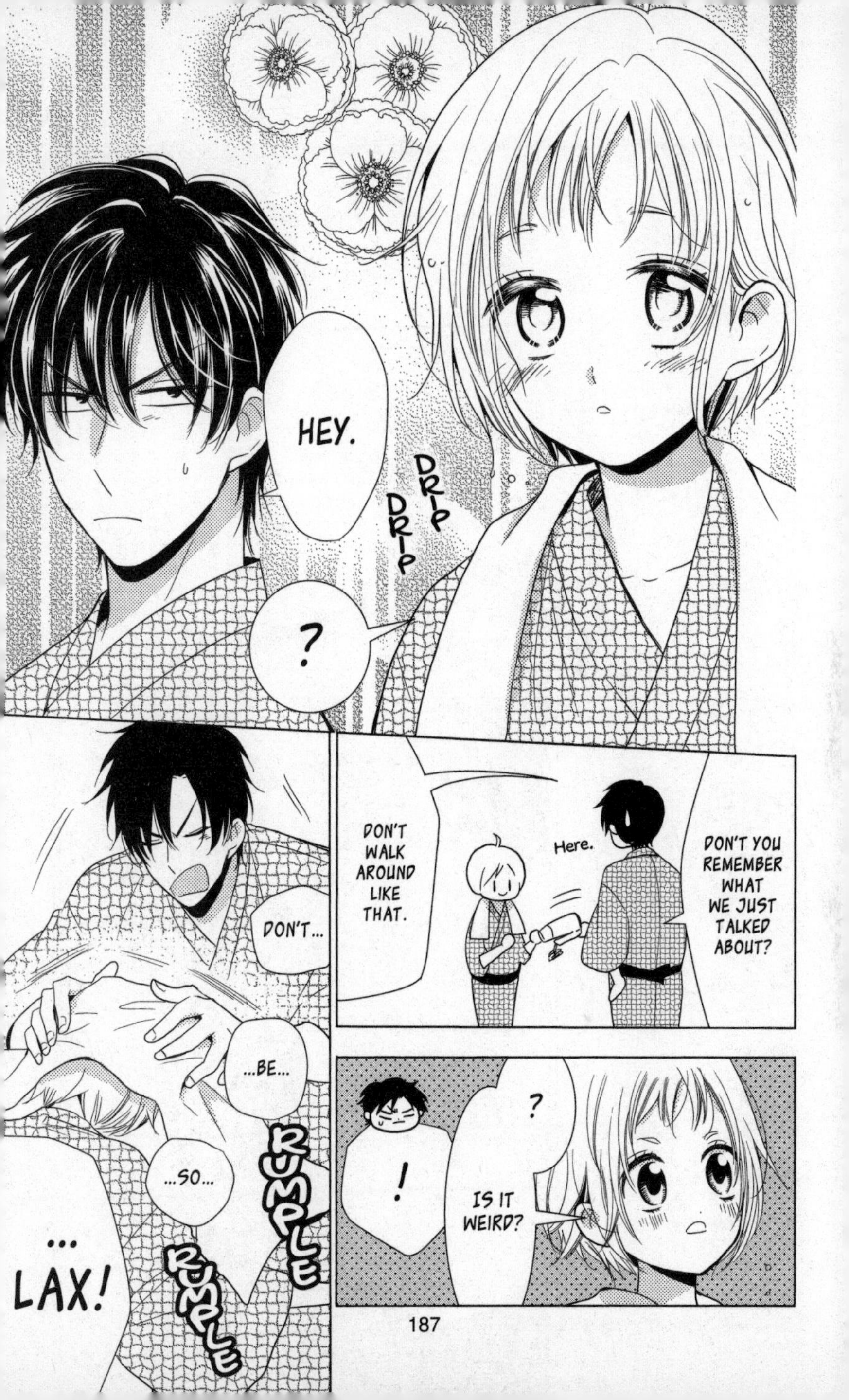

HEY.
DRIP DRIP
?
DON'T YOU REMEMBER WHAT WE JUST TALKED ABOUT?
Here.
DON'T WALK AROUND LIKE THAT.
?
IS IT WEIRD?
!
DON'T...
...BE...
...SO...
RUMPLE
RUMPLE
... LAX!

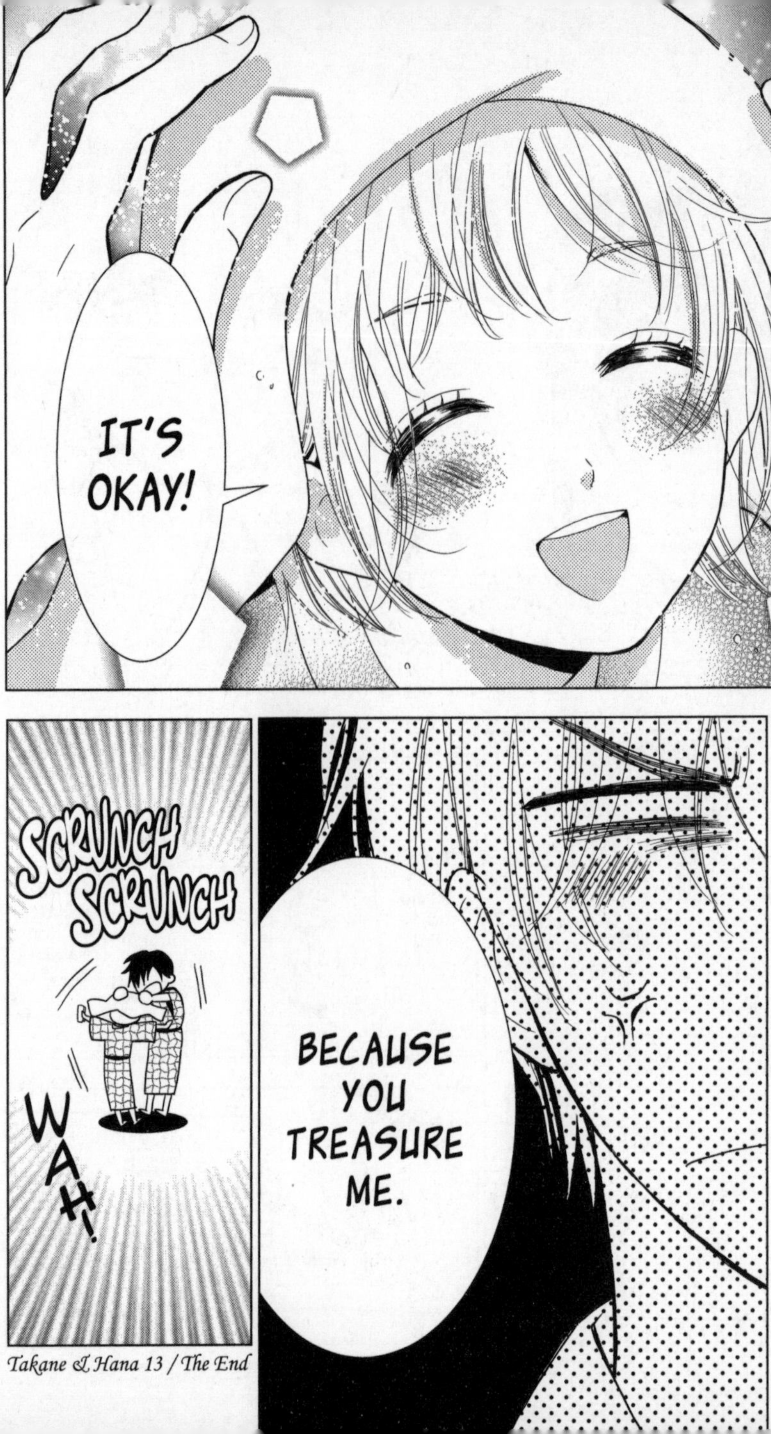
IT'S OKAY!
BECAUSE YOU TREASURE ME.
SCRUNCH SCRUNCH
WAH!

Takane & Hana 13 / The End

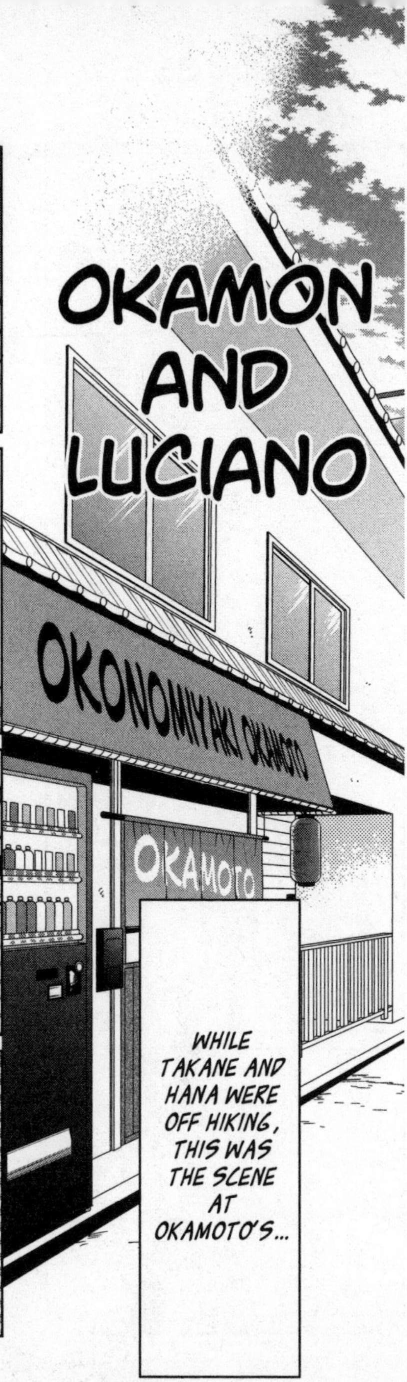
OKAMON AND LUCIANO
OKONOMIYAKI OKAMOTO
OKAMOTO
WHILE TAKANE AND HANA WERE OFF HIKING, THIS WAS THE SCENE AT OKAMOTO'S...

It's Brother Nicola!

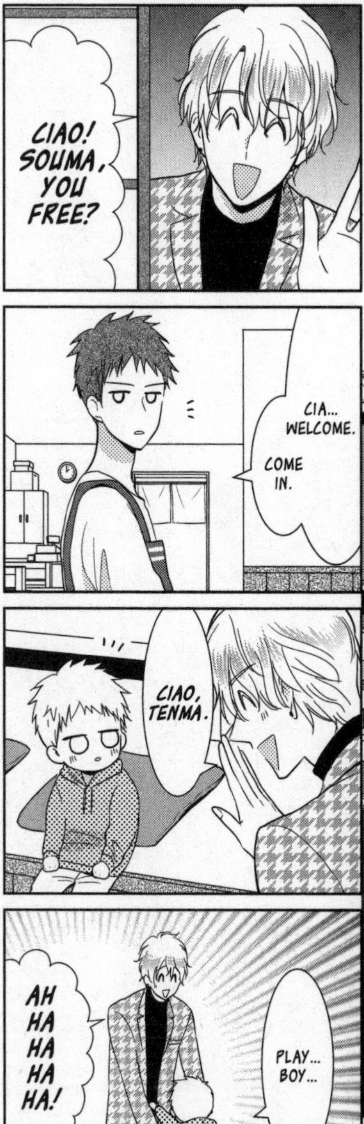
CIAO! SOUMA, YOU FREE?
CIA... WELCOME.
COME IN.
CIAO, TENMA.
PLAY... BOY...
AH HA HA HA HA!

Reading Each Other's Minds ④

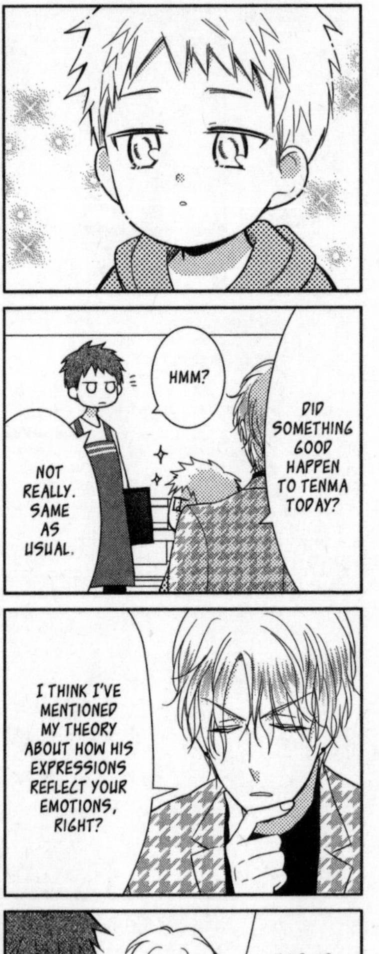
DID SOMETHING GOOD HAPPEN TO TENMA TODAY?
HMM?
NOT REALLY. SAME AS USUAL.
I THINK I'VE MENTIONED MY THEORY ABOUT HOW HIS EXPRESSIONS REFLECT YOUR EMOTIONS, RIGHT?
THIS...IS NOT THE WHOLESOME FACE OF A YOUNG BOY WHO JUST STARTED GOING OUT WITH A GIRL.
Is everything okay, Souma?

Reading Each Other's Minds ⑤

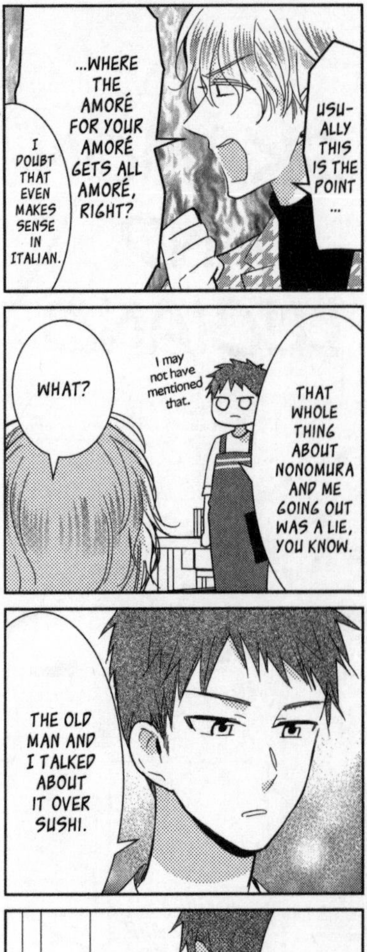
USUALLY THIS IS THE POINT...
...WHERE THE AMORÉ FOR YOUR AMORÉ GETS ALL AMORÉ, RIGHT?
I DOUBT THAT EVEN MAKES SENSE IN ITALIAN.
THAT WHOLE THING ABOUT NONOMURA AND ME GOING OUT WAS A LIE, YOU KNOW.
I may not have mentioned that.
WHAT?
THE OLD MAN AND I TALKED ABOUT IT OVER SUSHI.
SO IF ANYTHING, MAYBE IT'S THE FACE OF SOMEONE WHO'S GOTTEN OVER IT.
I SEE.

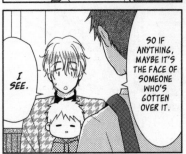

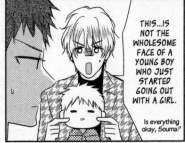

The Fabulous Force

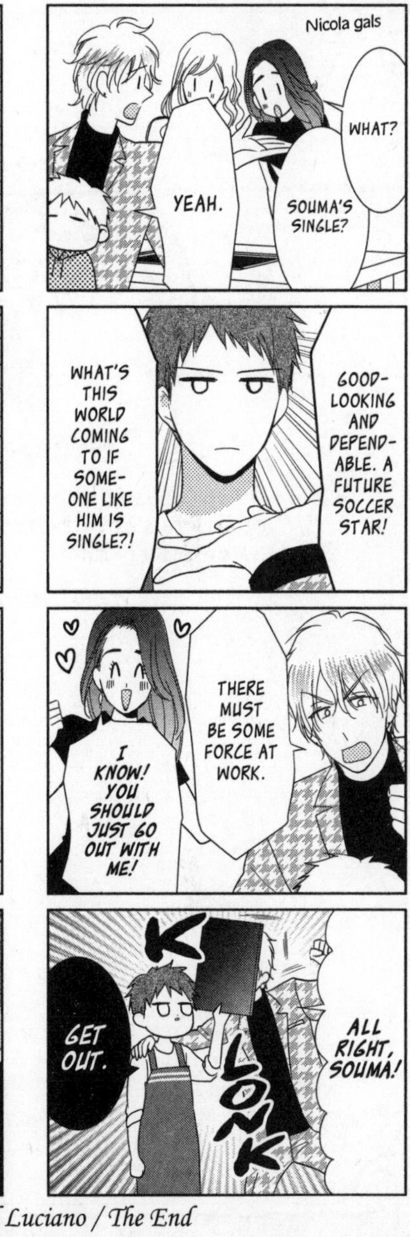

Nicola gals
WHAT?
SOUMA'S SINGLE?
YEAH.
GOOD-LOOKING AND DEPENDABLE. A FUTURE SOCCER STAR!
WHAT'S THIS WORLD COMING TO IF SOMEONE LIKE HIM IS SINGLE?!
THERE MUST BE SOME FORCE AT WORK.
I KNOW! YOU SHOULD JUST GO OUT WITH ME!
ALL RIGHT, SOUMA!
KLONK
GET OUT.

Leave Me Alone

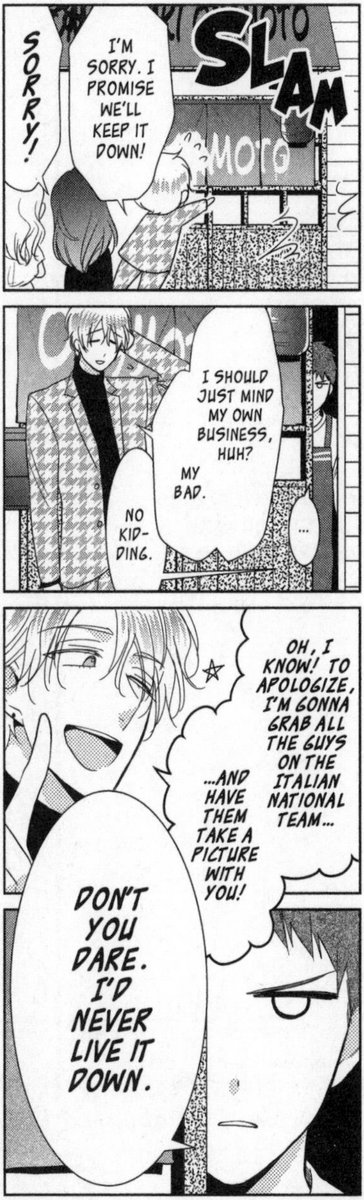

SLAM
I'M SORRY. I PROMISE WE'LL KEEP IT DOWN!
SORRY!
I SHOULD JUST MIND MY OWN BUSINESS, HUH?
...
MY BAD.
NO KIDDING.
OH, I KNOW! TO APOLOGIZE, I'M GONNA GRAB ALL THE GUYS ON THE ITALIAN NATIONAL TEAM...
...AND HAVE THEM TAKE A PICTURE WITH YOU!
DON'T YOU DARE. I'D NEVER LIVE IT DOWN.

Okamoto and Luciano / The End

I was so pleased to hear that you all loved
volume 12's cover! I decided to go with
a completely different vibe this time.

—YUKI SHIWASU

Born on March 7 in Fukuoka Prefecture, Japan,
Yuki Shiwasu began her career as a manga artist
after winning the top prize in the Hakusensha Athena
Newcomers' Awards from *Hana to Yume* magazine. She
is also the author of *Furou Kyoudai* (Immortal Siblings),
which was published by Hakusensha in Japan.

Takane &Hana

VOLUME 13
SHOJO BEAT EDITION

STORY & ART BY **YUKI SHIWASU**

ENGLISH ADAPTATION **Ysabet Reinhardt MacFarlane**
TRANSLATION **JN Productions**
TOUCH-UP ART & LETTERING **Annaliese Christman**
DESIGN **Shawn Carrico**
EDITOR **Amy Yu**

Takane to Hana by Yuki Shiwasu
© Yuki Shiwasu 2019
All rights reserved.
First published in Japan in 2019 by HAKUSENSHA, Inc., Tokyo.
English language translation rights arranged with HAKUSENSHA, Inc., Tokyo.

The stories, characters and incidents mentioned
in this publication are entirely fictional.

No portion of this book may be reproduced
or transmitted in any form or by any means without
written permission from the copyright holders.

Printed in the U.S.A.

Published by VIZ Media, LLC
P.O. Box 77010
San Francisco, CA 94107

10 9 8 7 6 5 4 3 2 1
First printing, February 2020

PARENTAL ADVISORY
TAKANE & HANA is rated T for Teen and
is recommended for ages 13 and up. This
volume contains suggestive themes.

 MEDIA
viz.com

shojobeat.com

IDOL dreams

STORY & ART BY ARINA TANEMURA

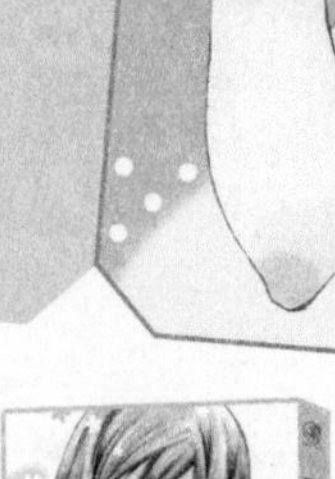

At age 31, office worker Chikage Deguchi feels she missed her chances at love and success. When word gets out that she's a virgin, Chikage is humiliated and wishes she could turn back time to when she was still young and popular. She takes an experimental drug that changes her appearance back to when she was 15. Now Chikage is determined to pursue everything she missed out on all those years ago—including becoming a star!

Thirty One Idream © Arina Tanemura 2014/HAKUSENSHA, Inc.

Ouran High School

Host Club BOX SET

Story and Art by
Bisco Hatori

Escape to the world of the young, rich and sexy

All 18 volumes
in a collector's box
with an Ouran High
School stationery
notepad!

In this screwball romantic
comedy, Haruhi, a poor girl at
a rich kids' school, is forced to
repay an $80,000 debt by working
for the school's swankiest, all-
male club—as a boy! There she
discovers just how wealthy the six
members are and how different
the rich are from everybody else...

www.viz.com

Ouran Koko Host Club © Bisco Hatori 2002/HAKUSENSHA, Inc.

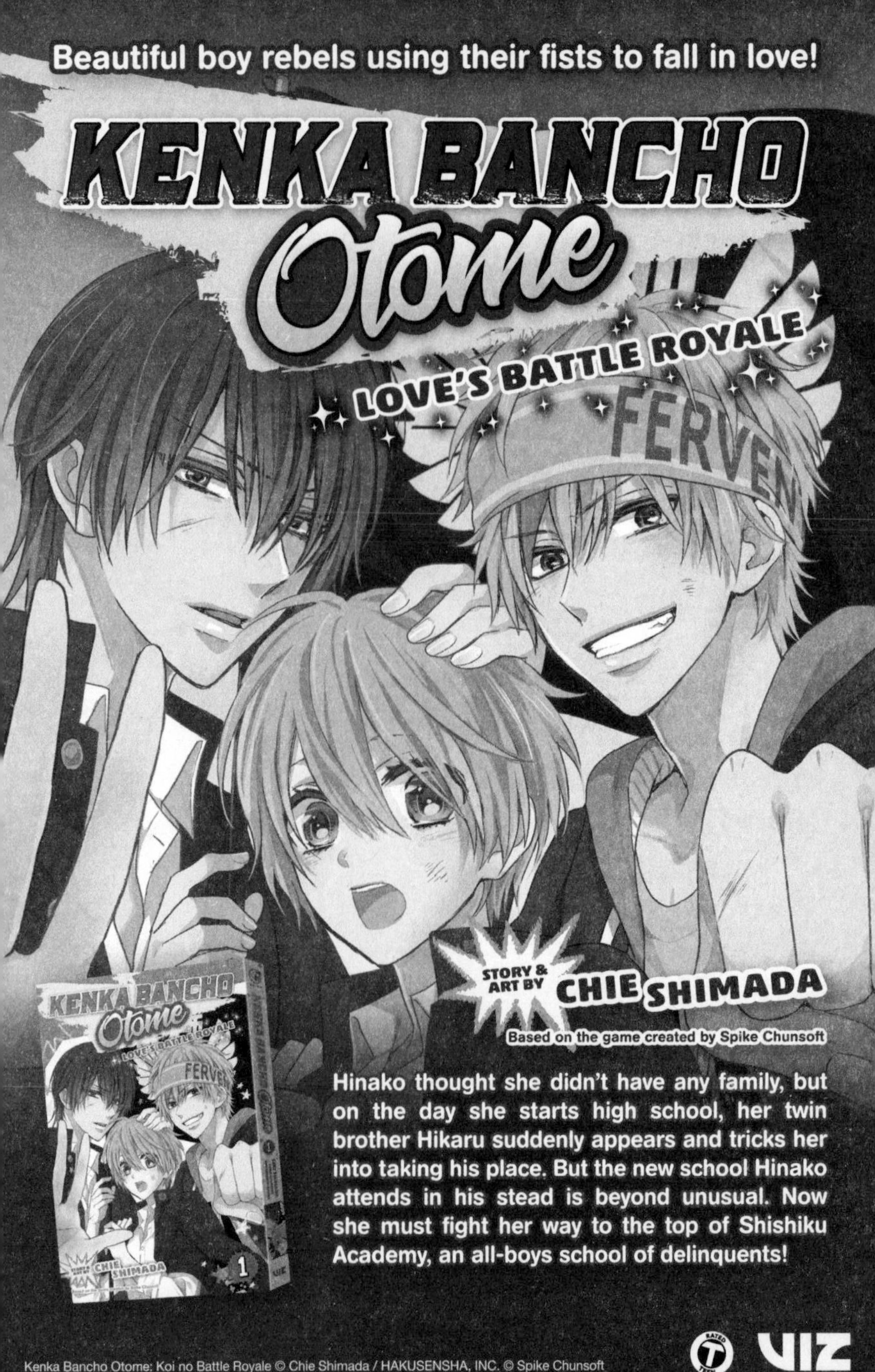
Beautiful boy rebels using their fists to fall in love!
KENKA BANCHO
Otome
LOVE'S BATTLE ROYALE
FERVEN
STORY & ART BY
CHIE SHIMADA
Based on the game created by Spike Chunsoft
Hinako thought she didn't have any family, but on the day she starts high school, her twin brother Hikaru suddenly appears and tricks her into taking his place. But the new school Hinako attends in his stead is beyond unusual. Now she must fight her way to the top of Shishiku Academy, an all-boys school of delinquents!
RATED T TEEN
VIZ

Behind the Scenes!!

STORY AND ART BY BISCO HATORI

From the creator of **Ouran High School Host Club**

Ranmaru Kurisu comes from a family of hardy, rough-and-tumble fisherfolk and he sticks out at home like a delicate, artistic sore thumb. It's given him a raging inferiority complex and a permanently pessimistic outlook. Now that he's in college, he's hoping to find a sense of belonging. But after a whole life of being left out, does he even know how to fit in?!

Urakata!! © Bisco Hatori 2015/HAKUSENSHA, Inc.

Natsume's BOOK of FRIENDS

STORY and ART by
Yuki Midorikawa

Make Some Unusual New Friends

The power to see hidden spirits has always felt like a curse to troubled high schooler Takashi Natsume. But he's about to discover he inherited a lot more than just the Sight from his mysterious grandmother!

Available at your local bookstore or comic store.

www.shojobeat.com

Natsume Yujincho © Yuki Midorikawa 2005/HAKUSENSHA, Inc.

RATED
T
FOR
TEEN
ratings.viz.com

www.viz.com

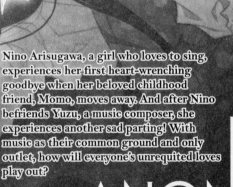

Nino Arisugawa, a girl who loves to sing, experiences her first heart-wrenching goodbye when her beloved childhood friend, Momo, moves away. And after Nino befriends Yuzu, a music composer, she experiences another sad parting! With music as their common ground and only outlet, how will everyone's unrequited loves play out?

ANONYMOUS NOISE

viz media
viz.com

Shojo
Beat

Story & Art by
Ryoko Fukuyama

Fukumenkei Noise © Ryoko Fukuyama 2013/HAKUSENSHA, Inc.

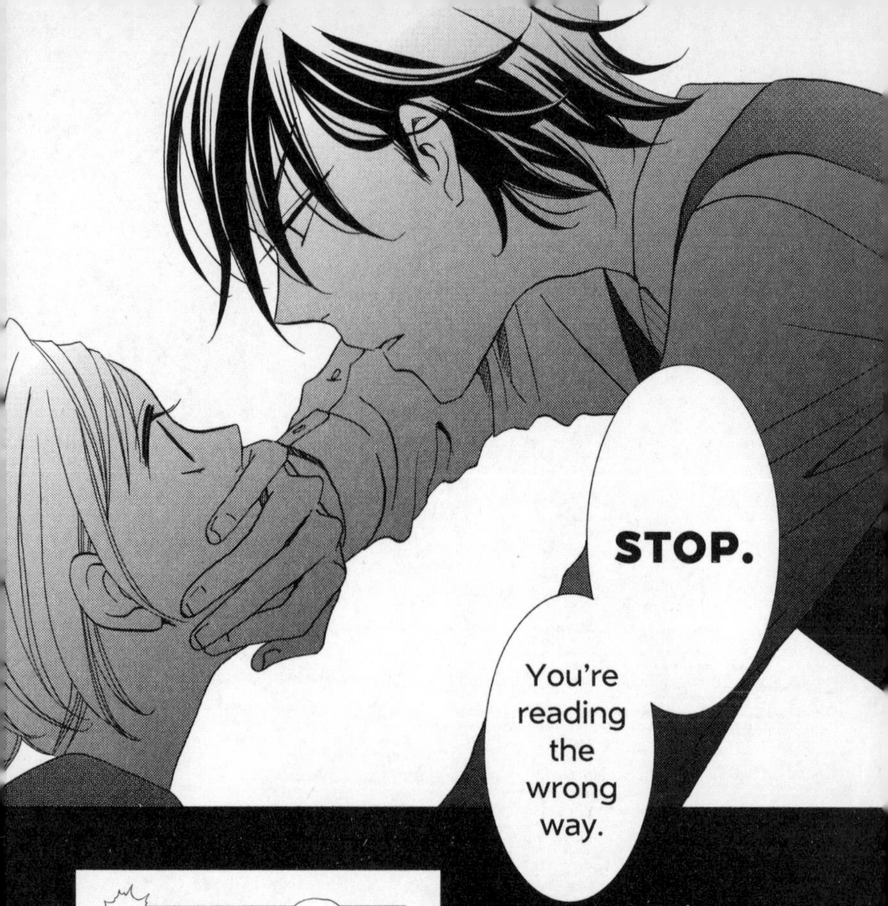
STOP.
You're reading the wrong way.

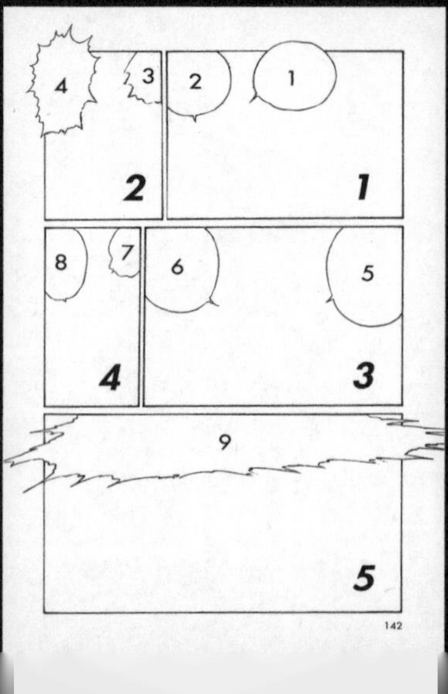

In keeping with the original Japanese comic format, this book reads from right to left—so action, sound effects and word balloons are completely reversed to preserve the orientation of the original artwork.

Check out the diagram shown here to get the hang of things, and then turn to the other side of the book to get started!